We Are Many

Modern Jewish History
Henry L. Feingold, *Series Editor*

Other titles in Modern Jewish History

Bearing Witness: How America and Its Jews Responded to the Holocaust
Henry L. Feingold

The Golden Tradition: Jewish Life and Thought in Eastern Europe
Lucy S. Dawidowicz

The Grandees: The Story of America's Sephardic Elite
Stephen Birmingham

Jews, Turks, Ottomans: A Shared History, Fifteenth Through Twentieth Centuries
Avigdor Levy, ed.

Lest Memory Cease: Finding Meaning in the American Jewish Past
Henry L. Feingold

New York Jews and the Decline of Urban Ethnicity, 1950–1970
Eli Lederhendler

New York Jews and the Great Depression: Uncertain Promise
Beth S. Wenger

Our Crowd: The Great Jewish Families of New York
Stephen Birmingham

Will to Freedom: A Perilous Journey Through Fascism and Communism
Egon Balas

WE ARE MANY

Reflections on American Jewish History and Identity

Edward S. Shapiro

Syracuse University Press

Syracuse, New York 13244-5160

First Edition 2005

05 06 07 08 09 10 6 5 4 3 2 1

The paper used in this publication meets the minimum requirements of American National Standard for Information Sciences—Permanence of Paper for Printed Library Materials, ANSI Z39.48-1984.∞™

Library of Congress Cataloging-in-Publication Data

Shapiro, Edward S.
We are many : reflections on American Jewish history and identity / Edward S. Shapiro.—1st ed.
p. cm. — (Modern Jewish history)
Includes bibliographical references and index.
ISBN 0–8156–3075–1 (pbk. : alk. paper)
1. Jews—United States—History—20th century. 2. Jews—United States—Identity. 3. Jews—United States—Politics and government—20th century. 4. Judaism—United States—History—20th century. I. Title. II. Series.
E184.355.S56 2004
973'.04924—dc22 2004028836

Manufactured in the United States of America

Do not say,
"How was it that former times were better than these?"
For that is not a question prompted by wisdom.
—Ecclesiastes 7:10

Lo, children are a heritage of the Lord. . . .
Happy is the man that hath his quiver full of them.
—Psalm 127

To my children—Marc Brooks, Alan Nahum,
David Jeffrey, and Evan Michael

Edward S. Shapiro, professor emeritus of history at Seton Hall University, specializes in twentieth-century American Jewish history. He is the author of *Letters of Sidney Hook: Democracy, Communism, and the Cold War* and *A Time for Healing: American Jewry since World War II,* the final volume in a five-volume series, *The Jewish People in America.*

Contents

Acknowledgments

ALL THE ESSAYS in this volume have been previously published. The appropriate citation and permission credit appear in a footnote at the beginning of each essay. I thank the respective publishers and journal staffs for graciously allowing me to reprint them in this book.

Also, I thank particularly Professor Marc Lee Raphael of the College of William and Mary for inviting me to a conference in Williamsburg, Virginia, where I presented a paper, "The Search for American Jewish Identity," and for inviting me to contribute essays to the special issues of *American Jewish History* devoted to Nathan Glazer and Charles S. Liebman. I am also grateful to Professor Henry L. Feingold of the City University of New York (CCNY) for thinking my essays worthy of publication by the Syracuse University Press. Professor Stephen Whitfield of Brandeis University has helped me clarify my ideas on American Jewish history and culture and has been a delightful houseguest.

As always, the staff of the Walsh Library at Seton Hall University Library have been courteous and supportive in responding to what must have seemed at times to be imperious requests. The library has also been helpful in providing me with a study where I escape from the academic demands that, although necessary, frequently impede scholarship. Seton Hall University's enlightened sabbatical policy provided the resources and time to research and write these essays. I also commend J. J. Lando, my computer consultant, for his conscientious and prompt efforts in my behalf.

My family should be listed on the title page of the book. My wife, Daryl, proofread many of the essays at a time when I had not yet discovered the beauties of a personal computer with its spell checker and thesaurus. My children have been my major inspiration, and the germ of many of my ideas regarding American Jewish history first appeared during our frequently boisterous conversations over the dining room table. Particularly helpful has been the bibliographic data provided by my eldest child, Marc B. Shapiro, the Harry and Jeannette Weinberg Professor of Jewish Studies at the University of Scranton.

Introduction

A HALF CENTURY AGO the Harvard historian Oscar Handlin published an essay in *Commentary* (February 1948) bemoaning the state of American Jewish historiography. Subtitled "Fact and Myth in History," "Our Unknown American Jewish Ancestors" noted that this history had been shaped by inaccurate historical paradigms, most notably the tripartite division of Jewish immigration into Sephardic, German, and East European streams, and that it had been suffused by an apologetic and filiopietistic ethos that detracted from its scholarly value. Not only had the writing of American Jewish history been "distorted and misleading," but important historical questions such as the impact of the American environment on American Judaism, the uniqueness of American Zionism, and the process of Jewish acculturation had been virtually ignored. "This is a deplorable situation," Handlin concluded, and "to be written right, the history must be freed of the burden of a defensive attitude. It must cease to be apologetic; it cannot afford to be distorted by the necessity for justification. The approach must be open and unhackneyed." In other words, American Jewish history must become the province of trained academic historians and not merely of amateur scribblers. Handlin's most significant contribution to rectifying this situation was his own book, *Adventure in Freedom: Three Hundred Years of Jewish Life in America* (1954). One of his students was Moses Rischin, whose doctoral dissertation, published by the Harvard University Press in 1962 and titled *The Promised City: New York's Jews, 1870–1914,* was precisely the kind of scholarly academic history Handlin had called for.

The writing of American Jewish history has certainly come a long way since 1948. Some of the nation's leading universities have chairs in American Jewish history; there are two journals in the field—*American Jewish Archives* and *American Jewish History;* and the publishing of books in the field by academic and commercial presses increases yearly. Most important, this history is now thankfully free of the defensive and filiopietistic tone Handlin had deplored. This does not mean, however, that all is well in the field.

Too few works have concerned themselves with comparative history. How rapid was Jewish economic and social mobility when compared to that of other ethnic groups? How does the political behavior of American Jews compare to that of Jews in other societies? Was American Zionism unique? What have been the major developments in the history of Judaism in the United States? These and other questions can be answered only by comparing the history of America's Jews to other ethnic groups and to Jews living elsewhere.

In his 1980 presidential address to the American Historical Association, Handlin's colleague and student Bernard Bailyn argued that the greatest challenge of modern historical scholarship is "to bring order into large areas of history . . . through synthetic works, narrative in structure, on major themes, works that explain some significant part of the story of how the present world came to be the way it is." The historians' task is to tell how the old "faded and blended into new configurations, how at every stage what was, was the product of what had been, and developed into what no one could have anticipated." Historical writing at its best necessarily entails asking important questions. Why did America win the Revolutionary War? What caused the Civil War? What was the effect of the frontier on American development?

Four decades ago, Jacob Rader Marcus, the dean of American Jewish historians, argued that the central theme of American Jewish history since the Civil War involved the "urge to unity" and the "will to survive." How were European and Sephardic Jews transformed into Americans while yet remaining Jews? How have America's Jews reconciled the two elements of their being? The weightiest historical question one can ask about America's Jews concerns the development and varieties of Jewish identity. The essays in this book attempt to answer this question.

Of all of America's ethnic subgroups, the Jews are certainly the most enigmatic. Part of their puzzling nature stems from the confusion surrounding what precisely is a Jew. The issue "Who is a Jew?" has vexed American Jewry just as it has the politics of Israel. The most contentious issues within American Jewry during the 1980s and 1990s have involved definitions of Jewish identity. In the early 1980s the American Reform movement cast aside the definition of Jewish identity that had delineated the Jewish community for thousands of years. According to this definition, a Jew had to have a Jewish mother or to have been converted according to Jewish law. The Reform movement rejected matrilineal descent as the sine qua non of Jewish identity and said that patrilineal descent was acceptable if the child was being raised as a Jew as evidenced by participation in religious services or enrollment in a religious school.

Spokesmen for Orthodox and Conservative Judaism vigorously dissented. They claimed that this would split American Jewry since Reform Jews could no longer be automatically considered as appropriate marriage partners for Jews who accepted the traditional definition of who is a Jew and who wished to avoid intermarriage. They also warned that they could no longer encourage the young members of their congregations to socially interact with their counterparts in Reform congregations, some of whom could not be considered Jewish even by the most lax standards of Jewish law, since this would encourage intermarriage.

In the 1990s the most important challenge to interdenominational harmony within American Judaism concerned the validity of religious conversions conducted under the auspices of Conservative and Reform rabbis. Under pressure from Orthodox religious circles in Israel, the Israeli government refused to recognize the legitimacy of non-Orthodox conversions. In addition, non-Orthodox groups were denied permission to conduct religious services at the Western Wall in Jerusalem, Judaism's most hallowed spot. While this controversy seemed to revolve around the questions of who is a rabbi and the legitimacy of non-Orthodox varieties of Judaism, many American Jews believed their Jewishness itself was being questioned.

The question of Jewish identity goes beyond this intramural conflict over the religious definition of who is a Jew. It encompasses the broader and more important issue of whether Jewishness is a matter of religion, history, culture, or ethnicity. When Will Herberg published *Protestant-Catholic-Jew* in 1955, he expressed the widely held assumption that Jews comprised one of the three great religions of American democracy. This conflating of Jewishness with Judaism is reflected in the academic practice of locating courses in Jewish studies, even when they are concerned with sociology and history, in departments of religion. One of the reasons that anti-Semitism in America has been a marginal phenomenon is the high value that Americans have placed on religion, and their tendency to equate Jewishness with Judaism.

But if Jews comprise a religious group, they have certainly been an idiosyncratic one. The pollsters and sociologists have noted that Jews have been and are today far less religious than Protestants, Catholics, and members of other American religions, if by "religious" we mean knowledge about the fundamentals of religious beliefs, the observance of religious holidays and rituals, and the application of religious teachings to one's daily life. Indeed, American Jews are deeply suspicious of any intrusion of religion into what Rev. Richard John Neuhaus has called "the public square," and their attitudes toward matters of church and state are more similar to those of secular organizations such as the American Civil Liberties Union and Common Cause than to those of most committed Christians.

The inadequacy of the religious definition of Judaism is revealed when it comes to the several hundred thousand immigrants from the Soviet Union and, after 1991, from Russia during the 1980s and 1990s. The Russian immigrants were almost totally estranged from Judaism, and the efforts of American synagogues to re-Judaize them have met with only limited success. Even Jews who rejected Judaism are still considered Jews in good standing. In fact, many of the fiercest critics of Judaism (and Jewishness) have been Jews, and modern-day Jewish movements such as Jewish socialism and Labor Zionism have opposed traditional Judaism. The ambiguous nature of Jewish identity is revealed when Jews are compared, say, to Irish Catholics. A lapsed Irish Catholic remains Irish, although he is no longer a Catholic in good standing. A Jewish atheist, by contrast, is still a Jew.

In the face of the secularism and indifference of most American Jews to Judaism, some observers of American Jewry have preferred to describe them as an ethnic group. But, here again, if Jews constitute an ethnic group, it is a peculiar one. Certainly the ethnic ties of Jews are not linguistic. Only a tiny segment of American Jewry uses a Jewish language, whether it be Yiddish or Ladino, as their primary language. Indeed, most American Jews are not fluent in any Jewish language, and even the Jewish *Forward,* at one time America's most widely read foreign-language newspaper, now has far more readers of its weekly English-language edition than of its Yiddish counterpart. And if language defines an ethnic group, what are we to make of the fact that the ancestors of today's American Jews spoke different languages in Europe, North Africa, and the Middle East? The language diversity of the first generation did not prevent the absorption of their descendants into a transcendent American Jewish community in which language plays no role.

But if a common language, or at least the memory of a common language, is not the core element of contemporary American Jewish ethnicity, what is? Some have argued that the study of Jewish history could play this role. Thus Henry L. Feingold, in his important essay "Jewish Survival in America," argued that Jewish communities in the Diaspora, including American Jewry, "have traditionally relied on history to invent themselves. . . . It is in history rather than in territory or sovereignty that Jews discover reasons to remain a people." In the absence of territory and sovereignty, "history is compelled to play the binding role that these more tangible factors play for others." The study of history was particularly imperative to American Jews because of "their waning sense of identity as a distinct people that is manifest everywhere in Jewish America." Indeed, Feingold claimed, without a sense of history the prognosis for Jewish survival in America was bleak. What else could provide American Jews with the sense that they comprise, in the words of the Bible, a "peculiar people"? History, Feingold concluded, was a survival mechanism, "for only by being armed with such self-knowledge can American Jewry become aware of where it is going and how it will get there."[1]

In order for history to play such a part, however, there must be a consensus among American Jews as to what constitutes their "usable past." But such a consensus is unlikely to result from the "full and objective" history that Feingold recommended. American Jewry is not an encapsulated shtetl. The history of American Jews has been too variegated, too divided along religious, social, and ideological lines, and subject to too many differing interpretations, for there to be any such agreement. It is a community, Feingold admits, with little "coherence and cohesiveness." Other observers agree. "Never had a Jewish community been to such an extent voluntary and so divided," the historian Robert Seltzer has written. Is it realistic to believe that American Jews could agree, for example, on the history of American Judaism or on the historic role of Jews in American politics? And without this it is not probable that history can play the role envisaged by Feingold. Although the United Jewish Appeal would like Jews to believe that "We are one," this is hardly the case. And yet American Jews still comprise a community. The attachment of Jews to Jewishness is far stronger than the loyalties of other ethnic groups, and their rate of exogamy was, until recently, far lower. Feingold noted that, in the face of massive acculturation, American Jews "retain something distinctive that is especially conspicuous in their abiding interest and concern for beleaguered Jewish communities abroad." But what that "something distinctive" is remains a puzzle. America's Jews, the sociologist Nathan Glazer declared, are "a social group with clearly marked boundaries . . . but the sources of the energies that hold [it] separate, and of the ties that bind it together, has become completely mysterious."

These ties are far weaker today than when Glazer wrote in 1950. In 1960 the sociologist Eric Rosenthal used the phrase "acculturation without assimilation" to describe how Jews had adapted to American life. While adjusting to the lifestyle and mind-set of the general population, they had separated from the rest of America in choosing marriage partners, friends, and places to live. Thirty years later "acculturation without assimilation" did not accurately describe the lives Jews had carved out for themselves in America. For Jewish survivalists, the most troubling statistic of the comprehensive National Jewish Population Survey of 1990 was the 52 percent of Jews who were marrying non-Jews. This, however, was to be expected since Jews now mainly live in suburbia where many of their neighbors are not Jews, and their children attend secondary schools and colleges where they are in a minority. Conservative rabbi Robert Gordis argued as early as 1966 in *Judaism in a Christian World,* at a time when Jews were first becoming aware of their skyrocketing intermarriage rate, that intermarriage was less a problem for which there was a solution than a condition Jews would have to live with. Intermarriage, Gordis wrote, "is part of the price that modern Jews must pay for freedom and equality in an open society."

In 1950 the Labor Zionist Hayim Greenberg predicted that American Jews were in "grave danger of becoming merely an ethnic group in the conventional sense of the term . . . but without the consciousness of a specific drama and tension in its life." Jews in the 1950s and 1960s believed such thinking to be unduly alarmist. During these years, Jews were moving rapidly up the social and economic ladder, building new and ornate synagogues, and listening to the good things that Jewish intellectuals were saying about Judaism and Jewishness. Today, however, some of Greenberg's warnings appear prescient. A 1988 national survey of American Jews by the *Los Angeles Times* reported that fully 25 percent of born Jews no longer saw themselves as Jews, and another 25 percent had no affiliation with any Jewish organization or contributed funds to any Jewish cause. Evidently the largest and fastest growing segment of American Jewry since the 1970s has been not Reform, Conservative, or Orthodox, but "none of the above."

American Jews had ceased to be a chosen people observing God's laws and instead had become a choosing people. Much as patrons at a Chinese restaurant will take items from Column A and from Column B, so American Jews became adept at selecting those aspects of Judaism and Jewishness that harmonized with their identity as modern Americans. As sociologists noted, these aspects did not interfere with acculturation, did not make Jews conspicuous, and conformed to "democratic" values. Jews were exhibiting that sense of individualism that commentators since the time of Alexis de Tocqueville have seen as quintessentially American. In the process, Judaism was being transformed into a religious "persuasion," to be accepted or rejected at will. No more than one-quarter of contemporary America's Jews make a stab at observing the dietary laws, fewer than 10 percent keep the Sabbath as a day of rest, and more than half of Jewish women do not light Sabbath candles. And yet most American Jews claim that being Jewish is very important to them and that they are "very good" Jews. This reflects the feel-good mood of modern America in which self-esteem is a mark of mental health.

In a sense most American Jews are "Jews by choice," the term generally applied to converts, since it is now so easy to cease being Jewish and since Jewishness weighs so lightly on their shoulders. There even exists a group of "messianic Jews," or "Jews for Jesus," who claim that being a good Jew does not conflict with accepting the divinity of Jesus. (They ignore Heinrich Heine's comment that Jews do not make good Christians because no Jew could believe in the divinity of another Jew.) With Jewish identity now a matter of prescription rather than ascription, what assurances are there that a sufficient number of American Jews would choose the same things, or, *pace* Feingold, read Jewish history in the same way?

American Jews are a troubled people and pessimism is in style. While not fearing for their physical safety, they are concerned about the future of American Jewry, which has experienced major demographic hemorrhaging due to a low birthrate, high exogamy, and religious and cultural apathy. "The despair and confusion of American Jewry in the face of this crisis," the historian Jack Wertheimer noted, "has no parallel in other religious communities." Certainly there is much to justify this pessimism, and also much to belie it as well. During the years since Greenberg's somber prognosis, American Jews have not become a "conventional" ethnic group. Instead, they have created a parochial school system encompassing more than six hundred day schools, their fund-raising efforts collect more than a billion dollars a year, and there is now an American Jewish intelligentsia that staffs the country's rabbinical seminaries and university programs in Jewish studies. While most of the nation's Jews can be described as Jewish Americans, there still remains a sizable minority of American Jews. It is of some comfort that whereas the buzzwords among Jews during the 1930s and 1940s were "survival" and "anti-Semitism," those of the 1980s and 1990s have been "continuity" and "identity." With anti-Semitism at an all-time low, it is comforting to know that Jews can focus on more subtle problems.

It is foolhardy to make predictions. As Francis Bacon said some four hundred years ago, predictions "ought to serve but for winter talk by the fireside." Who in 1988 could have predicted the end of the cold war, the break-up of the Soviet Union, and the election of an obscure governor from Arkansas as president? "Over and over again," wrote Jonathan Sarna, the historian of American Jewry, the Jewish community "has confounded those who predicted gloom and doom and has experienced surprising bursts of new life. There is no guarantee that this will happen again. . . . If history offers us no guarantee of success, it does at least provide us with a warrant for hope." Or, as that prominent student of American culture Lawrence P. (Yogi) Berra once said, it is déjà vu all over again.

Jews, the historian Simon Rawidowicz remarked, have been "an ever-dying people," and this remains as true today in America as it was in the Europe about which he wrote. On May 5, 1964, *Look* magazine published an article on "The Vanishing American Jew." The American Jew has not vanished, but *Look* soon did. Whether the magazine will have the last laugh, however, remains to be seen. Stephen J. Whitfield of Brandeis University has noted that the experience of Jews, more than that of America's other ethnic groups, "is the supreme test of how far acculturation can go without eroding the sense of distinctiveness." So far, he concluded, "American Jewry as a whole has not flunked this test of an open society. Sometimes they are in the dark, however."

The American Jewish experience has been sui generis. Little in the experience of Jews in Europe, Africa, or the Middle East prepared Jews for the social and intellectual demands of life in the United States. As an erstwhile corporate people, they now resided in a society in which individualism and personal gratification and not community obligations were idealized. A people for whom religion and ethnicity were inextricably linked now were surrounded by individuals who believed religion to be a private affair and described different religious ideologies and values as "persuasions." A people who had lived with the ever-present threat of exile and pogroms now resided in a land where anti-Semitism was mild and did not impede social and economic mobility. Nowhere else have the challenges and opportunities of modernity and liberalism for Jews been so stark as in the United States, the world's preeminent modernist and liberal nation. It is not accidental that the major theme of America's major Jewish writers has been the shock of acculturation and adaptation. One thinks, for example, of the novels of Abraham Cahan, Bernard Malamud, and Philip Roth.

Jews, of course, were not the only immigrant and ethnic group that had to live with the tensions of acculturation or who sought to reconcile the conflicting pressures of Americanization and group identity. The pressures were not as traumatic for Jews as they were, say, for American Blacks, but they were unique. Until quite recently Jews were the only major subgroup within American society that was not Christian. In addition, with the founding of the state of Israel in 1948, American Jews had to live with the question of why as Jews they chose not to live in the Jewish state. And because the social and economic upward mobility of Jews in America happened so quickly, Jews left the immigrant neighborhoods and adopted the style and values of mainstream America more quickly than other groups.

American Jews are by now accustomed to being verbally assaulted from pulpits and lecterns by jeremiads bemoaning the state of American Jewry and questioning whether it has any future. This anxiety about survival, Henry Feingold wrote, "has become American Jewry's most prominent characteristic." But in light of the rapid social and economic upward mobility of American Jews, perhaps the most important question one can ask about American Jews is not why they have acculturated, but why this process has not completely obliterated Jewish life in America. Within fifty years, a student named William Rosenblatt predicted, America's Jews would be "indistinguishable from the mass of humanity that surrounds them." He said this in 1872.

The essays in this book were published during the past two decades and were, in part, attempts to come to terms with the challenge that America has presented to Jewish identity and continuity. The essays are grouped into three parts: Identity, Acculturation, and Politics. Two essays in part 1, "The Search for American Jewish Identity" and "Jewishness and the New York Intellectuals," explore how American Jews, particularly intellectuals, have defined American Jewish identity. The second and third essays in this part, "World War II and American Jewish Identity" and "The Jew as Patriot: Herman Wouk and American Jewish Identity," argue that World War II was a watershed in the evolution of American Jewish identity. It was then that American Jews became fully comfortable in their dual roles as Americans and as Jews. Whatever importance anti-Semitism had had in American life prior to the war quickly dissipated after 1945.

During the early twentieth century, East European Jews in America commenced a remarkable movement up the social and economic ladders. This was slowed down during the depression years and the war, only to be resumed during the postwar decades. This transformed social, economic, and demographic profile is the focus of the six essays in the second part of the book titled "Acculturation." "The Ordeal of Success: American Jewry since World War II" surveys the extent of these changes. Within a few decades American Jewry would consist mainly of professionals, academicians, and successful businessmen (and women). Accustomed to thinking of themselves as workers and as victims of anti-Semitism, American Jews were ambivalent about their new social status and the economic success that accompanied it. "American Jews and the Business Mentality" and "Jews with Money" examine the roots of this discomfort and the attempts by some Jews to hold on to images of American Jews that were increasingly divorced from reality. This changing social composition of American Jews is particularly remarkable in academia, the focus of "The Friendly University: Jews in Academia since World War II." By the 1990s the three most famous universities in America—Harvard, Yale, and Princeton—had presidents named Rudenstine, Levin, and Shapiro, and Jews comprised anywhere from a quarter to a third of the faculty of America's most distinguished universities.

Part of the social transformation of American Jewry was the movement from the city to suburbia. By the 1960s, more than half of American Jews were living in suburbia. Most sociologists of American Jewry, including Nathan Glazer ("The Missing Element: Nathan Glazer and Modern Orthodoxy"), believed that Orthodoxy was a one-generation urban phenomenon and could not survive the acculturation and suburbanization of American Jewry. In fact, an Orthodoxy in modernist dress—Modern Orthodoxy—would sink roots in suburbia. The history of one synagogue in West Orange, New Jersey ("Orthodoxy in Pleasantdale"), illustrates some of the difficulties in attempting to remain faithful to Jewish law in the midst of suburban shopping malls, multiplex movie theaters, golf courses, and Gentiles.

If American Jews remain to a certain extent a "peculiar people," a major reason is their liberal political orientation. They are, Henry Feingold recently wrote, "America's liberals par excellence; and if no longer the most liberal, they remain the wealthiest constituency to make their political home in the left wing of the Democratic Party." The third part, "Politics," explores the content of this politics, particularly as it relates to the question of power ("Politics and American Jewish Identity"), Israel ("American Jewry and the State of Israel"), and race relations ("Blacks and Jews Entangled"). The essay "Charles S. Liebman and American Jewish Liberalism" analyzes one interpretation of American Jewish liberalism by a prominent Jewish academician. While other mobile ethnic groups have moved to the right politically, American Jews currently show little sign of deserting the left-wing politics they absorbed by osmosis in their families and neighborhoods. This is the case despite the existence of a small band of neoconservative Jewish intellectuals, a topic discussed in "The War among the Jews" and "Pat Buchanan and the Jews."

The careful reader will sense an ambivalence in this volume regarding the prospects of American Jewry. Most of the evidence from the social sciences is bleak, and this pessimism is reinforced by the melancholy of the rabbinate. The publication of this book, however, illustrates the other side of the coin. Most of these essays were published in American Jewish magazines, and their existence attests to the fact that not all is doom and gloom in the Jewish world. As an unabashed Jewish survivalist, I make no claim to a Rankean objectivity. Shortly before completing this introduction, a new museum concerned with Jewish history was dedicated in New York City. And shortly after the American Jewish Historical Society and several other Jewish cultural organizations opened their doors in a new cultural center in New York. One hopes that these institutions will be more than mere repositories of the records of the past. Perhaps they can help stimulate an intellectual and cultural renaissance within American Jewry.

PART ONE

Identity

ONE

The Search for American Jewish Identity

THE MOST IMPORTANT PROBLEM facing American Jews for the past century has been defining the nature of American Jewish identity. This had not been a major issue for Jews prior to the modern era, when traditional religious definitions of Jewishness, bolstered by state authority, held sway, and when anti-Semitism restricted the social and economic contacts of Jews with Gentiles. In America, however, religious authority was solely a private matter, and anti-Semitism was much less virulent. Since the saliency of the issue of Jewish identity was a response to Jewish emancipation and modernity, it is not surprising that it should have become important in the United States. Here emancipation was never a major political issue, and here also secularization, political and economic liberalism, and other aspects of modernization occurred earlier and were more pervasive than elsewhere.

American Jews were both Jews and Americans, and their efforts to define Jewish identity were influenced by the broader debate over the nature of American identity. More than two hundred years ago, in *Letters From An American Farmer*, Hector St. John de Crevecoeur, the French observer of American mores, asked the most famous and important question in American history: "What then is the American, this new man?" His answer stressed both the biological and intellectual uniqueness of the transplanted European. The American was an amalgamation of the ethnic strains of Europe, or at least those

Parts of this chapter were previously published as *What Is American about the American Jewish Experience* (Dept. of Religion, College of William and Mary, Williamsburg, Va., 1993), 108–22; and "Jewish-Americans," in *Multiculturalism in the United States: A Comparative Guide to Acculturation and Ethnicity*, ed. John D. Buenker and Lorman A. Ratner (New York: Greenwood Press, 1992), 149–72. Reprinted by permission. Greenwood Press is an imprint of Greenwood Publishing Group, Inc., Westport, Conn.

of Western Europe. "I could point out to you a family whose grandfather was an Englishman, whose wife was Dutch, whose son married a French woman, and whose present four sons have now four wives of different nations." The true American had also discarded European modes of thought. He is an American who, leaving behind him all the ancient prejudices and manners, "acts upon new principles, entertains new ideas, and forms new opinions."

Crevecoeur waxed poetic as he contemplated the future of this American new man and his land. "Here individuals of all nations are melted into a new race of men, whose labors and posterity will one day cause great changes in the world." American writers of the nineteenth century followed Crevecoeur's cue and stressed the theme of the newness of America and the American. Thus Ralph Waldo Emerson, in his famous 1837 "American Scholar" address delivered before Harvard's Phi Beta Kappa Society, declared that American dependence on the learning of other lands had ended. "The millions that around us are rushing into life cannot always be fed on the sere remains of foreign harvests. Events, actions arise, that must be sung, that will sing themselves." He concluded with one of the most famous sentences in American literature. Americans have "listened too long to the courtly muses of Europe. . . . What is the remedy? . . . We will walk on our own feet; we will work with our own hands; we will speak our own minds."

It is no coincidence that America's Jews, perhaps more than any other group, have followed the advice of Crevecoeur and Emerson to leave behind the prejudices and manners of Europe, "the sere remains of foreign harvests," and to sing of American events. This has been true not only in the defining of American nationality but also in the defining of American Jewish identity. Crevecoeur's "new modes of life" were especially new for the Jew. The definitions of Jewish identity developed elsewhere were hardly relevant for America. In Europe, Africa, and Asia, status and citizenship were based on religion, anti-Semitism was pervasive, Jews were denied citizenship until the nineteenth century, and the *kehillah,* the self-contained Jewish community, played a vital role and had an official, or at least semi-official position. In America, there was little public (as distinct from private) anti-Semitism, citizenship was a matter of right and not sufferance, there were few significant barriers to a Jew's social and economic advance, and the Jewish community had no standing in law, nor did it perform any official tasks. The Jewish attitude toward America was best expressed by Israel Baline (later Americanized to Irving Berlin), an immigrant from Eastern Europe who grew up in New York City's Lower East Side Jewish ghetto and wrote "God Bless America."

Pulled in seemingly opposite directions by the force of American hope and the power of Jewish memory, America's Jews were forced to define what it meant to be a Jew in America, to articulate the relationship between American and Jewish identities, and to develop lifestyles that were simultaneously both American and Jewish. No other ethnic group has been so concerned with defining its relationship to America. It is no coincidence that Jews wrote three of the most popular expressions of American identity: Emma Lazarus's poem "The New Colossus," Israel Zangwill's play *The Melting Pot,* and Horace Kallen's essay "Democracy Versus the Melting Pot." A disproportionate number of America's most prominent sociologists of ethnicity have been Jews—Arnold Rose, Milton Gordon, and Nathan Glazer, to name just a few. The Harvard historian Oscar Handlin wrote an important monograph on the history of America's Irish as well as *The Uprooted,* the most important monograph on American immigration history, and Jewish historians such as Gilbert Osofsky, Allan Spear, Lawrence Levine, and Herbert Gutman have provided much of the intellectual framework for understanding black history and culture. No American novel has probed more perceptively the costs of immigrant acculturation than Abraham Cahan's *The Rise of David Levinsky,* written by the longtime editor of the *Forward,* a Yiddish daily newspaper that during its heyday had the highest circulation of any foreign-language paper in American history.

Jews have had a more difficult problem in defining their status as Americans than any other major ethnic group. Not only did Jews have to adapt to a culture radically different from what they had known in Europe and the Arab lands, but they were also part of a society in which they were both a religious and an ethnic minority. Other immigrants were at least Christian and thus had a religious bond with native-born Americans. Furthermore, Jews in Europe, Africa, and Asia had been the most isolated and most communally organized of America's major immigrant groups, and they had to make a radical adaptation to the individualistic and liberal ethos of America.

The problem of defining American Jewish identity was complicated by the puzzling nature of Jewish identity itself. While most Christian Americans viewed Jews to be simply members of an exotic religion, the reality was quite different. Jewish identity had religious elements surely, but it also had ethnic and nationalistic elements as well. To an extent not true for other groups, the identity of Jews was idiosyncratic and not easily described by the categories familiar to historians and sociologists. Thus in the 1960s there appeared a group of atheistic Jews who used the seemingly oxymoronic term "humanistic Jews" to describe themselves. Other Jews did not deny the Jewish identity of these dissenters from God-centered Judaism.

American Jewish identity was further complicated by the eagerness of Jews to become Americans. Few other ethnic groups surpassed Jews in their ardor to become fully American. Jews had the lowest expatriation rate of any major immigrant group. The percentage of women among Jewish immigrants was higher than that of any other immigrant group except for the Irish. This was because Jews came over in families with the intention of never returning to Europe. Despite the nostalgia of *Fiddler on the Roof*, there was little longing among Jewish immigrants for the impoverished and brutal existences they had left behind in Europe. The passion of immigrant Jews for their new country was indicated by their high rates of attendance at night school and the rapidity with which they learned English, a process lovingly satirized by Leo Rosten in his stories of Hyman Kaplan, who was convinced that America's sixteenth president, Abraham Lincohen, must have been Jewish. Jews also tended to become citizens and to take part in electoral politics much sooner than other ethnic groups. And, as indicated by their participation down to the present day in various reform and good-government movements, Jews also took more seriously the pieties of democratic rhetoric than did, say the Irish, Italians, or blacks, who had fewer illusions about politics and who tended to view it as a means for personal or group advancement.

The defining of American Jewish identity was further complicated by the fluid and rather shapeless character of American identity. In contrast to other nations, America's population was too diverse to provide an identity based on ethnic or racial homogeneity. "Imagine, my dear friend, if you can," Alexis de Tocqueville wrote back to France more than a century and a half ago, "a society formed of all the nations of the world . . . people having different languages, beliefs, opinions: in a word, a society without roots, without memories, without prejudices, without routines, without common ideas, without a national character, yet a hundred times happier than our own." What could provide the cement of national unity for such a diverse community? The most popular answer was political ideology.

The self-evident "truths" that Jefferson laid out in the Declaration of Independence comprised not only the rationale for independence from Great Britain but also the ideological foundations of the republic. America was to be a *novus ordo seclorum*, a land where all people, or at least all white people, would enjoy the natural rights of "life, liberty, and the pursuit of happiness." Nationality was to be based on ideological affirmation and not on descent. A

Native-born American as well as an immigrant could be either un-American or pro-American depending on their ideological bent. "The genius of America, Arthur M. Schlesinger, Jr., wrote in *The Disuniting of America: Reflections on a Multicultural Society* (1991), "lies in its capacity to forge a single nation from peoples of remarkably diverse racial, religious, and ethnic origins. It has done so because democratic principles provide both the philosophical bond of union and practical experience in civil participation."

The precise nature of these principles that defined America was, of course, open to varying interpretations. The fact that Northerners and Southerners each believed they were faithful to the "truths" of the Founding Fathers did not prevent them from slaughtering each other during the Civil War. A significant percentage of Americans would disagree with Schlesinger, who wrote in his 1962 book, *The Politics of Hope* that "all of America is liberalism." American nationality has never been easy to define, when even the idea of a core American culture and an American literary canon has been challenged by proponents of "multiculturalism."

American Jews thus have never been more American than when pondering the nature of American nationality and asking what it means to be an American Jew. From the beginning, America's Jews sought to demonstrate that they were at home in America and that, at least for them, the travail of the wandering, homeless Jew had ended. In 1841, at the dedication of the Beth Elohim synagogue in Charleston, South Carolina, Rabbi Gustav Poznanski rebuked those American Jews who longed for a return to Zion. "This synagogue is our temple, this city our Jerusalem, this happy land our Palestine." This belief in the compatibility of Jewish and American identities was not something that could be taken for granted but had to be continually asserted and defended. This became the lifework of Rabbi Isaac Mayer Wise, the most important figure in the history of nineteenth-century American Judaism and the founder of Reform Judaism in America.

Wise preferred to use the term "American Judaism" rather than "Reform Judaism" to describe the changes in Jewish theology and ritual he sought in order to reconcile Judaism with the temper of America. He titled his 1857 prayer book *Minhag America* (American custom), his organization of synagogues was called the Union of American Hebrew Congregations, and his organization of rabbis was named the Central Conference of American Rabbis. The word "Hebrew" was frequently used by German Jews during the nineteenth century in describing themselves and in naming their institutions, partially to distinguish themselves from the Eastern European immigrant "Jews" whom they saw as backward and less Americanized. This Americanization of Judaism reached its logical conclusion in a seminal document drawn up by a group of Reform rabbis in Pittsburgh in 1885.

The Pittsburgh Platform not only emphasized the compatibility of Judaism with modern science and biblical criticism, but it also stressed the harmony between Judaism and America. It rejected those elements of Judaism that distinguished Jews from other Americans and cast doubt on their Americanness. "We consider ourselves," the rabbis solemnly declared, "no longer a nation, but a religious community, and therefore expect neither a return to Palestine, nor a sacrificial worship under the sons of Aaron, nor the restoration of any of the laws concerning the Jewish state." Rabbi Kaufmann Kohler called the Pittsburgh Platform the Reform movement's declaration of independence because it freed America's Jews from the nationalism and cultural and social separatism of "Mosaico-Talmudical Judaism."

Most Reform spokesmen were intense opponents of Zionism. They strongly opposed Zionism's emphasis on Jewish nationalism, its belief that anti-Semitism was a permanent aspect of European and American life, and its call for the ingathering of Jews into Palestine. Reform Judaism, in contrast, stressed the religious element of Jewish identity, claimed that the dispersion of the Jews was part of God's plan to spread the ethical teachings of Judaism, emphasized that American anti-Semitism was insignificant and transitory, and feared that Zionism would result in the raising of legitimate doubts about the patriotism of Jews. "As an American," Jacob Schiff wrote in 1907, "I cannot for a moment concede that one can be at the same time a true American and an honest adherent of the Zionist movement. . . . The Jew should not for a moment feel . . . that he is in exile and that his abode here is only a temporary or passing one."For some German Jews, even the tepid Judaism of the Reform movement was too particularistic. Felix Adler, the son of Rabbi Samuel Adler of New York, carried the rationalism and universalism of the left wing of Reform Judaism to their logical conclusion when he founded the Society for Ethical Culture in 1876. Wishing to free the Jew from any lingering effects of the ghetto and skeptical of traditional religion, Adler favored a humanistic religion that would transcend all racial and religious particularism. To this day a large percentage of the members of the Society for Ethical Culture and the Unitarian-Universalist Church are Jews seeking to escape from the remnants of an unwanted religious-ethnic heritage.

Despite the ideological challenge of Adler, the vast majority of nineteenth-century German Jews maintained that a denationalized Judaism was perfectly compatible with American identity. Rabbi David Philipson asserted, "From the hills of Palestine the prophet's voice floated down the vestibule of time, enjoining the soulful command, 'Hear O Israel, the Eternal is our God.' From the broad plains of the United States the answer is sent back, 'God is one.' " Reformers believed a universalistic Judaism shorn of any distinctive ethnic characteristics could make great strides in the United States, and Wise even rashly predicted that it could eventually become the majority American religion and lead to the salvation of the world.

From the Reform perspective, the mission of the Jew was no longer to preserve a distinctive religious culture and to observe Jewish law. Rather, it was to convert the Gentiles and to usher in the Messianic age. Reformers modified the Jewish liturgy to resemble upper-class Protestantism. Sermons became a central part of the religious service, decorum was stressed, and ethical behavior was emphasized. Religious services were often conducted in "temples," implying that the Jewish temple was here in America now and not in Zion at some future date.

Other Jews besides rabbis were also intent on showing that there was no incompatibility between being an American and being a Jew. In 1892, the American Jewish Historical Society, the nation's first ethnic historical society, was established to refute the claims that Jews were not patriotic, were interested solely in making money, could not be integrated into American life, and lacked ties to the colonial period of American history. One of the society's earliest publications had the revealing title *Christopher Columbus and the Participation of the Jews in the Spanish and Portuguese Discoveries.* The society's first president was Oscar Straus, who fancied himself an amateur historian. In 1885, Straus had published *The Origins of the Republican Form of Government in the United States,* which argued that the Founding Fathers had been influenced by the political ideas of the Jewish commonwealth.

Jewish writers during the late nineteenth and early twentieth centuries reinforced the efforts of the society to demonstrate that there was no inherent conflict between American and Jewish identities. The sociologist Milton Gordon, in *Assimilation in American Life* (1964), argued that the three most important paradigms of American immigrant acculturation have been Anglo-conformity, the melting pot, and cultural pluralism. Jews provided the most popular expressions of each model. Anglo-conformity, the belief that America was permanently shaped by the English character of the colonial period and that immigrants should make themselves over into good Yankees, is a central motif of Emma Lazarus's 1883 sonnet "The New Colossus." This poem was engraved on a memorial plaque and placed on the pedestal of the Statue of Liberty in 1903.

Lazarus was born in 1849 into an old, respected, and almost completely assimilated Sephardic New York family. One of her earliest references to Jews was in her poem "In the Jewish Synagogue at Newport," published in her 1871 collection, *Admetus and Other Poems.* The volume was dedicated to "My Friend, Ralph Waldo Emerson." The poem somberly contemplated the fate of Newport Jewry and, by implication, all of American Jewry. "No signs of life are here: the very prayers / Inscribed around are in a language dead."

Lazarus's nearly comatose Jewish identity was revived in the early 1880s when she read George Eliot's novel *Daniel Deronda,* learned of the Russian pogroms of 1881–82, and witnessed the beginning of the massive immigration of Eastern European Jews into New York City. She became involved in immigrant relief work and defended the Jewish immigrants against their detractors. According to the historian John Higham, she became "the first modern American laureate of their history and culture." In 1882, Lazarus wrote a series of essays in *Century* magazine attacking anti-Semitism and describing Jews as the agents of progress. In that same year, she published a volume of poems titled *Songs of a Semite,* which included the pro-Zionist poem "The Banner of the Jew." The poem denied that the "martial fire" and "mystic flame" of the Jews were spent. "With Moses' law and David's lyre, / Your ancient strength remains unbent." In *An Epistle to the Hebrews,* which appeared in 1883, Lazarus argued for a Jewish national and cultural revival in Palestine and the United States.

Lazarus thus undoubtedly had the immigrant Jews primarily in mind when it came time to write "The New Colossus." For Lazarus, the Statue of Liberty was a symbol of hope and welcome for Jews and other immigrants. For her it dwarfed in importance its venerable counterpart, the Colossus of Rhodes, a statue of the sun god Helios, one of the seven wonders of the ancient world. Initially Auguste Bartholdi's statue, "Liberty Enlightening the World," symbolized America as the land of liberty. Only later, and in part because of Lazarus's poem, did the statue come to symbolize America as a land of refuge for immigrants. "Mother of Exiles. From her beacon-hand / Glows world-wide welcome; her mild eyes command / The air-bridged harbor that twin cities frame."

And yet the words spoken by the statue seemingly conflict with the vision of an America whose "golden door" welcomes the immigrants. "Give me your tired, your poor, / Your huddled masses yearning to breathe free. / The wretched refuse of your teeming shore." Historians have puzzled over Lazarus's seemingly condescending description of the immigrants as "wretched refuse." One interpretation has argued that Lazarus did not use the phrase in a pejorative sense, since in the 1880s "wretched" was often used as a synonym for distressed, and "refuse" often described objects considered to be valueless rather than worthless. There was no doubt, however, as to the attitude of Lazarus's sister toward the immigrant Jews. She forbade the inclusion of "anything Jewish" when Emma's collected works appeared posthumously in 1889. Whatever the original intention of "The New Colossus," the poem was compatible with the ideology of Anglo-conformity, which asserted that Jews and other immigrants were acceptable only to the extent that they adopted the dominant social and intellectual patterns of American life and were purged of their foreign impurities. Otherwise, they remained "wretched refuse."

Israel Zangwill's 1908 play *The Melting Pot* was the most important literary answer to the doctrine of Anglo-conformity. Zangwill was born in 1864 in the Jewish ghetto of Whitechapel in London's East End. The son of poor Orthodox Russian immigrants, he was to become the most prominent Jewish writer of his generation in the English-speaking world. In 1856, eight years before his birth, Parliament granted complete civil rights to Jews. In a series of what he called "ghetto" novels, essays, and plays, Zangwill explored the challenge this grant of civil rights presented to Jewish identity.

Zangwill described himself as a man of "violent contraries." Deeply attached to Jewish history and the spiritual values of Judaism, he also believed Judaism was not a viable faith for modern man. The Jew, he wrote, was "like a mother who clasps her dead child to her breast and will not let it go." Although he translated portions of the Jewish liturgy into English, he also published *The Next Religion*, an attack on Judaism. Zangwill wrote nostalgically of the ghetto while proclaiming to be a militant assimilationist. He was one of the founders of British Zionism and a friend and supporter of Theodor Herzl, yet he advised Western Jews to forego any thought of settling in Palestine and to follow the path of assimilation that he himself had taken.

Zangwill yearned to be accepted as an English writer and not merely as a Jewish writer. Shortly before his marriage to Edith Ayrton, an English Christian, he defended intermarriage as the solution to anti-Semitism. "With Israelitish stiffneckedness we have spurned intermarriage, the only natural process by which two alien races can be welded into one. To speak most dispassionately, we have in the long run got only what we deserved." His wife shared his universalism, and the couple rejected all sectarian identifications such as Judaism and Christianity, preferring to support general causes, including peace and feminism. Their first son was neither baptized nor circumcised, and belonged, as did his parents, to an abstract humanity. The biological assimilation that Zangwill experienced in his own life was the theme of *The Melting Pot.*

Although an Englishman, Zangwill was entranced by the vision of an American nationality still in the process of evolving and combining the best that all of the world's ethnic groups had to offer. The purpose of his play *The Melting Pot,* he said, was to show how "the most violent antitheses of the past may be fused into a higher unity." Contrary to popular belief, Zangwill's melting pot did not refer to a process whereby immigrants were to be transformed into good Anglo-Saxons, but rather to a process whereby native-born Americans and immigrants alike were to be thrown together into the pot to create something entirely new. "America is God's crucible," he wrote, "the great melting pot where all the races of Europe are melting and reforming. . . . A fig for your feuds and vendettas, Germans and Frenchmen, Irishmen and Englishmen, Jews and Russians—into the Crucible with you all. God is making the American."

For Zangwill, intermarriage was the fuel that kept the melting pot bubbling. His play recounted the romance between two immigrants—David, a Russian Jew, and Vera, a Russian Christian, whose father was responsible for the pogrom that had caused the death of David's parents. The play's dramatic focus is on whether the love of David and Vera will survive amid the bitter memories of Europe and the opposition of their relatives. Will David remain true to his vision of America where the peoples of Europe are forgetting their Old World hostilities and fusing into a new nationality, or would the memories of Europe remain too strong? David's last name is Quixano, an unusual name for an eastern European Jew. Some scholars have speculated that this was an allusion to Cervantes' hero's belief in the power of love to conquer all. At one point David rejects Vera: "Christian love! For this I gave up my people—darkened the home that sheltered me. . . . Let me go home, let me go home." But, as could be predicted, love triumphs. At the play's end David pleads with Vera to "cling to me till all these ghosts are exorcised, cling to me till our love triumphs over death." In its melodramatic finale David proclaims to Vera his vision of an American national identity that is being shaped in the crucible of New York City. "Yes, East and West, and North and South, and palm and the pine, the pole and the equator, the crescent and the cross—how the great Alchemist melts and fuses them with his purging flame! Here shall they all unite to build the Republic of Man and the Kingdom of God. Ah, Vera, what is the glory of Rome and Jerusalem, where all nations and races come to worship and look back, compared with the glory of America, where all races and nations come to labor and look forward!" *The Melting Pot* made a deep impression on American audiences and was a great commercial success. President Theodore Roosevelt said, "I do not know when I have seen a play that stirred me as much." The magazine *Independent* praised Zangwill for allowing Americans "to see ourselves as others see us, to learn how the fair Goddess of Liberty looks to those who have fled to her protection from Russian pogroms."

Zangwill was not alone in favoring Jewish assimilation through intermarriage. During the era of the silent screen when Hollywood was dominated by Jewish producers, directors, and owners, dozens of films endorsing intermarriage appeared. Most of these films featured marriages between Jews and Irish. Love can conquer all, even religious differences, was the message of *Romance of the Jewess* (1908), *Becky Gets a Husband* (1912), *The Jew's Christmas* (1913), *For the Love of Mike and Rosie* (1916), *The Cohens and the Kellys* (1926), *Private Izzy Murphy* (1926), *Kosher Kitty Kelly* (1926), *Clancy's Kosher Wedding* (1927), and *Abie's Irish Rose* (1927).

The most famous treatment of intermarriage was *The Jazz Singer* (1927). The jazz singer, played by Al Jolson, changes his name from Jackie Rabinowitz to Jack Robin, rejects the religion and culture of his ancestors, sings in the Winter Garden and not in the synagogue, and marries the Gentile Mary Dale. "You're of the Old World," he tells his father. "Tradition is alright, but this is another day." In these films, the young Jew symbolizes Americanization and the melting pot, while their parents personify the anachronistic traditions of Europe.

Not all Americans, however, were so enthusiastic about the concept of the melting pot. Spokesmen for Anglo-Saxon Protestant Americans had no objection to immigrants jumping into the melting pot in order to purge themselves of their foreign impurities, but they had no intention of jumping into the pot themselves. Nor did they believe that American identity was still in the process of being formed. Rather, they maintained, the creation of American nationality had ended with the close of the eighteenth century. The *Forum*'s review of *The Melting Pot* suggested that its definition of American nationality could only have come from "an author who is himself foreign in nationality and alien in race." In *The Melting Pot Mistake,* which appeared in 1926, the year of Zangwill's death, Henry Pratt Fairchild, a fervent advocate of immigration restriction and a future president of the American Eugenics Society, warned that "a preponderinginfluence of foreigners . . . take away from a people its most precious possession—its soul."

Zangwill's message of "e pluribus unum" was particularly directed at America's Jews. He thought they had only two options. They could either renationalize themselves and migrate to Palestine, or they could renounce Jewish identity and throw themselves into the American melting pot. Zangwill did not believe that a strong Jewish identity could be reconciled with a strong American identity. Jewish assimilation was inevitable, although it could be slowed down by continued immigration from Europe and by anti-Semitism. For America's Jews, Zangwill's message was a prescription for cultural and religious extinction. "Not for this," the *American Hebrew* claimed, "have the million refugees from Russia sought America."

Mary Antin agreed with Zangwill that American and Jewish identities were incompatible. Four years after the appearance of *The Melting Pot,* she published *The Promised Land,* one of the most famous American Jewish autobiographies. Born in Plotzk in White Russia, Antin immigrated to Boston with her family while a child. Her memoir recounts how the promised land of America replaced the promised land of Zion. The autobiography's chapter recounting her passage across the Atlantic was appropriately titled "The Exodus." For Antin, life in America was a rebirth, and she was entranced by what she learned about America in the Boston Public Library, her American yeshiva. Her book ends with a panegyric to her new nation. "America is the youngest of the nations, and inherits all that went before in history. And I am the youngest of all America's children, and into my hands is given all her priceless heritage, to the last white star espied through the telescope, to the last great thought of the philosopher."

For Antin, as for David Quixano, the demands of American life required the putting aside of Old World traditions and hatreds. She married Madeus V. Grabau, a Columbia University professor of paleontology and the son of a Lutheran minister. One can only wonder whether she came to doubt her idealized view of America or her faith in assimilation when her husband left her in 1920 and settled in China.

In contrast to Antin, most American Jews sought to be both American and Jewish, and they welcomed Horace Kallen's attack on the melting pot concept in his 1915 essay "Democracy Versus the Melting Pot." Born in Silesia, Kallen settled in Boston with his family at the age of five. Although his father was an Orthodox rabbi, Kallen gave up any belief in God while a youth.

Breaking with Judaism was part of Kallen's repudiation of his Jewish identity, a repudiation that left him permanently estranged from his father. He initially saw Jewish identity as an encumbrance to full integration into American life and to becoming a Yankee.

Harvard, and one particular Harvard professor, Barrett Wendell, a professor of American literature, showed Kallen the great influence that the Hebraic spirit had had on American literature and culture. Wendell, as well as William James, the mentor of Kallen's Ph.D. dissertation, encouraged Kallen to think of American culture as diverse rather than monistic. While Harvard acquainted him with America's ideals, teaching at the University of Wisconsin prior to World War I acquainted him with American reality. He was impressed by the extent to which German, Scandinavian, and Irish immigrants had maintained their ethnic identities, and he mistakenly concluded that America was developing as a federation of nationalities similar to Switzerland. Rejecting his earlier efforts at assimilation, Kallen now claimed that being a good American and a good Jew were not antagonistic, as Zangwill had claimed, but complementary.

But how did Kallen define Jewishness? An atheist, his loyalties were not to Judaism but to Hebrew culture, and he referred to himself as a Hebraist rather than a Judaist. Defining Hebraism as "the total biography of the Jewish soul," Kallen became a secular Jewish nationalist, a fervent Zionist, and America's most important advocate of "cultural pluralism." In contrast to Reform Judaism's emphasis on Judaism as merely a religion, Kallen looked to the ethnic and nationalistic elements of Jewish identity. His was a message of ethnic, not religious, survival.

In "Democracy Versus the Melting Pot," which was a direct answer to Zangwill, Kallen replaced the metaphor of a melting pot with that of an orchestra. Just as the beauty of an orchestra stemmed from the different sounds of dozens of instruments harmonizing with one another, so the richness of American culture derived from the contributions of dozens of separate ethnic groups to the American mosaic. The American spirit, Kallen argued, consisted of "this union of the different," and was sustained by the equality among ethnic groups and by "the free trade between these different equals in every good thing the community's life and culture produce."

While comforting to some Jewish spokesmen, it is questionable whether Kallen's belief in a national mosaic of ethnic and religious groups was either accurate or desirable. There is much truth to the complaint of Nicholas Roosevelt that Kallen's scenario would have Balkanized America. In fact, ethnic identity was an unimportant factor in the lives of many Americans. Kallen, by contrast, argued that ethnic identity was the most intimate, important, and permanent element of a person's life, "the efficacious natural milieu or habitat of his temperament . . . the center at which he stands, the point of his most intimate social relations, therefore of his intensest emotional life." A person could change many things, he argued, but he could never change the ethnic character of his grandfather. This might be true, but a more important consideration was whether the grandfather could accurately predict the ethnic and religious identity of his grandchildren.

As the historian Arthur Mann has noted, Kallen did not anticipate that the intermarriage encouraged by Zangwill would become widespread. "Democracy Versus the Melting Pot" appeared during the heyday of American immigration from eastern and southern Europe. In 1915, ethnic loyalties remained strong, immigrant groups congregated together in ethnic neighborhoods, and exogamy was relatively rare. Jewish intermarriage in particular was quite low. Zangwill's own life should have alerted him to the malleability of American ethnic patterns.

He had married the daughter of a Methodist minister and hymn writer, his own daughter married a lapsed Quaker, and his grandchild was raised as a Jew. Today Abie's Irish Rose is a common phenomenon. If Irving Berlin could write "White Christmas" and "Easter Parade," if Leonard Bernstein could compose his *Mass*, and if Stephen Schwartz could write the popular musical *Godspell* (based on the Gospel according to St. Matthew), then it is possible at least to ignore one's grandparents. And, of course, it is always possible to change one's own name and one's identity. Bernie Schwartz became Tony Curtis, Julius Garfinkel became John Garfield, Theodosia Goodman became Theda Bara (an anagram of "Arab death"), and Max Aronson became Bronco Billy, America's first cowboy movie star.

All definitions of Jewish identity from the early twentieth century inevitably have had to confront Zionism and, after 1948, the Jewish state of Israel. Both Zangwill and Kallen were Zionists. For Zangwill, Zionism was the negation of the East European Diaspora, a movement with little relevance for Jews living in the West, few of whom had any intention of exchanging the good life of America, Canada, France, and Great Britain for the problems of Palestine. For Kallen, Zionism was an expression of that nationalistic cultural pluralism basic to American identity. American Zionists accepted neither of these formulations. They instead developed a Zionism that was appropriate both for Americans who had no plan to emigrate to the Holy Land and for a nation in which permanent nationalistic divisions were frowned upon.

The major figure in the "Americanizing" of Zionism was Louis D. Brandeis, the progressive reformer and advisor to Woodrow Wilson, and the first Jew to sit on the United States Supreme Court. The great mystery surrounding Brandeis is why he ever became a Zionist in the first place. There was little in his life before 1914 when he became a leader of the American Zionist movement at the age of fifty-eight to suggest such a possibility. A descendant of German Jews who had settled in Louisville, Kentucky in the mid-nineteenth century, Brandeis had not previously exhibited any particular interest in things Jewish. He was not a member of a synagogue or a Jewish fraternal group, he did not observe Jewish religious rituals, and he opposed the retention of ethnic differences. In 1910, for example, he stated, "Habits of living or of thought which tend to keep alive differences of origin or classify men according to their religious beliefs are inconsistent with the American ideal of brotherhood and are disloyal." And yet two years later, he joined the Federation of American Zionists and became an advocate of cultural pluralism. Various interpretations, ranging from the influence of Kallen to Brandeis's political ambitions, have been offered to explain such seemingly bizarre behavior. There is, however, no confusion as to his impact on American Zionism. He helped transform it from a plaything of unassimilated Jewish nationalists into a movement that could attract acculturated American Jews.

Under the influence of Brandeis, American Zionism was shorn of both its nationalistic thrust and its underlying assumption that the essence of Zionism was *aliyah,* a Hebrew term denoting emigration to Zion. Brandeisian Zionism saw Zionism as a philanthropy providing a refuge for persecuted Jews of *other* lands. American Jews had already migrated to the promised land of America, and they had no intention of migrating once more. One rather cynical definition of Brandeisian Zionism said that it was a movement in which one person gave money to a second person so that a third person could reach Palestine. As a result, American Zionism has been most popular when the needs of non-American Jews have been greatest, such as during World War I, World War II, and 1946–48, and after 1967 when Israel was directly threatened by her Arab neighbors. For many contemporary American Jews, Zionism rather than Judaism has become the most important manifestation of their Jewishness and the single most prominent factor shaping their identity as Jews. And yet only a tiny number of American Jews have resettled in the Holy Land—the thing that, more than anything else, defined one as a Zionist according to classic European Zionist ideology.

European Zionists lamented this transformation of American Zionism into a charity emphasizing refugee relief. They argued that Brandeisian Zionism divested the movement of its nationalistic raison d'être. They were convinced that anti-Semitism was so strong and economic conditions were so perilous for Jews, even those in America, that aliyah was the only realistic Jewish option. For East European Zionists such as Chaim Weizmann and David Ben-Gurion, any movement that rejected Jewish nationalism and the "negation of the Diaspora" was hardly Zionistic. Their European Zionist ideology, however, did not resonate in America, where there was no "Jewish question," nor any serious movement to deny American Jews the rights and responsibilities of full citizenship.

For Brandeis the legitimacy of Brandeisian Zionism stemmed precisely from what European Zionists objected to—its denial of Jewish nationalism and its definition of Zionism as a charitable effort, whose values and goals were compatible with the values and goals of America. He was careful to describe Jews as a "people" and not a "nation," in part because he did not want Zionists to appear un-American and guilty of "dual loyalty." American Jews who wished to succor Jews in Europe and elsewhere but did not wish to have their Americanism questioned welcomed Brandeis's revision of Zionism.

Brandeis argued that the basic impulses of Zionism resembled those of the American Progressive movement of the early twentieth century. Just as Zionism sought freedom, social justice, and democracy for the oppressed Jews of Europe, so Progressivism sought freedom, social justice, and democracy for under-privileged Americans. He was particularly impressed by the voluntary kibbutz movement, and helped found a kibbutz that was later named for him, Kibbutz Em HaShofet (Hebrew for spring of the judge). An American Zionist, Brandeis argued, was not only a better Jew but also a better American because Zionism exhibited precisely those impulses that Americans characterized as uniquely American. Zionism was thus a fulfillment and not a derogation of Americanism. "To be good Americans," he told a Jewish audience, "we must be better Jews, and to be better Jews, we must become Zionists." An American Zionist was thus by definition an ardent American patriot.

Brandeis's own life demonstrated this symbiosis between Zionism and Americanism. This leader of American Zionism was the first Jew to give the Fourth of July oration in Boston's Faneuil Hall. Brandeis and his supporters refused to turn their backs on America or Americanization. The relative unimportance of American anti-Semitism when compared to that of Europe, the improving social and economic status of America's Jews, and American democratic political and social traditions warranted neither a blanket condemnation of the nation nor a wholesale exodus to Palestine.

Supporters of classic Zionism strongly opposed the Brandeisian synthesis of American identity and Zionism. Chaim Weizmann, the future first president of the state of Israel, accused the Brandeisians of being ignorant of "all those questions in Zionism which have contributed so much towards the real life of the movement, like the Hebrew revival, like the desire of the Zionists to 'Judaize' the Jewish communities of the world . . . in short, for all those imponderabilia which form a national movement of which Palestine is merely a territorial aspect of a national political upheaval." Louis Lipsky, an American supporter of Weizmann, described Brandeisian Zionism as "a form of opiate for the Jewish masses, which would keep them in the bondage of a culture that could never lead to political rebirth."

Lipsky failed to realize that the political rebirth he sought for American Jews was already taking place in America. The character of Jewish immigration clearly showed the extent to which American Jews identified with their new homeland. When Jews came to the United States, they came with their wives and children, and they came to stay. Their rate of repatriation was far lower than that of other immigrant groups. Having little to return to in Europe, Jews decisively broke their ties with the old country. Only a minuscule minority ever contemplated exchanging the benefits of life in America for a problematic existence in Palestine or Israel. Their support for a Jewish homeland was limited to philanthropy, political lobbying, and tourism.

Undoubtedly the most important manifestation of Brandeisian Zionism was Hadassah, the women's auxiliary of the American Zionist Organization. Established by Henrietta Szold of Baltimore in 1912, Hadassah's mission was medical work in Palestine. Hadassah's eschewing of Jewish nationalism and aliyah, its ignoring of the political abstractions and ideology so dear to the hearts of European Zionists, and its emphasis on practical and concrete activities to alleviate suffering reflected the pragmatic, non-nationalistic, and charitable thrust of American Zionism. The Hadassah ideal, Szold stated, "can be embraced by all, no matter what their attitude may be to other Jewish questions." Hadassah would become the largest and arguably the most powerful Jewish organization in the world. By 1980 it had four hundred thousand members, approximately ten times the membership of the National Organization of Women.

The pragmatic Zionism of Brandeis and Szold was strongly opposed by a variety of ideological purists. Elements within the Reform movement, particularly at the Hebrew Union College in Cincinnati, believed all forms of Zionism were tainted, to a greater or lesser extent, by Jewish tribalism. For them, the Pittsburgh Platform remained the last word regarding Zionism, and they continued to oppose Zionism even when in 1937 in Columbus, Ohio, a new set of principles was adopted by the Central Conference of American Rabbis, the national association of Reform rabbis.

The Columbus Platform sharply revised the traditional American Reform position on Jewish identity and Zionism. No longer was Jewish identity viewed solely as a religious matter, and no longer was Zionism rejected out of hand. "We recognize in the group-loyalty of Jews who have become estranged from our religious tradition," the rabbis declared, "a bond that still unites them with us." Furthermore, they affirmed, "in the rehabilitation of Palestine, the land hallowed by memories and hopes, we behold the promise of renewed life for many of our brethren. . . . We affirm the obligation of all Jewry to aid in its upbuilding as a Jewish homeland by endeavoring to make it not only a refuge for the oppressed but also a center of Jewish culture and spiritual life."

The Columbus Platform was, of course, a response to the European catastrophe that was beginning to engulf European Jewry. The ideological consistency that had marked the Pittsburgh Platform retreated before the tragic reality of anti-Semitism and the Holocaust. The Reform rabbinate realized that there were more important things than ideological purity. American Jews had a responsibility for European Jews not merely because they were members of the same religion but because of ethnic loyalty. Some Reform spokesmen, however, remained anti-Zionist platonists and opposed any talk about the resurrection of a Jewish commonwealth.

These Reform Jews refused to allow facts, however disagreeable, to modify that classic Reform ideology that had emptied Jewish identity of all particularistic ethnic or nationalistic characteristics and had defined Judaism solely as a voluntaristic religion. In 1943, a dissenting group of Reform rabbis organized the American Council for Judaism after the Central Conference of American Rabbis in 1942 went on record in support of the formation of a Jewish army of Palestinian Jews. The initial statement of the Council supported the concept of Palestine as a refuge for Jews, but it adamantly opposed the creation of a Jewish state or a Jewish army. Such a state, the Council contended, would detract from the universal teachings of Judaism, would lead to accusations of dual loyalty directed at Jews, and would confuse "our fellow men about our place and function in society and also divert our own attention from our historical role to live as a religious community wherever we may dwell." As the manichean-like title of Rabbi Elmer Berger's book *Judaism or Jewish Nationalism* (1957) indicated, the American Council for Judaism believed the alternatives facing America's Jews were unambiguous.

The debate regarding a Jewish state became moot with the creation of Israel in 1948. American Jewry in general, and American Zionism in particular, then faced a vigorous challenge from Israeli officials and intellectuals who partially blamed American Zionism for the failure of American Jewry to migrate en masse to Israel. For them, American Zionism was a mere fund-raising operation and was unable to instill into American Jewry either a love of Zion or a commitment to aliyah. Abba Eban expressed the contempt of the Israelis for American Zionism in his quip that American Zionism demonstrated the truth of that fundamental religious belief that there can be life after death.

The confrontation between the Israelis and the Americans came to a head in 1950–51 over the Israelis' claim that all Jews were obligated to migrate to Israel. American Jewish leaders promptly demanded that Israel officially acknowledge that American Jews had no political obligations toward Israel. Because of Israeli concern for the future of Israeli-Diaspora relationships, David Ben-Gurion, Israel's prime minister, backed down in August 1950. He publicly acknowledged that Jews in America were not living in exile, and that "the state of Israel represents and speaks only on behalf of its own citizens and in no way presumes to represent or speak in the name of Jews who are citizens of any other country. We, the people of Israel, have no desire and no intention to interfere in any way with the internal affairs of Jewish communities abroad." Jacob Blaustein, then president of the American Jewish Committee, welcomed Ben-Gurion's statement, but warned that it was insufficient unless accompanied by unmistakable evidence that Israeli leaders recognized that relations between Israel and American Jews "must be based on mutual respect for one another's feelings and needs, and on the preservation of the integrity of the two communities and their institutions."

The attempt to define a proper American Jewish stance toward Israel that would allow for a close identification between American Jews and the Jewish state but not derogate from their Americanism masked a growing ideological, psychological, and emotional commitment to Israel. The secularization of American Jewry, the decline in the number of American Jews who identified with traditional Judaism, and the atrophying of Jewish socialism, Yiddish culture, and other forms of Jewish identity prevalent among first-generation Jews left a vacuum in Jewish identity that was partially filled by Zionism, American style. The importance of this expression of American Jewish identity became clear only after Israel's incredible victory in the 1967 Six Days' War. It was during the dark days of May and early June 1967 that American Jews realized the extent of their emotional identification with Israel and the degree to which support for Israel had become the lowest common denominator of American Jewish life.

This support, however, has been accompanied by sharp disagreements among American Jews regarding the wisdom of Israeli domestic and foreign policy. A majority of American Jews resent the power of the Israeli Orthodox religious establishment and question the wisdom of encouraging Jewish settlements in Judea and Samaria. A 1991 study by the Wilstein Institute of Jewish Policy Studies in Los Angeles revealed that 80 percent of those American Jews most actively involved in fund-raising for Israel opposed the settlement policy of the Likud government. Even more troubling was the finding of a 1990 study of American Jews that support for Israel among American Jews was declining.

On the other hand, the identification with Israel has been strengthened by another element within recent American Jewish culture—a growing interest in the Holocaust and a passion to learn its "lessons." American Jews attend numerous Holocaust remembrance events, write and read a continuing flow of novels and histories of the European catastrophe, and avidly view television shows and movies such as *The Holocaust, Playing for Time, The Sorrow and the Pity, The Pawnbroker, The Diary of Anne Frank, The Wall,* and *Shoah.* They endow university chairs and lecture series on the Holocaust, establish Holocaust museums and erect Holocaust statues, pressure state departments of education to establish Holocaust study programs in the high schools, and engage in numerable other Holocaust-related activities. The most popular course in many Judaic departments in American universities is the history of the Holocaust. The Hebrew word *zachor* (remember) has become the codeword for this obsession with the Holocaust.

By the 1970s, the American Jewish community was defining its agenda and judging its accomplishments partly by the extent to which they conformed to the Holocaust's purported teachings. The most important American explicator of the meaning of the Holocaust has been Elie Wiesel, the 1986 winner of the Nobel Peace Prize and himself a survivor of Auschwitz. His book *The Jews of Silence* (1966), which condemned the failure of world Jewry to work for the freedom of Soviet Jews, evoked bitter memories of the 1930s and 1940s when American Jews supposedly stood passively aside and allowed the slaughter of European Jews to occur unimpeded. Wiesel argued that the greatest sin of Jews in the post-Holocaust era was the sin of silence, the failure to hear the cries of fellow Jews for help.

Another eloquent voice in defining the meaning of the Holocaust has been Emil Fackenheim, a refugee from Hitler's Europe and a theologian at the University of Toronto. Fackenheim proclaimed in his *The Jewish Return into History: Reflections in the Age of Auschwitz and a New Jerusalem* (1978) the need for a 614th commandment to go with the 613 other commandments observed by devout Jews: "The authentic Jew of today is forbidden to hand Hitler yet another, posthumous victory." The book was dedicated to Jonathan Netanyahu, the hero of the Israeli Entebbe rescue of 1976, and it concluded with a segment from the official Israeli prayer for the state: "Our Father in Heaven, the Rock of Israel and her Redeemer, bless thou the state of Israel, the beginning of the dawn of our redemption. Shield her with the wings of Thy love, and spread over her the tabernacle of Thy peace." This determination not to allow Adolf Hitler another victory explains the outrage of American Jews in 1985 when President Ronald Reagan visited a military cemetery in Germany that contained the graves of SS soldiers.

Some American Jews have suggested that this consuming interest in the Holocaust has become counterproductive. Rabbi Daniel J. Silver of Cleveland, Ohio, for example, complained in 1986 that "the Holocaust cannot, and does not, provide the kind of vitalizing and informing myth around which American Jews could marshall their energies and construct a vital culture." Martyrs command respect, he argued, but the Jewish community's sense of sacred purpose must consist of something "more substantial than tears." Silver especially questioned the decision to build a Holocaust museum in Washington, D.C. "Such a museum," he feared, will speak of death, not of life, of victimization, not civilization—a less than appropriate statement of the spirit of a people who, throughout their long history, have obeyed God's command: 'Choose life.' " "The fires of Hell are mesmerizing," he concluded, but Jews would be mistaken to organize their future solely by this light.

While there is merit in Silver's concern, it slights the fact that the meaning of the Holocaust for America's Jews is intimately related to the greatest life-giving event in modern Jewish history, the establishment of the state of Israel. For American Jewry, Israel is a contra-Holocaust, rescuing recent Jewish history from its bleakness and providing meaning and purpose to Jewish existence. To emphasize the relationship between the Holocaust and the Jewish state, missions sponsored by the United Jewish Appeal will often first visit Auschwitz before going to Israel. Many of the most popular post-World War II novels by American Jewish writers examine implicitly or explicitly the connection between Israel and the Holocaust. Among the most notable are Herman Wouk's *War and Remembrance* and Leon Uris's *Exodus,* both runaway best-sellers. The American Jewish response to *Exodus* was particularly intense, and one observer dubbed it the Jewish *Uncle Tom's Cabin.*

The relationship between Israel and the Holocaust only became clear for most American Jews in 1967 before the Six Day's War, when Israel and world Jewry seemed to be confronted with the possibility of another holocaust. For Jews, the Gentile world in 1967 exhibited the same apathy toward Jewish suffering that had marked its behavior during the 1930s and 1940s. American Jews were convinced that the destruction of European Jewry could be explained in large part by the indifference of bystanders—officials in the Franklin D. Roosevelt administration fearful of the unfavorable political impact of welcoming a large number of Jewish immigrants to America, American Jewish organizations interested only in their own petty agendas, and British politicians concerned with preserving British interests in the Middle East. A series of historical and quasi-historical books with such titles as *While Six Million Died: A Chronicle of American Apathy* (Arthur D. Morse, 1967), *The Abandonment of the Jews: America and the Holocaust, 1941–1945* (David Wyman, 1984), and *Were We Our Brothers' Keepers?: The Public Response of Jews to the Holocaust, 1938–1944* (Haskel Lookstein, 1985) catered to this almost morbid obsession with allocating blame for the Holocaust among the Nazis' opponents.

The frantic response of American Jewry to the crisis of 1967—the unprecedented fundraising for Israel, the ears continually glued to radios for the latest news, the exultation at the amazing victory of Israeli arms—is understandable only against the backdrop of World War II. It was as if American Jews had spontaneously resolved to prevent another holocaust, to wash away the stain of guilt carried by American Jewry because of the apathy they and their parents had supposedly demonstrated a quarter of a century earlier, and to show to the non-Jewish world that the time of Jews "going like sheep to the slaughter," as the popular description put it, had ended. Since the 1960s, there has been an upsurge of militancy within American Jewry ranging from acts of violence to a vigorous and blatant political lobbying unknown prior to 1967 on behalf of distinctly Jewish causes. Throughout, the major concern of Jewish spokesmen has been that ancient and parochial question, "But is it good for the Jews?"

This militancy encompassed all strains of American Jewish life. Members of the Jewish Defense League and other organizations bombed pro-Palestinian and Soviet offices in the United States. Other Jews participated in giant demonstrations on behalf of Soviet Jewry and Israel. Jewish organizations and political action committees put unprecedented pressure on Congress and the White House to encourage the Soviet Union to allow its Jews to emigrate, to guarantee the military and economic security of Israel, and to speak up for Jewish interests in Ethiopia and elsewhere. This new Jewish militancy even modified individual behavior.

In the 1930s, the operative principle in Jewish life had been *shah*. Jews were advised to be as inconspicuous as possible for fear of provoking anti-Semitism. Beginning in the 1960s, however, it became common to see Jewish men wearing skullcaps outside the home, Jewish women wearing stars of David, and members of both sexes wearing buttons proclaiming "Kiss me, I'm Jewish"; and Jewish comedians such as Lenny Bruce and Woody Allen told Jewish jokes to largely Gentile audiences.

Jews also came out of the cinematic closet. In the 1960 film *Exodus*, the Israeli Ari Ben Canaan (Paul Newman) tells the Gentile Kitty Fremont (Eva Marie Saint) that she is wrong in believing that people are the same no matter where: "Don't believe it. People have a right to be different." And in the 1979 movie *Norma Rae*, the character Reuben Warshovsky, a northern Jewish union organizer, tells Norma Rae that they are different: "History makes us different." Indians speak Yiddish in *Cat Ballou* and *Blazing Saddles*, a black cabbie speaks Yiddish in *Bye Bye Braverman*, and a Japanese career woman speaks Yiddish in *Walk, Don't Run*. Barbara Streisand virtually built her Hollywood career playing Jewish characters. In *Funny Girl*, *The Way We Were*, *Yentl*, and other films she refused to dilute the Jewishness of the characters she portrayed, and she refused to get a nose job to modify her less than classic profile.

While these movies were being released, there was a dramatic upsurge of interest in Judaica on the American campus, and no major university was without its Jewish studies program offering courses in Jewish history, theology and philosophy, and Hebrew language. In the fall of 1985, the *New Yorker* magazine even published a lengthy three-part essay titled "Holy Days," which described in favorable terms the Lubavitch Hasidic sect in Brooklyn.

The overriding concern of this new Jewish militancy has been Jewish continuity. While the immediate threat of anti-Semitism receded, it was replaced by a fear of cultural assimilation and intermarriage. American Jewish leaders realized that the marriage altar rather than the pogrom was now the most direct threat to American Jewish identity. This fear even affected television programming. In the early 1970s the sitcom *Bridget Loves Bernie* featured the tribulations of an intermarried couple. (The show's hero and heroine—the Jewish David Birney and the Gentile Meredith Baxter—were an intermarried couple off the tube as well as in it.) Despite their longstanding commitment to freedom of speech, Jewish organizations succeeded in having the program taken off the air.

During the 1970s and 1980s, Jewish task forces examined the condition of the Jewish family and Jewish education, particularly the extent to which they discouraged intermarriage and transmitted Jewish identity. The studies of the task forces were generally somber in their conclusions, although Jewish sociologists such as Steven M. Cohen and Calvin Goldscheider claimed that the evidence was more ambiguous than generally assumed and that optimism was as warranted as pessimism regarding the future of American Jewry. Pessimism, however, fit the new mood of American Jewry with its overriding concern for demographic and cultural survival. This mood resulted in some startling changes on the American Jewish scene, particularly within the Reform movement, which previously had been eager to modify Judaism to conform to the temper of American life.

The Hebrew Union College, the Reform seminary in Cincinnati, has a branch in Jerusalem that all its students must attend prior to ordination. An even more startling development, because of its tradition of strong support of public schools and distrust of parochial education, was the establishment under Reform auspices of several Jewish day schools. But the movement's most controversial change was its modification of the very definition of a Jew. For millennia, to be considered a Jew required that one either have a Jewish mother or have been converted according to traditional Jewish law. In 1983, the Reform movement officially stated that it would consider a child of a Jewish father and a non-Jewish mother to be Jewish if the child was being raised as a Jew. This decision to recognize patrilineal descent stemmed from the growing intermarriage rate among American Jews. The Reform movement hoped the revised definition of a Jew along with a more open attitude toward religious conversion would provide a sufficiently large pool of people to ensure a vibrant American Jewish community in general and a strong Reform movement in particular.

For representatives of the Conservative and Orthodox wings of American Jewry, the Reform movement's approval of patrilineal descent was a direct challenge to the integrity of the Jewish legal process and to fundamental Jewish tradition. Traditionalists were adamant that Jewish law could not be made to conform to the Reform movement's latest sociological concerns, particularly if it encouraged a fraudulent Jewish identity. "We can't go half-way," Orthodox Rabbi Nosson Scherman declared. "I believe Torah is God-given, and I can't compromise on that." Traditionalists pointed out that if the Reform movement did not overturn its decision, no longer could those contemplating marriage assume that their spouses were Jewish. Some marriages between Jews would turn out, in fact, to be intermarriages, and this would present observant Jews and their children with a whole host of Jewish legal problems, including questions of illegitimacy. One prospect was that some Jews might not accept others as authentic Jews unless they provided family pedigrees.

Orthodox rabbis predicted dire consequences would flow from the patrilineal decision unless the Reform movement recanted. In December 1985, Rabbi Haskel Lookstein claimed the division within the American Jewish community was so deep that it threatened "to isolate Jew from Jew and to rend the fabric of Jewish peoplehood so that we will no longer be one people." Rabbi Irving Greenberg predicted that by 1990 "there will be between three-quarters of a million and a million people whose Jewishness is contested or whose marriageability is denied by a larger group of other Jews." You have, he lamented, "a situation ripe for schism."

This pervasive concern with Jewish survival and Jewish identity ultimately arose out of the revolutionary situation in which American Jews found themselves. While America was not the promised land, it was the land of promise. America's Jews have been perhaps the major beneficiaries of America's liberal and capitalist social, political, and economic order. America's Jews today comprise the wealthiest and most influential Diaspora community in history. Denied none of the benefits America has to offer, the nation's Jews have flocked to the universities, businesses, and professions in search of their share of the American Dream. Overall, they have not been disappointed. But the price Jews have had to pay for their rapid economic and social ascent has been an increasingly attenuated Jewish identity.

Most American Jews have eliminated those aspects of Jewish existence, such as distinctive dress and diet, that are barriers to economic and social mobility. Attendance at college—and approximately 85 percent of Jewish high school graduates enter college—puts Jews at an impressionable age in an intellectual and social environment in which parochial ethnic and religious identities and values are viewed as anachronistic. The secularism of American life and the religious skepticism characteristic of the campus have undermined Jewish identities derived from Judaism.

The slogan of the United Jewish Appeal was once "We are one." The oneness that holds Jews together is no longer Judaism or anti-Semitism but philanthropy, particularly that oriented toward Israel. The lowest common denominator of Jewish life is not attendance at the synagogue (even on Yom Kippur) or providing a Jewish education for one's children, but contributing at least a nominal sum to the United Jewish Appeal.

And status within the Jewish community is in large part determined by the size of one's charitable outlays and not by Jewish learning or piety. The local Jewish federation, rather than the synagogue or the yeshiva, has become the major focal point of Jewish life and the major dispenser of prestige. Many observers have severely criticized this "checkbook" Judaism, but they have been unable to suggest any alternative to even this attenuated Jewish identity that would appeal to acculturated and sophisticated Jews.

In 1900, Jacob David Wilowsky, a prominent rabbi from Slutsk, Russia, told a New York audience that Jews who had migrated to America were sinners because they had placed the spiritual welfare of themselves and their families in mortal peril. In coming to America, Jews had left behind "their Torah, their Talmud, their yeshivoth—in a word, their Yiddishkeit, their entire Jewish way of life." Three years later, Wilowsky himself settled in Chicago and became chief rabbi of a group of Orthodox congregations. If Wilowsky, one of the rabbinical giants of his age, could not resist the call of America, it was asking too much of less pious Jews to forego the lure of the "golden land." For every Jew who emigrated to Palestine during the late nineteenth and early twentieth centuries, perhaps fifty risked their souls by coming to the United States.

It has been the hospitality of a free and open society to Jewish aspirations that has provided the major challenge to American Jews—to be simultaneously both Jewish and American, to withstand the allure of cultural assimilation while affirming the right to be an integral part of America. Certainly Jews still bear the imprint of the Jewish cultural legacy—liberal and at times messianic politics, an educational elitism, and an occupational profile heavily tilted toward business and the professions. What is problematic is the ability of Jews to pass on to future generations a religious and cultural tradition that for many is no longer operative in their daily lives. Although valuable in themselves, cherishing Israel, commemorating the Holocaust, and contributing to Jewish charities are, in the long run, not weighty enough to support a strong Jewish identity. Perhaps nothing is as revealing about the contemporary status of American Jewish identity as the continual use by Jewish leaders of the word "agenda" when describing their objectives and activities. Philanthropic organizations, political movements, and interest groups have agendas, but cultures and religions don't have agendas. They simply exist. And yet by talking in terms of agendas, American Jews are merely exhibiting the pervasive impact that America has had in shaping their understanding of American Jewish identity. The same problem confronts today's Jews that confronted the first Jewish migrants to America—to establish the delicate balance that can satisfy the demands of both Jewishness and Americanness.

TWO

World War II and American Jewish Identity

PERHAPS NO OTHER EVENT was more important in shaping the nature of American Jewish identity during the twentieth century than World War II. From the perspective of more than half a century later, it is now becoming increasingly clear that the war was the great watershed of twentieth-century American history. "Even more than the Great Depression," the historian Charles C. Alexander wrote, "the war became the central, catalytic factor in American life." The United States emerged as a world power with international responsibilities as a result of the conflict. The war led to a radical change in the status of American women as well as in the nation's sexual mores. It also had a major impact on the history of America's racial and ethnic minorities, including the perceptions that members of these groups had of themselves as Americans. This was particularly true of America's Jews.[1]

While historians have emphasized the importance of the wartime years to the civil rights movement, they have not as yet fully grasped the impact of the war on America's ethnic groups, especially the fact that it was during the war that many ethnics for the first time felt themselves to be fully American. Nowhere was this process more evident than among American Jews. If World War II was a watershed for America's ethnic groups, it was doubly so for American Jews. Lucy S. Dawidowicz noted that the war had "a transfiguring effect on American Jews and on their ideas of themselves as Jews." But even she did not explore the implications of this insight.[2]

For Jews, two wartime events—one tragic and the other rather frivolous—were important milestones in the evolution of their identity as Americans and as Jews. The first, occurring in June 1941 just prior to American entry into

This chapter was previously published in *Modern Judaism* 10 (Feb. 1990): 65–84. Reprinted by permission of Johns Hopkins University Press.

World War II, involved the death of a Jewish congressman. The second, happening in September 1945 just after the end of the war, took place at America's most famous beauty pageant. For American Jews, the contrast between these two events could not have been more dramatic or significant, and it revealed a dramatic improvement in their individual and collective status. Never had American Jews felt more physically and psychologically secure than after World War II. For perhaps the first time in their history, American Jews believed that they had at last become fully American and that the relationship between their Jewish and American identities was to be one of symbiosis and not of conflict.

In 1941, M. Michael Edelstein represented New York City's Lower East Side in Congress. The Lower East Side, the initial destination for millions of immigrants, was the unofficial capital of American Jewry. Its tenements and storefronts housed the country's largest concentration of immigrant Jews as well as hundreds of synagogues and Jewish shops, theaters, schools, restaurants, charitable organizations, and newspapers. The early 1940s was a difficult time for the Jews of the Lower East Side. They were terrified for their European relatives now threatened by the advance of Hitler's armies, and they were worried by the spread of anti-Semitism in America. Their suspicion that America was not immune from the virulent Judaeophobia, that "it could happen here," seemed to be confirmed in June 1941.

The major issue facing Congress at this time was American policy toward the war in Europe. While public opinion and governmental policy were solidly pro-British, few Americans as yet wished to intervene in the conflict. A significant minority of Americans remained isolationist, and they were confident that the bulk of the population opposed involvement in the war. They were dismayed, however, by the growing tension between the United States and Germany, which threatened to bring America into the war. As they pondered the reasons for the Roosevelt administration's anti-German policies, they concluded that the country was being dragged into the conflict by a cabal that included influential Jews.

The most publicized expression of such sentiments, and the most controversial speech by any isolationist, was Charles Lindbergh's twenty-five-minute address "Who Are the War Agitators?" delivered in Des Moines, Iowa, on September 11, 1941, to an audience of America First supporters. For more than a year the aviator had been warning against the prowar influence of as yet unnamed powerful interest groups. By the fall of 1941 the danger of American involvement in the war had so increased that Lindbergh decided to speak with "the utmost frankness" at Des Moines and to name names.

For the first and only time, Lindbergh mentioned American Jews. He accused them, along with the Roosevelt administration and the British, of pushing America toward war with Germany. While expressing opposition to anti-Semitism and understanding for the reasons for the Jews' hatred of Hitler, he also cautioned Jews that "no person of honesty and vision can look on [Jews'] pro-war policy here today without seeing the dangers involved in such a policy, both for us and for them." Jews were particularly dangerous, he noted, because of "their large ownership and influence in our motion pictures, our press, our radio and our government." While they cannot be blamed "for looking out for what they believe to be their own interests," he said, "we also must look out for ours. We cannot allow the natural passions and prejudices of other peoples to lead our country to destruction." He predicted a worsening of American anti-Semitism should the United States go to war. "Tolerance is a virtue that depends upon peace and strength. History shows that it cannot survive war and devastation."[3]

Such talk was also heard in Congress. In February 1941, Senator Burton K. Wheeler of Montana warned against the Lend-Lease proposal, saying that it was supported by "the international bankers . . . the Sassoons . . . the Rothschilds . . . the Warburgs." Wheeler cautioned Americans about the prowar propaganda emanating from the immigrant and mostly Jewish "Hollywood Hitlers." "Gifted in the arts of corruption and bribery," the movie moguls have "debauched legislatures; they have elected and controlled governors. The tentacles of this octopus reach not only into the state legislatures but at times into the Congress of the United States."[4]

Senator Gerald R. Nye of North Dakota agreed with Wheeler. Nye was one of the original cosponsors of the 1941 resolution to establish a special congressional committee to investigate the movie industry. Testifying before the committee, he told American Jews that their support for an interventionist foreign policy would intensify anti-Semitism. Nye went on to describe foreign-born Jewish film executives as the country's "most potent and dangerous" fifth column, spewing forth "the most vicious propaganda that has ever been unloosed upon civilized people."[5]

Another zealous isolationist was Congressman John E. Rankin, an agrarian radical from Tupelo in northeast Mississippi. Rankin's rural congressional district was the exact opposite of Edelstein's Lower East Side. It probably had fewer immigrants, Catholics, and Jews than any other district in the country. A rabid anti-Semite and racist, Rankin was a self-proclaimed savior of what he called the "old-line Americans, Anglo-Saxon people who have been here for

200 years." Jews, he charged, were responsible for the economic plight of rural America, the triumph of Communism in Russia, the starvation of millions of Christian farmers in the Ukraine, the sit-down strikes in the American Midwest, urban crime, and racial agitation in the South. In 1939, he warned his House colleagues that "a certain international element that has no sympathy for Christianity was spending money by the barrel" in order to involve the United States in the war.[6]

Rankin's most important anti-Semitic diatribe was a brief speech in the House of Representatives on June 4, 1941. It was prompted by a news report of a rally in New York's financial district supporting American intervention in the European war. Although no Jew spoke at the rally or helped organize it, Rankin believed Jews were responsible for the rally. He denounced "a little group of our international Jewish brethren" for pressuring Congress and the president to declare war against Germany. According to Rankin, Jewish financiers feared that an English peace movement might succeed in halting hostilities prior to American involvement.[7]

Edelstein immediately responded. He charged Rankin with fanning hatred, noted that Jews had nothing to do with the rally and that few bankers were Jewish, and asserted that Jews were being used as scapegoats. "I say it is unfair and I say it is un-American. . . . All men are created equal, regardless of race, creed, or color; and whatever a man be, Jew or Gentile, he may think what he deems fit." The agitated Edelstein then walked up the aisle of the House chamber, began to sway, and was helped outside to the Capitol lobby. Within moments he was dead. Edelstein's colleagues were shocked. Congressman Samuel Dickstein of New York spoke for most congressmen. "The thing is so horrible that I cannot believe what has happened." In his final moments, Dickstein went on, Edelstein resembled an ancient prophet of Israel, denouncing "those forces of evil which ever threaten to engulf American democracy."[8]

Edelstein's funeral took place two days later in New York City. More than sixty policemen were needed to control a crowd of fifteen thousand mourners. Rabbi Bernard Bergman's eulogy emphasized the political and social significance of Edelstein's death during "these critical hours, when our dear country is being assailed from within and without by enemies of our American way of life." Edelstein had died "a martyr to democracy."[9]

Edelstein's death was further evidence to American Jews of their precarious and vulnerable position. It was obvious that many Americans still did not consider them to be fully American, despite their vigorous attempts to adapt to American life. For nearly two centuries American Jews had played down those aspects of their Jewish heritage that hindered their entry into the American mainstream. Jewish religious reformers in the nineteenth century had modified Judaism to approximate the outlook and flavor of upper-class Protestantism by introducing family pews, English sermons, and organs into Jewish services. Jewish spokesmen had rejected Zionism and its belief in a Jewish return to the Holy Land because it implied that Jews were not totally committed to the American "Zion." Jewish entertainers had changed their names to disguise their origins. Thus Nathan Birnbaum became George Burns, Julius Garfinkle became John Garfield, Emanuel Goldenberg became Edward G. Robinson, Leo Jacobi became Lee J. Cobb, Benjamin Kubelsky became Jack Benny, Marian Levy became Paulette Goddard, Laszlo Lowenstein became Peter Lorre, Betty Perske became Lauren Bacall, and Muni Weisenfreund became Paul Muni.

Their rapid acculturation had not as of 1941 earned Jews full acceptance as Americans. They faced quotas in the elite colleges and professional schools, restricted job opportunities in fields such as engineering, insurance, and banking, and the firm opposition of American public opinion to modifying the country's immigration laws to admit additional numbers of Jewish refugees. Public opinion polls in 1938 and 1940 revealed that nearly two-thirds of Americans believed Jews as a group had "objectionable traits," and more than 50 percent of Americans thought that German anti-Semitism stemmed either partially or wholly from the actions of the German Jews themselves. The Wagner-Rogers bill, which would have admitted several thousand Jewish children from Germany, could not pass Congress in the late 1930s without crippling amendments.[10]

This anti-Semitism escalated during the early 1940s. Employment opportunities for Jews remained limited, even in the defense industries. Approximately 30 percent of the employment advertisements in 1942 in the *New York Times* and the *New York Herald Tribune* expressed a preference for Christians. Wartime public opinion polls revealed that Americans distrusted Jews more than any other European group with the exception of Italians.[11]

In 1922 the eminent Harvard scholar Harry Austryn Wolfson had suggested to Jews that they accept the permanence of American anti-Semitism and realize that being Jewish was a disability they would have to live with forever. "There are certain problems of life for which no solution is possible," he wrote in a pamphlet aptly titled *Escaping Judaism*. "Because of our Judaism we must be prepared to give up some of the world's goods even as we must be prepared to make sacrifices because of other disadvantages with which we may happen to be born." Not all men are born equal. "Some are born blind, some deaf, some lame, and some are born Jews." The Jews' common lot, even in America, was "to be isolated, [and] to be deprived of many social goods and advantages."[12]

Other Jews, however, were unwilling to accept such a message of despair. Eager to become part of the American mainstream, they did not believe that escaping Jewishness was either undesirable or impossible. The journalist Walter Lippmann, for example, spent his life denying his Jewish background. Lippmann supported the efforts during the 1920s of A. Lawrence Lowell, the president of Harvard University, to limit the number of Jewish students admitted to Harvard College, Lippmann's alma mater. "I do not regard the Jews as innocent victims," he said. "They hand on unconsciously and uncritically from one generation to another many distressing personal and social habits." A decade later Lippmann rationalized away German anti-Semitism.[13]

Even those not afflicted with the extreme Jewish self-hatred of a Lippmann often viewed their Jewish background as an obstacle to Americanization. This was particularly true for leftist Jewish intellectuals of the thirties. One of the attractions of Marxism was its emphasis on class conflict, which transcended ethnic and religious particularities. Marxism provided Jewish radicals with a rationale for escaping the parochial world of their parents and a way of linking up with what they perceived to be a broader American culture. Ironically, in fleeing from Jewish ethnicity, the radicals became part of an encapsulated radical culture even more remote from the American mainstream.

Non-Marxist intellectuals also believed that a vibrant Jewish identity was incompatible with Americanization. Thus Jerome N. Frank, a former Harvard Law School professor, former chairman of the Securities and Exchange Commission, and a United States Circuit Court judge, reassured readers of the *Saturday Evening Post* that there was nothing offensive or distinctive about Jews. In order to propitiate his readers, he emptied American Jewish identity of any meaningful Jewish content and made it appear similar to membership in the Elks or Kiwanis. He was particularly opposed to Zionism. Zionists, he said, were mere "sojourners" in America and had little support among American Jews. Only immigrants accepted traditional Judaism, while, thankfully, the native born "have rejected all or most of the old Jewish customs." It was unlikely that this process of rapid assimilation could be slowed down, Frank asserted, since America would not be receiving many additional Jewish immigrants, a development he seemed to welcome. Finally, Frank mollified his readers by asserting they had nothing to fear from Jewish intellectuality. "The proportion of intellectuals or duds or bores or incompetents or mediocrities among American Jews is just about the same as one would find if he took any group selected at random—say, all red-headed or blue-eyed Americans." Frank's comments appeared in the magazine's December 6, 1941, issue. The next day the United States was at war.[14]

On March 28, 1942, with the Holocaust in full swing, the *Saturday Evening Post* published an even more disgraceful analysis of American Jewish identity by Milton S. Mayer, a Chicago Jewish journalist. Mayer's "The Case Against the Jew" was permeated with anti-Semitic stereotypes. While Frank had praised American Jews for assimilating to American conditions, Mayer complained that this assimilation was the source of the Jewish problem. While Frank rejoiced that American Jews had attempted to become just like everyone else, Mayer regretted it. "In their dream of 'assimilation,' " American Jews had "tried to shake the symbols of unassimilability from their coattails. . . . They tried to adjust, this pitiful people who once were proud." Jews had sought to adapt to a world dominated by a love of money, power, and fame. Jews had been willing to pay the price of admission to this world and as a result had become adept in financial speculation, shady business practices, and economic exploitation. "There was nothing that a Gentile would stoop to that a Jew wouldn't if he could."

Mayer noted that, despite (and perhaps because of) their feverish social climbing and attempts to become part of the modern world, the Jews were hated. "The Jews refused to be God's chosen people, and . . . in the end, they are Hitler's." The only way American Jews could save themselves was to stop hankering after the ways of the Gentiles and return to the teachings of the Prophets. Mayer advised the American Jew that before he could be saved he would have to learn "to walk humbly with his God." "Running away hasn't saved him. Resettlement hasn't saved him. Changing his name, his face, his clothes and his faith hasn't saved him." He could only save his "soul" by repudiating the materialism that, Mayer believed, was at the core of American culture.[15]

Even though they approached the question of American Jewish identity from different perspectives, Frank and Mayer both emphasized the difficulty of reconciling Jewishness with Americanization. Other American Jews agreed with them. In the February 1944 issue of the *Contemporary Jewish Record*, the critic Isaac Rosenfeld claimed that being Jewish "should occupy no more of a man's attention than any ordinary fact of his history." The literary scholar

Alfred Kazin echoed Rosenfeld. "The writing I have been most deeply influenced by," he said in 1944, "had no direct associations in my own mind with Jewish culture; it has every association, of course, with the fact that, like any other American, I have had to make my own culture." Kazin's conclusion was stark. "I have never seen much of what I admire in American Jewish culture."[16]

Lionel Trilling agreed. The first Jew to become a tenured member of Columbia University's English department, Trilling described American Jewish culture as a sterile response to the Jews' exclusion from more valued aspects of American life. American Jewish life, he avowed, "can give no sustenance to the American artist or intellectual who is born a Jew." American Jewry had as yet failed to produce "a single voice with the note of authority—of philosophical, or poetic, or even of rhetorical, let alone of religious authority." For Trilling, being Jewish was an accident of birth, an encumbrance rather than an identity that structured his vision of reality. While Wolfson wanted Jews to hold on to their Jewish identity, even if this meant they would never be fully accepted as Americans, Trilling believed that the loss of Jewish identity was a cheap price to pay for assimilation (and a position in Columbia University's English department). But both agreed that Jewish and American identities were, in certain respects, incongruous.[17]

After December 7, 1941, this sense of incongruity between American and Jewish identities dissipated as Jewish and American interests merged. America now stood for "the four freedoms," and anti-Semitic Germany was the mortal enemy of all Americans, Gentile as well as Jew. The need for wartime unity undermined such divisive appeals as Lindbergh's distinction between "our" interests and "their" interests and his reference to "other peoples." More appropriate was the sentiment expressed in one popular song of the period—"When those little Yellow-bellies meet the Cohens and the Kellys."

Anti-Semites were still around after the war, but by midcentury they had gone underground. Few Americans wished to be identified with the type of thinking that had led to the Holocaust or with an ideology that had been trumpeted by the most feared foe of the United States. Even polite anti-Semitism was no longer seen as a harmless form of social exclusiveness. Rather, it was now perceived to be another aspect of the thinking that had lead to Auschwitz. Anti-Semitism, which in the first half of the 1940s was more virulent than at any previous time in American history, was by 1950 at an all-time low. Pressured by the government, the universities repealed their quotas on Jewish students, corporations provided more employment opportunities for Jews, and residential areas dropped their restrictions against Jewish homeowners.[18]

The "dream factory" of Hollywood reflected this change in national sentiment and policy. For the first time in history, Hollywood producers believed that movies dealing with American anti-Semitism could be commercial successes. *Crossfire* and *Gentleman's Agreement* appeared in 1947 and were followed the next year by *Open Secret* and *Prejudice.* Ironically, influential Jews, slow to grasp the shift in public opinion, tried to prevent the production of *Crossfire* and *Gentleman's Agreement* because they feared an anti-Semitic backlash. *Crossfire* was based on Richard Brooks's novel *The Brick Foxhole,* which concerned the problems faced by a homosexual in the military. In a reversal of Hollywood's policy of playing down Jewish themes, the film's victim is Joseph Samuels, a Jew and a decorated war hero. He is murdered by Sergeant Montgomery, a sadistic bully.

Montgomery justifies his hatred for Samuels by claiming, "I've seen a lot of guys like Samuels, guys who played it safe during the war, scrounged around keeping themselves in civvies, had swell apartments and swell dames. Some are named Samuels and some got funnier names." Sergeant Keeley, disgusted by Montgomery's bigotry, responds, "He ought to look at the casualty list some time. There are a lot of funny names there too." When Montgomery is finally arrested, Keeley says to him, "My best friend, a Jew, is lying back in a foxhole at Guadalcanal. I'm gonna spit in your eye for him because we don't want people like you in the U.S.A. There's no place for racial discrimination now." While some critics panned the film, Bosley Crowther's *New York Times* review described it as "a frank and immediate demonstration of the brutality of religious bigotry." He gave the film an "unqualified A for effort."[19]

Gentleman's Agreement, based on Laura Z. Hobson's best-selling novel, is Hollywood's finest and best-known film about American anti-Semitism. It won the 1947 Academy Award for Best Picture (*Crossfire* was also nominated that year for the Oscar), and was Twentieth Century–Fox's most profitable film for that year. The critics praised it highly. *Time* claimed it to be "an almost-overpowering polemic film"; the *Hollywood Reporter* called its opening "a profound occurrence in the history of the motion picture industry"; and the *New York Times* noted its "dramatic forcefulness."

While *Crossfire* discussed the bigotry of the vicious and lower class, *Gentleman's Agreement* focused on the genteel anti-Semitism of the upper crust. The upper class would never dream of murdering a Jew, but they didn't want to live or work near him, either. The movie's major theme is that anti-

Semitism is un-American, and anti-Semites as well as timorous liberals who acquiesce in prejudice betray the values America fought for in the war.

The film's hero, Phil Green (Gregory Peck), is a writer for a magazine. He pretends to be Jewish in order to research and write an article on anti-Semitism to be titled "I Was a Jew for Eight Weeks." When questioned by his young son about Jews, he replies, "You can be an American and a Protestant or a Catholic or a Jew." At the end of the movie, Green's mother praises his article. "Wouldn't it be wonderful, Phil," she says, "if it turned out to be everybody's century, when people all over the world, free people, found a way to live together?" (A stagehand on the film missed the film's point. He told Moss Hart, the movie's scriptwriter, that he loved working on the picture because of its moral lesson. "I'll never be rude to a Jew again because he might turn out to be a Gentile.")[20]

The decline in anti-Semitism responsible for Hollywood's willingness to make films on American anti-Semitism was due in part to the unprecedented unity and militancy of American Jews resulting from the war. The traditional Jewish defensiveness was replaced by a vigorous espousal of Jewish interests. What Charles E. Silberman has described as the era of *"shah"*—the reluctance of Jews to draw attention to themselves—abruptly ended. For the first time in its history, American Jewry overcame class and ideological differences and presented a united front against anti-Semitism. After the war, the B'nai B'rith, the American Jewish Committee, and the American Jewish Congress sponsored research in the social and psychological roots of anti-Semitism (including the American Jewish Committee's *Studies in Prejudice,* one of whose volumes was T. W. Adorno's *The Authoritarian Personality*), lobbied on the state and federal levels for antidiscriminatory legislation, challenged discriminatory behavior in the courts, and sponsored community programs with other groups to overcome prejudice. These activities, Jews claimed, would not only improve conditions for Jews but would also strengthen American democracy. Anti-Semitism, in other words, was bad for Jews, but it was also bad for the country.[21]

The war impressed upon America's Jews the radical difference between their situation here and the conditions of Jews in Europe. Despite the prejudice they had encountered in America, American Jews had never experienced anything remotely resembling what Jews had gone through in Europe. If prior to 1941 American Jews tended to view their status as a glass half empty and emphasized the barriers to Jewish equality, after 1945 they viewed their status as a glass half full and stressed the opportunities for Jews in America.

Furthermore, in view of the Holocaust, assimilation appeared to be a cowardly betrayal of the six million European Jews who were murdered simply because they were Jewish. American Jews believed that at least they could dignify the memories of the slain by remaining true to their own Jewish heritage, however strong or attenuated that might be.

This was particularly true of Jewish soldiers who helped liberate the Nazi concentration camps and, in the process, became more conscious of their own Jewishness. The memory of one soldier regarding the Woebbelin camp in northern Germany was typical. "This horror was of such a nature that I couldn't wait to get away . . . and get that smell out of my nose and wipe the dirt off my feet, and yet I went back. . . . I don't know what I went back for, I don't know, maybe to get a souvenir or bring it back to have something tangible to think about." The novelist Meyer Levin, who was a war correspondent in 1945 and took part in the liberation of several Nazi camps, described the experience as penetrating "to the center of the black heart, to the very crawling inside of the vicious heart."[22]

Civilians responded similarly. Susan Sontag, the future cultural critic, remembered how photographs of the Bergen Belsen and Dachau camps had affected her three decades earlier. "Nothing I have ever seen—in photographs or in real life—ever cut me as sharply, deeply, instantaneously." When she looked at the pictures "something broke. Some limit had been reached, and not only that of horrors; I felt irrevocably grieved, wounded, but a part of my feelings started to tighten; something went dead; something still is crying."[23]

This new, symbiotic relationship between American and Jewish identities was reflected in the wartime portrayal of Jews in popular culture. News reports, films, and novels stressed the Jewish contribution to American victory. A total of 550,000 Jews served in the military during the war. They suffered more than forty thousand casualties, including eight thousand combat deaths. For Jews, the most important death was that of Rabbi Alexander Goode. Goode was one of the four chaplains killed in 1943 when the military transport SS *Dorchester* was sunk in the north Atlantic. The chaplains sacrificed their own lives by giving their life preservers to others on board. For Jews, Goode's death symbolized the Jewish contribution to the war effort, and it demonstrated their right to be considered as American as anyone else. A 1948 American postage stamp issued in memory of the four chaplains bolstered their argument. Its caption read, "These IMMORTAL CHAPLAINS. . . . Interfaith in Action."[24]

The federal government's wartime Office of War Information encouraged the writing of magazine stories and the production of films featuring Jewish military heroes with identifiably Jewish surnames. The military units in the war movies generally included a Jew from New York as well as other representatives from the American mosaic—a southern farmer, a Texas cowboy, an Ivy League intellectual, a Boston Irishman, and an Italian from Brooklyn. There were Jewish characters in "platoon movies" such as *Air Force* (1943), *Bataan* (1943), *Guadalcanal Diary* (1943), *Action in the North Atlantic* (1943), *The Purple Heart* (1944), *Winged Victory* (1944), *Objective, Burma!* (1945), *Pride of the Marines* (1945), and *A Walk in the Sun* (1945).

These war films reversed the "de-Semitizing" of Hollywood movies of the 1930s when Jewish film executives had feared that movies with Jewish characters and Jewish themes might exacerbate anti-Semitism and be unpopular with the public. When books with Jewish characters were brought to the screen, the names of the characters were frequently Anglo-Saxonized. Because of this emphasis on cultural homogeneity, even anti-Nazi films such as *Confessions of a Nazi Spy* (1939) and *The Mortal Storm* (1940) downplayed the role of Jews as victims of Nazi persecution.[25]

In the World War II platoon films, the Jew is generally street-smart, cynical, humorous, well liked by his comrades, and brave in battle. In a few of these films, it is the Jew who discusses the higher meaning of the war. In *Action in the North Atlantic,* Chips Abrams praises the American war effort. "You've got a right to say what you want. That's what we're fighting this war for. The Czechs and Poles, they didn't have a chance to say or do what they wanted." In *Pride of the Marines,* Lee Diamond says, "I know what I fought for. I fought for me, for the right to live in the United States. . . . One happy afternoon when God was feeling good, He sat down and thought up a beautiful country and named it the U.S.A. . . . Don't tell me we can't make it work in peace like we do in war. Don't tell me we can't pull together. Don't you see it, guys, can't you see it?" This speech is accompanied by the strains of "America the Beautiful" in the background. At the end of the film, Lee takes his leave of his childhood friend Al Schmid. He wishes him *"shalom aleichem"* (Hebrew for "peace be with you") and gives him a lesson in democracy. "Maybe some guys won't hire me because my name is Diamond and not Jones. 'Cause I celebrate Passover instead of Easter. . . . We need a country to live in where no one gets booted around for any reason."

The ethnic mix of World War II novels also frequently included a Jew. In Irwin Shaw's *The Young Lions,* Noah Ackerman, although small in stature, refuses to be pushed around by the bullies in his unit, wins the respect of his fellow soldiers, and proves himself under fire. Norman Mailer's *The Naked and the Dead* has two Jewish soldiers. Undoubtedly the most important fictional portrayal of the World War II symbiosis of Jewish and American identities is Herman Wouk's *The Caine Mutiny* (1952), which features the character of Lieutenant Barney Greenwald, a naval lawyer who defends the navy and the military virtues of discipline, honor, loyalty, and duty.[26]

World War II was unique in that for the first time Jewish novelists were recognized as legitimate chroniclers of the American military experience. Indeed, at no other time in the history of the Diaspora have Jews ever played this role. The same phenomenon occurred in music. Beginning with Morton Gould and his *An American Salute* (1942), American Jewish composers believed the war was a cause worth fighting and composing for. Patriotism permeated the wartime works of Aaron Copland. His *Lincoln Portrait* and *Rodeo* of 1942 were followed by *Appalachian Spring,* which won the Pulitzer Prize in 1945.

The most important American musical composition on World War II written by a Jew was Richard Rodgers's music for the 1952 television documentary *Victory at Sea.* The documentary won practically every major television award for which it was eligible, including an Emmy and the George Washington Medal from the Freedom's Foundation of Valley Forge, Pennsylvania. The year after the documentary appeared, the United States Navy awarded Distinguished Service Medals to three men, all Jews, involved in the twenty-six-part series: Rodgers, Henry Salomon, the series' producer, and Robert W. Sarnoff of the National Broadcasting Corporation, which owned the series.

Salomon was responsible for the series' dramatic cinematic impact. The critic Arthur Knight claimed *Victory at Sea* was a powerful demonstration of the film medium's ability "to mold raw fact into artistic, meaningful, even memorable statement." Salomon portrayed the war as a conflict between freedom, democracy, and liberty and bigotry, militarism, and dictatorship. Rodgers' music complements the film's emphasis on the inevitability of America's victory, the purity of her war aims, and the heroism of her sailors.[27]

If World War II was a watershed for American Jews, then it is fitting that the most dramatic event in their evolving perception of themselves as Jewish Americans should occur immediately after the conclusion of the fighting. On Saturday night, September 8, 1945, Bess Myerson of New York City became Miss America, the first (and to date the only) Jew to win this honor. Jews took an intense vicarious pleasure in Myerson's victory. Not only did it vindicate their pride in being Jews, but it was also a reproach to those who questioned their status as Americans. Myerson's victory was doubly sweet because she was so identifiably Jewish.

Myerson's parents were immigrants from Russia, and her father, a house-painter, was part of the Jewish working class of New York City. They lived in an all-Jewish apartment complex in the Bronx called the Shalom Aleichem Cooperative Houses, named after the great Yiddish writer. Its inhabitants' favorite pastime was arguing over politics in Yiddish. Bess herself was bilingual. Yiddish was spoken in her home, and for a time she attended both public school and an afternoon Yiddish school. Later she graduated from New York City's heavily Jewish Hunter College, a part of the city's college system. Before competing at Atlantic City, she rejected suggestions to change her last name to disguise her Jewish background.

Jews believed Myerson was their personal representative in Atlantic City. A Jewish clothing manufacturer provided her with free evening gowns. Jews, starved for good news in the wake of the Holocaust, came up to her in Atlantic City and said, "You've got to win, for all of us." After winning, she immediately became the most famous beautiful Jewish woman since Queen Esther in ancient Persia. For Jewish youth, a teenager at the time recalled, "Bess Myerson was the most important female image in your life. We didn't just know about her. We *felt* her." One survivor of the Holocaust recalled that he had first heard of Bess Myerson in a displaced-persons camp in Czechoslovakia.[28]

What Bess Myerson was for the Jewish masses, *Commentary* magazine, begun in 1945, was for the Jewish intellectuals—a demonstration of the compatibility of American and Jewish identities. The American Jewish Committee, the magazine's sponsor, believed that the time had come for the organized American Jewish community to become part of American intellectual life, and that American Jewish intellectuals, precisely because they were Jewish, had something valuable to say to their country. *Commentary* set out to explore issues of significance to America in general and to the American Jewish community in particular. *Commentary* had been preceded by the *Contemporary Jewish Record,* also sponsored by the American Jewish Committee. But the *Contemporary Jewish Record* was a small-scale operation, unable to serve either the American Jewish community or the larger American reading public.

While more highbrow and less parochial than its predecessor, *Commentary* nevertheless has been throughout its life an obviously Jewish publication. "The main difference between *Partisan Review* and *Commentary,*" Elliot Cohen, its first editor, remarked, "is that we admit to being a Jewish magazine and they don't." Among the magazine's initial group of contributing editors were Salo Baron and Jacob R. Marcus, two distinguished historians of the Jewish people. Norman Podhoretz, Cohen's successor as *Commentary*'s editor, believed Cohen had a "Grand Design" to augment the influence of the New York Jewish intellectual community by reconciling it to American culture and to the American Jewish establishment. This modern-day Moses, Podhoretz claimed, sought to lead it out of "the desert of alienation in which it had been wandering for so long and into the promised land of democratic, pluralistic, prosperous America where it would live as blessedly in its Jewishness as in its Americanness, safe and sound and forevermore, amen."[29]

Cohen's rationale for the magazine appeared in its initial issue. In his first editorial, "An Act of Affirmation," he asserted that the founding of *Commentary* was an act of faith of American Jewry "in the intellect, in the visions of visionary men, in the still, small voice of poets, and thinkers, and sages." It was particularly incumbent upon Jews to make this leap of faith since they, more than any other group, had experienced the hatred and irrationality that threatened modern civilization. It was also an act of faith in both the maturity of the Jewish community and in Jewish "possibilities in America." It was now the responsibility of American Jews, because of the devastation of European Jewry, to carry forward "our common Jewish cultural and spiritual heritage." "And, indeed," Cohen continued, "we have faith that, out of the opportunities of our experience here, there will evolve new patterns of living, new modes of thought, which will harmonize heritage and country into a true sense of at-homeness in the modern world. Surely, we who have survived catastrophe, can survive freedom, too."[30]

Three years after the founding of *Commentary,* the American Jewish community made its other great postwar contribution to American intellectual life when Brandeis University opened its doors. The establishment of Brandeis could not have come at a worse time as far as Jewish fund-raising was concerned. The proponents of a Jewish-sponsored university had to overcome the argument that, in the aftermath of World War II, the first priorities of Jewish philanthropy necessarily had to be refugee resettlement and support of the struggling Jewish community in Palestine. From this perspective, a university was a costly luxury.

Despite these caveats, the planning for the university proceeded. Prominent Jews, including the revered Albert Einstein, strongly supported the concept. The institution's early benefactors saw it as a way of repaying America for the freedom and opportunity she had provided Jews. It was, in the words of its first president, Abram L. Sachar, "a corporate gift of Jews to American higher education." Brandeis's unique mission was expressed in the title of Sachar's memoir of his presidency—*A Host at Last.*[31]

The reaction of the American Jewish establishment to the founding of Brandeis was quite different from its response to America's first Jewish-sponsored university, Yeshiva University, established in the 1920s. This difference was not only due to the fact that Yeshiva, in contrast to Brandeis, was an Orthodox institution that, it was argued, would perpetuate the backward religious mentality characteristic of Orthodox Jewish life in Eastern Europe. The Jewish establishment of the twenties believed that *any* Jewish-sponsored university would be too parochial. Their newspaper, the *American Hebrew,* termed the very idea of a Jewish college a "preposterous proposition . . . fraught with harmful possibilities." It indicated "a lamentable lack of confidence in the justice and fair play of the American people." Judaism "does not require cloistered walls or academic seclusion to retain its integrity." Fortunately, the proposal for a Jewish college was "not in any sense representative of the wishes of American Jewry."[32]

The influential attorney Louis Marshall, the unofficial spokesman of old-line American Jewry, also opposed a Jewish university. "I have no hesitation in saying that the establishment of a Jewish University would be most unfortunate," he declared. Jews such as Marshall failed to consider the possibility that a Jewish university could be an integral part of the American mainstream rather than a ghetto institution, or that it could benefit not only Jews but other Americans as well.[33]

Oscar Handlin and Will Herberg, two prominent Jewish intellectuals, manifested this postwar coming-of-age of American Jewry. Handlin, the first member of Harvard's history department with an Eastern European Jewish background, won the 1952 Pulitzer Prize in history for *The Uprooted,* a sensitive study of immigrant adjustment in America. The opening lines of the introduction to *The Uprooted* declared, "Once I thought to write a history of the immigrants in America. Then I discovered that the immigrants *were* American history." The legitimization of the immigrant experience would remain one of the central themes in Handlin's writing.

In 1950, Handlin published an essay in *Commentary* that clearly revealed how far American Jewry had come since World War II. "America Recognizes Diverse Loyalties" was a novel attack on one of the hoariest anti-Semitic canards—the accusation of dual loyalty. Handlin did not take the traditional tack of categorically denying that Jews had dual loyalties. Rather, he rejected the assumption that American nationality demanded unitary loyalty in the first place. Handlin's essay was opportune because the establishment of the state of Israel in 1948 had revived concern regarding the ultimate political loyalties of America's Jews. The existence of a Jewish state, Handlin said, "put into new and troubling forms the question as to the character of the loyalties" of the American Jew. His essay was a response to another *Commentary* article, by Dorothy Thompson, the columnist, and a critic of Zionism. In "America Demands a Single Loyalty," Thompson had raised precisely the question of dual loyalty.

Handlin reassured American Jews that their support of Israel did not imply disloyalty to America. Irish Americans, German Americans, and Polish Americans had preceded Jewish Americans in being concerned with the welfare of their homelands and their compatriots overseas. Such behavior fell into a well-established American pattern. It was not the eccentric thinking of unassimilated aliens, but rather "the normal outcome of the freedom of group life in a democracy." Multiple loyalties have never been a problem in America because the nation's dominant conception of nationality "was not totalitarian" and did not demand that its citizens love only the United States. In contrast to this "broad and expansive" patriotism was the "rigorous tribalism" propagated by those with little faith in the American democratic way of life. Handlin was confident that this was a minority position and that the more liberal traditional view of American nationality would hold sway.[34]

For a Jew to justify Zionism by defending the concept of diverse loyalties, and to have this defense published in America's leading Jewish magazine, reflected an unprecedented feeling of security and self-confidence among American Jews. Such a happening would have been inconceivable prior to World War II. Will Herberg's *Protestant-Catholic-Jew: A Study in American Religious Sociology*, the most famous sociological analysis of American religion published during the 1950s, carried this sense of the normalization of Jewish life in America to its logical conclusion. Herberg's central argument was that Americans, out of the need to answer the question of "Who am I," no longer identified themselves as ethnics. They now identified themselves in religious terms. Their social and cultural life took place within the three major American religious subcommunities.

Protestant-Catholic-Jew presented a fairly optimistic analysis of American Jewish identity. Published one year after the celebration of the Jewish tercentenary in America, it examined the revival of religiosity during the postwar years. Influenced by Marcus Lee Hansen, the dean of American immigration historians, Herberg argued that ethnic identity in America had gone through three stages. The first stage was that of the immigrant generation, who spoke the language of the old country and felt and acted deeply ethnic. The second generation, by contrast, was burdened by the fear of being considered foreign and was eager to become fully Americanized. Embarrassed by the accents and customs of their parents, the second generation moved out of the immigrant neighborhoods, often Anglicized its names, and discarded as rapidly as possible the ethnic ways of their parents.

The third generation, according to Herberg, faced the existential problem of defining their identity. It craved roots and meaning in an increasingly mobile and homogeneous society. In their effort to answer the question of "Who am I," they looked back to their grandparents. In Hansen's succinct formulation, "What the son wishes to forget, the grandson wishes to remember." Being fully Americanized, the third generation was unable to relate to the language and customs of the first generation. There was, however, one aspect of the immigrant world that could satisfy their need to belong—religion. The suitably Americanized religion of immigrants, Herberg wrote, was thus "accorded a place in the American scheme of things that made it at once both genuinely American and a familiar principle of group identification." The third generation turned to religion "to define their place in American society in a way that would sustain their Americanness and yet confirm the tie that bound them to their forebears." Religious association had become "the primary context of self-identification and social location for the third generation."

For Jews with long memories, the title and thesis of Herberg's book were mind-boggling. His book assumed that Jews, who made up only 3 percent of the American population, were no longer viewed as an exotic religious sect but instead had achieved parity with Protestants and Catholics. Gentiles no longer viewed Jews as tainted. Rather, Herberg claimed, they now perceived Protestantism, Catholicism, and Judaism as equally legitimate versions of what had come to be known as the American way of life. They were the three great religions of American democracy. Herberg's thesis seemed to be substantiated by the popularity of the interfaith movement after World War II and by the widespread use of the term "Judeo-Christian" to describe American culture. If Herberg was correct, Judaism was the means by which American Jews could become fully American. "Nothing is more characteristically American than the historical evolution of American Jewry," he concluded. "It is incontrovertible that the Jewish community in the United States has become a religious community in its own understanding, as well as in the understanding of the non-Jew." Americans were deeply respectful of religion, and American Jews, by being thought of as a religious community, shared in religion's elevated status. Herberg recognized, of course, that only a small minority of American Jews were actually religious, despite how Christians might see them.[35]

By the 1950s American Jewry was on the verge of a cultural flowering. Jewish studies had become a respectable field of study in academia, in contrast to the situation prior to World War II when Judaism was viewed as unworthy of serious academic interest. No longer did Jews feel any need to disguise their background. While David Kaminsky believed it necessary to be transformed into Danny Kaye, no such need was felt by David Steinberg, Richard Dreyfuss, or Jeff Goldblum. Indeed, a black comedian by the name of Caryn Johnson even thought it would be advantageous to change her name to, of all things, Whoopi Goldberg. But what could one expect in a nation in which the chief of police of Charleston, South Carolina, where the first shot of the Civil War was fired, was a black Jew named Greenberg. If in the 1930s and 1940s doctors could become wealthy by modifying the noses of Jewish girls to conform to an "American" standard, in 1968 Barbra Streisand (who refused to have a nose job of her own) could ask in *Funny Girl* whether "a nose with a deviation is a crime against the nation." The stigma of being Jewish had so receded that even Marilyn Monroe, Elizabeth Taylor, and Lynda Carter ("Wonder Woman") converted to Judaism.

While World War II was truly a watershed in Jewish identity, it was also a watershed in the American perception of American identity. The white Anglo-Saxon Protestant paradigm ceased to be equated with American nationality. The war helped end the exclusion of blacks from the American mainstream. Major-league baseball was integrated in 1947, and in 1954 the Supreme Court outlawed racial segregation in the public schools. Other racial and ethnic barriers soon fell. By the 1980s the racial mood of the country had so changed that a black was selected as Miss America and another black was even chosen Miss Mississippi. The first Italian American United States senator was elected in the immediate postwar years, the first Italian American to be a member of the president's cabinet was selected in the 1960s, and the first Italian American Supreme Court justice was chosen in the 1980s. In 1960 a Roman Catholic was elected president, and in 1988 it was not considered remarkable that the presidential candidates that year were a second-generation Greek married to a Jew and a white Anglo-Saxon Protestant with "little brown" grandchildren (the expression is George Bush's). While this opening up of American culture has not been without its tensions and problems, few Americans regret this development or doubt that the country has benefited enormously from it.

THREE

The Jew as Patriot

Herman Wouk and American Jewish Identity

THE MOST IMPORTANT EXPRESSION of the impact of World War II in defining American Jewish identity is to be found in the novels of Herman Wouk. No other American writer has been so closely identified with the war as the author of *The Caine Mutiny*, *The Winds of War*, and *War and Remembrance*. And no other author has been as successful in using the war as a backdrop against which to explore what it means to be an American Jew.

Despite, or perhaps because of, his enormous popularity with the reading public and his financial success since the 1940s, students of contemporary American literature have not been kind to Wouk. In their view, he is a mere storyteller with little feel for language or ideas. Thus Pearl K. Bell described *War and Remembrance* as a "good-bad book," bereft of "any daunting complexities of thought, craft, or human behavior," and suffused with a cloying sentimentality. The novel's major characters are "preposterous and irritating," and the book itself "never rises above the sentimental level of best-selling romance." This volume, she claimed, is part of a "sub-literary" genre that serious readers could safely ignore. Bell was particularly put off by Wouk's praise of "valor, gallantry, leadership, patriotism," traits that fail to resonate among a current generation aware of the lunacy of all war, including World War II. Bell was correct. Wouk did believe that World War II was a good war won by good men.[1]

Even those critical of Wouk's literary pretensions, however, admitted that he is a brilliant military historian of World War II, particularly when recount-

This chapter was previously published in *American Jewish History* 84 (Dec. 1996): 333–51. Reprinted by permission of the American Jewish Historical Society.

ing the naval history of the war. Bell noted that Wouk frequently provides the readers "a brilliantly evocative account of battle." Paul Fussell, a veteran of the Pacific Theater of World War II and a professor of literature at the University of Pennsylvania, agreed. For him, *War and Remembrance* is both a literary disaster and a historian's triumph. The novel is so "bad" and "embarrassing" that Fussell claimed its author was in reality a historian who had been attracted to fiction "by the emoluments now attaching to it and its residuals." In contrast to the novels of Joseph Heller and Kurt Vonnegut, Wouk's war novel "lacks the crucial dimension of the lunatic, the cruel, and the self-destructive." Fussell balanced his criticism of *War and Remembrance* as a literary work ("trash" and "soap-opera") with praise for Wouk the historian. As a historian of the war he ranks alongside Samuel Eliot Morison and B. H. Liddell Hart.[2]

Wouk has been a controversial figure within American intellectual circles since the appearance in 1951 of *The Caine Mutiny*, his Pulitzer Prize–winning novel of a mutiny on board a World War II destroyer-minesweeper in the Pacific. The mutiny against the insane Captain Queeg is encouraged by Lieutenant Thomas Keefer, a playwright, budding war novelist, and intellectual. The novel's conclusion, which defends Queeg, attacks Keefer, and argues that the ship's officers should have rallied around their captain, startled its readers, who had become accustomed to American novelists describing the military experience as dehumanizing. In Norman Mailer's *The Naked and the Dead*, for example, the commander of American forces on a Pacific island is a fascist obsessed with power. And in both *The Naked and the Dead* and Irwin Shaw's *The Young Lions*, the United States Army is permeated with anti-Semitism. Arthur M. Schlesinger Jr. called *The Caine Mutiny* "the great anti-intellectual novel, dedicated to the thesis that Keefer, the rootless critic, was a far greater threat to society than Queeg, the mad and cowardly embodiment of authority." Leslie A. Fiedler agreed with Schlesinger. Wouk defends "the whole military, the whole social order in all its smug security."[3]

Wouk's reputation as an enemy of the intelligentsia and a spokesman for conformity was solidified in 1955 with the publication of *Marjorie Morningstar*. This novel traces Marjorie's life from her rebellious teenage years, when she longs to become a "morning star" and part of New York's bohemian culture, to her mature years when the morning star has burned itself out and she is safely ensconced in Mamaroneck with her house, her attorney husband, Milton Schwartz, and her children. Marjorie, Fiedler noted, embodies "hundred per-cent Americanism." She is "the first fictional celebration of the mid-twentieth century detente between the Jews and middle-class America." In fact, Wouk's attitude toward his heroine is one of pathos and ambivalence. The most pitiful aspect of Marjorie's life, as one of the characters in the novel observes, is her belief that she could become anything other than a "Shirley," a respectable and dull suburban Hadassah matron.[4]

Norman Podhoretz's review of *Marjorie Morningstar* emphasized both Wouk's deficiencies as a writer and his banality. "Utterly incapable of rendering the feel of an emotion or a mood or a conversation," Wouk's imagination points "vaguely into space like a blind man trying to locate an object in an unfamiliar room." Even more troubling to Podhoretz than Wouk's "imaginative helplessness" and the "ugliness" of his prose are his jejune values. *Marjorie Morningstar* is a protest against all those who have "an appetite for diverse areas of experience, an unwillingness to settle into the common routines, a refusal to surrender one's demands on the world without a fight." Wouk writes as if Jewishness would disintegrate "if it ventures beyond the moral and spiritual confines of a Judaic bourgeois style."[5]

Wouk's low repute within the American intelligentsia increased on September 5, 1955, when he appeared on the cover of *Time*. The occasion was the publication of *Marjorie Morningstar*. The accompanying story lauded Wouk as the spokesman for conventional attitudes regarding morality and patriotism that, the magazine argued, have been repudiated by America's intellectual elite. Wouk "carries no chip on his shoulder and . . . gives the U.S. straight A's in his fictional report." He is at the vanguard of a rebellion against a literary establishment "dominated by skeptical criticism, sexual emancipation, social protest and psychoanalytic sermonizing."[6]

For students of American history, and particularly of American Jewish history, Wouk's significance lies not in his contribution to American literature or to the history of World War II. Rather it is in his definition of American Jewish identity. In his analysis of *Marjorie Morningstar*, Fiedler remarked that Wouk sought an end to "surly intransigence among the Jews." Wouk's view of American Jewish identity goes far beyond that. In six novels and in a preface to the letters of Jonathan Netanyahu, the hero of the Israeli rescue of the Jewish hostages at Entebbe in 1976, Wouk articulated a symbiosis between American identity and Jewish identity, an intertwining of American and Jewish fates in which the Jew is a patriot and the preeminent defender of American institutions and values. Wouk's own life anticipated this effort.[7]

Wouk's attempt to synthesize his American and Jewish identities was part of a broader effort to resolve the conflict between the two individuals who did the most to shape his outlook—his maternal grandfather, Rabbi Mendel Leib Levine, and the Columbia University professor Irwin Edman. One could hardly ask for a greater contrast than that between the Talmudist Levine, a former student at the famous Volozin Yeshiva in Lithuania who never read Western books, saw a movie or a play, or listened to classical music, and Edman, a distinguished intellectual, religious skeptic, and disciple of John Dewey. "The two teachers who most influenced my life," Wouk recalled, "were a man without a trace of Western culture and a man who is its embodiment." Wouk's working day, which began with an hour of study of the Talmud followed by many hours of writing, reflected this tension, which he sought to resolve in his fiction. Added to this was Wouk's service as an officer in the navy in the Pacific during World War II aboard the minesweepers *Zane* and *Southard*. At war's end he was the *Southard*'s executive officer and was slated to become the ship's captain until the ship was wrecked by a typhoon near Okinawa in October 1945. During the war Wouk took part in eight Pacific invasions and won four campaign stars and a unit citation. He described these years as "the greatest experience of my life. . . . In the Navy, I found out more than I ever had about people and about the United States." Among the things he learned during the war was that the navy could be tolerant of the peculiar dietary practices of Wouk, an Orthodox Jew.[8]

This theme of the Jew as patriot explains the otherwise puzzling dénouement of *The Caine Mutiny* involving Barney Greenwald, the attorney for the defendant, Lieutenant Stephen Maryk, the ship's executive officer. Captain Theodore Breakstone, the navy's district legal officer, is initially reluctant to have Greenwald, a reserve officer, fighter pilot, and graduate of Georgetown University Law School, represent Maryk, even though he is described as a "pretty red-hot officer" by one of Breakstone's subordinates. Greenwald is a Jew and a liberal and had built up a successful law practice in Albuquerque, New Mexico, defending American Indians. He is not the type of person one would expect to defend the institutional prerogatives of the navy or its code of discipline, loyalty, and honor. "Sounds like he might be pinko," Breakstone says, but he goes along with Greenwald's selection because he is the only remaining candidate for the assignment after eight other navy lawyers have rejected it.

Greenwald, in fact, is not sympathetic to those involved in the mutiny. He tells Breakstone, "These men are no underdogs, sir. They deserve to get slugged." A "halfway intelligent defense," he says, will likely get them off, and he does not want to be responsible should this occur. "I just don't want to defend these *Caine* people. Captain Queeg obviously is not crazy. The psychiatrist's report proves it. These fools find a paragraph in Navy Regs that gives them ideas, and they gang up on a skipper who's mean and stupid—as a lot of skippers are—and make jackasses of themselves, and put a ship out of action. I'm a damn good lawyer and a very expensive one, and I don't see contributing my services to get them acquitted." From the beginning of his pretrial investigation Greenwald is convinced that the intellectual Keefer is "the villain of this foul-up." He is eager to read Keefer's half-finished novel of the war. "I'm sure that it exposes this war in all its grim futility and waste, and shows up the military men for the stupid, Fascist-minded sadists they are," he sarcastically says to Maryk. "Bitching up all the campaigns and throwing away the lives of fatalistic, humorous, lovable citizen-soldiers." [9]

Contrary to what he told Breakstone, and contrary to the expectations of the prosecution, Greenwald ignores the charges against Maryk and instead puts Queeg on trial. He attempts to demonstrate during his questioning of Queeg and other witnesses at the trial that the captain is mentally ill, incompetent, and a coward (the officers of the *Caine* nicknamed him "Old Yellowstain") and that the defendant was thus justified in relieving him of his command. Greenwald adopts this strategy despite the fact that, if successful, it will ruin Queeg. He also knows that three navy psychiatrists and twenty crew members of the *Caine* are prepared to testify that Queeg always appeared sane and intelligent. In addition, Greenwald begins the trial conscious of the fact that Captain Blakely, the president of the court, doesn't like Jews. Wouk's description of Blakely is rather forbidding. He has "an alarming face; a sharp nose, a mouth like a black line, and small far-seeing eyes under heavy eyebrows, with a defiant, distrust glare." Nevertheless, Greenwald reassures Maryk that things will work out despite Blakely's prejudice. "You're not supposed to love Jews necessarily, just to give them a fair shake. I've always had a fair shake in the Navy, and I'll get it from Blakely, too, despite the eyebrows." And, in fact, the court does give Greenwald a fair shake, overruling most of the prosecution's objections to his mode of questioning.[10]

Greenwald's cross-examination of Queeg is devastating and leaves no doubt that the captain is suffering from extreme paranoia and should never have commanded any ship. At one time during the cross-examination Queeg blurts out, "I did not make a single mistake in fifteen months aboard the *Caine* and I can prove it and my record has been spotless until now and I don't want it smirched by a whole lot of lies and distortions by disloyal officers." After these and other outbursts, there is little doubt that the court will exonerate Maryk. Even Queeg senses that his navy career is over. He leaves the court a broken man, "shoulders hunched, head down, feet scurrying, the balls rolling in his fingers." During his closing argument, Greenwald is deferential and almost apologetic to the court. He realizes that he has ruined a naval officer and put the navy in a very bad position for having allowed Queeg to command the *Caine*. "It has been the most unpleasant duty I've ever had to perform," he tells the court. The navy court takes seventy minutes to acquit Maryk.[11]

In celebration, Keefer announces that he is going to host a dinner party at the Fairmont Hotel and will pay for it with the advance of a thousand dollars he has just received from the publisher of his novel. Greenwald is reluctant to go to a party whose purpose is not merely to cheer Maryk's acquittal but also to revel in Queeg's disgrace. Keefer tells him he is to be the guest of honor, and Maryk says that he will not come to the party if Greenwald is not there. Greenwald relents but shows up half drunk. When he arrives the officers of the *Caine* are making jokes at Queeg's expense, and Keefer proposes a toast in honor of the lawyer. "To Lieutenant Barney Greenwald . . . the forensic St. George who slew with his redoubtable tongue that most horrible of dragons—Old Yellowstain." Before toasting Keefer in return, Greenwald asks him whether his novel lambasts the navy and whether it contains a hero modeled on its author. Keefer responds affirmatively to both questions. "If I wrote a war novel," Greenwald replies, "I'd try to make a hero out of Old Yellowstain." The revelers are bewildered by this assertion. Greenwald then proceeds, in the most important section of the book, to explain why the officers of the *Caine* and not Queeg are the villains of the mutiny.

He begins by stating that he is a Jew and that his mother physically resembles Maryk's mother. But his mother would have a different fate than Maryk's mother and the mothers of all the other persons at the party if America did not win the war. "The Germans aren't kidding about the Jews. They're cooking us down to soap over there. . . . I just can't cotton to the idea of my mother melted down into a bar of soap." The *Caine*'s officers are puzzled by this seeming non sequitur. Greenwald explains. While Keefer and the other officers had been enjoying civilian life and looking down on the military, Queeg and the other "stuffy, stupid Prussians in the Navy and Army" were preparing to defend America from the Nazis. "Yes, even Queeg, poor sad guy, yes, and most of them not sad at all, fellows, a lot of them sharper boys than any of us, don't kid yourself, best men I've ever seen, you can't be good in the Army or Navy unless you're goddamn good. Though maybe not upon Proust 'n' *Finnegan's Wake* and all."

Greenwald says he will not stay for dinner since he does not wish to socialize with Keefer and the other mutineers. Before leaving, he tells Maryk that he was guilty of mutiny and was acquitted only because of "phony legal tricks." He then attacks Keefer for fomenting the mutiny, saying that he and not Maryk should have been tried. "I defended Steve because I found out the wrong guy was on trial. Only way I could defend him was to sink Queeg for you. I'm sore that I was pushed into that spot, and ashamed of what I did, and thass why I'm drunk. Queeg deserved better at my hands. I owed him a favor, don't you see? He stopped Hermann Goering from washing his fat behind with my mother." Instead of helping Queeg through his difficulties, the officers of the *Caine* conspired against him. They ruined Queeg, disgraced themselves, and undermined military authority. Greenwald throws a glass of wine in Keefer's face and walks out of the suite.

Later one of the officers admits that the mutiny was wrong. "The idea is, once you get an incompetent ass of a skipper—and it's a chance of war—there's nothing to do but serve him as though he were the wisest and the best, cover his mistakes, keep the ship going, and bear up." The person responsible for his change of opinion was "an amazing Jew named Greenwald."[12]

The attention of most readers of *The Caine Mutiny* focused on Wouk's defense of the military command structure. William H. Whyte Jr. argued that the novel's popularity indicated that many Americans were willing to conform to the demands of a new organizational ethos. The book, with its "astounding denial of individual responsibility," is "a landmark in the shift of American values" from the "Protestant Ethic" of individualism and self-reliance to the "Social Ethic" of organizational life. By contrast, Whyte called Greenwald's discussion of his mother being boiled down for soap "the most irrelevant climax in contemporary fiction." But for students of Wouk, Greenwald's conflating of American and Jewish destinies is the most important part of the book. This would also be the major theme of *The Winds of War* (1971) and *War and Remembrance* (1978), Wouk's two mammoth novels of World War II; *Inside/Outside* (1985); and *The Hope* (1993) and *The Glory* (1994), two novels of modern-day Israel.[13]

Thirteen years before the appearance of *The Winds of War,* Wouk published *This Is My God,* an apologia for Orthodox Judaism. Here he noted the similarity between the life of the religious Jew and that of navy men. "Are the sailors and officers less American because they are in the Navy? They have special commitments and disciplines, odd ways of dress, sharp limits on their freedom. They have, at least in their own minds, compensations of glory, or of vital service performed." This merging of Jewish and American identities was even more explicit in *The Winds of War* and *War and Remembrance*.[14]

These two novels tell the story of America's involvement in World War II through its effect on two families—the Henrys and the Jastrows. The plot reads like a soap opera. The patriarch of the Henry clan is Victor "Pug" Henry, a navy captain who acts as a personal emissary for President Roosevelt in Germany and the Soviet Union and then participates in several naval battles in the Pacific. Aaron Jastrow is a Jewish scholar living in Siena, Italy, with his niece Natalie, the wife of Byron Henry, Pug's younger son. The two Jastrows flee the Nazis, are eventually captured, and end up in Auschwitz, where Aaron is killed and Natalie barely survives. Wouk emphasizes the different backgrounds of the two families. Pug Henry is from an old-line white Anglo-Saxon Methodist family, while Aaron Jastrow, who is modeled on the art critic Bernard Berenson, had been a promising yeshiva *bocher* in his early years while growing up in Oswiecim (Auschwitz) in southern Poland. Aaron's family settles in Boston, he attends Harvard, becomes an agnostic, falls in love with a Christian, and secretly converts to Roman Catholicism. When his girlfriend refuses to marry him because of his Jewish background, Aaron relapses into naturalism.

Aaron's most famous book is *A Jew's Jesus,* which portrays Jesus not as the founder of a new religion but as a Jew who both loved and was loved by the Jewish common people. Aaron's Jesus is a student of the Talmud, an itinerant Palestinian preacher, and, finally a radical executed because of his political views. Another of Aaron's books is *A Jew Named Paul,* which emphasizes the rabbinic roots of Paul's thinking. Aaron is also an authority on the Italian Renaissance. This was a great blossoming of art and ideas, he tells Byron, that resulted when "paganism and the Hebrew spirit—in its Christian expression—briefly fertilized instead of fighting each other." Aaron calls himself a "hybrid" amalgamation of these two conflicting impulses.[15]

The marriage between Natalie and Byron symbolizes the union of American and Jewish identities and interests. Pug Henry tells Byron that he has no objection in principle to Byron's marrying Natalie. "I have nothing against Jewish people. . . . If I thought she could make you happy and give you some direction in life I'd welcome her, and take pleasure in personally punching in the nose anybody who upset her." Byron's Christianity is a religion without dogma, and he agrees with Aaron's view that Jesus was simply a "poor idealistic Jewish preacher from the back hills." That, he tells Aaron, is the Christianity he learned from his father. If American Christianity is different from that of Europe, so is America different from Europe. Thus a Polish soldier is incredulous when told that Byron Henry is married to a Jew. "No American Navy officer would ever marry a Jew," he says to Byron.[16]

This contrast between America and Europe is particularly sharp when it comes to Germany and anti-Semitism. In a conversation with a German in Berlin prior to the outbreak of the war, Rhoda Henry, Pug's wife, says, "I'm an American to the bone, going back six generations, and I'll never see eye to eye with you on this business of the Jews. It's absolutely awful." If the formative influences on America were classical paganism, Judaism, and Christianity, the formative influences on Germany were Hegelianism, Darwinism, nationalism, and romanticism. As Leslie Slote, an American diplomat in Warsaw, tells Byron, "Nazism is unthinkable without its roots in German nineteenth-century thought. . . . If you're not prepared to read every word of Hegel's *Philosophy of History,* for instance, give up. It's basic."[17]

Slote personifies the difference in attitude between the European nations and the United States toward their Jewish citizens. Shortly after the German invasion of Poland, a large number of European and American nationals fall into the hands of the SS. An SS officer orders that the Christians be separated from the Jews. While the Swiss, Hungarian, Rumanian, and Dutch citizens are divided between Christians and Jews, Slote adamantly refuses to allow American Jews to be singled out. "The policy of my country on religious groups is one of absolute equality of treatment," he tells the officer. "Look here, for your purposes you can assume we're all Jews." A retired American army officer also tells the SS that there are no Jews among the Americans. The difference between the United States and the European countries is clear. "In the rest of the waiting room the process of sorting out the Jews was over. People were glancing at the Americans, pointing and whispering."[18]

For historians the major problem with Wouk's effort to conflate American and Jewish fates during World War II was America's niggardly immigration policy, which provided a refuge for only a very small percentage of Europe's harried Jews. Wouk absolves Roosevelt of any responsibility for this, and he virtually ignores the growing anti-Semitism in America during the 1930s, which was one factor in the reluctance of Congress to liberalize the immigration laws. "What's one to do?" FDR asks Pug Henry in August 1941. "Scolding the Germans is so humiliating, and so *futile.* I've exhausted that line long ago. We've tried to get around the immigration laws, with this device and that, and we've had some luck, actually. But when I've got a Congress that's ready to disband the Army, can you imagine my going to them with a bill to admit more Jews."[19]

The entwining of American and Jewish destinies in *The Winds of War* occurs simultaneously with the awakening of Natalie Jastrow's Jewish identity. When she was eleven she dropped all religious practice and had never returned to it. As the novel opens, Natalie is single and working for her uncle as a research assistant in Siena. She travels to Warsaw just before the German invasion and, to her surprise, is fascinated by the large Jewish Quarter. She drags Byron to a Yiddish performance of a Eugene O'Neill play and is both amused and moved by the synthesis of American characters and Jewish emotion of the actors. Natalie tells Byron, "That was me, I guess. . . . That exact strange mixture. I never quite understood that, and I'm still sorting it out. It's disconcerting but exciting. Like seeing myself for the first time in a home movie." Byron, in turn, sees Natalie in a new light—a Jew one generation removed from the Jews he has encountered in Warsaw.[20]

At the same time, Natalie also experiences a change in her attitude toward the American military. During the 1930s she had accepted the conventional antimilitary thought fashionable among American leftists and had founded the Student Antiwar Committee while an undergraduate at Radcliffe. By 1940, however, she is engaged to Byron, is desperately seeking to escape from Italy with her uncle, and has abandoned her illusions about the military. "I never realized that there were people like you . . . and your father," she writes Byron. "I'm sure the stereotyped military men do exist in droves, the hard-drinking bigoted nincompoops. . . . The new thing is the Henrys. You're peculiarly unobtrusive on the American scene, don't know just why, but thank God you're there!"[21]

The Winds of War ends in December 1941 with Pug Henry viewing the fleet at Pearl Harbor. The sight of the sunken and damaged vessels is hideous, and he asks himself why he chose the navy as a career and why he now must risk his life. He provides his answer: "Because with all its rotten spots, the United States of America was not only his homeland but the hope of the world. Because if America's enemies dug up iron and made deadly engines of it, America had to do the same, and do it better or die." But who are these enemies? Wouk does not mention the Japanese. Rather, the sailors and pilots responsible for the destruction at Pearl Harbor "had obeyed orders of politicians working with Hitler." The major enemy of the Jews is now also the major enemy of the United States. "Until the life was beaten out of that monster, the world could not move an inch toward a more sane existence. There was nothing to do now but win the war."[22]

War and Remembrance picks up where *The Winds of War* ends. The sequel's epigram is from Exodus 17: "Write this for a remembrance in a book . . . that the Lord has a war with Amalek from generation to generation." The Amalek for the generation that fought World War II was, of course, Hitler, and the United States is the instrument of God's vengeance. The war transforms Aaron and Natalie. After a hiatus of half a century, Aaron resumes the study of the Talmud. He prays every morning with phylacteries purchased while in Theresienstadt with a diamond he had been saving for an emergency. While in Theresienstadt Aaron rips up the document of his conversion to Catholicism, which he has been carrying for possible protection. Another indication of return to the Jewishness of his youth is when he and Natalie begin conversing in Yiddish, a language she has not spoken for decades. Aaron also begins writing a spiritual meditation to be titled *A Jew's Journey.* This volume will not only present his thoughts on faith, the human condition, and his own biography but will also be "a salutary reckoning of the soul" now that he has returned to his people. He remains "at heart . . . the Oswiecim yeshiva boy." His last words before dying in the gas chamber at Auschwitz are from the Shema: "Hear O Israel, the Lord our God is One God."[23]

Natalie's embryonic Jewish feelings also grow during the war. Prior to her capture by the Nazis she begins to light Sabbath candles. Much to her surprise, she becomes a fervent Zionist. While waiting in Naples for a boat to take her, her son, Louis, and Aaron to Palestine, she tells Avram Rabinovitz, a representative of the Yishuv, "Look, don't you understand that I feel no emotion about Palestine? None! I am an American, completely irreligious, married to a Christian naval officer." "Bring your son to Palestine," Rabinovitz responds. "He'll grow up a man of action like his father." During her stay in the Theresienstadt concentration camp, Natalie comes to realize that Zionism is the only answer to the plight of Jews facing an Amalek such as Hitler and that she and her son belong in Palestine. Here she also discovers "the exaltation of being Jewish." Aaron welcomes Natalie's Zionism. "It seems to be for her the assertion of threatened identity that I have found in my old religion."[24]

Physically separated from her husband, Natalie is attracted to Rabinovitz. The suspense surrounding Natalie not only revolves around whether she will survive the war and be reunited with Louis, who was smuggled out of Theresienstadt, but also whether she will return to America with Byron or settle down with Avram in Palestine. "The contrast between Rabinovitz and Byron bit deep into her. . . . The white-haired stumpy Palestinian, his shoulders bowed, his expression in repose a mixture of weariness, sadness, and resolve, was of another breed than Byron. Her husband had the clear-eyed self-assured naive air of an American. . . . Byron Henry, if he lived to be ninety, and if all his years were hard, would never look like Avram Rabinovitz." The novel ends with Natalie reunited with Byron, but still the question remains whether she will return to the United States or settle in Palestine. Byron, however, intimates that the couple will be moving to Palestine when he asks Rabinovitz whether the Jews of Palestine have a navy. Louis is thus destined to personify the symbiosis of American and Jewish identities. The son of American parents, he will live as a Jew in a Jewish homeland.[25]

Since the publication of *War and Remembrance*, Wouk's ruminations on American Jewish identity have centered on Israel and Zionism. In 1980 he wrote the introduction to the letters of Jonathan Netanyahu. Netanyahu was killed while Americans were celebrating the two hundredth anniversary of the Declaration of Independence, a coincidence not lost on Wouk. Netanyahu was the son of a distinguished professor of Jewish history at Cornell University and the brother of a future prime minister of Israel. In *War and Remembrance*, Wouk had argued that saving the remnants of European Jewry depended on the United States defeating Germany. In his introduction to Netanyahu's letters, written while American hostages were being held in Iran by Ayatollah Khomeini, Wouk has the Jews of Israel repaying their debt to the United States.

Wouk describes the Entebbe raid as a beacon in the "dense gloom" of the struggle between civilization and terrorism. Netanyahu, an Israeli Pug Henry, died not merely for Jews but for free men everywhere. The same values and ideals that had animated Americans during World War II were now inspiring Netanyahu and other Israelis. Netanyahu demonstrated that "love of country is noble, that self-sacrifice is rewarding, that to be ready to fight for freedom fills a man with a sense of worth like nothing else." Wouk pays Netanyahu the highest compliment possible by comparing him to Admiral Raymond Spruance, hero of the battles of Midway and the Philippine Sea and an important figure in *War and Remembrance*. Both Netanyahu and Spruance "embody—by the cast of destiny—the virtue of their whole people in a great hour." If America, then experiencing a post-Vietnam backlash against the military, wished to remain "the great beacon in dense gloom, the promise to the hundreds of millions of the oppressed that liberty exists," she could profit from

Netanyahu's example. His sacrifice "may tell us Americans, in the greatest land of the free, something about honoring our own young guardians in the night."[26]

Wouk's belief that the values and interests of America and Israel are complementary is further developed in his semiautobiographical novel *Inside/ Outside*. The novel's protagonist is Israel David Goodkind (a "good kind"), who prefers not to use his first name until the final line of the book when, returning to the United States from Israel, he says to an El Al stewardess, "Call me Israel." This is an obvious allusion to that most famous of all first lines in American fiction, Herman Melville's "Call me Ishmael" in *Moby Dick*. It also indicates how Goodkind has resolved any conflict between his inside identity as a traditional Jew and his outside identity as a fervent American patriot and graduate of Columbia University. He simply denies that such a conflict exists. Significantly, Wouk has him observing the seven days of mourning for his deceased father when the Japanese attack Pearl Harbor. His personal grief commences at the same time that the nation begins its own period of suffering and sacrifice.[27]

At the beginning of the novel Goodkind has taken a temporary leave of absence from his successful New York corporate tax law practice to become a special assistant to President Nixon. This is in 1973, just prior to the outbreak of the Yom Kippur War and the emergence of the Watergate scandal. Before taking the job he tells the president that he will not work on the Sabbath. "I'm impressed, Mr. Goodkind," Nixon replies. "May I say that I've had numerous Jewish associates, but you're the first one who's made that stipulation, and I'm impressed. Very impressed." Although a lifelong Democrat, Goodkind does not share the visceral anti-Nixon sentiments of his friends and relatives. While not a Nixon enthusiast, he cautiously admires the president's commitment to peace, his struggle to preserve the authority of the president during the Watergate affair, and especially his support of Israel during the Yom Kippur War. Goodkind tells the president that the Jewish people will revere him forever if he sends arms to Israel, an American ally, to balance the arms being sent by the Soviet Union to the Arabs. "It will honor the man who showed greatness, by rising above his own desperate political predicament and coming to the rescue of the Jewish State." Nixon, in turn, praises Goodkind for not deserting his captain during the Watergate crisis. "You've stayed aboard while some others were jumping ship. It's been appreciated." Just as in the case of *The Caine Mutiny*, it is a Jew who defends duty, loyalty, and American institutions. Goodkind's (and presumably Wouk's) loyalty to Nixon, while understandable, is, however, misplaced. Nixon's desperate effort to maintain his authority challenged the Constitution and undermined the institutional prerogatives of the presidency.[28]

Wouk further developed the synthesis between Jewish and American identities in *The Hope* and *The Glory*. These novels span the history of Israel from its founding through the early 1980s. For Wouk, war has been the great experience of the twentieth century, and particularly has this been true for Israel. *The Hope* chronicles the Israeli wars of 1948, 1956, and 1967, while *The Glory* discusses the Yom Kippur War of 1973 and ends with the 1981 Israeli attack on the Iraqi nuclear reactor.

Mickey Marcus, a West Point graduate and veteran of World War II, is a key figure in the early pages of *The Hope*. At first this former Army officer is reluctant to help the Haganah during Israel's war of independence. Soon, however, he is caught up in the euphoria of helping fellow Jews. "You people are wonderful," he tells an Israeli. "You've pulled off a miracle, you've held on to the beachhead by your fingernails. . . . By God, maybe I was born to save Jerusalem." When Marcus calls Ben-Gurion the George Washington of Israel, an Israeli responds, "And you're our Lafayette." Marcus is skeptical of this analogy. "Lafayette brought over a trained army . . . and got the French fleet to fight on the American side. That's really how old George beat the redcoats. I bring you bopkess. If you know that military expression."

But Wouk is more impressed with the similarities than the differences between the history of America and Israel. An American Gentile woman explains to her Israeli lover why America is so supportive of Israel. "It's the resonance with American history," she says. "You've landed on a hostile shore, trying to bring forth a new nation conceived in liberty, haven't you? You and we both started as colonies that threw out the British. Both had early years of dangerous adversity, only yours are still going on. Almost a mirror image." He soon comes to agree with her. "The more I come to understand things, the more I perceive how our miracle of the return is linked to your older miracle of America."

This attempt to see Israel as America writ small was not unique to Wouk. Over three decades earlier Leon Uris's *Exodus* (1958) had done the same thing. Its portrayal of the Jewish national liberation struggle with the British resembles America's War of Independence. It also resembles an American Western movie, with the soldiers of the Haganah coming to the rescue of Jewish settlements encircled by the Arabs. It helped that Uris had recently worked on the script for *The Gunfight at the O.K. Corral*. One of the key characters in

Exodus is Kitty Fremont, a Gentile from Indiana. Initially skeptical of the Zionist goal of a Jewish state, she soon becomes a supporter of the Jewish cause. For Uris and millions of his readers, the Zionist cause was legitimized by a pro-Zionist American Gentile, who also was the lover of Ari Ben Canaan, the novel's hero.[29]

Wouk also draws an analogy between Israel's war of independence and the history of the American West. In a chapter in *The Hope* titled "The Alamo," Wouk has Ben-Gurion ordering Marcus to open a supply line to the besieged Jerusalem and then to hold on to the city, including the Jewish Quarter of the Old City. (A later chapter on the Israeli air strike to launch the Six Days' War is titled "Midway," and Anwar Sadat's visit to Jerusalem in 1977 is likened in *The Glory* to Lee's surrender at Appomattox.) Marcus compares the Jewish Quarter to the Alamo. "At West Point we used to argue whether that stand was heroism or folly. The Alamo was militarily indefensible. So's the Quarter. The boss man wants us to hang on for reasons of state, so that's that. Let's go." Although the Jewish Quarter is not liberated, Marcus's forces do open a corridor to the city. Marcus, however, is not able to enjoy this triumph for long; an Israeli sentry kills him by accident. Marcus's body is flown to the United States for burial in the cemetery at West Point. Zev Barak, an Israeli military officer, accompanies the body.[30]

For Wouk the circumstances surrounding the return of Marcus's body and the funeral symbolize the meaning of Israel's fight for independence and the nature of American Jewish identity.

> The plane landed and rolled to a stop. Through an opened side port, sunshine flooded the fuselage as three young officers in beribboned army uniforms, bristle-headed and stiff-backed, leaped in and saluted the Israelis. Reverently they removed the flag from the coffin. Two of them draped over the box an enormous Stars and Stripes, while the third folded the Star of David flag and handed it to Barak. He could see on the tarmac, under large American and Israeli flags flapping in the brisk wind, a long line of black limousines. An honor guard of policemen in dress blues—at least a hundred, Barak estimated—snapped salutes as the coffin was handed out of the plane, for Mickey Marcus had once been New York's commissioner of correction.

At West Point, Barak tells Marcus's widow how her husband once quoted to him a line from a poem by the English poet Rupert Brooke—"There is a corner of some foreign field that is forever England." Now, Barak says, "there's a corner of West Point that is forever Israel."[31]

One element in Wouk's belief in the compatibility of the interests of the United States, on the one hand, and the interests of American Jews and Israel, on the other, has been a hatred of communism and the Soviet Union. Wouk has always detested communism as a threat to religion, including Judaism, and to the United States and Israel. In his mind there was little to choose between Stalin, Hitler, and Mussolini, "the Caligulas, the Neroes, the Borgias of the twentieth century." *War and Remembrance* contains a devastating description of the pro-communist, Popular Front mentality at work in the person of a character named Leonard Spreregen. At a party prior to a pro-Soviet rally at the Hollywood Bowl in 1942, Spreregen, a successful screenwriter and an assimilated Jew, tries to convince Byron Henry of the need to launch an invasion of Europe in 1942 to take the pressure off the Soviet Union. Instead of holding a rally on behalf of a second front, Henry proposes that Spreregen and his fellow-traveling friends hold a rally for the suffering Jews in Europe. "Such big propaganda shows might do them some real good." Spreregen is dumbfounded by Henry's politically incorrect statement. He stops eating a slab of ham and responds, "Well, I'm not sure what's happening over there, my friend. I don't think anybody here really knows, but the way to end all that misery is by smashing Hitler with a second front now."[32]

In *The Hope* and *The Glory* Wouk argued that the close relations between the United States and Israel stemmed from their common enmity toward communism and the Soviet Union. A pro-Israel American CIA official tells Barak after Israel's remarkable victory in the Six Days' War, "You're handing Russian communism its first major setback on the battlefield and in world politics since Yalta. Only a people of God could pull that off." During the Yom Kippur War, Golda Meir, Israel's prime minister, says to Henry Kissinger, the American secretary of state, that the Israelis have "been fighting America's battle in the Middle East. You and I both know it. Were it not for the Soviet encouragement of their intransigence, the Arabs would long ago have come to terms with reality and made peace with Israel." In *The Glory,* an Israeli chief of staff says regarding the Arabs, "They can't get it into their head that we can live in peace side by side. One day they will, when they become good and tired of dying for the Russians."[33]

The most important part of *The Glory* involves the Yom Kippur War of 1973. As in *Inside/Outside,* Wouk describes a beleaguered Israel being rescued by Richard Nixon. Kissinger explains the president's thinking to Barak: "He may be distracted, but his instinct for foreign policy is still keen. The President knows that if you're defeated the Russians will dominate the Middle

East, the Arabs will be impossible to deal with, and the world balance will tilt against the United States." Wouk pictures Nixon as more eager to aid Israel than is Kissinger, a Jew. When an American airlift of military supplies finally commences, despite the foot-dragging of the State Department, it has an almost immediate effect on Israel's military fortunes. Moshe Dayan says, "They're phenomenal, the Americans, once they get going. . . . They're being magnificent." Golda Meir also effusively praises the American airlift. "We have kept the faith, and so has the American President."[34]

Three years after the Yom Kippur War, Israeli commandoes made their dramatic rescue of the Jewish hostages at Entebbe. Here also Wouk emphasizes the harmony between the American and Jewish experiences. The occasion is a celebration aboard the United States aircraft carrier *Forrestal* in New York in honor of America's bicentennial. Word of the Israeli raid reaches those in attendance shortly before the United States Marine Band plays "The Star-Spangled Banner" and a big bell tolls thirteen times for the original thirteen colonies. The general opinion of the diplomats in attendance is that "America should be more like Israel in dealing with its enemies and with terrorism."[35]

The Glory concludes with Barak pondering the future of Israel and the United States with his American girlfriend. "The old countries, Japan, England, Russia, worse off or better off, they just *are*. We're both still *trying to be*, you the giant of the world and we the crazy little nobody in the Middle East. Who knows whether we'll make it in the end, either of us?"

Wouk's belief in the similarity of interests of America and Israel and in the symbiosis of American and American Jewish identities is a by-product of the optimism of postwar America. With the dramatic decline of anti-Semitism after 1945, American Jews had never felt more at home. The fears of anti-Zionists that a Jewish state would call into question the patriotism of American Jews were unfounded as the cold war brought the United States and Israel into close cooperation. Similarly, the fears of religious reformers that the dietary laws and other restrictions of a fossilized Judaism would prevent observant Jews from entering into the American mainstream were also groundless. That Wouk was an Orthodox Jew did not prevent him from becoming one of America's most popular postwar novelists. The years of Wouk's popularity occurred while American Jewry was emerging from a psychological and geographical ghetto, and his message that Judaism and Jewishness facilitated rather than detracted from Americanization was very reassuring. A good Jew for him was almost by definition a good American.[36]

Recent developments, however, have called this optimism into question.

A symposium in the August 1996 issue of *Commentary* revealed that a number of America's leading Jewish religious thinkers now believe that dissonance rather than compatibility best describes the relationship between American culture and the future of American Jewry. While they do not fear for the physical safety of American Jews, they worry about the viability of an American Jewish population experiencing a major demographic hemorrhaging because of religious apathy, a low birthrate, growing intermarriage, and the lure of a secular culture emphasizing individual autonomy and personal gratification rather than individual religious obligation and communal commitment. "At greatest risk," the historian Jack Wertheimer said, "are those who are least prepared to regard Judaism as a unique system with a richly developed culture sometimes profoundly at odds with prevailing mores."[37]

These warnings are not new. Two decades earlier, in his *Letters to an American Jewish Friend: A Zionist's Polemic,* Hillel Halkin questioned whether American Jewry could withstand the social and economic forces encouraging acculturation and assimilation. "Where else in the history of the Diaspora," he asked, "has there ever been another Jewish community so well-organized with so little Jewish substance to its life?" Halkin, the scion of a prominent American Zionist family and an immigrant himself to Israel, warned American Jews that the only future for Jewish life was in Israel. "Jewish and Israeli history are two converging lines that are ultimately bound to meet, so that whoever wishes to be a point on one must be on the other as well."

Even some who had not chosen to settle in Israel, as had Halkin, were pessimistic. In his important volume *Rabbis and Lawyers: The Journey from Torah to Constitution,* Jerold S. Auerbach, a Wellesley College historian, challenged the widespread assumption that Judaism and Americanism and American and Israeli interests are in harmony. America's Jews are, Auerbach said, heirs to two disparate and, at times, contradictory traditions—Jewish and American. The "translation of the Jewish sacred law, and then Zionism, into American patriotism," Auerbach argued, ensures "that the struggle for 'the American Jewish soul' will persist." Committed Jews are fated to live in two competing and discordant worlds. "The synthesis of Judaism and Americanism," he concluded, is "a historical fiction." If so, then the historical fiction of Herman Wouk is partially to blame.[38]

FOUR

Jewishness and the New York Intellectuals

THE DISPROPORTIONATE IMPACT of Jewish intellectuals, particularly New York City Jewish intellectuals, on American intellectual life made it inevitable that Jewish identity would be a more important issue for the American intelligentsia than it has been, say, in Great Britain or France. With the publication of the memoirs of some of the leading figures among the New York intellectuals, including those of William Barrett, Sidney Hook, Irving Howe, Alfred Kazin, and William Phillips, and with the appearance of dissertations on the New York intellectuals, monographic studies of Daniel Bell, Will Herberg, and Lionel Trilling, and major books on the intellectuals by Alexander Bloom, Terry A. Cooney, and Alan Wald, their importance looms ever larger. Many of the major intellectual developments of modern America—the growth of socialism during the 1930s, the struggle over literary modernism, the emergence of neoconservatism, the debate over Jewish identity—seem to have been little more than intramural arguments within what Norman Podhoretz, the editor of *Commentary,* has called "the family."

This *mishpocha* of mostly Jewish intellectuals has assumed an almost mythic status. Elizabeth Hardwick once noted that she left Kentucky in order to become a New York Jewish intellectual (her conversion took place in the offices of the *New York Review of Books*). Hardwick was not alone in assuming that to be a New York intellectual (or any intellectual at all) it helped to be Jewish. As Victor Navasky, the editor of the *Nation,* jested in 1966, "Ru-

Parts of this chapter were previously published as "Jewishness and the New York Intellectuals," in *Judaism* 38 (summer 1989): 282–92, used by permission, and as "The Jewishness of the New York Intellectuals: Sidney Hook, a Case Study," in *American Pluralism and the Jewish Community,* ed. Seymour Martin Lipset (New Brunswick, N.J.: Transaction, 1990), 153–71. Reprinted by permission of Transaction Publishers, copyright 1990; all rights reserved

mors to the contrary notwithstanding, you don't have to be Jewish to be an intellectual."

During the past half century or so, the only other group that had a comparable impact on American intellectual life were the southern critics and writers. It would be difficult to conceive of two more different groups of intellectuals, yet the southern writers and the New York intellectuals were similar in at least one major respect: they were forced to come to terms with the conflict between the parochial and traditional cultures in which they had been raised and the cosmopolitan, intellectual communities of which they sought to become a part. The southern novelist and poet Allen Tate once said that the southern writers of the interwar years had a "peculiarly historical consciousness" because they lived at a time when the traditional South of cotton, the Lost Cause, and rural ways was being obliterated by a new South of cities, factories, and progressive ideas.[1]

The histories of the New York intellectuals have emphasized their sense of alienation and of living at a particularly crucial cultural and political crossroads. This was accentuated by their belief that they lived on the margins of both American and Jewish culture. Bloom's *Prodigal Sons: The New York Intellectuals and Their World,* Cooney's *The Rise of the New York Intellectuals: "Partisan Review" and Its Circle,* and Wald's *The New York Intellectuals: The Rise and Decline of the Anti-Stalinist Left from the 1930s to the 1980s* argue that the creativity of the New York intellectuals resulted, in part, precisely from their alienation from the religious and ethnic insularity of American Jewish life.

"These prodigal sons," Cooney noted, took their bearing from the recognition that "they stood outside two cultures. It was Jewishness that made possible the assertion of a double exile that promised exceptional insight." These cosmopolitan New York intellectuals "rejected the particularisms of nationality, race, religion, or philosophy, and they celebrated richness, complexity, and diversity. . . . Cosmopolitanism was by nature suspicious of dogma and quick to lash out against the narrowing of cultural possibilities." Their cosmopolitanism was evidenced by their affinity for Marxism with its rejection of ethnic and national distinctions, and for literary modernism with its stress on abstract literary modes of expression.[2]

The argument that there was a symbiotic relationship between, on the one hand, Jewish intellectuality and, on the other, marginality and alienation was not new. Beginning in the early nineteenth century, both supporters and opponents of Jewish emancipation in Europe noted that one of its side effects had been the emergence of cosmopolitan, secular, and, often, revolutionary intellectuals. The nineteenth-century German Jewish socialist J. L. Bernays rejoiced in the fact that the modern Jew had "rescued men from the narrow idea of an exclusive fatherland, from patriotism, by liberating men . . . from everything that reminded him of race, place of origin, dogma and faith." Three-quarters of a century later in his important 1928 essay, "Human Migration and the Marginal Man," the University of Chicago sociologist Robert E. Park argued that the modern Jew was the quintessential marginal man, existing "on the margin of two cultures and two societies . . . the first cosmopolite and citizen of the world."

In a famous address delivered in 1958 to the World Jewish Congress, the Marxist historian Isaac Deutscher used the term "non-Jewish Jew" to describe the phenomenon of Jewish intellectuals like Spinoza, Trotsky, and Freud who have "dwelt on the borderlines of various civilizations, religions, and national cultures . . . [and] lived on the margins or in the nooks and crannies of their respective nations." Deutscher himself was a prime example of the non-Jewish Jew. A child prodigy, he had been ordained as a rabbi when only thirteen. But even at this early age he had doubts regarding Judaism and the existence of God. The next year, Deutscher ate a buttered ham sandwich in a cemetery on Yom Kippur and was surprised that he was not struck down by God. He had crossed his Rubicon. He soon replaced Moses and the Talmud with Marx and Trotsky.[3]

The New York intellectuals themselves have emphasized their alienation from the world of their parents. In 1944, Alfred Kazin declared that of all the forces shaping his outlook, he had been "most deeply influenced by [his] struggle against a merely imposed faith, and against a sentimental chauvinism." What, he asked, was Jewish about the American Jew? "What does he believe, especially in these terrible years, that separates him at all from our national habits of acquisitiveness, showiness and ignorant brag? . . . What a pity that he should feel 'different,' when he believes so little; what a stupendous moral pity, historically, that the Fascist cut-throats should have their eyes on him, too, when he asks for so little—only to be safe, in all the Babbitt warrens." For Kazin and the other Marxist Jewish intellectuals, Jewishness and Judaism were particularistic anachronisms fated to disappear in a socialist and cosmopolitan utopia.[4]

Marginality is a major theme in Irving Howe's appropriately titled autobiography, *A Margin of Hope*. During the 1930s and early 1940s, he wrote, Jewishness "was not regarded as a major component of the culture I wanted to make my own, and I felt no particular responsibility for its survival or renewal. It was simply *there.* While it would be shameful to deny its presence or seek to flee its stigma, my friends and I could hardly be said to have thought Jewishness could do much for us or we for it." They resembled Deutscher's non-Jewish Jews. "Our partial assimilation—roots loosened in Jewish soil but still not torn out, roots lowered into American soil but still not fixed—gave us a seemingly endless range of possibilities." Above all, Howe and his friends were excited by "the idea of breaking away, of willing a new life." One manifestation of this universalism and repudiation of Jewish parochialism was Howe's opposition, during the early 1940s, to American entry into World War II. At that time he was a disciple of Trotsky, and he believed that American involvement would bolster British imperialism and strengthen capitalism. That was simply too high a price to pay for stopping the Nazis.[5]

The Jewish intellectuals seemingly took their Jewish ancestry for granted, but they denied that it had any significant influence on their thinking or any claim to their loyalties. Jewishness, they contended, was devoid of any positive content, and it was destined to fade away with social and economic acculturation and intellectual enlightenment. They would have agreed with Jean-Paul Sartre's *Anti-Semite and Jew* that Jewish identity was largely a response to anti-Semitism. A Jew, Sartre said, "is one whom other men consider a Jew." The intellectuals' major concern with Jewish matters prior to World War II was opposing anti-Semitism. For the Marxist true believers among them, and most of the Jewish intellectuals had been influenced in varying degrees by Marxism, the inevitable triumph of socialism would lead to the demise of modern anti-Semitism, since it stemmed from the social and economic maladjustments accompanying capitalism.

The cosmopolitan New York Jewish intellectuals rejected Zionism as a solution to the Jewish question. Jewish nationalism, they avowed, was simply too parochial and unrealistic. One of the most powerful expressions of this position was Morris Raphael Cohen's 1919 *New Republic* article, "Zionism: Tribalism or Liberalism?" It appeared while the Versailles Conference was debating the nationalistic claims of Europe's ethnic groups, including those of the Jews. Cohen, a professor of philosophy at New York's City College and a teacher of many members of the New York intelligentsia, rejected Zionist claims that Jewish assimilation was chimerical, that all Jews were united by indissoluable ties of ideology and blood, that Judaism and Jewishness could prosper only in a Jewish state, and that Palestine should be an exclusively Jewish state. He described the Zionist leaders as "zealous enthusiasts" and Zionism as a "mystic and romantic nationalism" that was "profoundly inimical to liberal or humanistic civilization." A Zionist Palestine would result in a state founded on a tribal religion, dominated by one ethnic group, and justified by a doctrine of radical supremacy. The amelioration of the Jewish condition depended not on any Zionist tribalistic fantasy, Cohen concluded, but on the spread of the liberal values of toleration, individual liberty, and reason.

Zionism, Cohen further claimed, was profoundly opposed to Americanism. He sharply dissented from Louis D. Brandeis's argument that Americanism and Zionism were mutually reinforcing, since both supported democracy and social and economic reform. Cohen contrasted the American belief in the separation of church and state and in individual freedom with the Zionist belief in the union of religion and state and the immutability of group loyalties. "The glory of Palestine is as nothing to the possible glory of America," Cohen concluded. "If history has any lesson at all it is that never have men accomplished anything great by trying to revive a dead past."

Those who criticize the New York intellectuals for their indifference to Jewish concerns would thus seem to have a good case. Ruth Wisse, a professor of Yiddish literature at McGill and then later at Harvard, has contended that the price the New York intellectuals paid for their intellectual independence and their cosmopolitanism was political irresponsibility and moral insensitivity. "One of the greatest moral and intellectual failures of the New York intellectuals," she said, "was their disregard of the Jewish fate, both before and during World War II and in the decades that followed." She quoted the Yiddish critic Shmuel Niger and his cry of anguish during World War II that European Jewry suffered from "Jews who are too coarse, but also from Jews who are too sensitive."[6]

But the problem with this picture of the New York intellectuals is that it is too pat and neat, too dependent on the sociological abstraction of the deracinated Jewish intellectual. The New York intellectuals, often much to their own surprise, were unable completely to withstand the ties of tradition and peoplehood. Just as the southern intellectuals sought to salvage something of value from the culture of the rural South, so the Jewish intellectuals remained tied to the culture of their immigrant Jewish neighborhoods. Even the seemingly most emancipated and cosmopolitan were reluctant to reject their Jewish background totally and, even if they could have, World War II would not allow them that luxury. As Norman Podhoretz remarked, the Holocaust demonstrated "the inescapability of Jewishness."

The Alfred Kazin who proclaimed his revolt from Jewish sentimental chauvinism was the same person who, in an autobiography titled *New York Jew,* described how the Holocaust became the consuming event of his life. "In my private history of the world I took down every morsel of fact and rumor relating to the murder of my people. . . . The line-up was always before my eyes. I could imagine my father and mother, my sister and myself . . . fuel for the flames, dying by a single flame that burned us all up at once." Kazin's book also contains a moving description of his trip to Israel after the Six Days' War.[7]

Irving Howe's relationship with Jewishness was also more important and tormented than one would assume at first glance. In the chapter "Jewish Quandaries" in his autobiography, he recounted his ambivalent relationship to things Jewish. He noted that what the New York intellectuals felt regarding Jewish matters "was rarely quite in accord with what we wrote or thought. . . . This was a kind of culture lag, recognition behind reality." The Holocaust had the same impact on Howe as it had on Kazin and other Jewish intellectuals. For Howe, the Holocaust was simply "the most terrible moment in human history." Rejecting efforts to transform the Holocaust into a symbol of universal moral turpitude, he argued that the Holocaust must be viewed primarily as a Jewish tragedy, "the culminating ordeal in the sequence of ordeals which comprises the experience of the Jewish people. One's first response—not the sole response, but the first—had to be a cry of Jewish grief." As a result of the Jewish catastrophe, Howe began what he called "timid reconsiderations of what it meant to be Jewish," reconsiderations that resulted in his editing several volumes of Yiddish literature and writing *World of Our Fathers* (1976), a prize-winning elegy on the culture of the Jewish immigrant, working-class generation.[8]

The acrimonious debate over Hannah Arendt's *Eichmann in Jerusalem* also played a part in the growing Jewish consciousness of Howe and other New York intellectuals. Arendt's volume forced them to come to terms with their own relationship to the Holocaust. The passions aroused in the intellectuals were, Howe said, "overwhelming. I cannot think of anything since then that has harassed me as much except perhaps the Vietnam War. You might say that it was a tacit recompense for our previous failure to respond."[9]

Howe admitted that this focus on the Holocaust "wasn't, of course, a very forthright way of confronting my own troubled sense of Jewishness, but that was the way I took." Being Jewish, he now realized, had always been an integral part of his life. He now described himself as a "partial Jew" and an advocate of secular Jewishness. Unsympathetic toward either Judaism or Zionism, Howe's Jewish identity had little of a positive nature to sustain it. It existed in "a state of prolonged interregnum, between the denied authority of total faith and the sterile prospects of assimilation." He admitted that his perspective on Jewishness "had reached a historical dead end," but "there, at ease or not," he chose to remain.[10]

Howe's recognition of the ambiguity of his newfound Jewish identity was typical of the situation that many of the Jewish intellectuals found themselves in. Feeling Jewish and, yet, not knowing what that meant, they found it difficult to locate the Jewish content of their lives. Inevitably they looked to Israel to bolster their fragile sense of Jewishness. Philip Rahv, in an act that amazed his friends, bequeathed his estate to an Israeli institution when he died in the 1970s. During the 1970s and 1980s, Howe wrote brooding essays from a non-Zionist and leftist perspective on Israeli politics and society. Although a supporter of the Jewish state, he feared that Israeli intransigence over the issue of the territories captured during the June 1967 war would lead to a tragic conflict between rival Arab and Jewish nationalisms.

Howe's friendly critic Sidney Hook has not often been thought of as a Jewish intellectual, yet for more than half a century, until his death in 1989, he wrestled with the question of American Jewish identity. Hook came to prominence during the 1930s when, as a philosopher at New York University, he was one of the few open Marxists on the faculty of a major American university. He participated in virtually all of the major internecine controversies that convulsed the Left during the depression. His *Towards the Understanding of Karl Marx: A Revolutionary Interpretation* (1933) and *From Hegel to Marx: Studies in the Intellectual Development of Karl Marx* (1936) were among the first serious American studies of Marx and Marxism. For orthodox Marxists, Hook's attempt to synthesize Marxism with the pluralism and instrumentalism of his teacher, John Dewey, was heretical. After World War II, Hook was a consistent and fervent opponent of communist totalitarianism and an equally strong supporter of democracy and of what Arthur M. Schlesinger Jr. termed "the vital center."

Hook's contribution to the debate over American Jewish identity was shaped by his commitment to democracy and Deweyite liberalism. The problem he confronted was the same one that has faced American Jewry since the late eighteenth century—reconciling the *pluribus* and the *unum* of America. Was the particularism of Jewish identity, he asked, compatible with an American identity that transcended ethnic and religious distinctions? For intellectuals, the problem was complicated by the contrast between the parochialism of

Jewish culture and the cosmopolitanism of Western culture of which they felt a part.

Hook was too much a child of the heavily Jewish Williamsburg section of Brooklyn to reject his ancestry, and too much a product of the City College of New York and Columbia University to affirm a particularistic religious or nationalistic definition of American Jewish identity. Instead, he sought to reconcile Jewish and American identities through the liberal and democratic pluralism of Dewey and Horace Kallen. For Hook, the most important element in American Jewish life was not religion or Zionism, but democratic values. There was, he contended, a symbiotic relationship between American Jewry and American democracy. Jewish identity strengthened democracy, while democracy strengthened Jewish identity.

As was true of Howe, Hook emphasized his initial estrangement from Jewish concerns. In recalling the stance of the New York intellectuals toward Jewishness, he said, "We took ourselves for granted as Jews and were concerned with the Jewish question primarily as a political one." On another occasion he denied any interest in Jewish affairs. "I suppose I have been in the thick of every controversy in the intellectual and political life of the nation during the last sixty years," he wrote in 1984. "But there is one area I *never* got involved in except in a civil libertarian way. That is Jewish affairs. A number of reasons account for this—the suspicion that its affairs are so tangled that if I got involved I would have no time for any other struggle, the fact that although I believe that the Jews ought to have a homeland of some kind, I have never been a *political* Zionist, etc."[11]

This claim of isolation from Jewish affairs is difficult to reconcile with Hook's deep involvement in Jewish concerns, particularly during the 1940s. (It is revealing that Hook did not discuss this in his 1987 autobiography, *Out of Step*.) He helped raise funds for the United Jewish Appeal within the New York University faculty; he was active in New York University's Jewish Culture Foundation and chaired the committee that planned the dedication of the foundation's library; he was a member of the Academic Council of the Hebrew University; he solicited funds on behalf of the Jewish magazine *Menorah Journal;* he prepared a lengthy self-study for the National Council of Jewish Women; he chaired the Advisory Committee of the Palestine Project of the National Council of Jewish Women; he was an advisor to several Jewish cultural agencies, including the Federation of Jewish Student Organizations of New York; he often spoke on Jewish themes before Jewish secular organizations and synagogues; and he was under contract to the Jewish Lecture Bureau of the Jewish Welfare Board and was a member of the bureau's Advisory Committee. While at the Hoover Institution at Stanford University during the 1970s and 1980s, he received (and read) the *San Francisco Jewish Bulletin* and contributed regularly to the annual campaign of the local United Jewish Appeal. He also published two significant essays on American Jewish identity: "Promise Without Dogma: A Social Philosophy for Jews" (1937) and "Reflections on the Jewish Question" (1949).

In contrast to Howe and other New York Jewish intellectuals, Hook never made a fetish of alienation. He was perfectly comfortable as an American and as a Jew. In 1952, for example, he noted that he was perplexed by the intellectuals' continual "laments about the 'alienation' of the creative artist in American culture." He never regretted being an American, and he was contemptuous toward those he termed "amateur Gentiles," self-hating Jews who denied their ancestry. His closest friends were Jews, particularly the philosopher Ernest Nagel, the political scientist Milton Konvitz, and the sociologists Lewis Feuer and Daniel Bell. Both of his wives were Jews, and for a short period he sent one of his sons to a Hebrew school in a Brooklyn synagogue.[12]

Hook's effort to carve out a Jewish identity was complicated by his opposition to the two most important modern manifestations of Jewish identity—Judaism and Zionism. Even before he was thirteen, Hook proclaimed himself to be an atheist and threatened not to take part in the hypocrisy of a bar mitzvah ceremony. He relented only after his parents pleaded with him not to shame them in front of their neighbors and relatives. Hook's rejection of religion was facilitated by his superficial Jewish education and by the primitive state of the Judaism of the immigrant generation. "Judaism seemed mainly a mass of superstitions taught by tyrannical old men who brooked no contradiction or honest doubt," he recounted. "There was little familiarity with enlightened, alternative versions of Judaism."[13]

Hook's initial rejection of theism stemmed from his inability to resolve the problem that philosophers have termed "theodicy"—reconciling the existence of evil with the goodness and sovereignty of God. Hook had first been drawn to the problem of theodicy when he learned that one of his siblings had died at an early age. The conclusion that Richard Rubinstein and other "God is dead" theologians reached during the 1960s as a result of thinking about the Holocaust, Hook had arrived at a half century before. The problem of theodicy would remain his major defense against the arguments of the religious. "I don't expect the innocent man to be vindicated tomorrow," he said in 1987, "but I do expect him to be vindicated before he goes to the scaffold. I don't expect the tyrant to be struck by a thunderbolt. But I would expect, if there is a God, that he would not die comfortably in his bed."[14]

Hook's atheism deepened when he became a student of John Dewey while in graduate school at Columbia University during the 1920s. Dewey's naturalism and faith in scientific experimentation bolstered Hook's denial of a supernatural God, and his emphasis on pluralism encouraged Hook to view America as a pluralistic and culturally diverse nation. Hook was also influenced by his friend Horace Kallen, America's most prominent exponent of ethnic cultural pluralism. Dewey and Kallen convinced Hook that democracy required cultural diversity. But what contribution should Jews make to this cultural mix? Neither Hook nor Kallen thought it should be Judaism.

Hook agreed with Kallen that ethnicity in general and Jewish ethnicity in particular had enriched American life; that religion need not be the central component of Jewish identity; and that the most valuable elements of Jewish culture were ethnic rather than religious. Hook was unfamiliar with Yiddish and Hebrew culture and with the classic Jewish texts. For him, therefore, the essence of American Jewish ethnic identity lay not in language, custom, literature, religion, or nationhood, but in Jewish "values," and these values were the same ones espoused by Dewey. The most important of these was democracy. "As Jews we plead guilty to the charge that we are defenders of the democratic way of life," Hook asserted in a lecture in the 1930s. "Our goal and our hope must be that without ceasing to be Jews, we can become its most zealous defenders."

According to Hook, the "democratic way" meant three things: (1) economic justice, particularly the elimination of economic insecurity; (2) the fostering of group differences and cultural pluralism; and (3) the pragmatic and scientific method of John Dewey. Hook asserted that the Jewish commitment to the democratic way meant that there was a mutually reinforcing relationship between Jewishness and Americanness. "As I interpret Jewish culture," he said in "Promise Without Dogma," "its noblest feature is the characteristic way in which its traditions have fused passion for social justice with respect for scientific method and knowledge. When Jews forsake this method, they reject a precious part of their tradition." American Jews were thus united not only by history but also by a commitment to American democracy and by traditions of science and justice. Hook omitted any mention of religious or national ties.[15]

As long as American democracy remained strong, Hook asserted, anti-

Semitism would have little appeal. His interpretation of the sources of anti-Semitism was a product of the 1930s as well as of his own affinity for an economic interpretation of history. Since Hitler had come to power during the Great Depression and promptly abolished German democracy, Hook naturally concluded that economic insecurity fostered anti-Semitic and anti-democratic sentiments. Hook did not flinch during the 1930s from carrying these assumptions regarding Jewishness, democracy, and social reform to their logical political conclusion. Democracy not only meant cultural diversity, the pragmatic method, and the complete separation of church and state, but also a socialist welfare state.

Socialism, he said, was the most acceptable social philosophy for Jews. It alone wedded "the ideals of the good life in the good society to the methods of intelligent analysis and action." Hook's ideal Jew thus combined the best of Marx and Dewey. For Jewish survivalists, the problem with Hook's approach was the absence of any positive and distinctive Jewish content since, as he readily admitted, the social philosophy he recommended to Jews was equally applicable to Gentiles, and its model practitioner was John Dewey. Furthermore, the twentieth century's experience with socialism hardly demonstrated that Jewish survival is most likely under socialist regimes.[16]

This ahistorical view of Jewish identity tells us more about the values of Hook and the editors of the *Menorah Journal* than it does about Jewish tradition. This tradition is, in fact, more theocratic than democratic, and while Jewish texts are eloquent regarding the charitable and moral responsibilities of the individual Jew, they offer little in the way of a blueprint for national economic planning. Furthermore, Jewish tradition is largely concerned with following God's laws and not with conforming to the dictates of the scientific method.

While both Kallen and Hook agreed as to the ethnic character of American Jewry, they differed regarding Zionism. For Kallen, Zionism was important in sustaining a vibrant American Jewish identity. Hook, in contrast, became an anti-Zionist when he became a Marxist while a teenager, and this anti-Zionism was probably reinforced during his undergraduate years at CCNY when he fell under the sway of Morris Raphael Cohen. For Marxists such as Hook, Zionism was a bourgeois nationalist ideology that distracted the Jewish proletariat from the economic and social reconstruction of their own societies. This view of Zionism was common among the New York Jewish intellectuals prior to the Holocaust and the establishment of the state of Israel. Socialism, not Zionism, was their answer to the Jewish question. "Having transcended American nationalism by our allegiance to a universalist ideal, in which all men were brothers, we were not going to settle for a more parochial national ideal," Hook recalled. "The Jewish problem—and we all knew what that was—would be solved when the classless society of the future was established." Hook (and Howe) also feared that Zionism would lead to war between Jews and the indigenous Arab population of Palestine.[17]

Prior to the establishment of Israel in 1948, Hook sympathized with Judah Magnes's proposal for a binational state in Palestine, a plan he later admitted was "utopian" because it lacked Arab support. In a letter published in the *New York Times* in 1948, Hook joined Albert Einstein, Hannah Arendt, and other leading Jewish intellectuals in protesting the racism, nationalism, chauvinism, terrorism, "religious mysticism," and even fascism that supposedly permeated Menachem Begin's right-wing Herut Party. (During the 1970s, Hook modified this harsh judgment of Begin, perhaps because he concluded that Begin's pessimistic view of the Arabs had merit, and perhaps because of Hook's antipathy toward Begin's critics on the Left.[18])

In his 1947 self-study of the National Council of Jewish Women, written at the height of the political debate over the proposed Jewish state, Hook supported the council's neutrality regarding Zionism. He agreed with the council that the major concern of America's Jews must be the future of American Jewry and that political Zionism caused legitimate questions to be raised regarding the loyalty of American Jews and their commitment to a future in America. His only caveat was that the council had been needlessly defensive because of an exaggerated fear of offending Zionist extremists.

Opposition to political Zionism did not mean, however, that Hook opposed American Jewry's efforts to assist financially the Yishuv and to lobby for unrestricted immigration into Palestine. American Jews, he said, were right in recognizing the cultural importance of Palestine for all Jews, in admiring the economic accomplishments of Palestine's Jews, and in sympathizing with the social and economic principles underlying the kibbutz. Hook's position was not far from that of mainstream American Zionism prior to the World War II Biltmore Conference when American Zionist leaders, for the first time, united in support of a Jewish state. Prior to that, American Zionism had emphasized the succoring of persecuted Jews and charitable efforts on behalf of the Yishuv rather than Jewish nationalism.[19]

After 1948, Hook's position regarding Israel resembled that of most

American Jews, including the New York intellectuals. He was interested in the country's welfare and supported the Israeli Labor Party and the Histadrut. But he had no intention of visiting Israel, much less settling in the Jewish state, despite invitations from Israeli academic circles, and he rejected the notion that as a Jew he had any special relationship or obligation to Israel. In 1949, Hook cautioned American Jews about the danger of ethnic chauvinism resulting from Israel's military victories in her war of independence. "A people that has, by and large, been rational and pacific," he warned, now sought through militarism, ultranationalism, and "the *mystique* of action . . . to prove that they are like everyone else—inconsistent, fanatical, atavistic."[20]

The Six Days' War of 1967 was a watershed in the attitude of the New York intellectuals and other American Jews toward Israel. It took the threat of an Israeli defeat to make them realize how much Israel actually meant to them. But while most New York intellectuals were driven primarily by fears of a second holocaust, Hook, a cold war warrior, was motivated chiefly by admiration for an Israel that had defeated the clients of the Soviet Union. Israel's primary significance for Hook was its role as an ally of the West in the struggle against the Soviet bloc and its Western dupes. His support for Israel was conditional on her remaining part of the Western coalition.

Hook did not share in the New York intellectuals' disenchantment with Israel after Begin's election in 1977 as prime minister. Hook defended the 1982 Israeli invasion of Lebanon, which most of the intellectuals firmly opposed, and he argued that the media's assault on Israel had generated "an atmosphere of pogrom-hatred against Jews." Accusations by Arthur Hertzberg, Irving Howe, and other intellectuals that Israel had "lost its soul" because of the Lebanese invasion struck Hook as nonsense. "Norman Podhoretz is closer to the truth in his order of priority of blame—the PLO first, and Israel last."[21]

Hook's attitude toward Israel was a by-product of his efforts, beginning in the 1930s, to shore up Western defenses against communism and the Soviet Union. In contrast to most of the other New York intellectuals during the 1930s and 1940s, he was more concerned with the danger of communism than fascism, and his anticommunism was deeper and more consuming. While fascism was a greater immediate military threat to the West, Hook believed communism to be the more important long-range threat to the "democratic way of life" because of its influence within the universities and the intellectual elite.

The Holocaust did not have the same impact on Hook as it had on Kazin or Howe. His infrequent writings on Nazism tended to downplay its unique demonic character, and he was too much the universalist to argue, as did Howe, that the significance of the Holocaust lay largely in its Jewish dimension. He implicitly rejected the argument—most forcefully presented by the historian Lucy Dawidowicz—that World War II was for Germany "a war against the Jews." According to Hook, Nazism was simply one manifestation of the totalitarian impulse, whose purest and most malignant form was Stalinism. This interpretation of totalitarianism differed sharply from that of other American Jewish intellectuals, and particularly from that of Jewish émigrés from Germany. For them the totalitarian paradigm was Nazism; for Hook it was Stalinism. Hook's relative lack of interest in Nazism also accounts for his uncharacteristic silence during the controversy of the early 1960s over Arendt's *Eichmann in Jerusalem.*

In a guest column in the November 26, 1938, *New Leader* titled "The Tragedy of German Jewry," published two weeks after Crystal Night, Hook claimed that Nazi Germany had learned from the Soviet Union how to deal with unpopular and vulnerable minorities. Stalin had taught Hitler "the art of uprooting and wiping out whole groups and classes of innocent citizens. . . . If, as it is rumored, Hitler intends to convert the Jews into serfs to work on canals, fortifications and roads, he will merely be tearing a leaf out of Stalin's own book." For Hook, the Nazis were evil, but their evil was hardly unique.[22]

Hook continually emphasized the importance of the communist theory of social fascism in facilitating Hitler's accession to office and in solidifying his authority. He believed that this theory, which declared the major threat to the German working class to be social democracy and not Nazism, had prevented the cooperation between the German socialists and communists that could have prevented the Nazis from coming to power. The Nazi-Soviet Pact of August 1939 and the cordial relations between the two dictatorships until the German invasion of Russia in June 1941 were not idiosyncratic but stemmed from the fundamental similarities between the two regimes.

One important aspect of Hook's interpretation of Nazism was its downplaying of anti-Semitism. Since anti-Semitism had no place in official Soviet ideology, an emphasis on Nazi anti-Semitism would have undermined Hook's argument that Nazism was derived largely from Stalinism and was not sui generis. "The Tragedy of German Jewry" contended that while the condition of German Jews was "one of the darkest shadows on our century" and could be resolved only by their mass exodus from Germany, it did not require a Western response different from that toward other minorities persecuted by Hitler and Stalin. In protesting against German anti-Semitism, he told his readers, "we are also protesting against his hounding of all other religious and political minorities. We are protesting against the murderous liquidation of all groups whose only fault has been that they have fallen foul of arbitrary, dictatorial decrees."[23]

Hook's most important analysis of National Socialism was the essay "Hitlerism: A Non-metaphysical View," which appeared in the February 1944 issue of the *Contemporary Jewish Record,* a magazine published by the American Jewish Committee. Its readers must have been surprised by its slighting of anti-Semitism as an explanation of the appeals of Nazism. According to Hook, anti-Semitism and other such "metaphysical" ideological factors were unimportant in the Nazi triumph in Germany. Nazi leaders had been attracted to Hitler solely by the promise of "material plunder and other perquisites of office and prestige," and his support from the masses stemmed from economic insecurity, rather than from any widespread sympathy for his racial fantasies. "It was not Hitler's rhetoric and propaganda they believed but his promises." Hook's solution to the Nazi problem followed logically. "Immunization from another plague of Nazism is conditional upon profound social and economic changes to be carried out by a democratic revolution which will give the masses security of existence without terror."[24]

This refutation of metaphysical explanations of the appeals of Nazism can be seen as a continuation of Hook's famous debate during the early 1940s with Mortimer J. Adler, the Thomistic philosopher at the University of Chicago. Adler had claimed that democracy must be grounded in metaphysics and theology, that philosophical relativism and agnosticism were greater threats to American democracy than Hitler, and that the West needed to counter the ideologies of its enemies with an ideology of its own. Hook attributed Adler's thinking to a "failure of nerve" and to a hankering for "transcendental consolation," which were incompatible with the nineteenth-century sources of liberal democracy and the methods of modern scientific inquiry. Adler's failure of nerve was "a desperate quest for quick and all-inclusive faith that will save us from the trouble of thinking about difficult problems." His philosophical monism was dangerous because, by repudiating secularism, pluralism, and respect for the "method of free, critical intelligence," it rejected the foundations of modern democracy. It also undermined the security of American Jews, which depended on secularism, democracy, and the scientific spirit.[25]

Hook's interpretation of American Jewish identity struck some new notes in the post-Holocaust era. The first was his ambivalence as to whether Jewish identity was a matter of fate or choice. He now said that the key element in Jewish identity was not democracy, the scientific method, or leftist economic planning; rather, it was the common lot of Jews that, "whether they like it or not or whether they like each other or not, cancels all their other not inconsiderable differences." The hold of this fate was so strong that even the most alienated of Jews were unable to separate themselves from it. Echoing Kallen, Hook now argued that it was psychologically destructive for Jews to hide their Jewishness, to capitulate to irrational prejudice, and to "deny kinship with their own fathers and mothers who, often against heroic odds, had courageously kept their integrity and faith whatever it was."

Hook was wrong. Many Jews did not feel any burden of a common fate with other Jews, nor were they afflicted with psychological traumas as a result of denying their ancestry. While rejecting the monistic definitions of Jewish identity of the Orthodox and the Zionists, Hook was close to accepting Kallen's monism of biological determinism and involuntary ethnic identity. Hook agreed with Kallen's famous statement that a person could change anything except his grandparents. There was, he said, "no dignity in denying one's origins or in living as if they were something to be apologetic about." These were strange conclusions for a disciple of Dewey.[26]

Dewey's open and pluralistic social philosophy affirmed the right to reject as well as the right to affirm group loyalties. The belief that a person must remain in the same social and cultural situation in which he was born, Hook had said, was "a piece of antidemocratic presumption." Whether a person chose to identify as a Jew in a democracy was a matter of voluntary choice. But Hook's commitment to Dewey's philosophy of openness and diversity was limited by his contempt for "amateur Gentiles" and his new ethnic interpretation of American Jewry.[27]

Hook now sought something more substantive and distinctive than liberalism and the scientific method to define Jewish identity. While liberalism allowed for group identity, the nature of this identity had still to be defined in Jewish terms, and it had to involve more than opposition to anti-Semitism. "The psychology of mere defense," he wrote, "is ultimately self-defeating unless there is some positive awareness of *what* we are defending, its significance and value." The challenge to American Jewry was to provide an identity that would be attractive even to college-educated youth afflicted with self-hatred. Hook's partial answer to the problem of Jewish identity among the young was to establish a nonsectarian university under Jewish auspices run on democratic, secular, and progressive principles. Such an institution appeared in 1948 when Brandeis University opened. But Brandeis would never be able to educate more than a tiny percentage of American Jewish youth.[28]

Hook's 1949 essay "Reflections on the Jewish Question" was prompted by the appearance of Jean-Paul Sartre's *Anti-Semite and Jew.* Here Sartre argued that Jewish identity was largely a response to anti-Semitism. For Sartre, the quintessential Jew was the victim—eliminate anti-Semitism and Jews would no longer feel any need to remain Jewish. Hook agreed that Jews were unified by a "negative togetherness." But Hook went beyond Sartre in affirming the possibility of a positive Jewish identity, although his distaste for ideological straitjackets and "muddy metaphysics" prevented him from advancing beyond vague generalities.[29]

A secular and democratic American Jewish culture could be the basis of American Jewish identity. Such a culture, Hook declared, would have to flow from indigenous American sources and be compatible with American social and political values. He proposed creating a host of artistic, literary, and philosophical organizations, journals, schools, theaters, and museums to stimulate American Jewish culture "through music, through art, through literature and drama, through common celebrations, religious or secular, and especially through study." Young Jews would not be attracted to Zionism and traditional religion, and a Judaism of Deweyite liberalism, Hook now said, was too tepid in the post–World War II environment of heightened American Jewish consciousness. A revived Jewish culture, by contrast, "interacting and integrated with whatever American life it can reach," would enable American Jews to avoid the extremes of acculturation and ethnic parochialism.[30]

But Hook was silent regarding the critical issue—what precisely would be the nature of this American culture. His pluralism and suspicion of ideologies prevented him from moving from process to content, from how to what. For Hook, the son of immigrants and the product of a Jewish neighborhood, defining culture was unnecessary. One does not have to define what is in your very bones. But definition would be necessary for later generations, whose ties to the Jewish past were more attenuated and whose Jewishness could not be taken for granted. Hook himself had been unable to provide any reason why such Jews should wish to be the cultural heirs of Moses rather than of Jesus or Marx.

Hook's report to the National Council of Jewish Women explored the nature of American Jewish identity. He began the study, he told the council, with only one major assumption—"a firm belief in the desirability of Jewish group survival in the United States." The report repeated familiar themes. It emphasized the right and duty of American Jews to create a separate collective existence, because democracy involved an equality of diversity and not an equality of unanimity. The report rejected all efforts to establish a single definition of Jewishness, since heterogeneity was the major characteristic of American Jews. Hook defined a Jew as "*anyone who for any reason calls himself such or is called such in any community which acts on the distinction*" (italics in the original). Jewish unity was a product not of beliefs but of "a common lot and destiny." Hook did not explain how a group that was so economically, socially, and geographically diverse could share a common lot and destiny.[31]

Instead of describing the specific contributions Jews could make to the American mosaic, Hook recommended that the council focus on strengthening cultural pluralism. This meant opposing all efforts to breach the wall of separation between church and state, supporting educational programs that emphasized the cultural and ethnic diversity of America, and attacking discrimination against any ethnic or racial group. The content of Jewish cultural activities seemed less important to Hook than the occasion they provided for Jews to interact. "Wherever Jews meet *as Jews* for a common purpose," he said, "an opportunity is at hand for the development of characteristic Jewish experiences." One of the beneficial results of Jewish education was that it led to such "ongoing activities."[32]

Certainly Hook was correct in seeing Jewish communal identity as important and not needing any justification. As Leonard Fein has noted, "The core method of Judaism is community. Ours is not a personal testament, but a collective and public commitment. . . . What defines the Jews *as Jews* is community; not values, not ideology." But a method is only a means to an end. Hook did not discuss why heterogeneous Jews would want to comprise a community. It is doubtful whether sociability for sociability's sake, what Hook called "continuing association and common activity," could sustain a continuing Jewish commitment in a nation where the barriers to assimilation are so easy to surmount. This is particularly true among young Jews for whom the campus provides a rival community.[33]

The surprising thing about Hook's muddled attempt to define an American Jewish identity along liberal and secular lines is not, as he later admitted, that it failed, but that it occurred at all. That an intellectual of Hook's stature should concern himself with the seemingly parochial question of American

Jewish identity is symptomatic of the inability of the New York intellectuals to divest themselves of their Jewishness, however they might define it. If Hook failed to resolve the tension between universalism and particularism, he is in good company; no one else has succeeded, either. This tension, Fein has written, "is not, as is so generally believed, a dilemma to be resolved but an existential condition to be lived and even savored. Alone, each is precarious; together . . . they are an arch, two weaknesses leaning into a strength."[34]

PART TWO

Acculturation

FIVE

The Ordeal of Success

American Jewry since World War II

PRIOR TO WORLD WAR II, the major underlying assumption of American Jewry was the compatibility of social and economic equality on the one hand and the maintenance of group identity on the other. Never was this assumption so challenged as in the years after 1945. This was not because American Jews diluted their commitment to Jewish survival but because American society had never been as open as it was after World War II. As Jews made their way up the social and economic ladders at an unprecedented rate, it became increasingly more difficult to presume that integration could be easily reconciled with group survival. Indeed, the struggle between the right to be equal and the right to be different has been the central theme of post–World War II American Jewish history. This conflict also laid out the parameters within which the debate over American Jewish identity took place.

The life of Hank Greenberg, the most popular and famous American Jew of the 1930s and 1940s, revealed the dilemma facing American Jews. Greenberg was the first great Jewish baseball player, and the first one to be voted into the Baseball Hall of Fame. He was the first baseman of the Detroit Tigers, and he won the American League Most Valuable Player Award in 1935 and 1940. American Jews revered Greenberg. He was the long and fervently anticipated baseball star whose exploits would demonstrate to the doubters that Jews could master this most American of games. Greenberg's achievements reassured Jews that they could be fully acculturated into American life. Jews were also proud of Greenberg because he had never tried to hide his Jewish background or backed down when taunted by anti-Semites. It was fitting that

This chapter was previously published in *American Jewish History* 81 (autumn 1993): 81–100. Reprinted by permission of the American Jewish Historical Society.

Greenberg played in Detroit, the home to both Henry Ford, the most prominent anti-Semite of the 1920s, and Charles E. Coughlin, the notorious anti-Semitic radio priest of the 1930s.

Greenberg's status among American Jews assumed mythic proportions in 1934 when he played in 153 of 154 games. His refusal to play on September 19 because it was Yom Kippur created a sensation. A poem by Edgar Guest praised the slugger.

> Came Yom Kippur—holy fast day world-wide over to the Jew—
> And Hank Greenberg to his teaching and the old tradition true
> Spent this day among his people and he didn't come to play.
> Said Murphy to Mulrooney, "We shall lose the game today!
> We shall miss him in the infield and shall miss him at the bat,
> But he's true to his religion—and I honor him for that!"

To his surprise, Greenberg was applauded when he attended Yom Kippur services in a Detroit synagogue.

Jews chose to overlook the circumstances surrounding Greenberg's decision not to play on Yom Kippur. He had played on the first day of Rosh Hashanah on September 10 when the Tigers were fighting the New York Yankees for the pennant. In fact, he had hit two home runs that day to help defeat the Red Sox, 2-1. In contrast to Greenberg, Barney Ross, the Jewish world welterweight boxing champion, refused in 1934 to allow a rained-out title fight to be rescheduled for Rosh Hashanah. By the time of Yom Kippur, the Tigers had clinched the pennant, and Greenberg's presence in the lineup was not required. Nothing, however, could tarnish the Jews' image of their hero.

In 1938 Greenberg captured the nation's attention when he almost surpassed Babe Ruth's legendary 1927 record of sixty home runs in a season. Greenberg remained ahead of Ruth's pace until the last week of the season, and finished with fifty-eight homers. This challenge to the then most famous record in American sports took place against the backdrop of the approaching European war and the rapid growth of anti-Semitism in the United States and abroad. Greenberg realized the significance of his assault on the Babe's record. "Sure, there was added pressure being Jewish," he recalled. "How the hell could you get up to home plate every day and have some son of a bitch call you a Jew bastard and a kike and a sheenie and get on your ass without feeling the pressure?" Greenberg knew he was a Jewish standard-bearer. "I just had to show them that a Jew could play ball. . . . I came to feel that if I, as a Jew, hit a home run, I was hitting one against Hitler."

In 1941, Greenberg's stature among Jews grew even further. Having been released from the army a few days before Pearl Harbor, he promptly enlisted in the army air corps, the first major leaguer to join the armed forces after December 7, 1941. To Jews, Greenberg was an authentic war hero. In reality, he enlisted in the air force in order to avoid serving in the army. Greenberg was in the military for forty-nine months. Gentiles admired him for having seemingly sacrificed his baseball career to serve his country. Jews cherished Greenberg for showing that Jews did not shirk their military obligations.

For Jewish baseball fans, World War II unofficially ended on June 14, 1945, when Greenberg became the first major league veteran to return to the big leagues. No player had ever successfully resumed a major league career after such a long hiatus. Greenberg surprised the skeptics by hitting .311 in seventy-eight games, including thirteen home runs. On September 30, the last day of the season, he hit a ninth-inning grand slam home run against the St. Louis Browns to win the American League pennant for the Tigers. "Goddam that dirty Jew bastard, he beat us again," muttered one member of the runner-up Washington Senators. Greenberg went on to lead the Tigers to victory over the Cubs in the World Series, hitting over .300 with two home runs and seven runs batted in.

A few months after the 1945 season, Greenberg married Carel Gimbel, the daughter of a New York department store magnate. They were married by a justice of the peace in Brunswick, Georgia, and not by a rabbi. This was more indicative of Greenberg's true Jewish identity than the mythology that had enveloped him for more than a decade. In fact, Greenberg had been alienated from Judaism at an early age. He was bored by Hebrew school and resented the time it took away from athletics. He identified Judaism and Jewishness with the drab immigrant life of his parents. He concluded that all organized religion was a con game. His second wife was the Gentile actress Mary Jo Tarola. Not surprisingly, there was no Jewish element in the memorial service at Greenberg's funeral in 1986.

After the 1947 season, Greenberg became an executive with the Cleveland Indians. While in Cleveland, neither Greenberg nor his wife was involved in Jewish affairs. They never joined a synagogue or even a Jewish country club. They never attended religious services nor celebrated any Jewish festivals. Their children did not receive a Jewish education and were scarcely conscious of being Jewish. Steve Greenberg, who had attended a New England prep school, was asked his religion when he entered Yale. His response was "Congregational."[1]

Hank Greenberg's ambition, his success in capitalizing on American opportunities, his secularism, his ambivalent relationship to his Jewish background, and his eagerness to leave behind the world of his immigrant parents were common among postwar second-generation Jews. In rooting for him they were rooting for themselves. In the conflict between individual opportunity and group survival, Greenberg had clearly voted for opportunity.

Three weeks before Greenberg hit the home run that won the pennant for the Tigers, Bess Myerson of the Bronx had been selected as Miss America. For Jews, there could have been no more dramatic contrast between the promise of American life and the reality of life in Europe than Myerson's victory. Myerson's triumph would come to symbolize the postwar movement of Jews into the American mainstream. Every young American Jewish girl could now strive to follow in her footsteps, to become a true Jewish American princess. (A decade later they would model themselves after the eponymous heroine of Herman Wouk's novel *Marjorie Morningstar.*) With a Jew as Miss America, there seemingly was nothing for which American Jews could not now aspire. Myerson became an American Jewish folk heroine, and ambitious New York City politicians eagerly sought her endorsement. The amalgam of ethnic pride, social mobility, and acculturation that infused this Jewish response to Myerson foreshadowed the postwar American Jewish experience. And, similar to Greenberg, Myerson would exhibit a hunger for social and economic mobility and a disdain for the values of the world of her immigrant parents characteristic of the second generation.[2]

In 1979, Andrew Kopkind, then a staff writer for the *Village Voice,* reflected back on what Myerson and Greenberg had meant to him in 1945. He was then ten years old and living in New Haven, Connecticut. "I can think of no public personages in all the succeeding years whom I've followed with such fawning," he wrote of Greenberg and Myerson. They were "secular saints . . . symbols of a sudden legitimacy which my family and friends seemed to sense in a nation under reconstruction. Hank and Bess were winners, like DiMaggio and Grable—only smarter. They were as American as apple pie and the Fourth of July—and as Jewish as *knishes* and Yom Kippur. For the first time, the Jews had successfully crossed over from ethnic favorites to national heroes without being isolated or absorbed; they had arrived without being assimilated or stereotyped."[3]

Such sentiments would have flabbergasted American Jews prior to World War II, familiar as they were with the anti-Semitism that was a daily presence in their lives. But after 1945 American Jews refused to accept anything less than full participation on their own terms in American life. They were now willing to publicize their distinctiveness. Advertisements in the New York subways reminded riders that they did not have to be Jewish to like Levy's Jewish rye. In the 1930s, the Ramaz Orthodox day school in New York City had discouraged its students from wearing skullcaps on the street. The skullcap, they were told, was an "indoor garment." After World War II, however, the wearing of skullcaps, Stars of David, and other Jewish accouterments became common. This displaying of Jewishness as well as a militant espousal of Jewish interests replaced the age-old fear of "what will the Gentiles think."[4]

The most striking example of American Jewry's willingness to go public occurred at the White House in 1985. Shortly after his reelection in 1984, President Ronald Reagan announced that he would be visiting Germany. On the itinerary was a wreath-laying ceremony at a military cemetery in Bitburg. It was soon discovered that the cemetery contained the graves of forty-seven members of the Waffen SS. Jews and other Americans were infuriated that the president would honor members of a German army that had engaged in atrocities. Elie Wiesel, a survivor of Auschwitz, expressed the anguish of Jews in a televised ceremony at the White House where he was to receive the Congressional Gold Medal of Achievement, the government's highest civilian honor.

Instead of politely and quietly accepting the honor, Wiesel gently reproved Reagan. The president of "the freest nation in the world, the moral nation," he said, had no business at Bitburg. "That place, Mr. President, is not your place. Your place is with the victims of the SS." Wiesel's statement, *Newsweek* wrote, was "surely one of the most remarkable moments in the annals of the White House." It was also, as Charles E. Silberman noted, one of the most remarkable moments in the annals of American Jewry. For a Holocaust survivor to receive the Congressional Gold Medal of Achievement was noteworthy enough. But for him to use the occasion to rebuke the president and to do this in the White House manifested a sense of security unprecedented in American Jewish history.[5]

One manifestation of this belief in the easy rapprochement of Jewish and American identities was the third version of the film *The Jazz Singer*, which came out in 1980. The original 1927 film starring Al Jolson had stressed the difficulty of reconciling Jewish tradition and American opportunities. Jolson quarrels with his father, a devout cantor, over his plans to become a jazz singer. His father wants his son to carry on the family tradition and become a cantor. The gulf between the two men is unbridgeable. In the 1980 film, director Richard Fleischer muted this conflict through the use of color. He used blue to represent the world of rock music and white to represent the Jewish world. Near the end of the film the two colors come together when the jazz singer, played by Neil Diamond, sings the Kol Nidre prayer at the beginning of the Yom Kippur service dressed in the traditional white robe and with a blue skullcap on his head. At the movie's conclusion, he performs at a concert attended by his beaming parents, who have been reconciled to their son's life. Dressed in a shiny blue shirt with a white scarf resembling a prayer shawl draped around his neck, he sings his own rock songs, including the rousing "Coming to America." The jazz singer's success symbolizes the prosperity Jews found in America. Certainly the jazz singer becomes a popular entertainer. But whether he successfully blends the blue of America and the white of Jewishness is doubtful. His good fortune comes only after he leaves his traditional Jewish wife, moves from New York to California, and becomes involved with a Gentile woman. Only in Israel does blue and white signify the harmonious integration of Jewish and national identities.

The new status of Jews in America after 1945 was confirmed by the rapid decline of anti-Semitism from its wartime heights. Virtually all the findings of public opinion polls and other sources pointed to a fundamental change in the attitude of Gentiles toward Jews. This, however, did not quell the fears of American Jews. They believed anti-Semitism had merely gone underground. During the 1980s, when American anti-Semitism was at an all-time low, the Simon Wiesenthal Center of Los Angeles had the most successful fund-raising operation of any domestic Jewish organization, even attracting the enthusiastic support of Frank Sinatra and Arnold Schwarzenegger. And during the 1990s, American Jews maintained that anti-Semitism was a more serious threat to Jewish continuity than intermarriage.

American Jews exhibited what social psychologists term "cognitive dissonance," the conflict between perception and reality that occurs when people are confronted with facts that clearly contradict deeply held beliefs. With American anti-Semitism declining, the *Jewish Press,* a Brooklyn weekly catering to religious zealots and right-wing Zionists, carried advertisements proclaiming that anti-Semitic movements were "growing quickly in membership and influence in America. They are gaining the sympathy and support of many of your neighbors. Hitler is their patron saint. Learn about them. The lesson might save your life." Such sentiments were not restricted to the unsophisticated, gullible, and uneducated. Jews, the sociologist Seymour Martin Lipset said in 1990, seemed to be living "under a permanent cloud." They felt "anxious, rejected and worried." Jews, Abba Eban once joked, are a people who can't take "yes" for an answer.[6]

The true status of postwar anti-Semitism was indicated by the inability of anti-Semites to capitalize on the trial of Julius and Ethel Rosenberg, the Jewish couple convicted of conveying secrets of the atomic bomb to the Soviet Union. Polls taken by the University of Chicago's National Opinion Research Center in July 1953, one month after the execution of the Rosenbergs, and in November 1954 revealed that only 1 percent of Americans identified "Jews" as a group "who are more likely than others to be Communists." The identification of Jews with other unsavory characteristics, such as dishonesty in business, clannishness, excessive power, pushiness, and lack of breeding, also became less popular. The shift in public opinion was both a cause and a result of the postwar efforts of local and state governments to outlaw employment and residential discrimination. Encouraged by these efforts in the public sector, universities repealed quotas on Jewish students and corporations lifted restrictions on the hiring of Jews. By the 1960s, according to public opinion surveys, hardly any Americans supported job discrimination against Jews, and very few objected to working alongside Jews.[7]

The polls also indicated a sharp decline immediately after World War II in political anti-Semitism. Much to its surprise, the Anti-Defamation League of B'nai B'rith discovered that there had been a "comparative absence of anti-Semitic activity" during the 1948 elections. A 1959 poll, the year before the election of the first Roman Catholic president, revealed that slightly more Americans were willing to vote for a Jew as president than for a Roman Catholic and that a far higher percentage would have voted for a Jewish man than for a Christian woman. By the 1980s, Jews had been elected to the United States Senate from states with minuscule Jewish populations such as Nebraska, Nevada, New Hampshire, Wisconsin, and Minnesota, and Jews had been elected to the House of Representatives from districts in Alabama, Colorado, Georgia, and Kansas. Not even in the South, where the support of northern Jews for the civil rights movement was widely resented, did politicians attempt to exploit anti-Semitism. The decline of political anti-Semitism paralleled a sharp decline in the percentage of Americans who feared Jews. By the 1960s, only one Gentile in a hundred believed Jews to be a national menace. Since World War II, Earl Raab observed in 1969, "there has been no serious trace of political anti-Semitism in America." For Raab, a prominent San Francisco Jewish leader, suggestions that "it could happen here" had "an antique flavor" and should be considered "phobic, paranoid, and even amusing."[8]

Perhaps the surest sign of the acceptance of Jews after the war was the increased willingness of Gentiles to marry Jews. By the 1980s, fewer than a third of American Gentiles categorically rejected the marriage of a child to a Jew. "Since marriage would seem to constitute the ultimate degree of acceptance," Charles Stember wrote, "the lessening resistance to Jews as potential wives or husbands probably is even more significant than the simultaneous lowering of barriers in other fields."[9]

Faced with the prospect of losing their raison d'àtre, Jewish professionals specializing in Jewish defense activities redefined the nature of anti-Semitism. In their 1974 book *The New Anti-Semitism,* Arnold Forster and Benjamin R. Epstein of the Anti-Defamation League admitted that American Jews possessed "a greater degree of economic and political security and social acceptance than has ever been achieved by any Jewish community since the Dispersion." But Jews should not relax, because they now faced "the new anti-Semitism." This involved neither physical assaults on Jews nor economic and social discrimination, but "a callous indifference to Jewish concerns," a failure to appreciate "the most profound apprehensions of the Jewish people," and "a blandness and apathy in dealing with anti-Jewish behavior," particularly when directed at the state of Israel.[10]

One of the reasons for this continuing stress on anti-Semitism at a time when it was actually in sharp decline was the belief that Jewish group solidarity depended on keeping the dread of Gentiles uppermost in the minds of Jews. It was feared that once Jews ceased to view Gentiles as "the enemy camp," the title of Jerome Weidman's popular postwar novel, they would choose the path of least resistance and assimilate. During the 1940s and 1950s, American Jews debated whether the American Jewish community could survive without ghetto walls. The pessimists convinced few Jews to reject the social and economic opportunities of America. Brownsville and the Grand Concourse could not compete with Park Avenue and Scarsdale, nor could CCNY and Brooklyn College compete with Princeton and Harvard.

Symptomatic of the level of American anti-Semitism was Jimmy Carter's speech accepting the 1976 Democratic nomination for president. Pledging to wage a war against prejudice, the former Georgia governor declared that now was the time "to guarantee an end to discrimination because of race and sex." He omitted any reference to ethnic or religious discrimination. More remarkable than Carter's failure to mention anti-Semitism was the fact that few people noted, or much less commented, on this oversight. Carter would not knowingly have antagonized Jews, an important bloc of voters and financial contributors to the Democratic Party. Apparently it never occurred to him or to his entourage that Jews were an oppressed minority requiring special treatment.

The opening up of American society to Jews was particularly noticeable in academia and business. The selection of Irving Shapiro as president of the Du Pont Corporation in 1973 and Harold T. Shapiro as president of Princeton University in 1987 exemplified the rapid social ascent of American Jewry. Few Jews prior to the 1970s would have predicted that Jews would eventually be in charge of Du Pont and Princeton, two of the nation's toniest institutions. "The Protestant caste system," Richard E. Rubinstein wrote in 1965, "remains as rigidly operative in the universities as it does in most business corporations." It was "almost impossible for a Jew to be appointed to an administrative position at any university not sponsored by Jews." Dartmouth, its president, Ernest M. Hopkins, had declared in 1945, "is a Christian college founded for the Christianization of its students." Within three decades Dartmouth would have had two Jewish presidents.[11]

It was only in 1968, when the University of Chicago selected Edward H. Levi to be its president, that a Jew would head a major American university not under Jewish auspices. Within the next quarter of a century Jews would serve as president of America's two most prestigious scientific institutions—the California Institute of Technology and the Massachusetts Institute of Technology—and of the University of Pennsylvania, Columbia, Harvard, Princeton, and Yale. In addition, Jews were appointed dean of the law schools at Columbia, Harvard, and Yale. Henry Rosovsky of Harvard even turned down the presidency of Yale in 1977. He said at the time that under different circumstances he might have accepted the appointment, but with the dropping of barriers against Jews in academia, his going to Yale would prove little, and he preferred to stay at Harvard. The Ivy League, one person quipped, was well on its way to becoming the "oi-vey" league.

The most unusual aspect of the selection of Shapiro as Princeton's president was, of course, the fact that he was Jewish. And yet neither the news article in the *New York Times* nor the paper's profile of him mentioned this. Evidently the *Times* believed a Jew becoming head of Princeton was not newsworthy. If so, the most remarkable thing about Shapiro's selection was that it was not considered remarkable.

During the 1920s, Harvard's president, A. Lawrence Lowell, sought to restrict the number of Jews admitted to Harvard College, supported the execution of Sacco and Vanzetti, and championed the restriction of immigration from southern and eastern Europe. In 1991, Lowell's Harvard selected Neil I. Rudenstine as its new president. Rudenstine's father was Jewish and his mother Italian. To add insult to injury, the teaching of the sacred literature of colonial New England at Harvard was now in the hands of a Jew, Sacvan Bercovitch, whose parents had named him after the two Italian immigrant anarchists.

An even more unusual anomaly occurred when Michael I. Sovern became president of Columbia University in 1980. Columbia had been founded as an Anglican institution in the mid-eighteenth century, and one of Sovern's ex officio responsibilities was to be a member of the board of trustees of the Cathedral of St. John the Divine, the Episcopal cathedral located a few blocks from the Columbia campus. Sovern was probably the first professing Jew in history to be a member of the governing body of any cathedral.

A similar ascent of Jews up the academic ladder also occurred within the professorate. Jewish academicians benefited from the explosive growth in college enrollments after the war. Between 1940 and 1975, college enrollments increased from 2,650,000 to 8,000,000, and university faculties went from 147,000 to more than 600,000. During these thirty-five years the percentage of professors who were Jews went from 2 percent to 10 percent. The percentage was even higher at elite institutions. By 1975 one-fourth of the faculty of the Ivy League universities were Jews. They were an even higher proportion among the faculty at elite law and medical schools.[12]

English and American literature had been one of the most difficult disciplines for Jews to break into. It was presumed that Jews were unable to appreciate the Anglo-Saxon literary tradition. In *The American Scene*, the novelist Henry James decried the cultural impact of the massive immigration from southern and eastern Europe. His greatest fear stemmed from what he termed "the Hebrew conquest of New York." The prominence of Jews in publishing and writing, James warned, was threatening to extinguish the English language. What Gentile can know "what the genius of Israel may, or may not, really be 'up to'?" [13] After the war, the definitive biography of James would be written by the Henry James Professor of English and American letters at New York University. He was a Jew by the name of Leon Edel.

History, particularly American history, was another field in which Jews had found it tough going. Prior to World War II, Jewish historians had a difficult time breaking into the academic big leagues. Jews, particularly those of an Eastern European background, were believed to lack gentility and to be too politically radical. Selig Perlman, a labor economist at the University of Wisconsin, reportedly warned Jewish graduate students in history to switch to economics or sociology. "History belongs to the Anglo-Saxons," he told them in his deep Yiddish accent. Jews specializing in American history had a particularly hard time getting jobs. Universities were reluctant to entrust the teaching of the nation's history to outsiders.

As late as 1962, Carl Bridenbaugh of Brown University, in his presidential address to the American Historical Association, complained about the distortions of American history being committed by those with immigrant and urban backgrounds. In this thinly veiled attack on Jewish historians, Bridenbaugh argued that they "find themselves in a very real sense outsiders to our past and feel themselves shut out. . . . What I fear is that the changes observed in the background . . . of the present generation will make it impossible for them to communicate to and reconstruct the past for future generations." Bridenbaugh's address was given in Chicago at a time when Daniel J. Boorstin of the University of Chicago, a descendant of Eastern European Jews and the future head of the Smithsonian Institution and the Library of Congress, was the city's most illustrious American historian.

Mentors of Jewish graduate students were forced to emphasize to prospective employers that their Jewish students did not have the unfortunate social characteristics associated with Eastern European Jews. Bert Loewenberg "measures up to the whitest Gentile I know," wrote Arthur M. Schlesinger of Harvard in 1930. Schlesinger himself was of partial Jewish descent, although he had overcome this disability by marrying into a distinguished New England family. On another occasion he wrote a prospective employer that his student Oscar Handlin "has none of the offensive traits which some people associate with his race." Handlin would become the first Jew with an Eastern European ancestry to receive tenure in Harvard's history department. After Schlesinger retired, Handlin would teach his course on the social history of the United States.

Handlin's student Bernard Bailyn, a Jew who grew up in Hartford, would become a professor of American colonial history at Harvard in the late 1950s. This field had previously been taught by such New England blue bloods as Edward Channing, the son of William Ellery Channing and the nephew of Margaret Fuller, and Samuel Eliot Morison, whose statue adorns Boston's Commonwealth Avenue along with those of his Puritan ancestors. Bailyn's dissertation was on New England merchants during the seventeenth century. By this time persons with a Jewish background could be found in the history departments of other leading American universities, including Richard Hofstadter (Columbia), Eric F. Goldman (Princeton), and John Morton Blum (Yale).[14]

Few of the leading Jewish academicians, however, had anything more than a tangential relationship to Jewish life. Jewish professors were part of a professional culture that viewed ethnic and religious loyalties as anachronistic and parochial. "The Jewish world is a sectarian world," one Boston-area Jewish academician said in 1973. It has "too narrow a basis, too narrow a spectrum for a man who wishes to make a contribution in international communicative ideas to feel comfortable in this group." Data collected by the Carnegie Commission on Higher Education in the 1960s revealed that two-thirds of Jewish professors were either indifferent to or opposed to religion. Jewish academicians observed fewer Jewish rituals, were more hostile to religion, affiliated with Jewish communal institutions less frequently, and intermarried more often than other Jews.[15]

Despite their prominence within academia, business remained the major avenue of economic ascent for Jews after the war. In *Today's American Jew* (1967), Morris N. Kertzer reported that, while Jews were as yet absent from the higher rungs of American business, merit considerations were slowly replacing "traditional clubhouse fraternalism." Six years later the great breakthrough occurred when Du Pont chose Irving Shapiro, the son of a Lithuanian-born pants presser, to be its chairman and chief executive officer. Du Pont was America's largest chemical company, the country's third largest manufacturing concern, and the nation's oldest corporation. It also had a reputation for being anti-Semitic. "I could understand a Jew becoming President of the United States," an American ambassador said in 1973, "but not the chief executive officer of Du Pont."[16]

The experience of Shapiro was not idiosyncratic. By the 1980s, Jews were in the highest echelons of such previously *judenrein* corporations as Disney and Ford. Jews also held important positions in New York City's major commercial banks and Wall Street law firms, two of the most socially elitist elements within the economy. "Jewishness," Shapiro remarked in 1983, "is simply not a relevant factor any more in most corporations."[17]

As Jews moved up the corporate and financial ladder, they came into closer social contact with Gentiles. It was impossible for them to remain within a hermetically sealed Jewish social environment, nor did they wish to do so. "Once they get affluence and mingle in the non-Jewish world," complained Laurence Tisch, the head of Loew's Corporation and one of America's wealthiest businessmen, "they think there's something socially more desirable perhaps over there." The inevitable result was intermarriage and an attenuating of Jewish loyalties. The September 1988 issue of *Moment* magazine contained two interviews with prominent Jewish industrialists—Shapiro of Du Pont and Alec Flamm, president of Union Carbide. While both were married to Jews, neither seemed particularly disturbed that their children had intermarried. One prominent Jewish businessman who intermarried was Leonard Stern, a billionaire New York City real estate magnate. Stern's father was Max Stern, the founder of Hartz Mountain Products and the benefactor of Stern College, the Orthodox women's college of Yeshiva University.[18]

By definition, only a small number of Jews could break into the American academic and business elite. Still the great majority of Jews after 1945 did move up the social and economic ladder. The Jewish demographic profile changed to more closely approximate that of non-Jews. Jews moved out of heavily Jewish urban neighborhoods into what was termed the "gilded ghetto" of suburbia. One out of every three Jews left the cities for suburbia between 1945 and 1965. Prior to World War II, the Bronx had more than half a million Jews and Brooklyn eight hundred fifty thousand Jews. By 1977, there were fewer than one hundred fifty thousand Jews in the Bronx and only half a million in Brooklyn. One suburb that experienced a heavy Jewish influx was Newton, Massachusetts, "the garden city." One wag claimed the nickname was because a Rosenbloom lived on every corner.

Jewish survivalists feared Jewish suburbanization would result in assimilation. In *This Is My God,* Herman Wouk described the prospect of Jewish oblivion in suburbia. It was "the threat of pleasantly vanishing down a broad highway at the wheel of a high-powered station wagon, with the golf clubs piled in the back." Mr. Abrahamson, our golfer, had not disappeared. "When his amnesia clears, he will be Mr. Adamson, and his wife and children will join him, and all will be well. But the Jewish question will be over in the United States." Philip Roth also wrote of the conflict between suburbanization and Jewish continuity. In his short story "Eli, the Fanatic," Jews react with horror when a European-born rabbi purchases a mansion in their quiet refuge in Woodenton, New York, in order to establish a yeshiva. "There's a good healthy relationship in the town because it's modern Jews and Protestants," one Jewish resident declares, "people who respect each other, and leave each other be. Common sense is the ruling thing. . . . I'm for common sense. Moderation."[19]

Another factor in the Jews' demographic "normalization" was the migration from the Northeast to the Sun Belt. By 1990, barely half of America's Jews lived in the Northeast. By then there were more Jews in San Francisco than in Baltimore, more in Phoenix than Pittsburgh, and as many in San Diego as in Detroit. The Jewish population of Greater Los Angeles exceeded that of any city in the world with the exception of New York, and more Jews lived in Los Angeles than in all of Latin America.

The Jewish influx into Florida transformed the southeast coastline of Florida into what was called a "garden of yidn." The approximately three hundred fifty thousand Jews in the Miami–Fort Lauderdale area was more than were found in any American metropolis except New York and Los Angeles. Miami Beach even had a 260-pound policeman with the unlikely name of Rocky Pomerance. He was undoubtedly the only police chief in the world with a daughter in the rabbinate. One airline provided blintzes, cheesecake, and celery tonic on its flights between New York and Miami. The Jewish presence in the Miami area was ubiquitous. Jews supported several weekly newspapers, and shops and restaurants catering to Jews were located throughout southern Florida. When the Miami Dolphins played at home during Chanukah, Lubavitch Hasidim lit a menorah at halftime to commemorate the Jewish victory over Hellenism and paganism. "We made Miami Beach a corned-beef and dill-pickle stand," one Jewish Floridian said, "and that's the way it's going to be!"[20]

The demographic and cultural transformation of American Jewry was one factor in the decline of the Jewish resort industry in the Catskills. By the 1990s, only a few out of the dozens of Jewish hotels that had existed in the "Jewish Alps" during the 1950s were still in business. Grossinger's, the major Jewish hotel along Route 17, "the derma road," had closed in 1985. "All day people stop to see the place," a security guard at Grossinger's said. "Their grandparents vacationed here, their parents were married here. They want to pay tribute."

The hotels that did remain catered to an increasingly non-Jewish clientele. "We don't even use the word borscht on our menu," the owner of the Pines Hotel said. "We just call it beet soup, because otherwise people wouldn't know what it was." The Nevele Hotel discarded its kosher menu and served bacon and shrimp cocktails. The Concord remained kosher, but provided its guests with a Japanese translation of its menu. One Korean American entrepreneur purchased the Imperial Hotel for Asian American vacationers. The kitchen remained kosher, but the menu was expanded to include kimchee and Korean rice. Before it closed, Brown's Hotel organized Irish and Greek heritage weekends, while the Women's Christian Temperance Union held its conventions in a previously Jewish Catskill resort. Symptomatic of the fate of the Jewish Catskills was the fact that the movie *Dirty Dancing,* which portrayed the mating habits at a Catskills hotel, was filmed at a resort in North Carolina, and the movie *Walk on the Moon,* which examined summer life at a Jewish bungalow colony in 1969, was filmed in Quebec.

After World War II, Jews moved en masse into the middle class, and the Jewish working class virtually disappeared. The second and third generations were not attracted to the small businesses established by the immigrant generation and instead found employment in government, the professions, academia, and big business. Going to college became virtually universal among Jewish youth, and a Jewish dropout was defined as a person with only a B.A. degree. In one of his most memorable skits, Lenny Bruce admitted Jewish responsibility for the death of Jesus. "We killed him because he didn't want to become a doctor, that's why we killed him." The Jews became the most middle-class and affluent of America's ethnic groups, with family income close to double that of Gentiles. Thomas Sowell, the black sociologist and economist, described this Jewish economic and social mobility as "unprecedented and unparalleled."[21]

Accompanying this ascent was the transformation of American Jews into Jewish Americans. Irving Howe believed the popularity among Jews for his prize-winning book *World of Our Fathers* (1976) did not stem from any authentic desire on their part "to 'find their roots' . . . but by a readiness to say farewell in a last fond gesture . . . an affectionate glance at the world of their fathers before turning their backs forever and moving on, as they had to, to a world their fathers would neither have accepted nor understood. My book was not a beginning, it was still another step to the end." While the Jewish identity of the immigrant generation was primarily religious and cultural, the Jewish identity of their children and grandchildren was primarily political and philanthropic. For the latter, American Jewry was not a distinct cultural entity but an interest group with distinctive claims. Reversing the advice of nineteenth-century German Jewish leaders to be Germans on the street and Jews at home, Jewish Americans became Americans at home and Jews in the street.[22]

By the 1980s, sociological data suggested that the future of American

Jewry was problematic. The Jewish family—supposedly the guarantor of Jewish survival—was under siege, and there seemed to be no relief on the horizon. The Jewish divorce rate was approaching the national norm, the birthrate was under replacement level, and intermarriage was more widespread than even the most pessimistic observers had assumed. For Jewish survivalists, intermarriage was the most troubling aspect of contemporary American Jewish life. Hand-wringing regarding intermarriage generally missed the point. Jews did not intermarry because they wished to assimilate; they intermarried because they were already largely assimilated.

Intermarriage presented Jews with a seemingly insoluble dilemma since it stemmed from diminishing anti-Semitism and rapid social and economic mobility, developments few Jews wished to see reversed. Jews were pleased that Caroline Kennedy, the daughter of President Kennedy, married Edwin Schlossberg. They were not pleased, however, that it took place in a Roman Catholic church. Jews, David Singer wrote in 1979, were now condemned to "living with intermarriage." One Jewish couple capitalized on this growing intermarriage rate by establishing a company called Mixed Blessing Inc. It produced greeting cards for the intermarried. One card pictured a Christian angel lighting the candles of a menorah.[23]

Jewish sociologists were not sanguine regarding the future of American Jewry. In his 1985 *Commentary* essay "On Jewish Forebodings," Nathan Glazer predicted that although Jews would continue to identify as Jews, "little by way of custom, belief, or loyalty" could be assumed as a result of this identification. This thinning of Jewish identity reflected itself in the growing number of Jews who were unaffiliated with any Jewish organization. During the 1970s and 1980s, the American Jewish Committee, B'nai B'rith, the American Jewish Congress, and other Jewish organizations saw their membership slowly shrink. There was much truth in the sardonic comment of the Israeli journalist Ze'ev Chafets that in most places in America, the land of his birth, "Judaism doesn't seem to be about anything. It is a holding operation—an effort to wring one more generation of allegiance from people who are no longer sure what being a Jew is all about."[24]

The problems facing American Jewry in the 1990s, the largest Jewish community in history, stemmed not from the hostility but from the openness of the host society. Indifference, not apostasy, was the threat. If intermarriage was the symptom, apathy was the disease. "In a free and open society the drift away from Jewish life is not surprising," the social scientist Daniel J. Elazar wrote. "Indeed, the way it occurs—so casually and without deliberate intent, so unlinked to ideology, and certainly not to any ideology of assimilationism—is . . . a reflection on the character of American society." But, as Marshall Sklare pointed out in his essay "American Jewry—the Ever Dying People," although the prospects for American Jewry have rarely appeared bright, Jews have survived countless crises. Perhaps they will also survive the challenge of American freedom and prosperity.[25]

SIX

American Jews and the Business Mentality

FOR CENTURIES anti-Semitism had limited the social and economic opportunities of Jews living in Europe and the Arab lands. Little wonder, then, that Jews emphasized the rabbinic restrictions separating themselves from their neighbors, that they sought solace in messianic movements such as Hasidim, and that they viewed themselves as outcasts and victims. These perceptions would be challenged by the social and economic realities of Jewish life in America. Here the absence of strong barriers against the social and economic advancement of Jews and of restrictions against Jewish participation in politics meant that the realities of Jewish life became increasingly remote from definitions of Jewish identity emphasizing victimhood. Jews, however, were reluctant to give up the old verities. A cultural lag resulted in which they continued to profess their identity as an oppressed people, while at the same time they benefited from all that this "golden land" offered.

American Jews have had an ambivalent attitude toward their financial success and commercial acquisitiveness. Their rapid economic and social mobility over the past seventy-five years, which far exceeds that of any other major American ethnic group during this period, enabled them to escape from the slums and radically transformed the occupational structure of American Jewry within two or three generations. The fervent desire of the first and second generations of East European Jews that their children not enter the sweatshops or live in tenements has been fulfilled beyond their wildest expectations. This particularly surprised American Jews of German descent who initially viewed the East European immigrants as *luftmenschen, schnorers*, and physically debilitated. While rapid Jewish social, economic, and occupational mo-

This chapter was previously published in *Judaism* 27 (spring 1978): 12–21. Reprinted by permission.

bility has become a staple of American sociology, there is, nevertheless, a tendency among many American Jews to ignore it or to underestimate its significance, and to refuse to recognize its source.

Some Jews deny that American Jews are now "haves" rather than "have-nots." Embarrassed by evidence of Jewish affluence, Jewish spokesmen in the 1960s and 1970s emphasized the tenacity of Jewish poverty. Not only did many of these seekers after Jewish poverty exaggerate its extent but they also often slighted its transitory character. In contrast to the poverty of other American ethnic groups that has persisted over several generations and has created what Oscar Lewis termed a "culture of poverty," Jewish poverty is a phenomenon found mainly among the elderly, recent immigrants, and the extremely pious. It is not a social condition that is passed on from generation to generation. Many of the elderly poor who are living out their last years on meager social security checks have children who are doctors, lawyers, and professors. Indeed, one of the psychological burdens carried by the elderly Jewish poor is the recognition that they have been largely forgotten by their successful offspring, whose concern is limited to a visit or two a year and a phone call once a week.

While most informed American Jews are aware of the financial success of American Jews, there is no widespread recognition of its cause. Perhaps the most widely held explanation is that American Jews took advantage of available educational opportunities, particularly the university, and especially the fabled City College of New York. The classrooms and cafeteria of CCNY have assumed in American Jewish folklore a position comparable to that of the playing fields of Eton and Harrow. The fact that Russian Jewish immigrants and their descendants in Latin America, the British Empire, and other areas where educational opportunities were not so easily available also experienced the same rapid economic mobility should have made the education explanation suspect.

Recent historical investigation has demolished the belief that scholastic achievement was responsible for American Jewish financial success. Professor Selma Berrol has shown that, prior to World War I, most American Jews did not even finish high school, much less go on to college, and that CCNY was far too small to account for any significant portion of Jewish mobility. In 1913, for example, there were only 209 graduates of City College, and it was not until the 1930s that the college was large enough to be a route of upward mobility for a significant number of Jews. By the 1930s, moreover, Jewish ascent was already well underway, as indicated by the large number of Jews who had been able to move from the Lower East Side. The Jewish population of the Lower East Side peaked well before World War I, and Jews continued to leave the area during the years after the war. The Lower East Side housed 353,000 Jews in 1916, but only 121,000 in 1930.[1]

The college explanation thus fails to account for the social and economic mobility of the first generation, and it is only a partial explanation for the ascent of the second and third generations. An alternative, and more persuasive, explanation of Jewish economic mobility stresses the ability of East European Jews and their descendants to take advantage of the economic and entrepreneurial opportunities offered by American capitalism. The East European Jewish immigrants of the late nineteenth and early twentieth centuries were overwhelmingly oriented toward business. In many areas of East Europe, Jews virtually monopolized commerce. The most frequently voiced criticism of Jews noted their supposed "parasitic" economic character. Jewish philanthropists and Zionists encouraged transforming Jews from peddlers and small businessmen into "productive" farmers and artisans. While these strictures overlooked the many Jewish artisans and the fact that hundreds of thousands of East European Jews had been proletarianized by the late nineteenth century, they correctly recognized that business was central to the life of East European Jewry.

The goal of most Jewish immigrants upon settling in America was to open their own business, and it was only as a temporary expedient that they entered the working class. The intense labor union activity in the New York ghetto early in the twentieth century was a response not only to the wretched working conditions of the sweatshops but also to the discontent of Jewish workers at being workers at all. The Jewish immigrant working class was a bourgeoisie temporarily posing as a proletariat. The major social characteristics of the Jewish working class, such as sobriety, temperance, frugality, willingness to defer gratification, and commitment to education, are generally associated with a mobile middle class.

While the East European Jewish immigrants possessed precisely those traits conducive for success, this would have been for naught if the American economy had not provided a hospitable environment for exercising their talents. Not only was the American urban economy burgeoning at the turn of the century, but there were no artificial barriers to enterprise. Licensing regulations, minimum-wage laws, and other government impediments to enterprise and social advancement either did not exist or were unimportant, and the labor movement in the garment industry and other Jewish-oriented industries was not yet strong enough to hamper economic mobility. As a result,

East European Jews gravitated toward business at a rate far higher than that of other immigrant groups.

"The Lower East Side," wrote the historian Moses Rischin, "developed a fervent commercial life, infused with a vitality that made it something more than a mass of tenements." It was this "fervent commercial life" that was responsible for Jewish social and economic mobility. "Jews joined the mainstream in seeking success through business," the historian Thomas Kessner said. "And indeed among the first generation immigrants it was not medicine, law or even their vaunted thirst for education that carried them forward. It was business." The same statements could be made of their children and grandchildren. The economic opportunities provided by the sweatshops and a much maligned capitalism enabled the grandchildren of the immigrants to criticize the economic system from the safety of their homes in Woodmere and Great Neck.[2]

But while the first generation tended to act as capitalists, they tended to think as radicals. The most popular Yiddish newspaper was Abraham Cahan's secular and socialist *Forward*. The Lower East Side was one of only a handful of districts ever to send a Socialist to Congress, electing Meyer London first in 1914. The Jewish labor unions were generally socialist in ideology, and most of the first-generation ghetto intellectuals were socialists of one variety or other. To this day, American Jewish social action organizations are to the "left," and they support a social and economic program that, it could be argued, has more relevance for Vilna of the 1890s than for contemporary America. Indeed, American Jewry has almost a knee-jerk suspicion of big business and capitalism, an attitude that has mystified conservatives and been a godsend for countless liberal causes and organizations.

This contempt for business has been a central motif in the recent resurgence of interest in American Jewish history, particularly the nostalgia for the immigrant generation and the old Lower East Side. The movies and books purporting to describe the "world of our fathers" have presented a picture at odds with the perceptions of the Jews who actually lived there. The residents of the Lower East Side knew that they were living in a slum, and they expended all possible efforts to escape from it. When Jacob Riis stated that thrift, "the watchword of Jewtown," was "its cardinal virtue and its foul disgrace," he was noting the willingness of Jews to scrimp and save in order to flee from the oppressive social conditions of the ghetto. They were under no illusions about the Lower East Side. For them it was neither quaint nor colorful.

One of the classic pictures of the Lower East Side as slum is *Jews Without Money,* published in 1930 by Michael Gold, a Communist and resident of the neighborhood. His description, when compared to later analyses such as Irving Howe's *World of Our Fathers,* clearly reveals the change in the Jewish radical sensibility. There is no sentimentality or nostalgia in Gold's portrait. Everything about the ghetto disgusted him. Not only did he exaggerate its social misery, but his Marxism prevented him from appreciating the difficult, yet partially successful struggle to establish traditional Jewish religious and cultural institutions in America.

Modern portraits of the Lower East Side, however, are concerned less with drawing attention to its social and economic conditions than with recapturing its cultural and religious yearnings. Some of this is an understandable quest for identity on the part of individuals for whom the Lower East Side is, at best, a vague memory. The pithy formula of Marcus Lee Hansen that what the son wishes to forget the grandson wants to remember explains some of the current interest in the early years of the East European Jewish settlement. This interest, however, involves something more than an understandable search for roots. The Lower East Side has become not merely a geographical location but also a standard by which to judge, evaluate, and censure modern American Jewry.

This is not the first time that the Lower East Side (and the East European shtetl) has been used in this way. At the turn of the twentieth century, many native-born Americans frequented the ghetto ("slumming," we might call it) in search of the excitement and local color that their own culture did not provide. The two most famous of these explorers were Lincoln Steffens and Hutchins Hapgood. According to Ronald Sanders, they "saw in the life of the Russian Jews a cultural integrity and vitality" lacking in American culture. The modern view of the shtetl and the Lower East Side, as presented, say, in *Fiddler on the Roof,* in Mark Zborowski and Elizabeth Herzog's *Life Is with People,* and in photograph volumes of the shtetl and the Lower East Side, is that of an anti-suburb.[3]

Suburbia is, after all, the habitat of the modern Jewish businessman who has "made it." For the modern Jewish intellectual, the memory of the ghetto is a welcome contrast to the ostentatiousness, materialism, spiritual vacuity, and aimlessness that supposedly characterize modern suburban American Jewry. The Lower East Side is idealized because of its intellectual intensity, its socialist politics, and its working-class culture, and because the immigrant generation never completely surrendered to bourgeois values. It has been romanticized to show just how far America's Jews have moved away from the ideals of their immigrant ancestors and have become enveloped within the commercialism and materialism of modern America.[4]

One is struck in viewing films about American Jewry by their pervasive antibusiness orientation and nostalgia for the ghetto. The showy wedding and bar mitzvah scenes in *Goodbye, Columbus* and *The Apprenticeship of Duddy Kravitz,* the wealthy but morally flawed uncle in *The Gambler,* and the corrupt businessmen in *Save the Tiger* exhibit a distaste for successful Jewish businessmen. When Duddy, a caricature of the capitalist hustler, asks his uncle why he never had time for him, the uncle answers, "Because you're a pusherke. A little Jewboy on the make. Guys like you make me sick and ashamed."

This animus toward business is perhaps best brought out in the overly praised film *Lies My Father Told Me.* The theme of the film is the struggle between the father and the grandfather for the mind of the young boy, David. Harry, the father, is pictured as the quintessential second-generation Jew in flight from the world of his father-in-law, and especially from Orthodox Judaism. He is an extreme materialist who has made money and social mobility his gods. He is continually thinking up inventions, including expandable cuff links and creaseless pants, that will enable him to escape from the Montreal ghetto. He views his father-in-law's religion as "nonsense," saying to him that "for you the world is still waiting for the Messiah." Zaideh makes his living by traveling through the narrow alleys of Montreal purchasing rags, clothes, and bottles. David often accompanies his grandfather on these journeys, and they frequently discuss religion and the coming of the Messiah. Zaideh personifies the effort of traditional religious and cultural values to survive in the face of the corrosive impact of materialism and the dream of capitalistic success. The film, while sympathetic to the grandfather's world, reluctantly recognizes that the future belongs to the Harrys.

The film *Hester Street* also has as its major theme the conflict between the values of traditional Yiddishkeit and the attraction of materialistic America. The movie's central figure is Jake, whose major goal is to be accepted as a "real American fella." Though living in this country for only three years, Jake has been thoroughly Americanized. He has changed his name from Yekl to Jake, wears a salon derby, punctuates his conversation with words about the latest happenings in the world of sports, and spends his evenings at Peltner's Dancing Academy in the company of the beautiful and Americanized Mamie. A cloud, however, comes into Jake's life with the arrival from Europe of his wife, Gitl, and their son, Yossele. Although Jake does succeed in changing his son's name to Joey and cutting his earlocks, he is unable to do much with Gitl, who holds on tightly to the religious customs and superstitions of Europe. Everything about her reminds Jake of the detested life in Europe, especially the wig Gitl insists on wearing, despite his strenuous objections. Jake's embarrassment soon turns to contempt and then loathing, and he divorces Gitl.

Jake is also at odds with his boarder and fellow worker Bernstein. Jake teases Bernstein for studying the Talmud and for being a "greenhorn." Bernstein, in turn, curses Columbus, saying that when a Jewish immigrant leaves for the United States, he should cry out to God, "Goodbye, O Lord, I'm going to America." The film ends with Mamie and Jake going to city hall to be married, and with Gitl and Bernstein making marriage plans of their own after the conclusion of the waiting period for a female divorcée required by Jewish law. They talk of opening a grocery store, which Gitl will operate while Bernstein studies the Talmud.

Everything about *Hester Street* is designed to portray traditional Jewish immigrant life on the Lower East Side in as favorable a light as possible. But, to quote the film critic Stanley Kaufmann, it is "phony to the eye," since it fails to convey any sense of its poverty, filth, and deprivation. The audience is unable to comprehend why Jake would choose the meretricious and Americanized Mamie over Gitl, nor can they understand, much less sympathize with, Jake's desire to escape the ghetto and become a "Yenkee."[5]

Another important attempt to portray American Jewish culture prior to its seduction by materialism is Irving Howe's *World of Our Fathers*. The book's jacket describes it as an analysis of "the journey of the east European Jews to America and the life they found and made," a rather loose characterization since Howe's 650 pages of text barely discuss the commercial world of the immigrant generation. There is no mention of David Sarnoff, but there are long accounts of the labor lawyer Joseph Barondess, the Socialist politician Meyer London, and the Yiddish literary critic Shmuel Niger.

According to Howe, the life of the Jewish immigrants revolved around Yiddish culture, Socialist politics, and the Jewish labor movement. Certainly this is part of the truth, especially in New York City. But, along with this, there was also a passion to flee from the ghettos, a hunger to climb the economic and social ladder, and an eagerness to seize the economic opportunities available in America. Abraham Cahan, that sounding board of Lower East Side life, reflected this immigrant ambivalence. Not only was he editor of the *Forward*, the most important foreign-language socialist newspaper, but he was also the author of *The Rise of David Levinsky*, the classic picture of the parvenu immigrant Jewish businessman.

American Jews, Howe claimed, can look back to the immigrant world for "images of rectitude and purities of devotion." But devotion to what? For Howe, the essence of immigrant Jewish culture was "a readiness to live for ideals beyond the clamor of self, a sense of plebeian fraternity, an ability to forge a community of moral order even while remaining subject to a society of social disorder, and a persuasion that human existence is a deeply serious matter for which all of us are finally accountable." If this strikes Jews as a rather extravagant description of the motives of their parents and grandparents, it is because Howe did not concern himself with the average Jewish immigrant.

World of Our Fathers is an elitist interpretation of the Lower East Side written by a Jewish intellectual who became a socialist at the age of fourteen and an editor of a socialist weekly when he was twenty-one. Most Jewish immigrants were not overly concerned with what Howe saw as the essence of the Yiddish cultural experience in America: "the messianic impulse of secular Judaism" and the discovery of "modes of conduct" in order to "establish a genuine community." The one overpowering goal for most immigrant Jews was "My children will not work in the shops."

Jews can take pleasure, Howe writes, "in having been related to those self-educated workers, those sustaining women, those almost-forgotten writers and speakers devoted to excitements of controversy and thought." Can't Jews also take pleasure in the businessmen and artisans whose enterprise and hard work enabled the immigrant generation to leave the ghettos, and can't Jews also be grateful to the immigrant generation for passing on to their descendants middle-class virtues and ambitions that would stand them in good stead? *World of Our Fathers* is an elegy on the old Lower East Side, and, like all elegies, it recalls those qualities of the deceased that one wishes to be remembered. A history of the world of our fathers, however, must make room for the Sammy Glicks and the David Levinskys as well as for the victims of the Triangle Shirtwaist fire and the pioneers of the Yiddish stage.

Howe's interpretation of the Lower East Side experience is infused with a wistfulness totally lacking in Gold's *Jews Without Money*. While Gold believed that a "garden for the human spirit" could emerge out of the eagerly awaited destruction of the ghetto, Howe laments the rapid obliteration of the Yiddish cultural and socialist values resulting from the decline of the old Jewish Lower East Side. This difference should not, however, obscure Howe's basic agreement with Gold regarding the insignificance of the nonradical aspects of Jewish life on the Lower East Side. A case in point is Howe's virtual ignoring of religion. There is no discussion of Orthodox Judaism, Yeshiva University, or the yeshivot of the Lower East Side, such as Moshe Feinstein's Mesivta Tifereth Jerusalem on East Broadway or the Rabbi Jacob Joseph Yeshiva on Henry Street. In addition to slighting religious traditionalism, Howe also passes over the Zionist activity of the ghetto. Indeed, *World of Our Fathers* focuses on some of the most transitory aspects of Jewish life on the East Side, while disregarding precisely those elements that, since they have been able to weather the migration to suburbia and the shock of acculturation, have proven to be the most lasting and important.

There is something ironic, indeed, about the second and third generation, who, safely ensconced in suburbia, nostalgically yearn to recapture the intellectual intensity, the spirit of community, and even the radical politics that supposedly were the hallmarks of the immigrant ghettos. Seventy-five years ago German Jews in America questioned whether the Jewish immigrants from Eastern Europe could make it economically and culturally in the United States. Now the descendants of the Russian immigrants question the value of their success and acculturation. The contrast between *Hester Street* and *Lies My Father Told Me* and films of the 1920s featuring Jews reveals the extent of this contemporary alienation from modern America. Movies such as *Bleeding Hearts, The Heart of the Jewess, Child of the Ghetto,* and *The Jazz Singer* associated the ghetto with poverty and ethnic parochialism and stressed the benefits of assimilation and social mobility. Today, when many have become cynical about mainstream American culture, it is natural to sentimentalize the immigrants, who were not yet acculturated and affluent and had not moved to suburbia. Jews, in particular, have become what Dan Isaac called "a mythic symbol for ethnic survival."[6]

American Jews will have to come to terms with their history if Jewish identity and cultural pluralism are to rest on more than mere sentimentality. This means recognizing that their history encompasses Inland Steel as well as the ILGWU, Revlon as well as Delancey Street, and Federated Department Stores as well as Jacob Adler. American Jewish historical consciousness must acknowledge American Jewry's persistent middle-class character and the enormous benefit that America's Jews have derived from American capitalism.

S E V E N

Jews with Money

THE ECONOMIC STATUS of America's Jews presents a challenge to those Jews for whom Jewish identity involves an identification with the oppressed. Jews, either individually or collectively, are certainly not oppressed in the United States, and in fact, they are among America's most affluent groups. Elements within American Jewry, however, are eager to maintain ties to the political Left, and this requires that they ignore the realities of American Jewish affluence in order to promulgate a Jewish identity redolent of East Europe in the early twentieth century.

One needs little imagination to fancy what Michael Gold would have thought of the special issue that *Forbes* magazine publishes every fall listing the four hundred richest Americans. Gold was the American Communist Party's literary guru of the 1930s. Described by Allen Guttmann as "the first important document of proletarian literature," Gold's *Jews Without Money* was his answer to the anti-Semitic canard that most Jews were affluent and had a special affinity for making money.

Gold's Jews, by contrast, were hard working, poor, and exploited. They worked and lived under horrible conditions, thanks to American capitalism. At one point in the book, Gold's father, a former housepainter and now an impoverished banana peddler, pleads with his son: "What a rich country America is! What an easy place to make one's fortune! Look at all the rich Jews! Why has it been so easy for them, so hard for me? I am just a poor little Jew without money. . . . It's better to be dead in this country than not to have money. Promise me you'll be rich when you grow up, Mikey! . . . This is my one hope now! This is all that makes me happy! I am a greenhorn, but you are an American! You will have it easier than I; you will have luck in America!"

This chapter was previously published in *Judaism* 36 (winter 1987): 7–16. Reprinted by permission.

For Gold, of course, the idea of becoming rich was a fantasy. Unable to share his father's "naive optimism," Gold's heart sank as he "remembered the past and thought of the future." For a brief time he embraced religion before concluding that socialism and revolution, not the Jewish Messiah or economic opportunity, were to be the salvation of East Side Jewry. "O workers' Revolution, you brought hope to me, a lonely, suicidal boy. You are the true Messiah. You will destroy the East Side when you come, and build there a garden for the human spirit. O Revolution, that forced me to think, to struggle and to live. O great beginning!"[1]

The *Forbes* list is so intriguing for students of American Jewish culture because, out of the four hundred richest Americans, more than one hundred are Jews. Thus more than 25 percent of the richest Americans come from a group that is no more than two and a half percent of the general population. By contrast, the *Forbes* list contains only a handful of Italians, Hispanics, blacks, and East Europeans. All of these groups vastly outnumber Jews. (A disproportionate number of America's ordinary millionaires are also Jewish, and the per capita income of American Jews is far higher than that of the general population. In part, this reflects the high percentage of Jews who are in business and the professions and who live in urban and suburban areas.) Furthermore, of the fourteen American billionaires on the first *Forbes* list, which appeared in 1982, at least four were Jewish: Marvin Davis, the Denver oil mogul and former owner of Twentieth Century Fox; Leslie Wexner, the founder of The Limited, Inc. women's apparel shops; and the Newhouse brothers, Samuel and Donald, who control America's largest privately owned newspaper, magazine, and book publishing empire. Although the wealthy of Canada are not included in the *Forbes* list, it is noteworthy that the three most prominent Canadian business families are Jewish: the Belzbergs of Vancouver, the Reichmanns of Toronto, and the Bronfmans of Montreal.

The economic and political influence of American Jews is not, however, commensurate with their wealth. An Irving Shapiro, the former chief executive officer of the Du Pont Corporation, is still rare in corporate America. Power is in the hands of the insurance companies, banks, and industrial corporations, and these are usually controlled by Gentiles. Much of the Jewish wealth has been acquired in "marginal" fields—entertainment, retailing, real estate speculation—where the economic rewards are often great but are not accompanied by significant power or status.

Some Jews are embarrassed by references to Jewish affluence for fear that they will encourage the anti-Semitic stereotype of vast Jewish wealth and economic power. The association of Jews with money was a staple of American, as well as of British, literature of the nineteenth and early twentieth century. Jews have an "unquenchable lust for lucre," the American poet William Cullen Bryant wrote. The novelist Henry James used the Jew to symbolize greed, commercial exploitation, and the nouveaux riches. In *McTeague,* Frank Norris wrote that it was impossible to look at the Jew Zerkow and not immediately recognize that "great—inordinate, insatiable greed—as the dominant passion of the man." Even Mark Twain, normally considered a friend of the Jews, claimed in his essay "Concerning the Jews" that "the Jew is a money-getter. . . . He made it the end and aim of his life to get it."

The American press also drew attention to this relationship between Jews and money. In the mid-nineteenth century, the *New York Sunday Dispatch* described Jews as "a nation so fond of money that it would sell its own mother and its own soul for a dime." The *Quarterly Sentinel* concurred. Economic rapacity was "the Jew's second nature. . . . The lust for gain is so strongly rooted in his organism, that it extinguishes every other feeling, every other passion." In his muckraking book *How the Other Half Lives,* the Progressive-era reformer Jacob A. Riis claimed that the God of "Jewtown" was money. "Life itself is of little value compared with even the leanest bank account. In no other spot does life wear so intensely bald and materialistic an aspect as in Ludlow Street."

The belief that the Jews have a unique ability to make money has remained a staple of anti-Semitic demonology. (According to one contemporary joke, when the pope sang "Ave Maria," one thousand persons became Catholics; when Billy Graham sang "Onward Christian Soldiers" five thousand became Protestants; when Pat Boone sang "There's a Gold Mine in the Sky," fifty thousand Jews joined the air force.) Marxists, true to the teachings of the founder of their cult, have identified Jews and Judaism (and now Israel) with commercial exploitation and capitalism.

Little wonder, then, that Jews and their friends, despite evidence to the contrary and even though they themselves know better, prefer to deny, ignore, or explain away American Jewish wealth. (A noteworthy exception is Gerald Krefetz's 1982 *Jews and Money: The Myths and Reality.*) In 1936, for example, the editors of *Fortune* published a small volume titled *Jews in America,* which vigorously argued that, except for the clothing and movie industries, Jewish economic influence in America was insignificant. American Jews themselves have claimed that real economic power remains in the hands of Anglo-Saxon Protestants, who control the banks, insurance companies, and major industrial corporations. Arthur Liebman's *Jews and the Left* (1979) evidences another stratagem of minimizing American Jewish wealth by emphasizing its marginality and precariousness.

This reluctance to deal openly with the reality of the American Jewish economic condition is due in part to the novelty of the situation. Jews, after all, are hardly familiar with status and security, even if these phenomena stem only from money, and it is not surprising that they should view their situation as exceptional and temporary. "Never in modern history," Gerald Krefetz wrote, have Jews "been in such an enviable position of wealth and power." But Jews would prefer to believe, and have others believe, that when it comes to economics, they are like everyone else, only more so. This stance has the advantage of not attracting attention. History, they believe, teaches that safety stems from anonymity and not from being part of any elite, even if it is only an economic elite. This refusal to admit the reality of American Jewish economic success and the discomfort this new status causes reflect an obsessive sensitivity to Gentile opinion and a lack of confidence in American democratic institutions. A continuing psychology of marginality makes it difficult for Jews to conclude that this is, after all, their country too, and that they need not be embarrassed by their achievements.

Those who contend that drawing attention to Jewish wealth will lead to anti-Semitism can point to the example of the German sociologist Werner Sombart, whose volume *The Jews and Modern Capitalism* (1911) argued that greed and materialism lay at the heart of both capitalism and Judaism. (Not surprisingly, two decades later Sombart supported the Third Reich.) Influenced by Max Weber's *The Protestant Ethic and the Spirit of Capitalism,* Sombart attributed the rise of capitalism not to Weber's hardworking Calvinists but to Jewish merchants and bankers. As the historian Paul Gottfried has pointed out, although Sombart's scholarship was suspect and permeated with malice toward Jews and Judaism, he was correct in emphasizing the productive role of Jews in the economic modernization of Europe. Despite his "deplorable political judgments," Sombart did provide a real service by challenging the accepted view that Jewish capitalists were "merely products of Jewish self-alienation and Christian discrimination."[2]

Jews, however, attacked Sombart's association of Jews with capitalism, partly because of the anti-Semitic uses to which his thesis could be put and partly because of their own animus toward capitalism. Thus, Michael Gold's essential argument—that capitalism was hostile to the interests of Jews—was, prior to World War II, shared in one form or another by many leading Jews, including David Dubinsky, Abe Cahan, Morris Hilquit, Sidney Hillman, and Stephen S. Wise. Capitalism was supposedly one element in a conservative ideology that encompassed anti-Semitism, autocracy, militarism, and the exploitation of the working class. The Jewish Lower East Side, the historian Stephen Whitfield has noted, resembled the "burnt-over district" of upstate New York prior to the Civil War because of the popularity of radical political movements.

And yet there is no reason why American Jews need be embarrassed by their economic success or by the advantages accruing to them from capitalism. The rags-to-riches myth occupies a central role in the American mythology, and, of all the immigrant economic success stories, none has equaled that of the Jews. (It was appropriate that Horatio Alger, the most famous exponent of the success myth, was employed by the German Jewish Seligman family to tutor their children.) The Jew has become a symbol of capitalist achievement and a living proof of the reality of the American dream. While many of the Gentiles on the *Forbes* list made their money in the old-fashioned way through inheritance, the overwhelming majority of the wealthy Jews are self-made, having achieved success through their own talents, determination, successful exploitation of the tax laws, and the good fortune to have been located in sectors of the economy and areas of the country that boomed after World War II. They are the latest chapter in that American cult of success that stretches back to Cotton Mather and Benjamin Franklin.

Just as Mather and Franklin stressed the social responsibilities of wealth, so have most of the Jewish rich contributed munificent sums to cultural, educational, religious, and medical institutions. "Money," the businessman Max Fisher stated, "should not control the individual, the individual must control the money." Wealthy (and middle-class) Jews contribute more to charity than do their Gentile counterparts. The greatest philanthropic enterprise in contemporary America is the annual campaign conducted by local Jewish federations, which raise more than three-quarters of a billion dollars from a donor pool of less than 3 percent of the population.

Alexis de Tocqueville's classic commentary, *Democracy in America*, written in the 1830s, noted the crucial role of money in defining American nationality. "I know of no other country where love of money has such a grip on men's hearts or where stronger scorn is expressed for the theory of permanent equality of property. No stigma attaches to the love of money in America, and provided it does not exceed the bounds imposed by public order, it is held in honor." This quest for riches, Tocqueville wrote, flowed ineluctably from the democratic character of the United States. While aristocratic societies admired the "turbulent virtues" leading to conquest and warfare, democratic societies admired the "quiet virtues" and "regular habits" conducive to commerce and industry. And while people living in aristocratic societies were differentiated on the basis of "birth, standing, or profession," those living in democracies were distinguished from one another primarily by the possession of money. "Distinction based on wealth," Tocqueville reasoned, "is increased by the disappearance or diminution of all other distinctions." Hence, money became the standard by which Americans kept score, and one "usually finds that love of money is either the chief or a secondary motive at the bottom of everything the Americans do."

If Tocqueville was correct, then the American Jewish nabobs are part of the classic American saga, and their success stamps them as super-Americans. As an editorial in the *Philadelphia Evening Telegraph* in 1872 noted, "Wherever there is a chance for enterprise and energy the Jew is to be found. He brings into every community wealth and qualities which materially assist to strengthen and consolidate its polity." The historian John Higham concluded that the Jewish emphasis on the materialistic and competitive values of business is "deeply ingrained in American life." [3]

Ethnic groups have different backgrounds and values, and they pass on these values to future generations. Each has made a contribution to American life, but they have been different contributions. It is naïve to suppose that each group possesses the same political skills, intellectual ambitions, and economic talents, or that each group has contributed to American life in the same way and to the same degree. Jews should be no more embarrassed by their millionaires (or their violinists, chess players, and Nobel Prize–winning economists) than blacks should be by their athletes and entertainers, Irish by their politicians, or Asians by their scientists and academicians.

The difference between the Christian and Jewish attitudes toward wealth is striking. The Sermon on the Mount proclaims that "blessed are the poor," and the New Testament states that "it is easier for a camel to go through the eye of a needle, than for a rich man to enter into the kingdom of God." The Mishnah, by contrast, asks, *"Mi hu ashir? Hasaneah be-helko,"* which can he rendered as "Who is rich? He who enjoys his wealth." The Saturday night services ending the Sabbath proclaim, "Blessed shall be your basket and your kneading trough. Blessed shall be the fruit of your body and the fruit of your land, your cattle and your flocks of sheep. The Lord will command the blessing upon you in your barns and in every enterprise to which you put your hand, and will bless you in the land which the Lord your God gives you. The Lord will open his good treasures of heaven for you, to bestow rain in due season on your land, and to bless all your labor, so that you shall lend to many nations but never need to borrow from them." Jewish thinkers have never viewed poverty as a desirable condition, and there is nothing in Jewish tradition similar to the vow of poverty assumed by monks and nuns. Maimonides' highest degree of charity was providing the destitute with sufficient capital to become self-supporting.

There is a strong strain within Christianity arguing for the nobility of the poor. Martin Luther King Jr., for example, claimed that the poor better appreciated the teachings of Christianity since they had not been corrupted by materialism. J. Andrew Kirk's *The Good News of the Kingdom Coming: The Marriage of Evangelism and Social Responsibility* (1983), a defense of Christian socialism, claims that according to Scripture, the private accumulation of wealth "was considered contrary to the terms of God's covenant with his people." Marxism, in contrast, "has exalted collective freedom—the freedom to enjoy a basically dignified life."

There has never been a Judaic counterpart to Christian socialism or liberation theology with their rejection of private property and private enterprise. Although there have been Jewish socialists, they have generally been estranged from, and even hostile to, Judaism, and traditional Jews from the beginning have abhorred socialism. Pious Jews have not been reluctant to become involved in commerce, and many great rabbis have also been businessmen. For Jews, Irving Kristol correctly said, the spirit of commerce "is perfectly compatible with full religious faith and full religious practice."[4]

The sociologist Robert Merton noted in his essay "The Self-Fulfilling Prophecy" the irony in the reluctance of American Jews to acknowledge their economic and social accomplishments. "In a culture which consistently judges the professionals higher in social value than even the most skilled hewers of wood and drawers of water," he wrote, "the out-group finds itself in the anomalous position of pointing with defensive relief to the large number of Jewish painters and paper hangers, plasterers and electricians, plumbers and sheet-metal workers." Furthermore, living in a society that "looks upon wealth as a warrant of ability," American Jews feel impelled to deny the very success American culture most admires. They bend over backward to convince others that they do not play a significant role in the American economy. By contrast, they are not reluctant to trumpet the accomplishments of the Koufaxes, Menuhins, Jolsons, and Salks.

This fear that acknowledging the reality of American Jewish economic success will encourage anti-Semitism reflects a psychological insecurity incompatible with the social, political, and economic position of contemporary American Jewry, the openness of American society, and the contemporary insignificance of American anti-Semitism. Thus three-quarters of American Jews are convinced that most American Gentiles believe Jews have too much economic power, a belief totally at variance with the data revealed by the surveys on Gentiles' attitudes toward Jews.[5]

It should not surprise us that it was a Gentile, Stephen Birmingham, who chronicled the history of wealthy American Jews. In three books—*Our Crowd, The Grandees,* and *The Rest of Us*—he described the economic success of America's German, Sephardic, and Eastern European Jews, observing at one point that the success of those "brash and young, ambitious and daring" Eastern European Jewish entrepreneurs "has been accepted by the rest of the populace with equanimity and respect, without envy or rancor." It is the inability of Jews to believe that this can possibly be true that explains their reluctance to publicize the American Jewish economic success story.[6]

Perhaps half of the Jewish superrich are in real estate. ("The Jew runs to real estate," Jacob Riis wrote, "as soon as he can save up enough for a deposit to clinch the bargain.") In New York City, except for a few Gentile interlopers such as Donald Trump and Harry Helmsley, the great majority of the most successful real estate entrepreneurs are Jews. They include Samuel LeFrak, Leonard Stern, Peter Kalikow, Jack and Lewis Rudin, Leonard Marx, and Seymour Cohn. Other cities have their own Jewish real estate barons: Alfred Taubman in Detroit, Walter Shorenstein in San Francisco, Melvin Simon in Indianapolis, Monte and Alfred Goldman in Oklahoma City, Mortimer Zuckerman in Boston, Stephen Muss in Miami, and Laszlo Tauber in Washington. Because of the secrecy surrounding real estate, there is good reason to believe that *Forbes* has understated the number and wealth of the Jewish superrich real estate investors.

The Jewish real estate moguls exhibit a refreshing and earthy attitude regarding their success. "I'm not very smart and have mediocre ability," Leonard Marx of New York noted. "I make up for it with hard work." Peter Kalikow's advice was to "assume the person you're dealing with is at least as smart as you are. Then you won't get hurt thinking you can outsmart him." His humility, however, had a limit. "We don't have time to deal with idiots. It takes time from my day." When asked how much he was worth, Samuel

LeFrak replied that he didn't know. "If I could count it, it couldn't be very much." He also is fond of the morally obtuse, hackneyed parvenu line: "I follow the Golden Rule: those with the gold make the rules."

The affinity of Jews for real estate has not attracted the attention of many scholars. One exception is Nathan Glazer and Daniel P. Moynihan's *Beyond the Melting Pot: The Negroes, Puerto Ricans, Jews, Italians, and Irish of New York City.* Jews, they speculated, have gravitated to real estate because it was more open than, say, insurance and investment banking and could be run as a family operation. "Perhaps there is among Jews an accumulation of business acumen, supported by a relatively strong family system, that permits mobilization of capital (even if in small sums), and that makes it possible to move into new areas with opportunities for great growth and high profits." Walter Shorenstein asserted that real estate was an ideal industry for ambitious Jewish entrepreneurs who lacked capital and contacts. "You don't need a factory, you don't need a product, you don't have to invest in inventory, and you don't need to go to school for eight or ten years." Perhaps also there is something in the Jewish experience of geographical mobility that has influenced Jews, in contrast to Italians, to prize not land but land values.[7]

Not surprisingly, several of the wealthiest Jews made their fortunes in retailing: Leslie Wexner of The Limited, Milton Petrie of Petrie Stores, Leon Levine, the founder of Family Dollar Stores, Sy Syms Merns of the Syms retail clothing chain, Sol Price of California, and the Rosenwald family of Sears, Roebuck.

Several of the Jewish moguls are in publishing. In addition to the Newhouse brothers, there is the Annenberg family, which once owned Triangle Publications (*TV Guide, Seventeen,* and the *Daily Racing Form*), the newspaper publishers Paul and William Block, Arthur Sackler, whose wealth was partially derived from several medical magazines, and the Sulzberger family of the *New York Times.* There are also a handful of extremely wealthy Jews in the entertainment industry. Sumner Murray Redstone and Richard Alan Smith of Boston each owns a chain of movie theaters, Steven Spielberg is the most successful movie director in history, Norman Lear is an independent television producer, William Paley founded CBS, and Lew Wasserman established MCA.

It is not surprising that there are wealthy Jewish real estate investors, merchants, publishers, and entertainment moguls. But what is unexpected is the presence of wealthy Jews in American industries not generally associated with Jewish economic enterprise. Paul Kalmanovitz was a brewer, Max Fisher,

Leon Hess, the Blaustein family of Baltimore, Armand Hammer, Arthur Belfer, and Marvin Davis made their fortunes in oil, Maurice Greenberg is an insurance magnate, and Russell Berrie manufactures teddy bears.

Jews have also begun to accumulate sizable fortunes in high technology. Glazer and Moynihan predicted that the first important breakthrough of Jews in heavy industry would be in electronics and other highly technical forms of manufacturing, these being areas where Jews would profit handsomely because of their investment in education. (One can also assume that Glazer and Moynihan were pessimistic regarding the prospects of Jews storming the citadels of big business and high finance.) The emergence of the Internet has provided countless new roads to wealth, many of which do not require the initial outlay of vast sums of capital. The Jewish affinity to science and the intellectual pursuits has also encouraged young Jews to establish businesses involved in high tech.

One of the contemporary fears of American Jewish communal leaders is that too many young Jews are going into the professions and academia and not enough into business, where the real money is. From whom will Jewish philanthropies continue to receive the major gifts on which they depend if Jews desert business? (Ironically, this is the same Jewish establishment that has downplayed Jewish economic achievement and rarely held up the businessman as a role model.) Their concern seems to be needlessly alarmist. Judging from the *Forbes* list and other scattered evidence in the sociological literature, there is little indication that the American Jewish passion for "making it" has diminished.

The founders of Amoco Gas, Federated Department Stores, Hyatt Hotels, Consolidated Foods, and Levi Strauss have been as significant a part of the American Jewish experience as Louis Brandeis, Woody Allen, Saul Bellow, David Dubinsky, and Emma Goldman. These businesses should occasion pride and not embarrassment among Jews, for, as Samuel Johnson remarked in the eighteenth century, "there are few ways in which a man can be more innocently employed than in getting money."

EIGHT

The Friendly University

Jews in Academia since World War II

AS ACADEMIC CREDENTIALS PLAYED an increasingly large role in modern America, it was important for Jews, an upwardly mobile group, that anti-Semitic barriers in faculty hiring and student selection, particularly among America's elite institutions, be eliminated. That Jews in large numbers eagerly sought admission after 1945 to places such as Princeton and Yale revealed the extent of their acculturation and the nature of their Jewish identity. For a while in the 1930s and 1940s the City College of New York was known as the "Jewish Harvard." By the 1950s, however, Jews sought out the real thing. No longer did they view the Ivy League and the Seven Sisters as the enemy camp. Growing affluence enabled more Jewish parents to send their offspring to more expensive residential colleges, while acculturation convinced them that their children were deserving of the best that America had to offer. Four years spent at CCNY or Brooklyn College were not the same as four years in New Haven or Ithaca, and this was precisely why Jewish families were willing to go into debt to pay their children's tuition.

In the movie *Pete and Tillie,* the character played by Walter Matthau was asked why, since he was three-quarters Lutheran and only one-quarter Jewish, he insisted on calling himself Jewish. "I'm a social climber," he replied. Nowhere in American culture has this rise in the status of Jews been more evident than in academia. Prior to the 1960s, the presidency of the leading American universities was monopolized by white Anglo-Saxon Protestant males. In his 1966 annual report as president of the American Jewish Committee, Morris Abram claimed that not one Jew could be found among the

This chapter was previously published in *Judaism* 46 (summer 1997): 365–74. Reprinted by permission.

approximately one thousand persons who had been named president of public colleges and universities during the preceding seventeen years.[1]

Abram did not anticipate that major changes in the status of Jews within the highest levels of academia were imminent. According to the rabbi-historian Arthur Hertzberg, the universities were "the first established American institutional arena in which Jews entered and even joined the elite." It was in the Ivy League that the ascent of Jews up the academic ladder was most noticeable and remarkable. By the 1990s, only Cornell and Brown had not had a Jewish president, and by the middle of the decade five of the eight Ivy League institutions were headed by persons with a Jewish background.[2]

Perhaps the most surprising development involved Harvard University. In May 1990, Derek Bok, Harvard's president, announced his plans to retire. In the eyes of Cambridge, the Harvard presidency was the most prestigious academic position in America, if not in all the world. One is reminded of the response early in the twentieth century of the secretary of A. Lawrence Lowell, Harvard's president, to a visitor inquiring as to Lowell's whereabouts. The president, she replied, had gone to Washington to meet with Mr. Taft.[3]

After a grueling selection process in which more than seven hundred sixty applicants were considered, including Indiana University president Thomas Ehrlich and Dartmouth College president James O. Freedman, Harvard narrowed the search to four candidates: a Harvard economist, a Harvard Medical School geneticist, the provost of the University of Chicago, and the executive vice president of the Mellon Foundation. On March 24, 1991, the Harvard Corporation formally selected as its new president the Mellon Foundation official. According to reports in the *New York Times* and *Time,* the most unusual and noteworthy characteristic of Harvard's new president was that he had not attended Harvard College. (He had earned his B.A. at Princeton.) This, however, was not a fatal flaw since he had a Ph.D. from Harvard in English literature. Also of interest was the fact that his father had been a guard at Sing Sing prison.[4]

For those interested in the history and sociology of American ethnic succession, however, the most notable fact about the selection of Harvard's new president was its Jewish aspect. Two of the three unsuccessful candidates—the economist Martin Feldstein and the geneticist Philip Leder—were Jews, and the parents of the successful candidate, Neil I. Rudenstine, were a Jewish immigrant from Russia and a second-generation Italian. Moreover, the Harvard dean who had been sent to broach the idea to Rudenstine was Henry Rosovsky, who himself had been a serious candidate for the presidency until he withdrew his name from consideration. Rosovsky, the first Jew to sit on the Harvard Corporation, had been born in Danzig (now Gdansk), Poland, and was married to an Israeli. Neither the *Times* nor *Time* mentioned Rudenstine's ethnic background, evidently believing it to be unimportant.

A. Lawrence Lowell, a vice president of the Immigration Restriction League, undoubtedly rolled over in his grave after hearing of Rudenstine's appointment. Lowell was not enamored of immigrants from southern and eastern Europe, particularly Jews and Italians. "I long ago came to the conclusion that no democracy could be successful unless it was tolerably homogeneous," he said in 1918. One can only imagine Lowell's response to the successful effort in 1923 of a Philadelphia couple, Myrtle and Henry H. Kobotchnik, to change their name to Cabot. Over the opposition of the Pennsylvania branch of the Order of Founders and Patriots, the Historical Society of Pennsylvania, the Genealogical Society of Pennsylvania, and several Cabots, a judge in the Philadelphia Court of Common Pleas approved the Kobotchniks' request. One anonymous newspaper poet of the time emphasized the hardship this would cause the Lowell family.

> And this is good old Boston,
> The home of the bean and the cod.
> Where the Lowells have no one to talk to,
> Since the Cabots talk Yiddish, by God![5]

Robert Morss Lovett noted that in dealing with immigrants, Lowell was "no longer straight-forward and scrupulous, but indirect and tortuous, his behavior a mixture of insolence and cunning." The most famous example of this "cunning," besides Lowell's role in the execution of the Italian anarchists Nicola Sacco and Bartolomeo Vanzetti, was his 1922 proposal to solve Harvard's "Jew problem" by limiting the Jewish enrollment in Harvard College. Lowell claimed his suggestion had only the Jews' best interests at heart, since it would diminish the anti-Semitism caused by the Hebrew invasion of Cambridge. Actually Lowell disliked Jews, believed they could not be both Americans and Jews, and asserted that they would have to give up their "peculiar practices" if they wished to be treated equally. Lowell and other Harvard administrators claimed that Jews lacked the proper "character" for Harvard. Character denoted personality, manners, morals, and other vague qualities, which were to be used to restrict Jewish enrollment. Thus Henry Pennypacker, the chairman of Harvard's admissions committee, warned in

1926 of applicants with "extreme racial characteristics," who did not have the requisite "character, personality, and promise."[6]

Some Harvard students vigorously supported Lowell's goal of restricting Jewish enrollment at Harvard. They argued that the proper Bostonians, "the men who have made Harvard what it is today," would not continue sending their sons and bequests to Harvard if the transformation in the university's student body was not reversed. "Were it only a matter of scholarship," one group of undergraduates declared, "there could be no objection to Jews at all. But they do not mix. They destroy the unity of the college."[7]

One wonders whether Jews at Harvard who wanted to "mix" would have been welcomed by those undergraduates for whom Harvard was almost a family possession. A group of students even reproached the aristocratic Grenville Clark for conducting a tour during World War II of the Porcellian Club, Harvard's most elite undergraduate club. That Clark's guest was Dwight D. Eisenhower hardly justified such chutzpah. After all, Eisenhower's boss, Franklin D. Roosevelt, had not been good enough to make Porcellian when he had been a Harvard undergraduate.[8]

The history of Jews at Columbia, Princeton, and Yale paralleled their history at Harvard. Columbia's "Jewish problem" had been more acute than any other Ivy League institution because its location in New York City made it particularly attractive to the city's huge Jewish population. A college song of the 1910s expressed the common view that Columbia was overrun with Jews.

> Oh, Harvard's run by millionaires,
> And Yale is run by booze.
> Cornell is run by farmers' sons,
> Columbia's run by Jews.
> So give a cheer for Baxter Street,
> Another one for Pell.
> And when the little sheenies die,
> Their souls will go to hell.[9]

As early as the eve of World War I, Columbia officials expressed concern that, as a result of the university's large Jewish enrollment, future members of the American social and economic elite would enroll at other institutions, such as Williams and Amherst, where there were few Jews. At this time about 40 percent of Columbia's undergraduate students were Jews. "Isn't Columbia overrun with European Jews, who are most unpleasant persons socially?" Dean Frederick P. Keppel of Columbia College asked rhetorically. In response to such fears, Columbia pioneered in devising means to limit the Jewish invasion. These included geographical quotas, personal interviews, tests for "character," and a requirement that applicants furnish photographs and their mothers' maiden names. Other universities followed Columbia's example, confident that these stratagems would enable them to weed out undesirables. Six decades later, Columbia University chose Michael Sovern, who grew up in the Bronx near Yankee Stadium, to be its president. Had he applied to Columbia College between the world wars he might have been turned down because of the unpleasant social traits associated with Eastern European Jews.

In 1987 Princeton University appointed Harold T. Shapiro to succeed William G. Bowen as its president. (Rudenstine had been rumored to be Bowen's successor, but he chose to accompany Bowen to the Mellon Foundation.) A native of Montreal, where his family owned Ruby Foo's, the city's most elegant and expensive Chinese restaurant, Shapiro had earned a Ph.D. in economics from Princeton. He was president of the University of Michigan at the time of his appointment, and he was a leading candidate for the presidency of Yale before he withdrew his name from consideration when the Princeton presidency became open. This was the second time that a Jew jilted Yale.

The selection of Shapiro was a quantum leap in the social mobility of Jews. Princeton was probably the most socially exclusive of American universities, and it had always prided itself on its cachet. When the *Social Register* began publishing early in the twentieth century, it chose Princeton's colors, orange and black, for its binding. Princeton's selective admissions policy, its informal quota for Jewish applicants, and its eating clubs reinforced its elitist reputation. The class of 1935, for example, had only five Jews, and the university's Jewish students were made to feel that, as a group, they were aliens and lacked status.[10]

Princeton's pecking order was most evident in its eating clubs, where undergraduates took their meals and relaxed. The social status of undergraduates was indicated by the clubs to which they belonged. Few Jews were invited to join the most prestigious clubs. During World War II the university's administration insisted that all students, even Jews, who applied for membership in an eating club must be placed. It would have been embarrassing for Princeton if Jews and other undesirables were blackballed at the same time that their relatives and friends were fighting in defense of Princeton and the American way of life. This system worked well until 1958, when twenty-three students failed to receive bids from any of the seventeen eating clubs. More than half of these were Jews.[11]

It soon became clear that the Jews had been rejected because the clubmen considered them to be excessively bookish, lacking in the social graces, and ill at ease among their social betters. These were the same complaints that had been voiced at other Ivy League institutions prior to World War II. Jews, one Princeton undergraduate declared, were academic "grinds" and "poor mixers who did not fit well into a purely social organization." The preppy anti-intellectualism that characterized Princeton, the "country club of the Ivy League," would dissipate in the following decades.[12]

Yale's selection of a Jewish president came later than that of Harvard, Columbia, and Princeton, but it was not for lack of trying. In 1977, Henry Rosovsky rejected the Yale presidency over the protests of his wife. (He also rejected the presidency of the University of Chicago that same year.) Yale then turned to A. Bartlett Giamatti, a member of its modern language faculty. Although half Italian, Giamatti was at least a Protestant. After serving as its president for a decade, Giamatti deserted Yale for his first love, baseball, becoming president of the National League. He would move on from that position to become the commissioner of major league baseball.

Prior to World War II, Yale's leaders would never have considered people named Rosovsky and Giamatti. Yale's unofficial policy was to limit the Jewish presence among its faculty and students. No Jew received tenure on the Yale College faculty before World War II. As was true of other Ivy League institutions, Yale feared that its traditional student clientele could not or would not compete with intellectually aggressive and ambitious Jews. According to Robert N. Corwin, chairman of Yale's admission committee in 1922, Yale's typical Jewish student was "as naked of all the attributes of refinement and honor as when born into it. His wits have probably been sharpened but he has not gained wisdom, at least not the kind expected of college men." Corwin forgot to mention that Jews, more than any other group, were also the most likely to be able to read the Hebrew inscription on the Yale seal.[13]

Yale's officials pondered whether the university would be able to civilize its Jewish students before its Jewish students Judaized Yale. Roswell Angier, a psychologist and the dean of freshman, claimed that Jews "are more or less in the nature of a foreign body in the class organism. They contribute very little to class life." Frederick S. Jones, dean of Yale College, also feared the impact of Jews on Yale. "We should do something to improve them. If we do not educate them, they will overrun us," he exclaimed in 1918. "We have got to change our policies and get them into shape. A few years ago every single scholarship of any value was won by a Jew. . . . We must put a ban on the Jews." Jones suggested that Jewish upperclassmen be denied honorary scholarships, since these had been established by and for Christians, and he blamed Jews for the worsening academic performance of Yale's Gentile students. Christians, he claimed, refused to compete for academic honors if it meant having to match wits with "greasy grind" Jews. Seven decades after Jones made this statement, the dean of Yale College would be a distinguished classical historian named Donald Kagan, a Jew born in Lithuania with a B.A. degree from Brooklyn College.[14]

Yale's effort to restrict Jewish enrollment was supported by the student-run *Yale Daily News.* A 1926 editorial claimed that Yale should "institute immigration laws more prohibitive than those of the United States government." This would filter out the "unkempt" and prevent Yale from being transformed into "a brains plant." The paper proposed that Yale go even further than Columbia and Harvard, which required prospective freshmen to submit personal photographs. Yale should demand that applicants furnish photographs of their fathers as well! While the Yale administration did not go that far, it did drastically reduce the number of Jewish undergraduates. The class of 1927 was 13.3 percent Jewish, but the class of 1934 was only 8.2 percent Jewish. Eugene Rostow, while an undergraduate at Yale in the early 1930s, strenuously protested Yale's anti-Jewish policy. Three decades later he was dean of the Yale Law School.[15]

In April 1993, Yale selected Richard C. Levin, one of Roswell Angier's "foreign" bodies, as its president. Previously Levin had been chairman of Yale's economics department and dean of its Graduate School of Arts and Sciences. Yale's new leader had precisely the "unkempt" and "brains plant" traits that the *Yale Daily News* had condemned seven decades earlier. His family background contrasted dramatically with that of the northeast Protestant social and economic establishment from which Yale had traditionally drawn its leaders. Levin's father was a salesman for a liquor importer, and his mother's family owned a theatrical costume company. After graduating from Stanford, he did postgraduate work at Oxford, where he knew Bill Clinton, and then received a Ph.D. in economics from Yale.

Jewish enrollment at Yale, Harvard, Princeton, and Columbia increased dramatically after World War II. By the 1970s, approximately one-quarter of their undergraduates were Jews. Jewish enrollment at the other four Ivy

League schools also increased. Princeton's Hillel chapter even assisted the university's admission office in recruiting Jewish students. A comment in 1962 by Yale's dean of admissions reflected this change in policy. When asked by a prospective Orthodox student whether eating kosher would be held against him, he responded, "Absolutely not, although it's something you might want to hold against us." A few years later Yale's Whiffenpoof singers selected an Orthodox Jew to join its ranks. Much to the surprise of old Yalies in the audiences, he wore a skullcap during concerts.[16]

With a larger percentage of Jewish students, the Ivy League institutions became more sensitive to Jewish concerns such as providing kosher food, exempting Jews from Saturday examinations and classes, and not scheduling university events on Jewish holidays. In 1985, for the first time in its history, Princeton rescheduled the opening day of classes so that it would not conflict with the Jewish New Year. When one of Harvard's commencements in the 1980s inadvertently fell on the Jewish holiday of Shavuoth, the university vowed this would never happen again. The increase in Jewish enrollment resulted in an active Jewish cultural life on Ivy League campuses. Princeton students sponsored a Jewish quarterly newspaper, Israeli and Yiddish film festivals, a Hebrew choir, lectures and concerts, religious services ranging from Reform to Orthodox, and a "free Jewish University" offering a variety of courses in Judaism and Jewish culture. Princeton also had a kosher kitchen. It was dedicated in 1971 on the eve of Hanukkah, a holiday that celebrates the Jewish victory over Hellenism.[17]

These Jewish activities were due not only to the increased number of Jews on the campus but also to the fact that Jewish students, in contrast to their parents and grandparents, were not reluctant to display publicly their Jewishness. It was common to see Jewish students in skullcaps walking across college campuses. In responding to complaints that Jews controlled Brown University's newspaper, the paper published a tongue-in-cheek editorial assuring Gentiles that they would not meet prejudice if they wished to work on it. Jewish professors and administrators were also more vigorous in making their Jewish identity visible and in protesting policies that worked against Jews. Several Harvard law professors opened a kosher delicatessen in Harvard Square in the late 1980s called Maven's Kosher Court. Another Harvard professor publicly objected to the university's admission policy that, as one university official explained, was designed to limit the number of students from the "donut" suburban communities surrounding the large eastern cities. They were not donuts, the professor said. They were "bagels."[18]

The increased Jewish presence in academia was equally impressive within the faculty. Prior to the 1940s, Jewish professors were a rarity in the elite universities. This was also true in England and Germany. Until the late nineteenth century, Oxford and Cambridge were Anglican institutions providing a liberal education for a privileged class destined for the clergy or government service. Protestant dissenters, Roman Catholics, and Jews were excluded both as students and as dons. Only when the control of the Church loosened in the late nineteenth century were non-Anglicans made to feel welcome at Oxbridge, and it would not be until half a century later that there would be a significant number of Jewish students and faculty at the two universities.[19]

Jews were also unwelcome in German universities during the late nineteenth and early twentieth centuries. One of the tasks of the German university was the inculcation of *bildung*—culture and cultivation—that, it was widely believed, was alien to the Jewish temperament. Although there were many Jews in the lower professorial ranks, it was very difficult for them to become associate and full professors. Academic advancement required recommendations by full professors, and these were often hard to secure. The eminent sociologist Robert Michels was forced to accept a position in Italy despite the efforts of his teacher Max Weber to secure him an academic appointment. The sociologist Georg Simmel became a professor in 1914 when he was fifty-six years old, four years before his death. The eminent philosopher Ernst Cassirer made full professor only when he was forty-five, and then at the new University of Hamburg.

"In Germany," Weber said, "the freedom of learning exists only within the limits of officially accepted political and religious views." German academia, the historian Fritz K. Ringer has shown, was a highly integrated, homogeneous nationalistic "mandarin" community. German professors were united by "their common educational background, their social status, and the threat to their position which . . . they all felt deeply." To some, Jews were a force for national decomposition. The historian Georg von Below, for example, argued that Jews tended "to acquire influence by indulging and arousing the instincts of the proletariat and to make unpatriotic politics with this influence." Not surprisingly, Jewish intellectuals often found careers outside the university—in journalism, publishing, private institutions, and, as in Michels's case, by leaving Germany.[20]

As was true for many other aspects of American life, World War II was a watershed for higher education. Encouraged by the GI bill of rights and by the economic opportunities available to those with undergraduate and advanced degrees, college enrollments soared after 1945. With universities competing for personnel with a booming private sector, religious and ethnic barriers in the hiring and retention of faculty were lowered. Jewish academicians also benefited from the revulsion against all forms of anti-Semitism, including the elitist anti-Semitism of academia, that occurred after the Holocaust. Prodded by Jewish organizations, New York, Massachusetts, and other states outlawed discrimination in employment and college admissions after the war. The federal government also looked askance at anti-Semitism in higher education. These political pressures were particularly important because the federal and state governments rapidly increased their funding of higher education. With the doors of academia now ajar, Jews interested in a teaching career no longer had to settle, as they had during the 1930s, for positions in second-rate institutions or in secondary education. Jews, who had made up only 2 percent of America's professors in 1940, were 10 percent of academia by the 1970s.[21]

Jewish professors were notable not only for their increased numbers but also for their high academic status. A 1937 report of the American Jewish Committee had noted that it was "very difficult these days for Jews to become full professors in the leading universities." Less than four decades later the sociologists Everett Carll Ladd Jr. and Seymour Martin Lipset said that by every possible criteria, Jewish academicians had "far surpassed their Gentiles colleagues." Jews tended to publish more frequently, were more committed to research, were promoted at an earlier age, and made more money than their colleagues. They also tended to be in the most intellectually demanding fields, particularly those stressing abstract and theoretical reasoning. They gravitated to anthropology, economics, history, mathematics, physics, and sociology, rather than agriculture, education, home economics, journalism, library science, nursing, and physical education. Electrical engineering, the most theoretical branch of engineering, had a greater proportion of Jews than mechanical, civil, or chemical engineering. Jews were particularly numerous in the teaching of medicine and in allied disciplines such as biochemistry, bacteriology, physiology, and psychology.[22]

A greater appreciation of ethnic, cultural, and religious diversity within the university was another cause of the increased Jewish presence in academia. One aspect of the democratization of academia was recounted by Ari L. Goldman, the former religion reporter of the *New York Times,* in *The Search for God at Harvard,* a memoir of the year he spent as a student at the Harvard Divinity School. For a century and a half the HDS had been a bastion for the training of Protestant clergy. Goldman was amazed that his first act in 1985 as an HDS student was attending the funeral mass of the school's acting dean, George W. MacRae, a Jesuit priest who had died while leading a spiritual retreat at a Catholic seminary.[23]

Changes in the culture of the elite universities also opened up these institutions to members of previously excluded racial, religious, ethnic, and gender groups. Before World War II they had been self-consciously Protestant institutions committed to the education and cultivation of America's future economic, political, and cultural elite. Jews were perceived to be guests who had been admitted at the sufferance of their hosts. The presence of imposing Gothic chapels and divinity schools on the campuses of Yale, Princeton, Duke, Harvard, and the University of Chicago attested to their Christian character. It was not until 1926 that Yale abolished compulsory chapel for its students, but this did not eliminate the university's image of itself as a Christian institution. Charles Seymour stated in his 1938 inaugural address on becoming the president of Yale that "Yale was dedicated to the upraising of spiritual leaders. . . . The simple and direct way is through the maintenance and upbuilding of the Christian religion as a vital part of university life."[24]

After 1945, however, these universities, along with Oxford and Cambridge in England, became almost totally secular institutions little interested in their charges' character and moral and religious development. Christianity, the historian George M. Marsden wrote, became not merely peripheral to higher education "but also often came to be considered absolutely alien to whatever is important to the enterprise." The task of the universities now was perceived to be fostering intellectual distinction as defined by scientific and professional criteria. The modern research university, which began in the late nineteenth century when the nation's leading universities established graduate schools and began awarding the Ph.D. degree, became the standard for judging academic excellence. "In the light of such commitments," Marsden notes, "academic expressions of Christianity seemed at best superfluous and at worst unscientific and unprofessional." The exclusion of Jewish "brains plants" from this meritocracy ran counter to the new academic ideals. In addition, the country's leading universities aspired to be national institutions, and this required the attenuating of parochial religious attachments. One indication of the spirit of secularism pervading the academy (and the country) was Harvey Cox's 1965 book, *The Secular City,* which sold more than a quarter of a million copies. Although a professor at the Harvard Divinity School, Cox celebrated the secularization of the university and firmly rejected the notion of Christian higher education. The effort to retain a Christian presence in the academy, he wrote, was a "cumulative catastrophe."[25]

The social disabilities that previously had made Jews unwelcome on the campus had also become less important. Their supposedly uncouth urban manners and their reputation as academic grinds no longer stamped them as outsiders to the new university ethos. The lack of interest of Jews in athletics fit in well with the Ivy League's de-emphasizing of sports, particularly football. The elite universities no longer included among their responsibilities the inculcation of bravery and physical prowess.

The friendlier attitude of America's elite universities toward Jews was also due to changes in the values and behavior of Jews themselves. Jews no longer stood out from other students as a result of their acculturation, their movement up the social and economic ladder, and their migration from Jewish neighborhoods in the inner cities to suburbia. Their personalities, interests, values, and mannerisms no longer bore the mark of the ghetto. Indeed, the unofficial arbiters of American manners were now two sisters of Eastern European Jewish background who went under the names Dear Abby and Ann Landers.

The emphasis on merit that enabled Jews to advance in academia both as students and as faculty did not go unchallenged. In the 1970s and 1980s the major objection to the principle of merit came not from old-line Americans wishing to restore their prewar position, but from blacks, Hispanics, feminists, and other aggrieved minorities. Devaluing traditional indicators of competence, they sought through what the Harvard sociologist Nathan Glazer called "affirmative discrimination" and what they termed "affirmative action" to increase the number of students and faculty from among those who were otherwise unqualified on the basis of impersonal tests, publications, and degrees. Those concerned with maintaining academic integrity argued that affirmative action would lower academic standards, devalue academic degrees, create an academic spoils system, and balkanize education into competing ethnic, racial, gender, religious, and political factions. For Jews, affirmative action was reminiscent of the anti-Jewish quotas of European and American universities prior to World War II, and they feared it would close an important avenue of social ascent. Ironically, affirmative action was encouraged, or at least tacitly accepted, by some Jewish academicians and administrators, whose own advancement had resulted from the spread of the merit principle.[26]

A particularly egregious example of this was Stephen Steinberg, a sociologist at the City University of New York. Steinberg's book *The Ethnic Myth* strongly protested the opposition of Jewish organizations to affirmative action. According to Steinberg, Jews were "privileged" because they had the economic and educational prerequisites to take advantage of the meritocracy of academia. Members of other groups, however, who through no fault of their own lacked these prerequisites, were excluded from the university. Steinberg termed this "institutionalized racism." He maintained there was little resemblance between the quotas favored by A. Lawrence Lowell that had sought to exclude Jews and affirmative action that sought to open up academia to hitherto barred groups.

The fact that some individuals were hurt by affirmative action just as Jews had been hurt by pre–World War II quotas was "the price of a societal commitment to achieving racial parity in the professions." While some whites might be injured in the process, "it is due not to racism, but to an effort to combat racism." Steinberg asked fellow Jews whether they "will erect barriers behind them to protect their hard-won gains, or whether they will continue their historic battle against privilege." Such idealism was small consolation to those who, in contrast to Steinberg, lacked an academic position, much less tenure, and had only the comfort of knowing that they were being discriminated against for supposedly benign reasons.[27]

The Ethnic Myth clearly delineated the differences between the proponents and opponents of affirmative action. On the one side were those such as Steinberg who talked in terms of societal commitments, racial disparities, and the historic claims that blacks, women, and other groups have on American society. On the other side were those who believed that the purpose of law is to protect individuals, that the interests of individuals should not be sacrificed for the sake of abstractions such as ethnic, racial, and gender egalitarianism no matter how well-meaning these abstractions might be, that people should be judged on their own qualifications and not as members of a group, and that government policy should encourage the removal of all barriers that limit individual opportunities. Affirmative action, it was argued, is antithetical to the merit principle, which is the basis of the modern university. It is no coincidence that the successful campaign in 1996 to amend the California state constitution to forbid discriminatory practices by the state and local governments was initiated by two academicians.

A major effect of affirmative action has been to intensify the politicizing of the university. Some of its proponents argue that the university is a political institution, and as such, political considerations as well as intellectual distinction should be taken into consideration in the hiring and tenuring of faculty and in the admission of students. Opponents of affirmative action, on the other hand, agree with Randolph Bourne's 1913 statement that "scholarship is fundamentally democratic. Before the bar of marks and grades, penniless adventurer and rich man's son stand equal." Jews have a particularly good reason for opposing affirmative action. Making up less than 3 percent of the population, they are not in a good bargaining position if academic decisions are to be based on ethnic and racial considerations. The future of Jews (and Asians) in American academia will be determined in part by the extent to which the university remains faithful to the ideal of merit. As yet it does not appear that their proportionately high representation in the academy has been significantly affected by affirmative action. Whether this will continue to be true remains to be seen. Election returns and surveys of public opinion seem to indicate that there are good reasons to be cautiously optimistic about the future.[28]

N I N E

Orthodoxy in Pleasantdale

PRIOR TO THE 1970s, most sociologists and historians of American Judaism believed Orthodoxy to be a transient first-generation, urban phenomenon that would not follow American Jews as they poured after World War II onto the crabgrass trail leading to the land of split-level houses, patios, and outdoor barbecues. Thus Albert I. Gordon's *Jews in Suburbia* noted as early as 1959 that "Jews in suburbia are preponderantly non-Orthodox in religious ideas and practices." Orthodoxy, it was commonly believed, would play no role in the evolution of American Jewish identity in modern America. Only Americanized versions of Judaism would survive the acculturation of American Jewry.[1]

The classic sociological argument for the irrelevance of Orthodoxy in America is Louis Wirth's *The Ghetto* (1928), a revised version of his University of Chicago dissertation. Wirth's teachers at Chicago, particularly Robert E. Park, believed the removal of discrimination against immigrants would result in ethnic assimilation. Wirth agreed. The "medieval rabbinism" of Orthodoxy, he avowed, had little appeal for second-generation American Jews, who were bored by its rituals and resentful of its restrictions. For him, Orthodoxy was solely a lower-class and foreign phenomenon. American Jews would abandon it as they prospered and moved out of the immigrant ghetto. This analysis was not value-free. Wirth was an ardent assimilationist, and the demise of Orthodoxy was a development he eagerly anticipated.

The postwar suburbanization of American Jewry was accompanied by the growth of the Conservative movement, whose large temples attracted upwardly mobile professionals in the midst of family formation and flight from the inner city. Suburbanites tended to identify Orthodoxy with the world

This chapter was previously published in *Judaism* 34 (spring 1985): 163–70. Reprinted by permission.

from which they were escaping: crowded urban living conditions, the poverty and Yiddish speech of their parents, and archaic European religious practices. The Conservative and, to a smaller extent, the Reform movements provided the suburbanites with a religious and ethnic identity and a decorous and elevated religious rite that comported with their newly acquired economic and social status. Orthodoxy, it was predicted, was fated to become an anachronism, a victim of its own obscurantist ideology, its inability to transplant itself to suburbia, and the inexorable processes of immigrant acculturation. When in 1966 Immanuel Jakobovits resigned the pulpit of the Fifth Avenue Synagogue in New York to become the chief rabbi of Great Britain, he recalled that the major challenge he faced when he arrived in New York in 1958 had been "to make Orthodoxy elegant and fashionable and to show that you don't have to live on the Lower East Side in squalor to be a strictly traditional Jew." Despite his efforts, the popular and scholarly correlation of Orthodoxy with low social and economic status persisted.

The last two decades, however, have confounded these prophecies of Orthodox ruin. Orthodoxy has managed to put down roots in the suburbs of virtually all major American cities. For the first time in American history, wrote the sociologist Solomon Poll in 1969, "second and third generation Jewish Americans followed the social and religious patterns of their parents." An Orthodox "edifice complex" resulted in the construction of numerous spacious suburban synagogues, day schools, yeshivot, and mikvehs (ritual baths). The suburbanization of Orthodoxy occurred at the same time as the emergence of the *baal teshuvah* movement, the growing influence of the yeshiva world on American Orthodoxy, and the coming to maturity of the children of the Holocaust survivors. These developments revitalized American Orthodoxy, particularly in the New York area with its many yeshivahs and large Holocaust population.[2]

Since 1969 I have lived in the Pleasantdale section of West Orange, New Jersey, and have been a member of Congregation Ahawas Achim, B'nai Jacob and David. It is by far the largest Orthodox synagogue in Essex County, which encompasses Newark and its environs. West Orange, located six miles west of Newark and fifteen miles west of New York City, is within five miles of the Garden State Parkway, the state's major north–south highway, while Route 280, one of the most important east–west highways in the northern part of the state, bisects Pleasantdale. A variety of buses and trains connect Pleasantdale to downtown Newark and New York. Commuting to New York by public transportation takes approximately one hour.

Pleasantdale, along with Teaneck and Englewood in Bergen County and Fair Lawn and Passaic in Passaic County, is convenient for young Orthodox couples contemplating a move to New Jersey suburbia. The community has a roomy synagogue and a mikveh located across the street from the synagogue. Several day schools and yeshivot provide busing for West Orange children. In 1969 Pleasantdale did not have a sufficient Orthodox population to support stores catering to Orthodox needs. Now it has a kosher bakery, a kosher delicatessen, and a kosher restaurant, and neighboring Livingston has two kosher restaurants. The local supermarkets stock a variety of kosher and kosher-for-Passover products.

Pleasantdale was not always like this. Its initial claim to Jewish fame was as an alternative to the borscht belt. It had several hotels and boardinghouses, which Jews from New York and Newark visited in search of fresh air and good food. Today the hotels and boardinghouses are gone. The last hotel was purchased by Italian Americans in the 1970s, and its name was changed from Goldman's to The Town and Campus. As late as 1948 only thirteen hundred Jews lived in all of West Orange, of which Pleasantdale is a small part; ten years later the town's Jewish population had increased to seven thousand.

Much of this growth consisted of refugees from Newark. During these ten years, Newark's Jewish population declined from fifty-seven thousand to forty-one thousand. Philip Roth, the poet laureate of Newark Jewry, described in "Goodbye, Columbus" the process whereby Jews "had struggled and prospered, and moved further and further west, towards the edge of Newark, then out of it, and up the slope of the Orange Mountains, until they had reached the crest and started down the other side, pouring into Gentiles territory as the Scotch-Irish had poured through the Cumberland Gap."

Perhaps half of West Orange's growth in Jewish population after World War II was in Pleasantdale. The Conservative Jewish Center of West Orange, located in Pleasantdale, had fewer than 40 families in 1933, when it acquired its first structure, and only 45 families as late as 1945. It grew rapidly after the war. By 1950 it had 150 families, and by 1958 there were 600 families on its membership rolls. Rabbi Stuart E. Rosenberg's autobiography, *The Real Jewish World: A Rabbi's Second Thoughts,* contains a corrosive portrait of Pleasantdale Jewish life during World War II prior to this demographic explosion. Rosenberg was then a student at the Jewish Theological Seminary and served as the community's weekend rabbi. Pleasantdale in the 1940s, Rosenberg wrote, was "a foretaste of all that was . . . wrong with 'suburban Judaism' in America." For one thousand dollars a year, Rosenberg was the *rov* of West

Orange, conducting services on Friday night, Saturday morning and evening, and Sunday morning, and teaching the children on Wednesday afternoon and Sunday morning. He thoroughly detested the experience. His congregants, having moved to West Orange for its suburban lifestyle, were ignorant of Jewish culture, theology, and history and were mainly concerned with securing a modicum of *yiddishkeit* for their children. They led a vicarious Jewish existence, basking in the glow of their rabbi's religiosity.[3]

Sabbath services were poorly attended, and they frequently lacked a minyan. Rosenberg attributed this not merely to a lack of interest but also to his congregants' embarrassment over their ignorance of Hebrew and Jewish ritual. He recounts the time when the president of the congregation was called to the *bimah* after the weekly portion had been read in order to place the crown on top of the Torah. Not knowing what to do with the crown, he became flustered and finally put it on his own head. "I knew then," Rosenberg said, "that I could not spend the rest of my life in suburbia, teaching grown-ups materials that were really intended for children." He believed that he was supervising a "super-kindergarten." Looking back forty years later, he continues to see a barren suburban Jewish landscape and wonders whether Jews are ready to "finally settle down to a maturer and deeper Jewish life."

Until the 1960s there was no Orthodox presence in Pleasantdale. Then, as a result of the inevitable quarrel within the Jewish Center, dissident elements left it, merged with an Orthodox Newark synagogue seeking to relocate to the suburbs, and held services in a building that previously had served as an animal hospital. Soon the new congregation purchased a Baptist church (steeple and all) on Pleasant Valley Way, the area's major thoroughfare. In 1969, it had fewer than twenty Sabbath-observant families. By 1985 it had approximately one hundred fifty observant families, and by 1998 more than four hundred such families. Some of these families are headed by children of Holocaust survivors. As the Orthodox congregations of Newark folded, several merged with Ahawas Achim. A local joke is that the "Cong." in the synagogue name refers to "conglomerate" and not to "congregation." In addition to Ahawas Achim, Pleasantdale also has a small Young Israel synagogue with about twenty families, which relocated from Orange, and a new congregation, Ohr Torah, which was established in the 1990s and is located a mile and a quarter north of the main synagogue on Pleasant Valley Way. Pleasantdale thus has the variety of congregations that every Orthodox community requires: the one I attend and the ones I wouldn't step foot into.

The most salient characteristics of Pleasantdale's Orthodox are their advanced education, affluence, and large families. The average number of children per family is more than three, and families with five or six children are not unusual. The classic sociological relationship between Orthodoxy and poverty is certainly not true of Pleasantdale or of other new suburban Orthodox communities. As a matter of fact, one of the problems facing Pleasantdale's Orthodox has been to carry out the religious commandments to provide food for the poor on Purim and Passover. Poor Jews are not to be found in Pleasantdale, and it is necessary that the local rabbis forward the money to the needy in Israel and elsewhere.

Suburban affluence stems from the professional status of the Pleasantdale Orthodox, who include physicians, accountants, lawyers, computer programmers, engineers, and a large number of scientists working in New Jersey's chemical and pharmaceutical industries. As befits a congregation including many scientists, the handing out of honors on the Sabbath is computerized. Very few of the Pleasantdale Orthodox work in business and the trades, which was the usual place for employment for the first-generation Orthodox. Nor does the community have many teachers and academicians.

It is not surprising that many of Pleasantdale's Orthodox population are scientists since science poses less of a threat to traditional Judaism than do the humanities. One wonders whether religious fundamentalists gravitate to the sciences or whether science-oriented individuals find it easier to accept the intellectual demands of Orthodoxy. The scientific orientation of the Orthodox is responsible, in part, for the community's intellectual flaccidity, a characteristic that, according to the sociologist Charles Liebman, afflicts Yeshiva University also, the major American modern Orthodox institution and the alma mater of the congregation's rabbi and many of its members.

The social background and religious commitment of Pleasantdale's Orthodox determines the character of their children's higher education. Actually, "education" is a misnomer. There is very little desire for education per se. Instead, education is viewed in its most pragmatic and instrumental sense. For the Orthodox, the university is a place where their children can be trained in a profession as expeditiously as possible. There is little understanding of the university years as a time for playing with ideas, for intellectual challenges, and for ideological dialogue. In fact, education, in contrast to professional training, is suspect since it is seen as a threat to religious pieties and could lead to intermarriage. This anti-intellectualism is strengthened by the social background of many of Pleasantdale's Orthodox, which leads them to place an inordinate importance on financial success. Thus, many of Pleasantdale's young end up at Touro, Stern College, or Yeshiva College, the triad of New York's Orthodox colleges, where they will be safe from intellectual contamination and can receive preprofessional training.

The Orthodox of Pleasantdale are what sociologists have termed "Modern Orthodox." The community also has a small number of sectarian Orthodox, who are oriented toward the world of the yeshiva. No problem has troubled the community more than defining its own identity, of locating itself within the Orthodox spectrum, and of relating itself to the general Jewish population. In this they are not unique. Modern Orthodox Jews, Samuel C. Heilman has written, "stand between two sources of stigmatization: the contemporary, which considers their Orthodoxy a stigma, and the traditional Orthodox community which looks upon their modernity with disapproval. As such, modern Orthodox Jews have only themselves."[4]

Pleasantdale believes it is situated between the general mass of largely indifferent Jews who are on the road to assimilation and Orthodox right-wing sectarians who are an anachronism in modern suburbia. The sectarian Orthodox are a constant reminder to Pleasantdale of the extent to which it falls short of being truly Orthodox. At stake is Pleasantdale's view of itself as a legitimate Orthodox community. On the other hand, there is a communal fear of becoming "black hat," of moving too far to the right. Boro Park, Brooklyn, with its completely encapsulated right-wing Orthodox life, is an anti-model for the Modern Orthodox. Ahawas Achim once even sponsored a Friday night Oneg Shabbat at which the topic for discussion was whether Pleasantdale was doomed to become another Boro Park.

Thus, the stance of the Pleasantdale Orthodox is ambivalence—defining themselves as Orthodox, guilty for not being more traditional, willingly participating in the delights of contemporary secular culture, and suspicious of the non-Orthodox and their sectarian coreligionists. They fit the pattern described by Heilman as "cosmopolitan parochialism." Compartmentalization, the dividing of lives into Jewish and secular existences, enables Pleasantdale's Orthodox to deal with the antithetical impulses of modernity and tradition. Another way is through hypocrisy. The famous aphorism that hypocrisy is the tribute that vice pays to virtue fits certain aspects of Pleasantdale's religious life. Thus, the constitution of Ahawas Achim states that the congregation must follow the Shulhan Arukh (the code of Jewish law). This, however, is not taken seriously since it would be too divisive and would violate the community's religious consensus. "The Modern Orthodox Jew," Heilman wrote, "has learned to live with the sociological ambivalence inherent in his dualistic identity. A genuine *homo duplex,* burnished with a cosmopolitan parochialism, he waits for the Messiah to solve his problem."[5]

A few families have left Pleasantdale because it was insufficiently Orthodox. They wanted a higher voltage religious environment in which to raise their families. Most families, however, are familiar with the community's religious ethos before moving in and have no difficulty reconciling the conflicting demands of Orthodoxy and modernity. They may fail to come to terms with what Heilman calls "the sociological ambivalence inherent in (their) dualistic identity," yet they do not exhibit that "patterned desperation" that, he believes, characterizes Modern Orthodoxy.

The fear that Pleasantdale might go "black hat" is unrealistic in light of the sociological and economic background of its residents. While there have been divisive religious issues within Pleasantdale, these have been debated within a religious consensus. This consensus moved gradually to the right during the 1970s, 1980s, and 1990s as a result of the settling in Pleasantdale of a more right-wing Modern Orthodox element. The divisiveness within Pleasantdale's Orthodox is a microcosm of the divisiveness within the larger American Orthodox community, and it stems from the same source—religious one-upmanship. Status among the Orthodox comes in part from being more religious than one's neighbor. This results in continual religious bickering, which is viewed with incomprehension, if not ridicule, by the non-Orthodox. This need for religious status is particularly prevalent among newer and younger members of the community who are less affluent and influential than those who have lived in Pleasantdale longer. One achieves religious status by the size and nature of one's *kippot,* by wearing a tallis over the head during the silent devotion, and by *shokel*ing (rocking back and forth during prayer). The religious consensus excludes the wearing of black hats during services, although guests often wear them.[6]

One important religious issue that has bedeviled Ahawas Achim (and this is true of other Modern Orthodox congregations as well) is the size and configuration of its *mehizah,* the barrier separating men from women during prayer. The controversy over it is an opportunity for members to voice their religiosity without significantly changing their lifestyle. Quarrels over the *mehizah* and other religious items are symbolic, resembling the interminable sectarian infighting between obscure left-wing sects that marked American radicalism during the 1930s, but nevertheless are quite intense because the stakes are so small.

The role of the rabbi at a Modern Orthodox congregation such as

Ahawas Achim is not an enviable one. The laity are constantly on the alert for rabbinic religious transgressions that can be a source of status for themselves ("I am even more religious than the rabbi"). Denigration of the rabbi provides psychic pleasure to those seeking religious recognition, and the problem is accentuated when, as in the case of Ahawas Achim, the rabbi emeritus had at one time filled a pulpit in a Conservative congregation. Furthermore, Ahawas Achim has many members who believed, rightly or not, that their ritual observance and knowledge of Torah were superior to that of the rabbi.

Buffeted by the left and right and fearful of splitting the congregation, Ahawas Achim's rabbi emeritus had adopted a tactic of compromise and movement by consensus, a tactic that also suited him temperamentally. This was most evident in his Sabbath sermons. A learned Talmudic discourse would go over the heads of many of his listeners and cause concern that he was going "black hat." He thus was forced to pitch his message to the lowest common denominator. The sermons focused on innocuous topics such as support for Israel, eliminating community gossip, and the need for silence during prayer. A constant theme was the need for greater unity among Jews and the danger of dissension. (Ahawas Achim means "brotherly love.") Throughout there was a reluctance to discuss theology, ideology, or halachic observance because of the possibility of antagonizing some of the listeners. The rabbi, a graduate of Yeshiva University, fit Charles Liebman's description of the typical YU product: "church-oriented, communally involved, and very much aware of the necessity for compromise." He presented no threat to the congregation's cultural dissonance.[7]

Paralleling the rightward movement in American Judaism generally, Ahawas Achim moved to the right, but only after a consensus was reached. This did not satisfy everyone, particularly those whom the historian Jeffrey Gurock has called the "fellow-traveling Orthodox." Several of the congregation's original families, uncomfortable with its shift to the right, left the synagogue to join the West Orange Jewish Center. The most serious threats to congregational unity, however, came from the right wing, among the "card-carrying Orthodox." Almost any occasion had the potential to cause religious dissension. Thus when a dinner was held to honor the person responsible for building the new *mikveh,* a group insisted on separate seating for themselves and for their wives, even though the dinner's major speaker, an Orthodox rabbi, sat at a table with women. These same individuals also refused to eat meat at the dinner, despite the fact that the caterer was *glatt* kosher and a member of the congregation. What better opportunity to exhibit one's religiosity than at a mikveh dinner?

The synagogue's annual dinner also was a source of divisiveness. A strict interpretation of halacha forbids mixed dancing, yet for years Ahawas Achim's annual dinner had both social and traditional Jewish dancing. At one time the synagogue even had square dances. As the community moved to the right, the amount of social dancing at the annual dinner gradually decreased. When it came time for the congregation to honor the rabbi, he asked that there be no mixed dancing, ostensibly in deference to rabbinic colleagues who would be in attendance. Since then there has been no mixed dancing. Change in religious practice thus resulted from the desire to maintain the community's religious consensus and as a consequence of a fait accompli rather than from an ideological confrontation. This is characteristic of Modern Orthodoxy.

The building of Pleasantdale's *eruv,* the boundary line surrounding the community that allows Jews to carry items on the Sabbath, also revealed the religious dynamics within the community. To construct an *eruv,* even under the best of circumstances, is a difficult undertaking. Many rabbis prefer not to have one since there is always the possibility that Jews might unknowingly desecrate the Sabbath at those times when the *eruv* was not properly functioning. The building of West Orange's *eruv* was begun only when the community got the approval of Rabbi Moshe Feinstein, then the most prominent contemporary authority on Jewish law, and its construction was supervised by one of his disciples from the Lakewood (New Jersey) yeshiva, a bastion of right-wing Orthodoxy. Even then, it took more than four years and had to surmount the opposition of those who feared it would attract more "black hatters."

Women were particularly eager to have the *eruv* built since it would enable them to visit the synagogue on the Sabbath with their infant children. The *eruv* allows one to push a carriage with small children to the synagogue, even though halachic authorities have asserted that children who are incontinent and under the age of education are a distraction and do not belong in synagogue. Men and women attending religious services together, however, conforms to the general pattern of American religious behavior, even though they do not sit together in an Orthodox sanctuary. The building of the *eruv* was thus an acknowledgment of the power of the secular culture to mold the behavior of the Modern Orthodox.

Another event that revealed the tensions within Modern Orthodoxy was the selection of a new rabbi in Pleasantdale in 1998. In Reform and Conservative congregations, where the laity are largely nonobservant, the rabbis are selected and judged by their skills in human relations rather than by the level of their religious observance and their knowledge of Torah, and they have learned not to make religious demands on their members. In Orthodox congregations, by contrast, religious observance is not a monopoly of the clergy, and the religious behavior of the rabbi (or any prospective rabbi) is watched carefully. Depending on who is talking, the rabbi will be judged to be too religious or not religious enough, and too cosmopolitan and open to the general Jewish world or too parochial and fundamentalist. The selection of a rabbi for a Modern Orthodox congregation is also troubling because of the potential challenge he could pose to the congregation's religious consensus, particularly to the manner in which the community's members have synthesized the often conflicting demands of modernity and Orthodoxy.

By 1998, the Pleasantdale congregation had grown to more than four hundred families and met in a large building worth five million dollars. When it came time to choose a new rabbi, it was made clear from the beginning that he would have to be similar to the incumbent. That is, he could not be a product of the right-wing sectarian yeshiva world, that he would have to work with and relate well to the non-Orthodox world, particularly the federation, the annual United Jewish Appeal campaign, and the local modernist day school, and that he would attract families to relocate to Pleasantdale. But even within these broad parameters, tensions accompanied the selection of the new rabbi.

One candidate, Rabbi O, was in the mold of the incumbent. During his visit to West Orange he emphasized his involvement in the general Jewish community and his interest in pastoral counseling. He was no threat to the congregation's religious consensus, or to the compromises by which the community's families had reconciled modernity and Orthodoxy. Unfortunately he did not project the charisma or religiosity that many congregants were seeking. It is revealing that the candidate who exhibited the balance and spirit of compromise of the then current rabbi was not selected. By 1998 the community was looking for something different.

The second candidate was Rabbi S, and he presented a different model of a rabbi. He was a Torah scholar and a member of the faculty at the Boston Hebrew College. He came strongly recommended by his former teachers and rabbinic mentors, who predicted that he would become one of American Orthodoxy's intellectual luminaries. Some members of the community were enthusiastic about Rabbi S and believed he would bring intellectual distinction to the community. Rabbi S, however, withdrew his candidacy after visiting West Orange and before the final vote took place. The best informed claimed that this was because he realized that the myriad tasks of a rabbi of a congregation the size of Pleasantdale would leave little time for study and writing. It is also possible that he found the prospects of dealing with the various religious factions in the synagogue rather daunting.

The successful candidate was Rabbi SP. His image was not that of a pastor or a scholar but of a communal *rov*. His dress, personal appearance, and demeanor projected a more right-wing outlook. His candidacy provoked discussion as to whether he would seek to change the reigning religious ethos of West Orange and whether he could relate to the non-Orthodox Jewish world. Another set of concerns involved the issue of feminism. He was asked his opinion of women's prayer meetings, when women would read from Torah scrolls (he opposed them), and his attitude toward women wearing slacks (he hoped that women would wear appropriate clothing when meeting with him).

It is not surprising that the question of feminism loomed large during the selection process. As is true of the larger American Jewish world, feminism has been among the most contentious issues facing contemporary Modern Orthodoxy. Modern Orthodox women have demanded a greater role in liturgical matters and synagogue governance and changes in Jewish law regarding birth control and other matters of particular interest to women. As is true of Modern Orthodoxy in general, Modern Orthodox women are poised between two worlds. On the one hand, they identify with a religion that has very traditional views regarding the place of women. But on the other hand, they have been influenced by a modernist social ethos that strongly opposes gender differentiation in employment, education, and social life. They, and their husbands, were particularly sensitive to any indication that the rabbinic candidates were less than fully sympathetic to the idea that their daughters should be allowed to realize their full economic, social, and intellectual potential. The fact that Rabbi SP was married to the daughter of the head of a prominent yeshiva was not reassuring in this regard.

Another important consideration for some in the community, but not for those on the search committee, was what schools the rabbi would select for his children. Would he send his children to the local day school, which was modern and latitudinarian in outlook, or would he send them to more right-wing institutions? This was largely a symbolic issue, since the schooling of the rabbi's children would not have any impact on the population of Pleasantdale. But symbolism was important, because the rabbi defined how the community viewed itself and how it defined Orthodoxy. For some it was reassuring to have a rabbi who was more to the right and hence "more religious," even though their own level of religious observance would not change. As Samuel Heilman has noted, the American Orthodox rabbi, in addition to being a teacher, scholar, and preacher, has also been a "symbolic model Jew."[8]

The selection of Rabbi SP reflects the right-wing move of Pleasantdale (and of Orthodoxy in general) during the past several decades. Behavior that was acceptable a quarter of a century ago, such as mixed dancing at the synagogue's annual dinner, square dancing in the synagogue building, and women singing at synagogue events, no longer takes place. There is more study of Jewish sacred texts, and there is a group of approximately eight men in the synagogue who participate in the *daf yomi*, the daily one-hour study of the Talmud.

There are many reasons for this turn to the right. One is the fact that the children of Pleasantdale spend a year or two studying in Israeli yeshivas and women's seminaries before returning to the United States for college. The sociologist Charles Selengut has noted the impact on Modern Orthodoxy of this "yeshivization." In such schools, he wrote, "theological and halachic pluralism, once the hallmark of the modernist camp, now gives way to increasingly fundamentalist and rigid interpretations of religious law and practice code. . . . Living amid the certainty of yeshiva life is a relief and release from the ambiguities of modernity."[9]

In addition, the Orthodox have been responding to the seeming unraveling of moral standards in America. The Orthodox have resisted this unraveling, and this resistance increases the further one moves rightward. Orthodoxy, and particularly right-wing Orthodoxy, also appears to have the formula for resisting the demographic problems plaguing American Jewry, such as divorce, intermarriage, and a low birthrate. Finally, right-wing Orthodoxy has benefited from the contemporary popularity of multiculturalism. To a much greater extent than the Modern Orthodox, the right-wing Orthodox live in heavily Jewish neighborhoods, wear distinctive clothing, support distinctive ethnic-religious institutions, and are more isolated from the American cultural and social mainstream.

In this atmosphere, the virtues of Modern Orthodoxy—its accommodation to modernity, its greater doctrinal flexibility, and its openness to social trends such as feminism—appear as spineless compromises. "More than before," Heilman and Steven M. Cohen have noted in their appropriately titled book *Cosmopolitans and Parochials: Modern Orthodox Jews in America*, "these tendencies came to signify surrender (even if unwitting) to a Jewish (or an American) world plagued by many of the ills Orthodoxy was committed to countering."[10]

Charles Liebman argued in 1965 that "the only remaining vestige of Jewish passion in America resides in the Orthodox community." While this is an exaggeration, as witness the enthusiasm on behalf of the annual United Jewish Appeal campaigns and the involvement of volunteers in federation work, Orthodoxy is certainly the most dynamic force on the American Jewish religious scene. The future of Orthodoxy as well as the future of American Judaism generally is being determined in suburbia. And it is in suburbia where the compromises and assumptions of Modern Orthodoxy are most evident, where, to quote Liebman again, Jews live in "a half-pagan, half-halachic world."

TEN

The Missing Element

Nathan Glazer and Modern Orthodoxy

FOR THE PAST FORTY YEARS Nathan Glazer has been one of America's most astute and prolific authorities on ethnic identity. A graduate of City College of New York and a prominent member of the New York Jewish intelligentsia, Glazer undoubtedly was led to this interest in ethnicity by his Jewish background. In fact, Glazer has considered Jews the quintessential American ethnic group. His most important contribution to the study of American Judaism and American Jewish identity is his 1957 volume *American Judaism*. Its treatment of Orthodoxy, especially its glaring omission of any mention of Modern Orthodoxy, reflected the then current assumptions of American sociologists, particularly American Jewish sociologists, regarding American ethnicity in general and American Judaism and American Jewish identity in particular.

When *American Judaism* appeared, the United States was experiencing a supposed religious revival. Academic interest in theology was high, and Jacques Maritain, Reinhold Niebuhr, Paul Tillich, and Martin Buber had become almost cult heroes on the campus. On the popular level, the evidence of the religious revival was pervasive. In 1954 the words "under God" were added to the Pledge of Allegiance, and the next year "In God We Trust" was put on all American currency. During the fifties, Bishop Fulton J. Sheen was a media star, films with religious themes were commercial successes, newspapers increased their coverage of religious affairs, the songs "Vaya con Dios," "I Believe," and "Big Fellow in the Sky" made the charts, one toy manufacturer sold a doll that bowed when stroked, Mickey Spillane became a Jehovah's Witness, television spot commercials proclaimed that "the family that prays

This chapter was previously published in *American Jewish History* 77 (Dec. 1987): 260–76. Reprinted by permission of the American Jewish Historical Society together stays together," DIAL-A-PRAYER was available to residents of New York City ("One minute of inspiration in prayer"), and the best-seller lists regularly included religious books, or at least books by religious figures, including Rabbi Joshua Loth Liebman's *Peace of Mind,* Billy Graham's *Peace with God,* Fulton J. Sheen's *Peace of Soul,* and especially Norman Vincent Peale's *The Power of Positive Thinking,* which broke every American record for book sales. For those with specific problems, the bookstores offered *The Power of Prayer on Plants* and *Pray Your Weight Away.*[1]

President Eisenhower went out of his way to emphasize the unique relationship between the United States and the Almighty: "America is the mightiest power which God has yet seen fit to put upon his footstool." The actress and sex goddess Jane Russell professed her deep religious commitment in the pages of *Modern Screen* magazine. "I love God. And when you get to know Him, you find He's a living doll." By 1957, 62 percent of the American people were members of some formal religious organization, compared with fewer than 50 percent in 1940, and half of the American people claimed to have attended a religious service the previous week. Many of these services were in the buildings erected with the billions of dollars raised annually during the 1950s for religious edifices.[2]

American Jews were part of the religious revival. Synagogue membership reached an all-time high as did the funds expended to build synagogues and religious schools. Judaism received a respectful hearing even among deracinated Jewish intellectuals, who had previously prided themselves on their skepticism and universalism. In 1951, Will Herberg's *Judaism and Modern Man* and Abraham Joshua Heschel's *Man Is Not Alone* were published, heralding a miniboom in Jewish theology.

There were many interpretations of the causes of the religious revival. Postwar suburbanization, it was argued, had resulted in a new middle-class lifestyle centering around the home and children in which religion played a vital part. Another interpretation stressed the impact of America's rivalry with the Soviet Union, a self-professed atheistic nation. Will Herberg's *Protestant-Catholic-Jew: An Essay in American Religious Sociology* argued that the religious revival was due to the emergence of the third-generation American for whom the question "Who am I" could be answered only in a religious, rather than an ethnic, context.[3]

The religious revival was not without its critics. The Protestant theologian Reinhold Niebuhr believed it was superficial and meretricious and due less to a faith in God or to a concern with personal salvation than to extraneous sociological and political considerations of questionable merit. "Our religiosity," he said in 1955, "seems to have as little to do with the Christian faith as the religiosity of the Athenians." The " 'unknown God' . . . in America seems to be faith itself." Herberg agreed. *Protestant-Catholic-Jew* argued that the three major American religions were simply alternative expressions of the American way of life, and that religion was valued because it sanctified Americanism.[4]

Glazer was also skeptical regarding the supposed religious revival. He believed it was due more to sociological factors, particularly the coming of age of the third generation of eastern and southern European ethnics and the adoption of the norms of middle-class respectability by the majority of the population, than to any faith in God. He was pessimistic regarding religion's future. The spread of science and skepticism, he claimed, had so undermined the credibility of religion that, except for the intellectually sophisticated, religion was important not because of faith and dogma but because of its social utility.

Glazer noted the extent to which American Protestantism had become modernized and religious fundamentalism had become irrelevant. "The last decades of the nineteenth century," he wrote in 1955, "marked the end of revivalism and the faith of the Puritans (even in its transmuted forms) as a serious force in American life; from that time on no religious leader was also a leader in American intellectual or spiritual life. . . . By the time of the Scopes trial, no one could take the old-time religion seriously; and no one has since."[5] This was written at the same time that Billy Graham, one of the most important figures in the history of American revivalism, was the nation's most significant religious personality. Graham was regularly listed among the ten most admired Americans, his *Hour of Decision* appeared on both radio and television, and his revivals were probably the most significant mass religious phenomenon of the decade. (One of his converts was the Los Angeles gangster Mickey Cohen, who, after converting, promptly borrowed five thousand dollars from the Graham organization that he never repaid. Cohen was later murdered in his mistress's apartment.) Glazer's belief in the decisive impact of modernity on right-wing religion also shaped his interpretation of American Judaism.[6]

Most American Jews, Glazer claimed, had been influenced by the dramatic decline in the intellectual credibility of religion. They valued Judaism because it encouraged Jewish ethnic solidarity, not because its doctrines and practices were God-given. Judaism served the Jewish people; the Jewish people did not serve Judaism. Glazer pointed out that only a small minority of

American Jews believed they were part of a holy and chosen people. Furthermore, there was a distinct absence of any intense religious experience among Jews, and, in fact, strong religious feeling was "looked upon with suspicion in the Jewish community and often considered a harbinger of conversion to Christianity." Even Orthodoxy was bereft of any sense of spirituality that could speak to the modern world, and its emphasis on such religious minutiae as the exact height of the synagogue's barrier separating men from women made it unattractive to any except a small number of true believers. For Glazer, the most significant fact about America's Jews was a negative one: they had refused to become something other than Jews. Jewish institutions flourished in the 1950s because of this commitment to Jewish survival and not out of any intense religious striving.[7]

As a sociologist, Glazer was largely concerned with understanding the social dynamics of Judaism, and his discussion of Orthodoxy mirrored the major assumption of contemporary students of American Judaism. This assumption, most persuasively presented by Marshall Sklare in his *Conservative Judaism: An American Religious Movement*, was that Orthodoxy was an anachronism and that the religious synthesis of the Conservative movement was the version of American Judaism most compatible with Jewish tradition and American social realities. Virtually all major postwar analyses of American Judaism agreed with Sklare. Thus Will Herberg claimed that Conservatism and not Reform had been "the primary beneficiary of the Americanization of Judaism in this country." At the same time, the major spokesmen for Conservatism were quite optimistic as to their movement's future. Rabbi Robert Gordis stated that Conservatism was "the most vital and promising tendency for the future," and Rabbi Louis Finkelstein, the chancellor of the Jewish Theological Seminary and the dominant figure in the movement, predicted that "the Judaism of the next generation will be saved by us."[8]

Glazer agreed. Conservatism, he said, harmonized with the upward social and economic strivings of America's Jews. Furthermore, its emphasis on "Jewishness" appealed to a suburban Jewish population that was "remarkably resistant to religious feeling" but wished to interact culturally, socially, and intellectually with other Jews. Conservative congregations, which often had the word "Center" in their names, uniquely catered to this sense of Jewish peoplehood by providing a center for Jewish activities of all sorts and for all ages without making undue demands in the area of ritual observance. This was important since suburbanites organized their social activities primarily along denominational lines. "It is the social needs of the individual Jew, and the communal needs of the entire community," Glazer wrote, "that the synagogue has met, and as an institution it is flourishing." By offering a variety of programs for the young and by reshaping the liturgy to make it more attractive to youth, the Conservative synagogue had become an important instrument for instilling into future generations a sense of Jewish identity. "Conservatism," Glazer said, "became the movement of those Jewish people who were friendly to all 'positive' tendencies, hoping that out of them would emerge, somehow, an American Judaism." [9]

Glazer believed the Jewish religious revival resulted from the movement of the second and third generations from areas of second settlement to more affluent urban neighborhoods and to suburbia. These new locations contained a high percentage of Gentiles and were distinguished by what Glazer called "middle-class respectability." Here Jews were more self-conscious regarding their Jewishness, and they joined synagogues because religious identification and religious education for their children were part of the respectability they so highly prized. The Jewish culture of suburbia, Glazer correctly noted, was child centered, and parents identified with the Jewish religion in large part for their children's welfare. "Judaism," he wrote, was "being re-created for the children, who play a surprisingly large role in the services of the suburban synagogue and for whom religious festivals are recast so as to emphasize the pleasant and attractive elements." [10] The flip side of this belief that the torch of traditional Judaism had been passed for safekeeping into the hands of the Conservative movement was the assumption that Orthodoxy was doomed in America. It was too European, too identified with the immigrant generation, too hostile to the lifestyle of suburbia, too obscurantist for a population increasingly made up of college graduates. The history of American Orthodoxy, Marshall Sklare said, "can be written in terms of a case study of institutional decay." [11]

The belief that religious fundamentalism, including Orthodoxy, is a lower-class phenomenon has been a staple of twentieth-century sociology. Sociologists and historians emphasized that religious behavior was associated with social class and that education and social mobility resulted in changes in religious identity. The correlation of acculturation, Americanization, and social and economic mobility with the decline of fundamentalist religion is one of the themes of H. Richard Niebuhr's famous book *The Social Sources of Denominationalism* (1929). Niebuhr noted that the religion of "the untutored and economically disfranchised classes" was characterized by emotional fervor, informality, and intellectual naïveté, while the religion of the middle classes was marked by decorum, a stress on individual sobriety and prudence, and an educated clergy. In his chapter "The Churches of the Immigrants," Niebuhr pointed out that as the immigrants became acculturated and more prosperous, their religious practices gradually approximated the American middle-class norm.[12]

This picture of Orthodoxy as an anachronism became a cliché of American Jewish sociology. Sociologists such as Louis Wirth and Howard W. Polsky emphasized that the Orthodox were poorer, older, and less acculturated, and tended to congregate in the first areas of settlement. Polsky's study of Orthodoxy in Milwaukee showed that even the Orthodox had a "survivalist" mentality. They believed they comprised a beleaguered and diminishing minority, and that their own congregations would eventually become Conservative synagogues. The popularity of modernization theory, a major theme of contemporary social science after World War II, strengthened this tendency to view right-wing religion as doomed in America. Using the concept of "ideal types" popularized by the German sociologist Max Weber, modernization enthusiasts stressed the sharp distinction between traditional and modern societies and saw a worldwide tendency toward economic and social modernization and the destruction of the rural, static, and traditional order by bureaucratization, secularism, egalitarianism, democracy, social and demographic mobility, capitalism, political and economic centralization, the rationalization of authority, industrialization, urbanization, technology, nationalism, higher education, and the rise of the masses. The influence of modernization on religion, it was claimed, encouraged modernity, intellectual sophistication, and rationality at the expense of fundamentalist ideas and charismatic practices.[13]

American Judaism was quite pessimistic regarding the future of American Orthodoxy. By and large, Glazer claimed, Orthodoxy appealed only to poorer and less Americanized Jews. By 1957, hundreds of small Orthodox congregations had folded because of the emergence of the more acculturated second and third generations, changing urban demography, and the social and economic rise of American Jewry. Children of the Orthodox had defected because Orthodoxy did not conform to their vision of middle-class respectability. While American Orthodoxy still exhibited a "remarkable vigor," Glazer wrote, its survival was problematic.[14]

The bright spots in Glazer's otherwise dismal portrait of Orthodoxy included Yeshiva University, the right-wing yeshiva world, the Orthodox elementary and secondary day-school movement, and the European Hasidic groups, which had immigrated to America after World War II. And yet despite its "considerable strength," Orthodoxy was declining in numbers and was experiencing difficulty in penetrating "the more prosperous and Americanized sections of the Jewish community." Glazer contended that Orthodoxy in America resembled " 'a saving remnant' that supplies the fund of Jewish knowledge on which all the rest draw. It is fated to become the smallest, if most intense, tendency in Judaism." (In the second edition of *American Judaism,* which appeared in 1972, these two sentences were omitted. By then students of American Orthodoxy had concluded that it consisted of more than a saving remnant, that it had become a permanent aspect of the American Jewish landscape, and that its importance was not limited to the support it provided for other elements within the American Jewish mosaic.)[15]

The inability of Glazer and other sociologists of the 1950s to anticipate the emergence of Modern Orthodoxy stemmed from their sociological model in which acculturation and social and economic mobility went hand in hand with the flight from Orthodoxy. Orthodoxy was such an integral part of the warp and woof of Jewish ethnicity that it would inevitably fade with the emergence of the acculturated second and third generations. This prognosis was strengthened by the assumption that secularization would continue, particularly in the United States, the most industrially advanced nation, and especially among Jews, the most urban, educated, and intellectually sophisticated of American ethnic groups.

American Judaism is completely silent about the phenomenon of Modern Orthodoxy, perhaps because Glazer's identification of Orthodoxy with the "exotic" and the poor had no place in it for those Orthodox who are quintessentially middle class, American born, and economically and professionally successful. For Glazer (and other sociologists of the fifties), American Jews were divided between those attracted to "either Hasidism or the Judaism of past ages" and "the rest of American Jews." His sociological model of American Judaism, which divided Orthodoxy from Conservatism and Reform along distinct socioeconomic lines, could not account for an Orthodox group that was equal in status and education to the non-Orthodox.[16]

American Judaism contains a surprisingly flattering picture of the Hasidim of Brooklyn that stands in stark contrast to its ignoring of Modern Orthodoxy. At one point Glazer speculated on what American Judaism would look like if a sizeable number of Jews rejected the "bland religious life of middle-class" America. To illustrate, he pointed to that most incongruous element within American Jewry, the Satmar Hasidim of the Williamsburg section of Brooklyn. Glazer looked to this "exotic" Jewish community as an example of that intense and authentic commitment to Judaism and the "good and holy life" that was so radically different from the ersatz Judaism of middle-class suburbia. For Glazer, Williamsburg was a contrasuburb and thus a true religious community.[17]

This distaste for suburbia was common among urban intellectuals of the post–World War II years. At this time, suburbia was frequently described as bland, homogeneous, and conformist. William H. Whyte's *The Organization Man* provided the most popular and supposedly most accurate portrait of the typical suburban resident. Songwriters attacked the "ticky-tacky" homes of suburbia. John Keats's *The Crack in the Picture Window* spoke of housing developments "conceived in error, nurtured by greed, corroding everything they touch," of real estate speculators defacing the countryside with "identical boxes spreading like gangrene," and of suburban dwellers resembling "swarms of neuter drones . . . [who] cannot be said to have lives of their own." It is thus not surprising that Glazer, one of the authors of *The Lonely Crowd,* would contrast the intense Judaism of Williamsburg with the insipid Judaism of suburbia.[18]

Except for those addicted to intellectual slumming, the Judaism of Williamsburg has very little appeal. But traditional Judaism in the postwar years was not restricted to declining neighborhoods in Brooklyn. By 1957, Modern Orthodoxy had begun to put down roots in American suburbia and among the professional middle class. The Lincoln Square Synagogue in Manhattan and the Orthodox community of the Five Towns on Long Island was more indicative of the future of American Orthodoxy than the Hasidim of Williamsburg.

Glazer's relegating of Orthodoxy to an anthropological "survival" was common, and few scholars anticipated any revival in Orthodoxy's fortunes. The sociologist Milton M. Gordon, for example, shared Glazer's assumption that traditional Judaism and acculturation were incompatible. His influential 1964 book *Assimilation in American Life: The Role of Race, Religion, and National Origins* noted that the social and economic mobility and acculturation of America's Jews had resulted in the decline of Orthodoxy and in the Jews' "adaptation to American middle-class values." He also omitted any mention of Modern Orthodoxy, and claimed that kashrut, "except on ceremonial occasions, is fast disappearing." In fact, far from vanishing, kashrut actually experienced a resurgence during this period.[19]

One year before Gordon's book appeared, a headline in the *Wall Street Journal* proclaimed, "Kosher Label Covers More Name Brands from Aspirin to Pizza" (Apr. 8, 1963). During the 1960s, Jewish organizations began to observe the dietary laws at their annual banquets in order to placate and attract the Modern Orthodox. Today kosher Chinese, French, and Italian cuisine is available; kosher meals are provided in hospitals, airplanes, and even prisons; McDovid's, an establishment in Manhattan, offers kosher fast food; and many rabbinic organizations certify food products purchased in stores as kosher. The devout can even sample kosher bacon as well as cheeseburgers using ersatz cheese. An interesting recent phenomenon of American Jewish life in the major cities and resorts has been the opening of dozens of kosher restaurants and dining facilities. This indicates not only the growing affluence of the Orthodox but also their willingness to make their religious commitment visible outside the privacy of their homes. This revival of kashrut has occurred in a nation that European Jewish leaders of the early twentieth century described as a *"trefa"* land unsuitable for religious Jews.

The impact of Modern Orthodoxy has been evident in other areas of American life besides food. There has been a phenomenal growth in the enrollment and number of Jewish day schools over the past four decades. There are now well over five hundred Jewish Orthodox day schools in America, the great majority of which are under Modern Orthodox auspices. Another bright spot has been the birthrate among the Modern Orthodox, which is much higher than that of nonreligious Jews with similar economic and social characteristics.

The traditional sociological analysis of American Orthodoxy was unable to account for the recent growth or affluence of the Modern Orthodox. Modern Orthodoxy includes a disproportionate number of professionals and successful businessmen, and their families do not exhibit the generation gap associated with the families of the Jewish immigrants of the early twentieth century. Children of the Modern Orthodox have been more loyal to Orthodoxy than previous generations of Orthodox-reared children.[20]

The modernist-acculturation paradigm of American religious sociology has also been unable to explain the contemporary resurgence of fundamentalist Protestantism. The dominant interpretation of fundamentalism—seen for example in the movie *Inherit the Wind* and in Ray Ginger's book *Six Days or Forever?*—has emphasized its affinity with the anti-intellectualism and primitivism of rural America, especially the rural South. The upsurge of fundamentalism, however, has not been a uniquely rural phenomenon, and whatever else one can say about it, it certainly is not a rural atavism.

Since the 1960s, Jewish sociologists have paid more attention to Orthodoxy in general and to Modern Orthodoxy in particular, and they have ceased viewing it as an anachronism. The second edition of Marshall Sklare's *Conservative Judaism,* which appeared in 1972, modified the first edition's pessimism regarding Orthodoxy. While the second edition of *American Judaism* continued to ignore Modern Orthodoxy, Sklare in 1972 noted an amazing "renaissance of American Orthodoxy" and its ideological challenge to Conservatism. No longer, Sklare argued, could Conservative leaders assume that they were the guardians of the only version of traditional Judaism with a chance of surviving in America. "Unaccountably, Orthodoxy has refused to assume the role of invalid," he wrote. "Rather, it has transformed itself into a growing force in American Jewish life. It has reasserted its claim of being the authentic interpretation of Judaism." Sklare was not referring to the Hasidim of Brooklyn, who in any case were viewed by Conservative leaders as irrelevant to American life, but to Modern Orthodoxy. Orthodox synagogues, he noted, had even relocated to "upper-class and upper-middle-class areas."[21]

By the early seventies, Conservative leaders had clearly recognized the ideological challenge of Modem Orthodoxy. Traditionalist Jews had been joining the Modern Orthodox synagogues springing up in suburbia, leaving Conservative congregations with just a handful of the ritually devout. In 1972, Conservative rabbi Gilbert Rosenthal complained about the lack of Jewish ritual observance among the Conservative laity. "We have missed the boat in not making demands on our people," he wrote. We have made "a virtue of nonpartisanship. . . . He who seeks to be all things to all men, ends up being nothing to too many." And a decade later, Gerson Cohen, the reform-minded chancellor of the Jewish Theological Seminary, called for a renewal of halakah within the Conservative movement. In 1987, Conservative rabbi Mordecai Waxman perceptively analyzed the challenge of Modern Orthodoxy to Conservatism. Orthodoxy, he noted, had "finally come to grips with the American scene," producing a laity and a rabbinate capable of assuming major roles in Jewish social and organizational life.[22]

One of the most comprehensive analyses of the Orthodox challenge to Conservatism was Stuart E. Rosenberg's 1985 book *The New Jewish Identity in America.* Rosenberg, a Conservative rabbi and historian of Canadian and American Jewry, argued that the revived emphasis on ethnicity in the United

States during the 1960s and 1970s had been a boon to Modern Orthodoxy. "To be Orthodox," he wrote, was "no longer regarded as 'un-American.' Rather, it often came to be seen as the fullest, surest way to ensure Jewish survival. Indeed, the 'fall and rise of Orthodoxy' also helped to re-ethnicize and re-traditionalize other, more liberal synagogue groups." Among other causes of the revival of American Orthodoxy that Rosenberg mentioned were the Orthodox day-school movement; the emergence of the third generation of American Jewry, who did not flee from tradition as had their parents; the move to the right in American life generally; the improved quality of Orthodox institutions, schools, and journals; the *baal teshuvah* movement resulting from disillusionment with political and social radicalism; and the higher economic and social status of the Orthodox.

Rosenberg pointed out that, in contrast to the European rabbis of the late nineteenth and early twentieth centuries, Modern Orthodox spokesmen emphasized the compatibility of Orthodoxy and America. As Samuel Belkin, president of Yeshiva University, said during the 1950s, "We firmly deny that our integration in the American community in any way implies the abrogation of even one iota of our sacred tradition. More than two generations of our people have been lost to us because of the erroneous belief that there exists a serious conflict between our spiritual heritage and the American way of life, which is itself deeply rooted in Hebraic spiritual values."[23]

While Conservatism was experiencing a crisis of faith and seemed to be in disarray, Orthodoxy in general, and Modern Orthodoxy in particular, was in the midst of an unanticipated resurgence. "Orthodoxy," Rabbi Louis Bernstein of Yeshiva University said in 1987, "is flourishing in the United States and brims with a self-confidence bordering on triumphalism." Two of the factors he emphasized were a high Orthodox birthrate ("the only positive population factor on the American Jewish scene") and the emergence of a new generation who, although committed to Torah, were "thoroughly at home in the American milieu." Furthermore, the Modern Orthodox rabbinate and laity were playing a more significant role in the general Jewish community. Bernstein concluded that the challenges facing American Orthodoxy no longer emanated from such external sources as Conservatism and secular Judaism but were internal, in particular Orthodoxy's incessant divisiveness.[24]

While there was much merit in the mainstream sociological interpretation in the 1950s and 1960s of Orthodoxy, it suffered from a too deterministic framework. Can sociology explain why Orthodoxy was able to transplant itself to suburbia? Can sociology explain why physicians, scientists, lawyers, and accountants, with educational levels and incomes placing them in the highest social and economic categories, would voluntarily assume a religious lifestyle that supposedly does not conform to their social positions? Can sociology explain the simultaneous revival of Orthodox morale and the decline of Conservative morale? Marshall Sklare's comment of 1972 is apt. The Orthodox resurgence seemed to have repealed "the laws of religious gravity." For historical, psychological, and theological reasons, a group of socially mobile Jews found Orthodoxy intellectually, emotionally, and socially attractive and compatible with the modern lifestyle they prized.[25]

Ironically, Glazer had criticized the tendency of sociologists to explain religious phenomena solely in sociological terms. Two years before the publication of *American Judaism,* he had reviewed Marshall Sklare's *Conservative Judaism* in the pages of *Commentary.* While very enthusiastic about the volume, he gently chided its author for believing that the appeals of Conservative Judaism could be explained solely in terms of such sociological concepts as "anomie." Sklare, Glazer wrote, "narrows his canvas too much. . . . Never in his book does one find a hint that Jewish tradition also plays a role in the matter, and that this tradition leads an existence quite independent of surrounding social forms." He criticized Sklare for picturing Jewish tradition as without an independent existence of its own, forced willy-nilly to adapt itself to American society. Glazer found Sklare's approach too pessimistic regarding the ability of Jewish tradition to withstand the pressures of inevitable acculturation. "Sociological analysis," he said, "must take all forces into account, and the existence of a religious tradition that makes strong demands, and is still accepted by many thousands of people, is one such force." The greatest weakness of sociologists, Glazer concluded, was in not according an independent status to religions and ideologies, seeing them as only "passive elements given by history and molded by social forces and individual needs."

Glazer predicted that American Jewry, or at least a significant part of it, might remain faithful to Jewish tradition and withstand the appeals of acculturation, an eventuality that sociologists, who reduced all phenomena to social forms, would find inexplicable. Glazer's failure to anticipate the growing importance of Modern Orthodoxy, his belief that Orthodoxy in America would increasingly become centered among exotic and unacculturated groups in Brooklyn, and his inability to transcend the modernization paradigm, at least as far as Orthodoxy is concerned, is an example of precisely what he warned against in 1955.[26]

For Glazer, the most significant (and mysterious) fact about American

Jews has been their continued commitment to some form of Jewish identity. He believed America's Jews were essentially an ethnic group, and that acculturation would divest them of their most prominent ethnic elements, including Orthodoxy. Under the pressure of acculturation, the rituals and doctrines of American Judaism would presumably come to approximate American (i.e., Protestant) norms. Here is the source of Glazer's befuddlement regarding Modern Orthodoxy's continuing vitality.

Glazer has remained unconvinced that traditional Judaism can be reconciled with modernity and middle-class cultural norms. In his 1985 *Commentary* essay "On Jewish Forebodings," he argued that Louis Wirth had not been wrong in predicting the dissolution of Jewish identity and culture in America. "Jews will survive, yes, and perhaps even continue to identify themselves as Jews," Glazer said, but "little by way of custom, belief, or loyalty will be assumed as a result of their identity as Jews." That same year he wrote a book review in the *New York Times Book Review* that claimed that financial success and religious separatism were mutually exclusive and that only the isolated Hasidic sects would be able to withstand assimilation. "Jewish life," he wrote, is "maintained better in conditions of poverty and modest comfort—in which one interacted with the larger world little, if at all—than in conditions of worldly success." He continued to refuse to consider the possibility that a symbiosis could take place between what he termed "historical Judaism" and American social and religious norms. An *American* Orthodoxy remained for him a contradiction in terms. The question worth pondering, Glazer concluded, was not whether historic Judaism could take root in America, but whether its "American version can develop the confidence to maintain itself worthily as a parallel second branch of Judaism."[27]

Modern Orthodoxy has been able to transcend the identification of Orthodoxy with the immigrant Jewish culture of East Europe, and to withstand the pressures of modernization and secularism. Some American Orthodox leaders of the early twentieth century believed America did not have to be a cemetery for Orthodoxy, but Orthodoxy would have to be acculturated if it was to attract the upwardly mobile. This required a university, both to educate the faithful and to provide an Americanized religious leadership for the Orthodox community. In 1928, Yeshiva College, the most important American Modern Orthodox institution, opened its doors to provide a liberal arts education under Orthodox auspices. It has been this commitment to both the secular world and the world of Torah that has marked Modern Orthodoxy from the beginning.

Educated in Jewish day schools and universities (including Yeshiva and Stern Colleges) and employed in the professions, by government, and by major financial, scientific, and industrial corporations, the Modern Orthodox are comfortable in the symbiosis they have created between their American and religious identities. In fact, the major intellectual challenge to Modern Orthodoxy has been the overly comfortable fit between it and Americanism and not the incompatibility between the two that sociologists had emphasized. A small but growing number of prosperous, well-educated, and totally Americanized Jews have identified with Modern Orthodoxy. According to sociologists and Conservative leaders, this should not have happened. Only Conservative Judaism, or a variant of it, could supposedly minister to the social and religious needs of upwardly mobile and religiously traditional Jews. From the perspective of the 1990s, this prophecy ignored the possibility of Orthodoxy adapting itself to American conditions; it underestimated the openness of America to a traditionalist expression of Jewish identity; and it had an overly confident faith in the ability of sociology to correlate religious behavior with social and economic status. History, Orthodox rabbi Reuven P. Bulka said, "should have taught the prognosticators that religious commitment has the unique power to enable the Jewish minority to survive, even to flourish, in alien environments."[28]

PART THREE

Politics

E L E V E N

Politics and American Jewish Identity

IT IS NO SECRET that American Jews are deeply troubled about their future. The sociologist Samuel C. Heilman, for example, ended his 1995 volume *Portrait of American Jews* by expressing his fear that Judaism and Jewishness had no future in America. "If I am to be certain that my children and their children will continue to be actively Jewish," he wrote, "then the boat that brought my family here to America in 1950 may still have another trip to make," namely to Israel. There is nothing new about American Jews being pessimistic. Today's fears, however, are quite different from previous periods in which the buzzwords were "anti-Semitism" and "survival." By contrast, the contemporary buzzwords are "continuity" and "identity."[1]

Jews now stand at the pinnacle of American life, politically, socially, culturally, and socially. The widespread custom of rabbis delivering invocations and benedictions at social and athletic events and the presence of courses in Jewish history and learning in American academia attest to the fact that Jews are perceived to be an integral part of American culture. No informed observer of the contemporary American Jewish scene takes domestic anti-Semitism seriously, although anti-Semitism in Europe and the Middle East is another story. Alan M. Dershowitz's book *The Vanishing American Jew* noted that the threat today to Jews comes not from anti-Semitism but from those who would "kill us with kindness—by assimilating us, marrying us, and merging with us out of respect, admiration, and even love."[2] In the half century since the end of World War II, a revolution has occurred in the status of American Jews and in the attitude of American Gentiles toward Jews. Jews no longer are viewed as an exotic segment of the American population, similar to the Amish of Pennsylvania or the Cajuns of southern Louisiana. This revolu-

This chapter was previously published in *Judaism* 47 (fall 1998): 425–36. Reprinted by permission.

tion has been both a cause and a result of the acculturation and assimilation of American Jews that has been so worrisome to Jewish leaders. The most troubling statistic for American Jews is no longer the annual Anti-Defamation League figures on anti-Semitic incidents but the skyrocketing intermarriage rate, which the 1990 National Jewish Population Survey put at 52 percent. Many scholars are skeptical about the 52 percent figure, but even the most optimistic believe that it exceeds 40 percent. American Jews have survived anti-Semitism, but whether they will be able to survive as Jews in the face of this widespread social acceptance by the majority population is another question.

The most disturbing aspect of the high rate of exogamy is not the rate itself but what it says about the capacity and willingness of American Jews to maintain their distinctive institutions and values. Jewish survivalists are befuddled by what to do about intermarriage. They recognize that it results from a development that no one wants to change—the lowering of barriers that previously had limited the interaction of Jews and Gentiles in the university, at work, or in leisure time activities. How can the rate of intermarriage be reversed or at least slowed down without also reducing the economic and social opportunities of Jews, which brings Jews and Gentiles into closer proximity to each other and leads to intermarriage? In view of the massive movement of American Jews up the social and economic ladder, intermarriage would seem to be inevitable and less a problem for which there is a solution than a condition with which Jews would have to learn to live. With nearly one out of every two Jews choosing a spouse who is not Jewish, the prospects of Jewish identity in America would appear to be bleak.

Two articles in 1997 drew attention to the problem of Jewish identity and the future of American Jewry. The first was Jack Wertheimer's essay in the July 1997 issue of *Commentary*, titled "Judaism Without Limits." Wertheimer, the provost and professor of history at the Jewish Theological Seminary in New York, the leading institution of Conservative Judaism, argued that American Jews and Judaism faced a crisis stemming from an excessively latitudinarian attitude toward Judaism and Jewish identity. This inclusiveness has put an imprimatur on practices and impulses hostile to traditional Judaism. The result is a Judaism without limits in which traditional values and practices have given way to experimentation and syncretism. "As more Jews intermarry," Wertheimer said, "institutions conclude that they must blur formerly clear dividing lines lest they suffer a steep decline in membership and financial support. But the more the lines are blurred, the greater the confusion sown among Jews and non-Jews alike as to the limits of Jewish identity." The end result is not pluralism and growth but "anarchy and self-extinction."[3]

The second article appeared in the July 14, 1997, issue of *New York* magazine under the provocative title "Are American Jews Disappearing?" "Are American Jews assimilating themselves out of existence?" asked the essay's author, Craig Horowitz. Horowitz noted that Jews were assimilating in record numbers and that the American Jewish population has been declining relatively and perhaps in absolute numbers at a time when American Jewry is "the most vibrant, diverse, productive, creative, and powerful Diaspora Jewish community in history." The problem stemmed from intermarriage, a low birthrate, the rejection of organized religion, and a widespread indifference to things Jewish. American Jewish parents, Horowitz concluded, rightly "wonder, with good demographic reason, whether their grandchildren will be Jewish." "For all practical purposes, the American Jewish community is committing suicide, and no one is saying anything about it," Horowitz quoted Rabbi Ephraim Buchwald, the founder and director of the National Jewish Outreach Program. Actually American Jewish leaders have been talking about little else.[4]

"How do we become good Jews? Can we fully embrace modernity and an open society and live fully engaged Jewish lives?" John Ruskay, the vice president of the United Jewish Appeal, asked Horowitz. This question goes to the heart of the most fundamental conflict in American Jewish life. On the one hand, Jews have been universalists, loudly claiming that Jews are like everyone else only more so, and that they should seek to break down all barriers impeding their full integration into American life. A prominent example of this type of thinking was Rabbi Morris N. Kertzer's article, "What Is a Jew?" published in June 1952 in the American weekly magazine *Look*. Kertzer emphasized that Jews and Christians "share the rich heritage of the Old Testament. They both believe in the fatherhood of one God, in the sanctity of the Ten Commandments, the wisdom of the prophets and the brotherhood of man."

If Kertzer was correct that Jews were like everyone else, then why should they choose to remain Jewish? They would not experience any fundamental change should they convert to Christianity. On the other hand, Jews have recognized that they were, in fact, different from Gentiles, that they wished to pass down these differences to their children, and that converting to Christianity was unthinkable. While American Jews have accepted the presence within their ranks of homosexual Jews, Buddhist Jews, communist Jews, and humanistic (i.e., atheist) Jews, they have drawn the line at "messianic Jews" or "Jews for Jesus." America's Jews thus have been schizophrenic, espousing the seemingly contradictory goals of integration and distinctiveness, of equality and pluralism. The American Jew, Charles S. Liebman said in his book *The Ambivalent American Jew*, "desperately sought to participate in the society and rejected sectarianism as a survival strategy, yet at the same time refused to make his own Jewishness irrelevant." The contemporary crisis of Jewish identity stems from the fact that the tensions between these competing values can no longer be papered over by euphemisms and bromides.[5]

Despite the pressures of acculturation and assimilation, in certain respects Jews have remained a "peculiar people," as the Bible puts it. The Jewish economic and social profile diverges dramatically from that of Gentile Americans. Jews are wealthier and more likely to be found in the professions, academia, and the upper ranks of business, and they attend universities, especially the elite universities, in greater numbers. Jews also give more money to charity, and they are far more inclined to support institutions involved in the advocacy of civil liberties, human rights, and economic issues. These traits are not sui generis to America. Jews in Canada, Central and South America, and Europe exhibit the same characteristics.

Another area in which American Jews have differed from Gentiles is politics. Marshall Sklare's "Lakeville" studies of the 1960s revealed that residents of this Chicago suburb believed that supporting humanitarian causes, aiding the underprivileged, and helping blacks achieve equality was more important to being a good Jew than supporting Israel or observing the basic tenets of Judaism. Such thinking has survived the post-1960s eclipse of liberalism and the self-destructive impulses of certain segments of the black population. A survey among Los Angeles Jews in the 1980s, the second largest concentration of American Jewry, revealed that the most important element in the Jewish identity of 59 percent of those surveyed was neither Judaism nor supporting Israel but a commitment to social equality. For American Jews, the sociologists Charles S. Liebman and Steven M. Cohen wrote, "liberalism is not merely a characteristic but clearly a major component of their understanding of what it means to be a Jew."[6]

The role of liberal politics in defining Jewish identity has been far more important in the United States than in, say, France. This is partially explained by the difference in the size of the respective Jewish communities of France and the United States. The far larger American Jewish population created a virtually autonomous left-wing subculture with its own newspapers, cultural institutions, labor unions, schools, and summer camps. Furthermore, by the 1960s French Jewry consisted primarily of refugees from French North Africa. The political values of these Sephardic Jews are different from those of East European immigrants and their offspring.

Dominique Schnapper's *Jewish Identities in France: An Analysis of Contemporary French Jews* emphasizes the extent to which French Jews—and this includes even French Jews who are areligious or even antireligious—see Jewishness as a matter of religious observance and belief rather than of culture or politics. In part this is due to the reigning cultural traditions of France. The French have never considered themselves to be a nation of immigrants, nor did their heritage of what Schnapper calls "cultural centralism" leave much scope for the idea of cultural pluralism. After the emancipation of the Jews following the 1789 Revolution, the French presumed that French Jews would eventually be fully integrated within French culture. The essence of Jewishness, they assumed, was religious, and the only thing that supposedly distinguished French Jews, or should distinguish French Jews, was Judaism. Their Jewishness involved religion and not ethnicity, a part of which is politics. "Collective Jewish politics," wrote the historian Paula Hyman about French Jewry prior to World War I, "except to serve the needs of the state or defend their own equality, would be suspect in the eyes of Frenchmen." As a result, French Jews expressed their solidarity with one another "in religious terminology." Furthermore, the importance of Roman Catholicism and the often bitter conflict between church and state in France after the Revolution gave the religious question a greater saliency in France. It is not surprising, therefore, that French Jews conflated Jewishness with Judaism.[7]

In America, by contrast, liberal politics has played a significant role in defining Jewish identity. The politics of Jews is not what one would expect from a population whose economic and social status far exceeds the American norm. The sociologically aberrant political behavior of Jews has not gone unnoticed by non-Jews, particularly conservatives who have waited expectantly for Jewish political behavior to conform to their economic and social profile. Richard Brookhiser, the conservative writer and senior editor of William F. Buckley's *National Review*, once quipped that the only difference between Reform Judaism and the Democratic Party was their respective holidays. Brookhiser was touching on a major element in modern American Jewish history—the extent to which liberal politics for many Jews has filled the vacuum created by the decline and even disappearance of conventional religious beliefs. Except for Orthodox Jews, who comprise less than 10 percent of

American Jewry, and a small segment of Conservative Jews, American Jews are largely indifferent to the demands of Judaism. They attend religious services far less frequently than Protestants or Catholics, and religion appears to have little influence in their daily lives. Even under the loosest definition of kashrut, no more than 20 percent of American Jews observe the Jewish dietary laws. A majority of Jewish women do not light Sabbath candles, and fewer than 10 percent of Jewish men pray daily. Forty percent of American Jews do not even attend services on Rosh Hashanah and Yom Kippur. At the same time, these same persons claimed that being Jewish was very important to them and that they considered themselves to be "very good" Jews. This does not mean that American Jews are fooling themselves or are bereft of a Jewish identity, for, as Steven Cohen has noted, "modern political movements have served as functional alternatives to conventional religion."[8]

The liberalism of American Jews is particularly evident in presidential elections. Every Democratic candidate for president since the 1920s, except for Jimmy Carter in 1980, has received a majority of the Jewish vote, and generally the Democratic candidate received at least two-thirds of these votes. (Carter would also have received a majority of Jewish votes had it not been for the third-party candidacy of John Anderson.) At times the difference between the voting behavior of Jews and of Gentiles has been bizarre. In 1972, for example, George McGovern received 65 percent of the votes of Jews, while nationally he garnered only 30 percent of the votes of other white Americans. The gap between Jewish and Gentile white voters was an astounding 35 percent. In 1976, Jimmy Carter, the first southerner to run for president since the Civil War, received a minority of the votes of white southerners, but he gained 65 percent of the votes of Jews. Thirty-nine percent of American Jews voted for Ronald Reagan in 1980, but only 29 percent voted for him four years later. Jews were the only major group besides the unemployed who did not increase their vote for Reagan between 1980 and 1984. In 1984 a lower percentage of Jews voted for Reagan than did Hispanics or union members. Whereas 71 percent of Jews voted for Walter Mondale in 1984, no more than a third of Gentile white voters voted for him. Four years later, a higher percentage of Jews than Greeks voted for Michael Dukakis. In 1992 no more than 15 percent of Jews cast their ballots for George Bush, and in 1996, according to a survey by the American Jewish Committee, 76 percent of Jews voted for Clinton, 5 percent for Ross Perot, and only 17 percent for Bob Dole.[9]

From where does this continuing commitment to liberalism come? The consistency of the voting statistics indicates that Jewish voting is a product not of transient issues but of an ethnic political culture passed down from one generation to the next. Most American Jews are descendants of the great wave of Jewish immigration of the late nineteenth and early twentieth century when perhaps two million Jews from central and eastern Europe settled in the United States. Politics was very important to the Jews of central and eastern Europe, and they believed that what was called the "Jewish question" could be solved through politics. In Europe they participated in a host of political movements and parties, each with a unique analysis of what ailed European Jewry. These included religious parties, Jewish socialist parties, and Zionist parties, as well as the general socialist, communist, anarchist, and conservative parties.[10]

When the Jews of Eastern Europe came to America they brought their interest in politics with them. They established dozens of Yiddish newspapers with different political ideologies. Another indication of the interest of Jews in politics was their speedy acquisition of citizenship. Jews became citizens at a rate faster than probably that of any other major immigrant group. Jews also brought with them from Europe a distinctive political outlook. Perhaps the most important element in this outlook was the belief that Jews were victims and outsiders, a natural-enough stance in view of the history of European Jewry, particularly in the Russian Empire. This attitude existed, as David Biale has noted in his *Power and Powerlessness in Jewish History,* at the same time that East European Jewry was entering a new political era based on "mass mobilization and organization" and on "a quest for power." The proponents of this new Jewish politics were tragically naïve regarding the likelihood that Jews could ever acquire sufficient power to protect their interests. The weak political position of Jews did not prevent anti-Semites from claiming that Jews possessed superhuman power, which they were using to subvert European Christian society.[11]

This emphasis on the Jew as victim was important in shaping the politics of European Jews, and, eight decades after the end of the massive immigration from Eastern Europe, it continues to resonate among the descendants of these immigrants. The image of the Jew as a victim was reinforced by the Holocaust. According to surveys of public opinion by the National Opinion Research Center, American Jews are less at ease and more distrustful than other white ethnic groups. And this image is also responsible for the thrust of American Jewish humor, which, as in the case of the Jerry Seinfeld television show, is replete with neurotic and angst-ridden individuals who are continually defeated in their search for spouses, sexual fulfillment, and financial success.[12] For radicals such as Ellen Willis, victimization is central to their understanding of themselves as Jews. "It seems like such a negative thing to define Jewish identity in terms of anti-Semitism," Willis said. "But I've come to the conclusion that's really a false issue, because the very identity of the Jews—who we are in history, what we represent is totally bound up with anti-Semitism. . . . Every Jew is a victim of anti-Semitism—a member of a pariah people." This reminds one of Jean-Paul Sartre's famous statement in his book *Anti-Semite and Jew* that "it is the anti-Semite who creates the Jew."

Sartre did not see anything in the Judaism or Jewishness of the France of his day that might be attractive to Jews. Rather, Jews remained Jews because they had no choice. "The Jews have neither community of interests nor community of belief," he wrote in the same year that saw the establishment of the state of Israel. "They do not have the same fatherland; they have no history. The sole tie that binds them is the hostility and disdain of the societies which surround them." The sense of the Jew as victim helps explain why radical Jews support other groups also perceived to be victims, such as Palestinians, grape pickers, and garment workers in Central America. This image of the Jew as victim permeates the pages of the radical bimonthly Jewish magazine *Tikkun*. If Jews are, by definition, victims, then those Jews who do not sympathize with this cult of victimization are unauthentic Jews who betray the essence of Jewishness. From the perspective of Willis and *Tikkun*, a conservative Jew is a contradiction in terms.[13]

Even for those Jews who don't share Willis's radical politics, the sense of being a victim, an emphasis on the "oyes" rather than the joys of Jewishness, has been important in shaping their politics. This is particularly evident in attitudes toward anti-Semitism, Israel, the Holocaust, civil liberties, blacks, and church-state issues. Despite the findings of social scientists and the clear evidence before their eyes, Jews find it difficult to believe that anti-Semitism is not important in contemporary America. According to the 1990 National Jewish Population Survey, more than 80 percent of American Jews believed anti-Semitism to be a serious problem in the United States. Another poll by the American Jewish Committee revealed that, by a 2-1 margin, American Jews saw anti-Semitism as a greater threat to Jews than intermarriage.

Their self-definition "was so inextricably bound to battling anti-Semitism," the historian Gerald Sorin wrote, "that it was extremely difficult for Jewish Americans to believe what the pollsters and sociologists were saying. . . . Some observers in the 1980s and 1990s suggested that Jews clung to the notion of a persisting anti-Semitism because their Jewishness had been hollowed out, that it was based on nothing more solid than paranoia." Indeed, when it comes to the Jewish view of anti-Semitism, we have an example of what social scientists call cognitive dissonance—the gap between reality and the perception of reality. Even the Anti-Defamation League, which has an interest in stressing the presence of anti-Semitism, is hesitant to argue that anti-Semitism is more than a peripheral phenomenon, and yet Jews continue to exaggerate its importance.[14]

For Jews wallowing in victimhood, a decline of anti-Semitism is unwelcome since it requires that they rethink the content of their own Jewish identity. This is why Jews in America continue to believe they are a beleaguered people, despite all the evidence to the contrary, and why they inflate the importance of minor anti-Semitic incidents. It also helps in part to explain the nature of their attachment to the state of Israel. American Jews were eager to see the establishment of a Jewish state, and they were proud of Israel's growth and accomplishments during the first two decades of her existence. But the attitude toward Israel changed radically in 1967 when Israel was threatened with annihilation by her Arab neighbors. At this time the emotional stake of American Jewry in Israel intensified dramatically. The thought of a Jewish holocaust in the Middle East coming a quarter of a century after the European Holocaust was too frightful to contemplate. The visceral response of Jews to Israel's plight stemmed from their perception of Israel as a potential victim.

Israel's stunning victory in the Six Days' War of June 1967 revealed Israel's military might. The image of a triumphant, militarily powerful Jewish state was extremely troubling for Jews accustomed to thinking in terms of Jewish powerlessness and victimization. American Jews also found it difficult to accept the suggestion of some Israelis, voiced during the 1990s, that Israel had matured and was no longer in need of the financial assistance of world Jewry. Such thinking threatened the Jewish raison d'être of those whose Jewish identity involved raising funds for a threatened Israel.

For radical Jews, the display of Israeli power in 1967 was almost anti-Jewish. Thus Michael Selzer, writing from the safety of America in the aftermath of the Six Days' War, argued in his book *Zionism Reconsidered* that Zionism, by seeking to empower Jews, violated Jewish ethics and purpose. The very essence of Judaism, Selzer asserted, "involved a revolution to radicalize the world through Jewish powerlessness and suffering." American Jews, radicals and nonradicals alike, were disturbed by the continuing Israeli occupation of lands captured during the Six Days' War containing large numbers of Arabs. This could not be reconciled with the image of the Jew as victim. The Jew was supposed to be the occupied and not the occupying power.[15]

Perhaps the two most important American exponents of the Jew as marginal and politically powerless are the brothers Jonathan and Daniel Boyarin. Jonathan Boyarin wrote his dissertation in anthropology on Yiddish-speaking political immigrants in Paris because he and they shared a "marginality," and he was attracted to Orthodoxy and living on the Lower East Side of New York City because they held out the prospect of "enjoying the possibilities offered by marginality." The same impulse that drew him to Orthodoxy repelled him and his brother from an Israel that exercised state power in ways similar to other states. In his book *A Radical Jew,* Daniel Boyarin argued that political Zionism is a form of "tribal warfare" and "fascism," and Israel is "a product of European colonialism and cultural imperialism." The paramount sin of Israel has been the desire for "political hegemony" and its quest for "exclusivist and dominating power." Political Zionism and Israel subverted Jewish culture because they rejected the traditional Jewish goal of sharing political power. Daniel Boyarin's goal of severing Judaism from territorialism draws on the seemingly opposed cultural Zionism of Judah Magnes and Martin Buber and the antipolitical Zionism of Netorei Karta, a small group of anti-Zionist religious extremists living in the Mea Shearim neighborhood of Jerusalem.[16]

American Jews' image of themselves as impotent victims also accounts for their involvement in the building of Holocaust museums and their support of civil liberties. Samuel Heilman predicted in 1995 that the Holocaust museum in Washington, D.C., "may become the single most outstanding monument to Jewish identity in America (and its most visited shrine). Of course, if it does, it will be a monument to Jews as victims—not necessarily something upon which to build a future." Through their financial contributions and pro bono legal work, Jews have been the backbone of American civil liberty organizations. Jews, to an extent greater than that of other Americans, exaggerate threats to civil liberties and are far more likely to defend unpopular minorities such as political radicals and homosexuals. This explains the seemingly paradoxical situation in the late 1970s when Jewish civil liberties lawyers defended the right of Nazis to march through the streets of Skokie, Illinois, a suburb of Chicago containing a large number of Holocaust survivors. It also explains the intense support of Jewish women for abortion rights. Judging by their low birthrate, Jewish women cannot possibly see themselves as beneficiaries of the abortion rights movement. They have been successful on their own in limiting the number of their children. While abortion rights are not a matter of self-interest for American Jewish women, it is important to them since it reflects the long-standing Jewish distrust of authority and the equally long-standing defense of individual rights. Jewish women have also been important in the feminist movement all out of proportion to their percentage of the American population. They accept the feminist image of women being oppressed by a patriarchal society and of a "sisterhood" of the victimized and the powerless.[17]

Accustomed to thinking of themselves as powerless, Jews have an almost reflexive fear of government and authority. When the rabbi in *Fiddler on the Roof* is asked to say a prayer in behalf of the anti-Semitic czar, he is at first nonplussed. He thinks for a moment and then responds that God should keep the czar—far away from Anatekva. This Jewish distrust of authority is particularly evident in matters of church and state. No group has been more active than Jews in ensuring that the wall between church and state not be breached. Jewish sensitivity is particularly acute here because of memories of Europe where the established Christian Church, in league with the government, often encouraged anti-Semitism. Steven Cohen, an expert on American Jewish opinion, noted that one of the more curious phenomena revealed by public opinion polls is that there were "far more Gentiles than Jews expressing a readiness to accept the public display of a menorah."[18]

There is an obvious dissonance between a Jewish political culture based on an imagery of victimization and powerlessness and the situation of Jews in contemporary America, not to mention in Israel. Jews have great power in America, if not as Jews then certainly as individuals. A Jew heads the Federal Reserve System, two Jews are on the Supreme Court, and for a while during President Clinton's first term, six Jews were simultaneously members of his cabinet. "The movement of Jews into the American political elite," David Biale wrote, "marks one of the most radical social transformations in Jewish history and probably, for that matter, in history in general." Jews have also served as president of some of America's leading corporations, including United Airlines, Disney, Du Pont, and Bank of America. The prominence of Jews in the mass media, the entertainment industry, and Wall Street hardly needs mention. Jews also have a role in American intellectual and cultural life disproportionate to their numbers. Isaac Stern once defined a cultural exchange between the Soviet Union and the United States as an event in which the Soviets send their Jewish violinists from Odessa to the United States and the Americans, in turn, send their Jewish violinists from Odessa to the Soviet Union.[19]

But Jews continue to behave politically as if they are victims and outsiders. "Memories of powerlessness," Biale wrote, "have created an embarrassment over power," so much so that it is difficult for American Jews to acknowledge their actual status in contemporary America. One of the challenges facing American Jewry, Alan Dershowitz recently noted, "is to move the Jewish state of mind beyond its past obsession with victimization, pain, and problems and point it in a new, more positive direction, capable of thriving in an open society." Such a shift would also reconcile the politics of Jews with their economic and social status. Charles Liebman once wrote that the future of American Jewish liberalism depended on "the continued state of Jewish estrangement." He himself was not optimistic about the future of Jewish liberalism because he believed this sense of estrangement to be dying out. But there have been many such predictions during the last thirty years of the imminent passing of Jewish liberalism. Liebman's words were published more than two decades ago, and American Jews have not yet given up on their romance with political liberalism. Indeed, in some respects this romance is more ardent than ever.[20]

TWELVE

Charles S. Liebman and American Jewish Liberalism

IN AUGUST 1977 the sociologist Charles S. Liebman published a brief essay in *Commentary* titled "American Jews: Still a Distinctive Group." Here he disagreed with students of American Jewry such as Seymour Martin Lipset and Joseph Blau who had argued that the dominant motif of Jewish identity in America was accommodation to the dominant cultural patterns of Gentile society. According to the accommodationists, Jewish behavior, both institutional and individual, increasingly reflected that of the general society. Liebman noted that the accommodationist thesis had been welcomed by Jews at opposite poles of the ideological spectrum. Assimilationists advised American Jews to accept the inevitable and throw themselves into the American mainstream, while Zionists argued that Jews who were committed to Jewish continuity had no choice but to relocate to Israel.

Liebman admitted that it was "a self-evidently true proposition" that American Jewry was no different from other Jewish communities in its adoption of the mores of the host culture. The real debate concerned the degree of this adaptation and its nature. Had American Jews simply adopted in toto the ways of the general culture, Liebman wondered, or had they significantly modified these ways to conform to Jewish needs and values? "The question," he said, "is which elements of that culture have they simply assimilated and adopted without change, which elements have they transformed in the process of absorbing them, which elements have they resisted, and which important elements, if any, have they ignored." The answer could not simply be left to the dispassionate and impartial investigations of sociologists, because it involved value judgments regarding the opposing stances of accommodation

This chapter was previously published in *American Jewish History* 80 (summer 1991): 451–64. Reprinted by permission of the American Jewish Historical Society.

and resistance to the general culture as well as predictions about the future of American Jewry.

Rejecting the accommodationist thesis, Liebman pointed to four areas of American Jewish life that had been relatively untouched by the general culture. The first was a sense of Jewish peoplehood, which manifested itself in the political and philanthropic support of American Jews for Israel and for beleaguered Jewish communities throughout the world. The second was an emphasis on communalism in Jewish life, particularly seen in the important role of Jewish federations and community-wide fund-raising campaigns. The third was the significant place of the synagogue among Jews, which Liebman believed was far greater than that of the church among American Christians. The final element of American Jewish life that Liebman pointed to as evidence that American Jews were still a distinctive group concerned religious observance. While the reigning norm among Gentile Americans regarding religious obligation stressed moral behavior, Jews continued to see ritual observance and synagogue participation as the essence of Judaism. Even completely nonobservant Jews believed that keeping kosher and observing the Sabbath were more important than ethical conduct in defining who was a religious Jew. Liebman concluded his essay with a caveat: "The impact of America on American Judaism . . . is not so simple or so unambiguous as has sometimes been maintained. American Jews have done more than accommodate themselves to their environment. They have not only transformed that environment in some instances, and resisted it in others, but have even remained utterly indifferent to it in areas that touch their deepest concerns and values as Jews. And therein, perhaps, lies some basis for a continued hope for distinctive Jewish survival."[1]

Liebman's examples were questionable. Based on the percentage of Americans who had visited Israel and who worked on behalf of Jews overseas, he probably exaggerated their sense of Jewish peoplehood. In addition, the number of Jews who took part in federation fund-raising campaigns and were involved in communal institutions, particularly in places of growing Jewish population such as Los Angeles, were a small percentage of the total Jewish population. And despite the recognition among Jews regarding the synagogue's mission, there was little evidence that Liebman was correct in predicting that the sense of peoplehood was "as likely to lead to a greater affinity for the religious aspects of Judaism as it [was] to act as a surrogate for religious affiliation." Finally, while Jews might believe that the essence of Judaism involved observance more than morality, there was no indication that the level of observance, minimal at best, was increasing.

Considering the doubtful status of Liebman's four examples, it is surprising that he did not discuss that area of American Jewish life that, perhaps more than any other, would have most strongly confirmed his argument for the continuing distinctiveness of American Jewry. One trait that most clearly distinguished American Jews from their Gentile neighbors and which seemed most impervious to change involved politics. No other white American ethnic group has been so committed to political liberalism, a commitment that has persisted despite fundamental changes in the economic and social status of Jews. Jews, Milton Himmelfarb quipped in 1969, earn money like Episcopalians but vote like Puerto Ricans.

Himmelfarb believed the romance of American Jews with liberalism had become increasingly counterproductive to Jewish interests, and he, along with other political observers, has been predicting for several decades an imminent transformation of Jewish political behavior. As yet, however, voting statistics have given little comfort to conservatives.

The Jewish political profile has deviated sharply from what one would expect from an upwardly mobile ethnic group. Contrary to other groups, Jews have persisted in voting liberal despite a rapid rise in their social and economic status. Jewish neighborhoods in affluent suburbs around New York City strongly supported Democratic presidential candidates during the 1980s, while Ronald Reagan had more support in less affluent Jewish neighborhoods in Brooklyn such as Boro Park. Sociologists noted the anomaly of the Jewish electorate in which conservative voting patterns were to be found in *poorer* Jewish neighborhoods.[2]

Such was the affinity between Jews and liberalism that important Jewish spokesmen asserted that it would be sacrilegious to desert liberalism. In an op-ed piece in the November 2, 1984, *New York Times,* Rabbi Arthur Hertzberg warned Jews that voting for Ronald Reagan and the Republicans in order to benefit their pocketbooks would be to repudiate that which gave meaning to their Jewish lives. Jews, Hertzberg claimed, instinctively knew that politics was about "life and death," the creation of a "world of justice," and "the nature of democracy." The emphasis of conservative Jews on Jewish self-interest was "ignoble" and reduced "the meaning of the Jewish struggle in America to a quest for success and abandons those who are still friendless and foreign to fend for themselves." Leonard Fein agreed. Only a commitment to economic and social justice, Fein wrote, can be "our preeminent motive, the path through which our past is vindicated, our present warranted, and our future affirmed."[3]

Liebman's reluctance to mention politics in order to substantiate his argument that American Jews had remained a distinctive group, despite his own awareness of the significance of liberalism for Jews, was not accidental. It resulted from his understanding of Jewishness, Judaism, and liberalism. For him, the essence of Jewish identity was religion, and what was Jewish about Jews was Judaism. Liebman emphasized that Judaism bore little resemblance to Christianity, in which religious beliefs and declarations of faith were central. Judaism, by contrast, was an ethnic or folk religion, and its most authentic version existed in eastern and central Europe prior to the revolutionary changes accompanying the Enlightenment and emancipation. His interpretation of Judaism was similar to that of Mordecai Kaplan's vision of "Judaism as a civilization." In fact, Liebman described traditional Judaism as a "religious civilization."[4]

The theme of declension dominates Liebman's interpretation of the recent history of Jews and Judaism. In contrast to premodern Jews who lived in tightly knit Jewish communities and for whom Judaism was the all-encompassing fact of their existence, Jews in the Diaspora for the past century have been partial Jews, torn between the competing attractions of the general society and an increasingly attenuated Jewish subculture. A new Jew has emerged "to whom the interrelationships of ethnicity, nationality, culture, and religion had lost resonance. . . . The individual Jew and eventually the entire Jewish community increasingly oriented themselves toward achieving a new position and status within Gentile society."[5]

This was particularly evident in the United States. According to Liebman (and Steven M. Cohen), American Jews had Americanized Judaism by emphasizing its liberalism and universalism. By stressing that "Judaism is a system of shared views they deny the ethnocentricity of their heritage, by making Judaism accessible to those who share these values they universalize it, and by affirming the values as 'liberal' they moralize them." For Liebman, this diminishing of Jewish ethnicity struck at the very essence of Jewish identity. He rejected a "Quaker-like future for American Judaism" bereft of a sense of community and external religious obligation. Instead he argued in *The Ambivalent American Jew* (1973) that the sine qua non of Jewish identity was a sense of Jewish peoplehood, a commitment to the observance of Torah, and the study of Torah and Jewish texts.[6]

Liebman claimed that American Jews were caught "between two sets of values—those of integration and acceptance into American society and those of Jewish group survival." He observed, "These values appear to me to be incompatible. . . . My own position . . . is that if the Jewish community is to survive, it must become more explicit and conscious about the incompatibility of integration and survival." In his own personal life Liebman resolved this conflict by relocating to Israel, the only society in the world where there was no conflict for Jews between national identity and religio-ethnic identity. This, however, was not very helpful for the vast majority of American Jews, who had no intention of making aliyah. For them the question remained regarding the Jewish "values" they were willing to perpetuate in the Diaspora and their conception of what American Jewish survival demanded.[7]

The emergence of alternative forms of Jewish identity during the past two centuries, Liebman believed, was not a sign of cultural creativity but of a Judaism in decay. Zionism, Bundism, and other Jewish movements were ersatz efforts to fill the void created by the decline of Judaism as a religious civilization. In contrast to those who described modern left-wing Jewish politics as the fulfillment of Jewish values and impulses, Liebman saw it as their negation. The Jewish affinity for such politics evidenced an integrationist mentality that threatened American Jewish continuity. "To many Jews, Judaism has meant the fight for social justice, civil rights, and civil liberties," he wrote in 1973. "The difficulty with this conception of Judaism is that on the surface it has very little to do with what is uniquely Jewish."[8]

Liebman suggested that liberalism and Jewish survival were incompatible. The classic goal of liberalism since the late eighteenth century, he emphasized, has been to eliminate all social distinctions among individuals and all intermediary social bodies that stand between the citizen and the state. Liberals rejected Judaism's sharp distinction between Jews and Gentiles, and they opposed the communal thrust of Jewish life. Liberals were also skeptical of the sense of peoplehood that lay at the core of Jewish identity. For liberalism, the individual and not the community was important. Liberalism also rejected the moral absolutism found in all religions, including Judaism.

Commentators from Alexis de Tocqueville in the 1830s to Louis Hartz in the 1950s have emphasized that liberalism has been more dominant in America than in any other society, that America was a liberal society par excellence. Insofar as Liebman saw Judaism endangered in America, it was partially because of the universalism and individualism inherent in liberalism. Judaism was "threatened by contemporary currents in American life," he noted in *The Ambivalent American Jew.* "Fewer and fewer areas today are even neutral to Jewish values. Literature, theater, art, scholarship, politics—all seem to undermine what I consider to be the essentials of Judaism. More than ever before, the values of integration and survival are mutually contradictory. At least until we enter a post-modern world, it seems to me that Jewish survival requires a turning against the integrationist response." This book's pessimism was strikingly different from the rather upbeat argument of Liebman's *Commentary* essay published four years later.[9]

Liebman's fullest exploration of the relationship between politics and Jewish identity was his 1969 essay "Toward a Theory of Jewish Liberalism" (reprinted with minor changes in *The Ambivalent American Jew*). Here he attempted to explain why Jews continued to vote liberal, in contrast to other groups with similar socioeconomic characteristics. He rejected three popular contemporary explanations for Jewish liberalism. The first was best presented in Lawrence Fuchs's *The Political Behavior of American Jews* (1956). Fuchs claimed that Jewish liberalism was a logical outgrowth of Jewish values. These values included a respect for intellectuals and freedom of thought, communal responsibility for the less fortunate, and a rejection of asceticism and otherworldliness.

In response, Liebman noted that traditional Jewish culture had few of the characteristics ascribed to it by Fuchs. It was folk oriented and ethnocentric, not universalistic and cosmopolitan, and it was skeptical of attempts to mold the world through reason. The study of the Torah did not lead to faith in rationality and a commitment to social planning. Traditional Judaism preached instead that prosperity and suffering resulted from God's will, not from man's efforts. Liebman also questioned Fuchs's argument that Jewish intellectuality could be traced back to Judaism. In fact, Jewish traditionalists have been quite skeptical of secular education and intellectuals, believing correctly that the values and lifestyles of the university and the salon had little in common with those of the Torah. Finally, Liebman noted that if liberalism was a product of Jewish values, then the most Jewish of Jews should have been the most liberal. This has not been the case. The most alienated of Jews have tended to be the most liberal and radical, while the most traditional of Jews have inclined to be the least liberal. "The evidence seems to indicate," Liebman concluded, "that one cannot find the source of Jewish political liberalism in the religious values of Judaism."[10]

The sociologist Seymour Martin Lipset offered another theory of the origins of Jewish liberalism, which emphasized the disparity between the economic and the social status of Jews. American Jews, Lipset claimed, deeply resented the fact that their economic accomplishments had not earned them commensurate social status. As a result, Jews were attracted to political movements that sought to overthrow the economic and social status quo. Liebman correctly noted that Lipset's thesis helped explain a Jewish affinity to radicalism, but not to liberalism, and that only a small minority of Jews had been drawn to radical movements. Also, Lipset's arguments could not possibly explain the leftist political preferences of Jewish garment workers who felt no disparity between their economic and their social positions. The inferior-status hypothesis, Liebman said, "leaves unanswered the more specific question of interpreting Jewish response to the political environment; why should the Jews respond to society's image of them rather than their own self-image?"[11]

The third and most popular interpretation of the origins of Jewish liberalism stressed its historical roots. The historical interpretation argued that Jews had been attracted to European left-of-center political movements because of their support for Jewish emancipation and their opposition to restrictions on Jewish social and economic opportunities, while Jews had been repelled by conservative parties, which were aligned with the anti-Semitic Russian Orthodox, Roman Catholic, and Lutheran Churches. This historical interpretation, Liebman said, failed to explain why, prior to the Great Depression, American Jews divided their votes among Socialists, Democrats, and Republicans, why the Orthodox Yiddish press on New York's Lower East Side was Republican in the early twentieth century, why Jews born in America have been more liberal than their immigrant ancestors, why Jewish political parties in Poland often aligned themselves with conservative rather than with left-of-center parties, and why Jews should welcome emancipation at all since it threatened traditional religious and communal institutions and loyalties.

While recognizing that the historical argument was not without merit, Liebman nevertheless claimed that it "posits too much for a particular historical condition and it fails to account for distinctions among Jews." There must have been other sociological and historical factors in America that reinforced any initial Jewish commitment to the political Left. The last part of "Toward a Theory of Jewish Liberalism" describes these factors.[12]

According to Liebman, the flowering of Jewish liberalism in America resulted from a decline in Jewish identity. Liberalism appealed to Jews because of a cosmopolitanism and a universalistic ethic "which is seemingly irrelevant to specific Jewish concerns." A prime example of this was liberalism's defense of the strict separation of church and state and its assumption that religion was solely a private matter. Jews living in a society governed by liberal principles did not have to make their Jewishness public. Liberalism thus went hand in hand with acculturation and assimilation. But, Liebman maintained, the future of Judaism and the Jewish people depended on making distinctions between Jews and Gentiles, and between the sacred and the profane.[13]

Liebman's interpretation of the source of Jewish liberalism bears a striking resemblance to the pre–World War II complaints of anti-Semites regarding the political impact of Jews. The cosmopolitanism and universalism of liberalism, Liebman contended, was a modern manifestation of the traditional Jewish estrangement from Gentile society. Liberalism was a philosophy of the alienated, "an ethic which could be posed against society's traditions." In contrast to Zionists and the Orthodox, who sought to overcome their estrangement by creating a Jewish state or by living within a totally encapsulated religious environment, Jewish liberals attempted to surmount their disaffection by creating a society free of religious and ethnic distinctions. According to Liebman, Jewish liberals were engaged in a virtual conspiracy to facilitate the entry of Jews into American society. They wished, he wrote, "to impose the Jewish condition of estrangement upon society" at large. Jews gravitated to liberalism not because it promised to repair the world but because it fostered Jewish acceptance.[14]

While liberalism might be good for the social and economic advancement of individual Jews, Liebman said, its popularity reflected a weakening of Jewish commitments. This analysis, however, was not readily accepted by Jews. Liberal Jews sought the best of two worlds. On the one hand, liberalism did not demand that they cease identifying as Jews. On the other, liberalism encouraged the casting aside of those Jewish characteristics that sharply distinguished Jews from non-Jews. Liberalism was popular among Jews who were "most estranged from their own traditions and hence most concerned with finding a value that supports Jewish acceptance without overtly destroying Jewish group ties."[15]

The dismal prognosis regarding the American Jewish condition in "Toward a Theory of Jewish Liberalism" helps explain why Liebman chose to reprint it in the equally gloomy *The Ambivalent American Jew.* Liebman's caveats regarding liberalism, specifically his image of liberalism as the politics of the alienated, resulted from his overall pessimism regarding the future of American Jewry. He is a Jewish survivalist and believes that the essence of Jewishness is Judaism. He was disturbed by the phenomenon of Jews who defined Jewishness in terms of liberal politics, for whom being Jewish meant having a Jewish heart. Liebman was not impressed by a Jewish identity that revolved around liberalism, since there was nothing uniquely Jewish about liberalism (or anything uniquely un-Jewish about conservatism). Franklin D. Roosevelt, Hubert Humphrey, John Dewey, and Hugo Black demonstrated that one did not have to be Jewish to be a liberal.

"Toward a Theory of Jewish Liberalism" concluded with a brief paragraph regarding the prospects of Jewish liberalism. "Its future is no more assured than is the continued state of Jewish estrangement," Liebman wrote. "My own impression is that the future of Jewish liberalism is a bleak one." If assimilation reached the point where Jews no longer felt alienated from Christian America, or, conversely, if Jewish identity was intensified, Jews would no longer be attracted to a politics that spoke to their estrangement and emphasized universalism and cosmopolitanism. By the 1970s, according to Liebman, even Jewish liberals realized that the marriage between liberalism and Jewishness was unraveling. The typical Jewish liberal now "felt himself increasingly alienated from his traditional ideological concerns, so that social justice was no longer a satisfactory vehicle by which to define his focus of expression."[16]

The years since 1969 have not confirmed Liebman's prognosis for the future of Jewish liberalism. Despite frequent predictions that Jews were moving to the right, they have remained wedded as strongly as ever to liberal politics. Notwithstanding the friendliness of Republican administrations during the 1970s and 1980s toward Israel, Jews continued to vote overwhelmingly Democratic and to be the major source of campaign contributions for liberal politicians. Neither individual Jewish leaders nor Jewish organizations such as the American Jewish Congress evidenced any tendency to break with liberalism. The rightward movement of *Commentary* was idiosyncratic and hardly indicative of general Jewish political sentiments. "American Jewish liberalism persists," Liebman noted in *Two Worlds of Judaism*.[17]

The reason for this continuing commitment to liberalism lay in the evolution of American Jewish identity. With the dying out of the immigrant generation, there remained only a smattering of Jews for whom Jewishness involved immersion in a distinctively Jewish culture. And despite the tendency of American culture to define Jewishness in religious terms, only a minority of Jews took traditional Judaism seriously. Acculturated and secular Jews filled this cultural and religious void with liberal politics and support for Israel and other Jewish interests. Rather than facilitating assimilation, as Liebman contended, liberalism enabled Jews to identify with a Jewish history and a Jewish community from which they were otherwise estranged.

The fears of Jews regarding the issue of church and state intensified their commitment to liberalism. With the exception of Israel's security, no political issue of the 1980s concerned Jews more than the impact of the Christian Right. This was particularly true in 1984 when President Reagan professed sympathy for the politics of right-wing evangelical Christians. Despite Reagan's staunch support for Israel, the economic recovery of the early 1980s, and the avid Republican courting of Jews in 1984, the Jewish vote for Reagan was less in 1984 than in 1980. Instead of recognizing Reagan's overtures to conservative Christians as typical campaign boilerplate, Jews worried that the United States was on the verge of being transformed into a Christian state. It is not surprising that Jews would have such a distorted understanding of the nature of American politics.

Among the most salient characteristics of the Jewish political ethic is an intense distrust of political power. Because of their unfortunate experiences with political authorities and their exclusion from politics while living in Eastern Europe and the Arab lands, Jews have almost a visceral distrust of politics, politicians, and officials such as the police and the military who exercise political power. In contrast, say, to the Irish, Jews have tended to view politics idealistically rather than as an opportunity for personal advancement. Jews did not look to politics as a career. "The only excuse for a Jewish [bloc] vote," Rabbi Stephen S. Wise once asserted, was "to keep bad Jews out of office. We can leave it to the fairness of the American public to elect good Jews."[18]

This fear of governmental power and support for the rights of individuals threatened by the state is manifested in the many civil liberties lawyers who are Jews; in the financial contributions of Jews to the American Civil Liberties Union and other civil libertarian organizations; in the advocacy of Jews for civilian review boards to monitor the police and for laws protecting the rights of communists, homosexuals, and abortionists; in the tendency of Jews to give the benefit of the doubt to the powerless in any conflict with government or powerful economic interests; and in the relatively small number of Jews who choose law enforcement or the military as a career. One survey in the 1980s of American Jewish attitudes regarding marriage and divorce, censorship and pornography, and the use of drugs reported that only 11 percent of American Jews favored more government involvement and stricter law enforcement in these areas, while 60 percent wanted less. Jews, particularly more affluent Jews, became even more sympathetic to liberalism during the 1980s, when issues of culture, lifestyles, and individual rights became more important on the liberal agenda than economic concerns.[19]

A good example of the Jewish attitude toward politics concerns abortion.

Conservative Jews such as Irving Kristol were puzzled by the strong support of secular American Jewish organizations for the pro-choice movement. Such a stance, Kristol noted, appeared incongruous in view of the low Jewish birthrate, the hemorrhaging of the American Jewish population due to intermarriage and assimilation, the effectiveness with which Jewish women use birth control devices, the low rate of illegitimacy among Jewish women, and the opposition of Jewish tradition to permissive abortions. Jews, it would appear, are less concerned with the pro-life movement's direct effect on them than with what they perceive to be its attempt to use political authority to limit the rights of individuals.[20]

Alan Fisher, an authority on American Jewish political behavior, has emphasized the relationship between this Jewish distrust of political authority and foreign policy issues. Three decades of research into Jewish voting patterns convinced him that there were "no greater and more consistent differences between Jews and non-Jews than on the topic of violence, including support for war." This was true even regarding the Gulf War, a conflict that, if America had been successful, would have destroyed the military might of Iraq, a major threat to Israel. That Jews were less supportive of military action against Iraq, Fisher concluded, "conforms with their extreme reluctance to resort to arms." The fears of Jews regarding international violence have also been responsible for their exaggerated faith in the United Nations as an arbiter of international disputes.[21]

An alienation from a sense of community has accompanied this Jewish fear of political authority. On at least one occasion Liebman discussed this alienation without, however, commenting on its political ramifications. In "The Sociology of Religion and the Study of American Jews," an essay published in 1971, Liebman praised the Orthodox home for inculcating a sense of community:

> The Orthodox home is related to a *kashrut*-observing community of time and place. The Orthodox Jew lives with the sense of an omnipresent community which mediates relationships to other Jews, to Jewish history, and to major Jewish symbols. At the simplest level this means that the relationships to the local Jewish community, the national Jewish community and even to Israel take place through a network of institutions (the synagogue, the day school, American counterparts of Israeli political parties, hospitals and other philanthropic societies, and so on) which share an Orthodox orientation. On the other hand, relationships at the most intimate level, family and peers, are, at least to some extent, governed by a sense of obligation toward the rules and customs of that community.[22]

The Yiddish novelist Chaim Grade, in describing the traditional Jewish community of Eastern Europe, emphasized this sense of community. "With us Jews the individual doesn't exist; it's the community that counts." Here, perhaps, is the key to understanding the differing political orientations of the Orthodox and the other 90 percent of American Jews. Emancipated from the demands of community and lacking the respect for authority found among the religious, the non-Orthodox majority inevitably regard politics, politicians, and the demands of community with suspicion. They are estranged not only from the traditional Jewish community but also from American society. What matters to them is individual self-fulfillment, not the maintenance of institutions, tradition, and communal norms. The Orthodox, for a variety of reasons, have tended to view liberalism with skepticism. These reasons include, according to Samuel C. Heilman and Steven M. Cohen, "clear *halachic* dictates, unambiguous institutional interests, a preference for more traditional personal life styles, an interest in public policies that protect traditional mores in private life, and insular personal networks."[23]

Why did Liebman not highlight the relationship between the alienation of American Jews from, and distrust of, power and community on the one hand and their commitment to liberalism on the other, particularly when it would have confirmed his pessimism regarding the future of American Jewry? Perhaps the answer is to be found in the nature of his discipline. Although trained as a political scientist, his primary research for the past several decades has been in sociology. Sociology studies the variety of relationships—religious, political, and social—people form with one another. As the eminent sociologist Robert A. Nisbet frequently noted, sociology emerged in the late eighteenth and early nineteenth centuries as a protest against the atomizing effects of the French Revolution. While the revolutionists preached the rights of man, the earliest sociologists emphasized the role of institutions; while the revolutionists stressed individualism, the sociologists underscored the primacy of community; while the revolutionists argued that life belonged to the living, the sociologists stressed the significance of historical memory.

For liberal Jews, politics involves acting apart from, and frequently in opposition to, the institutions, social structures, and traditions that are the very essence of sociological study. Is it surprising, then, that as a working sociologist Liebman would not dwell at length on the American Jews' almost anarchic attitude toward political power? Perhaps this also explains why he has written at greater length on politics in Israel where, he has noted, there is "very little relationship between Judaism and liberalism."[24]

THIRTEEN

The War among the Jews

AMERICAN JEWRY during the 1970s and 1980s experienced a series of political controversies that involved, among other things, differences over the place of political liberalism in defining Jewish identity. One such conflict in the early 1980s concerned Jacobo Timerman, an Argentinian Jew and prominent journalist. The response of Jews to Timerman was one aspect of an incipient struggle within American Jewry between a regnant liberalism and what came to be known as "neoconservatism."

In the spring of 1981 Timerman published *Prisoner Without a Name, Cell Without a Number,* a harrowing description of his imprisonment and house arrest by Argentinian military authorities from April 1977 through September 1979. Timerman recounted in graphic detail the agonies of his confinement, stressing throughout the anti-Semitism permeating the Argentinian military dictatorship, the harsh treatment meted out to him because of his Jewish background, and the pusillanimous attitude of the Jewish leadership of Argentina. *Prisoner Without a Name* also sketched Timerman's biography and his involvement in Jewish affairs. From an early age he had been involved in left-wing Zionist activities, although he had never played any role in the established Jewish community of Argentina. His Jewish identity centered on leftist politics. Proclaiming himself "passionately Jewish," Timerman noted that "my Judaism was a political act."[1]

Prisoner Without a Name created a storm of controversy. Those sympathetic to Timerman used his memoir to indict the Argentinian regime and to criticize the efforts of the Reagan administration to forge better relations with Buenos Aires and to modify the human rights theme that had played such a prominent role in the diplomacy of the Carter government. Timerman even

This chapter was previously published in *Intercollegiate Review* 18 (fall–winter 1982): 25–38. Reprinted by permission of the Intercollegiate Studies Institute, Inc.

appeared as a silent witness at the hearings of the Senate Foreign Relations Committee to protest the nomination of Ernest Lefever as assistant secretary of state for human rights and humanitarian affairs. Timerman became an instant celebrity. He appeared on Bill Moyers's television show, and his book received a front-page review by Anthony Lewis in the *New York Times Book Review.* After his release and deportation from Argentina, Timerman settled in Israel. He soon became a vocal critic of the Begin government's policies regarding the Palestinian issue. "I see that this country is going to totalitarianism and fanaticism. . . . I see very clearly a repetition of what happened in Argentina," he claimed. In future elections, "if there is a good general as a candidate, he will win. There is always a democratic way to elect a fascist government."[2]

Timerman also injected himself into the controversy over the Reagan administration's policy toward violations of human rights by governments sympathetic to the United States. The rationale for this policy had been laid down by Jeane Kirkpatrick in her famous article, "Dictatorships and Double Standards," which caught the future president's attention when it appeared in *Commentary* magazine in November 1979. The essay was prompted by what Kirkpatrick saw as American complicity in the overthrow of the shah in Iran and the Somoza regime in Nicaragua. She argued that the Carter administration had cooperated in replacing pro-American, moderate autocrats with anti-American revolutionary governments. The United States, she contended, should not attempt to impose democracy and liberalism on governments fighting for their very existence. Any such attempts would merely hasten the coming to power of regimes that would deprive their people of their remaining rights. Furthermore, it was unrealistic to expect democratic governments to arise in those parts of the world where social conditions and history were different from those of the West. Kirkpatrick also maintained that a right-wing autocracy was far likelier than a revolutionary government to evolve into a liberal regime. In addition, right-wing governments were generally more sympathetic to the United States than revolutionary ones. She believed the Carter administration's failures in foreign policy were due in part to a "lack of realism about the nature of traditional versus revolutionary autocracies and the relation of each to the American national interest."

Kirkpatrick provided Reagan with the rationale for changing American policies toward right-wing, pro-American regimes such as those in South Korea, Chile, Taiwan, and Argentina. Kirkpatrick would soon be called upon to defend the new American stance regarding violations of human rights when she was selected as the Reagan administration's ambassador to the United Nations. The Reagan government was particularly interested in overturning the embargo on the shipment of arms to Argentina, which had been imposed during the Carter years. Timerman, naturally, vigorously dissented from the American government's new attitude toward Buenos Aires. He claimed that Kirkpatrick, Reagan, and Secretary of State Alexander Haig were oblivious to the issue of human rights, unconcerned with human rights, authoritarian in outlook, and monomaniacal regarding communism.[3]

One aspect of the Timerman controversy overlooked by the general public was that Timerman and his book were the focus of a serious debate among American Jews. This controversy not only reflected the extreme sensitivity among Jews regarding anything evoking memories of the Holocaust, but it also highlighted the rightward drift of some American Jewish intellectuals who sought to transform American Jewish political and social attitudes. The controversy surrounding Timerman tells us as much about the metamorphosis of the American Jewish community as it does about the status of Argentina's four hundred thousand Jews.

For decades the liberalism of American Jews has been viewed as one of the unchangeables of American politics, having withstood rapid Jewish economic and cultural mobility, the breakdown of the political coalition forged by Franklin Roosevelt in the 1930s, and the decline of modern liberalism. Of all ethnic groups, none seemed to ignore with such consistency their economic self-interest as the Jews, and none seemed to be so wedded to the liberal wing of the Democratic Party. "Jews," the onetime radical sociologist Irving Louis Horowitz once wrote, "have proven to be a unique force in American politics in that, despite their class backgrounds or interests, they have exhibited the capacity to vote and act beyond their class and interest group constraints." It is not coincidental that New York City is home to both the largest single concentration of Jews in the world and the most liberal city in the nation.[4]

Jews, it was said by a Jewish Republican during the 1940s, had three "velten" (worlds): "die velt" (this world); "yene velt" (the future world); and Roosevelt. The liberalism of Jews shaped their understanding of other countries and foreign relations. Jews had traditionally identified anti-Semitism with the Right, and they interpreted Nazism as a right-wing reactionary movement. They ignored the fact that the Nazi Party professed a commitment to "national socialism." Jews attributed the rise of Hitler to the social dislocations and economic misery resulting from the Great Depression. Liberal reforms to alleviate social discontent by providing good housing, jobs, unemployment insurance, free health care, and subsidized educational benefits were seen as barriers to the spread of anti-Semitism. Jews in America thus assumed that liberalism and Jewish welfare went hand in hand. A Jewish conservative verged on being a political exotic, if not an oxymoron.

In the 1960s and 1970s, however, a minority of Jews moved politically to the right. Their numbers included some of America's most prominent conservative and neoconservative intellectuals. In April 1973 Irving Kristol, the so-called godfather of neoconservatism, prematurely declared in *Congress Bi-Weekly* that the alliance between the Left and the Jews had ended. "This is not a temporary phenomenon. Jewish politics in the decades to come are going to be very different from what Jewish politics have been in the past century and a half." This was contested by a small clique of Jewish socialists associated with *Dissent* magazine.[5]

In the mid-1970s Bernard Rosenberg and Irving Howe published an essay that asked, "Are American Jews Turning to the Right?" They noted that this question had become a matter of great concern since "the overwhelming thrust of Jewish thought and writing in America these past several decades has been liberal, notably more so than in the population at large; and whatever radicalism we have had in America has found disproportionate support among Jews." Although skeptical that the Jewish commitment to the Left had been shattered, Rosenberg and Howe pointed to Norman Podhoretz's *Commentary,* published by the American Jewish Committee, as evidence of a rightward shift among some Jewish intellectuals. They did not believe *Commentary* was as yet a conservative magazine. Rather it remained a liberal magazine, although one opposed to the "vulgarizations of liberalism." *Commentary*'s drift to the right was symptomatic of a growing Jewish disillusionment with some of the more outlandish aspects of the liberalism of the 1960s, Rosenberg and Howe claimed, but it would require more than mere disillusionment for a Jewish conservatism to appear. It would demand a positive and coherent ideology.[6]

Howe and Rosenberg admitted there were certain factors with the potential for fostering a Jewish conservatism. These included upward economic mobility, the decline of the Jewish labor movement, cultural assimilation, fear of black anti-Semitism, a greater concern for ethnic survival, and anxiety over the security of Israel. They predicted that Jewish political attitudes would exhibit a greater emphasis on class and group interest. "We are witnessing," Rosenberg and Howe wrote, "a regrouping of forces and ideas within the Jewish world that will bring into existence a stronger conservative wing, which will in time enable the emergence of a conservative Jewish intelligentsia. . . . Certainly, we are witnessing a regrouping of forces within the Jewish world, which will result in a conservatizing of its dominant liberalism." And yet they believed that liberalism had a fighting chance to retain its hold on the Jewish community. But this would occur only if the majority of Jews remained faithful to Jewish values of moral compassion and social commitment.[7]

Podhoretz directly confronted his socialist critics in 1979 when he published *Breaking Ranks,* his memoir of the intellectual wars of the 1960s. Here he admitted to being a "neoconservative" and attacked the socialism of Irving Howe's *Dissent* for having "no discernible content" and for resembling a religious faith. Only the fact that socialism had become a surrogate religion impervious to the realities of contemporary life, Podhoretz said, explained Howe's continuing commitment to socialism. The less socialist content there remained in Howe's thinking, "the more desperate he was to affirm his socialist faith. And since there was so little of a positive nature left to affirm, what he mainly did was to attack other intellectuals for deserting the true faith." Podhoretz also attributed a darker side to Howe's attacks on *Commentary.* Howe's personal position within the American Left depended on remaining an advocate of socialism, although he had long since ceased believing in it. This could be most easily achieved by criticizing *Commentary,* the most prominent opponent of liberal and socialist pieties.[8]

Dissent's response to *Breaking Ranks* was not long in coming. Its spring 1981 issue contained a long "special feature" by Bernard Avishai, a professor at the Massachusetts Institute of Technology, titled "Breaking Faith: *Commentary* and the American Jews." Ironically, Avishai's title and his twenty pages of turgid prose confirmed Podhoretz's argument that *Dissent*'s socialism had degenerated into a secularist religion. Avishai contrasted the self-satisfied conservatism of *Commentary* with the *Jewish Daily Forward,* the radical labor movement, and the "heroes, sensibilities, moral taste, the *civil religion to which we try to make converts.*" (Avishai's emphasis) Not only had *Commentary* deserted Jewish interests, but it had also rejected its own previous commitment to "social action" as a Jewish "vocation," as well as its previous opposition to military adventurism and evangelical anticommunism. *Commentary* in its golden years had believed that Jews "belonged with the utilitarians, the socialists and democrats; with people who took the emerging social good and not the individual's sensuous pleasure as the preeminent moral problem."

Avishai attributed *Commentary*'s initial fall from a state of grace to the Six Day War of 1967. This injected into the magazine a Jewish jingoism, which overwhelmed the intellectual detachment and commitment to radicalism that had been the sources of the magazine's creativity during its golden years of the early 1960s. Podhoretz had thus broken ranks "with those people who were holding to the radically democratic view of politics with which *Commentary* had justifiably tried to identify American Jews for a decade." The new *Commentary* had become a house organ for the Jewish establishment and a spokesman for its crassest interests. This was accompanied by a "narrow and reckless style of argument" and a mean-spirited attitude toward social reform in general and affirmative action in particular. *Commentary,* Avishai wrote in prose characteristic of the true believer contemplating the apostate, had been "wrong in the most discreditable way, violating common standards of fairness." It was the responsibility of thinking Jews to "respond in public and repudiate the politics that the magazine claims to be pursuing for our 'own good.' "

Avishai even doubted that *Commentary*'s renowned support for Israel was good for the Jews. By focusing on the strategic value of Israel to America, the journal had weakened the support for the Jewish state among her most reliable allies—"liberal politicians, progressive journalists, labor leaders." They supported Israel because it was democratic and socialist, not because of the Jewish state's importance as a cold-war ally of America. *Commentary* had thus helped discredit Israel on college campuses, in the liberal press, and wherever there was a well-educated "progressive constituency" opposed to the escalation of the cold war. Avishai concluded his diatribe by accusing the magazine of contributing to "wide-scale disillusionment with democratic humanism," to the growth of the New Right and Christian fundamentalism, and to a decline in federal funding of Jewish philanthropic institutions. Only a return to "the urbane, communitarian values of the Left," the same values that had been espoused by Podhoretz before he turned nasty and which traditionally had been the authentic values of American Jews, could guarantee the continuing social and intellectual relevance of American Jewry.[9]

As if to answer Avishai's accusation that it did not speak for Jewish interests and values, *Commentary* published an essay in its December 1981 issue by Murray Friedman espousing "A New Direction for American Jews." Friedman called for a radical change in the activities and goals of Jewish community relations organizations, such as the American Jewish Congress, the American Jewish Committee, and the Anti-Defamation League of B'nai B'rith. Since the New Deal, Friedman noted, Jewish community relations personnel had supported legislation and judicial decisions strengthening civil rights for minorities, a strict secularist interpretation of church-state relations, and the expansion of federal social welfare programs. Possessing a "liberal-left perspective," the professionals believed that the fates of liberalism and Jews were inextricably bound together. Friedman contended this perspective was out of date and that there was an urgent need for a reshaping of the Jewish political outlook.

Among the factors that he believed might cause Jews to rethink their commitment to liberalism were the seemingly inexorable growth of government, taxes, and the dependent class; evidence that liberalism was undermining the moral fiber of the nation; and the weakened position of America in world affairs. Friedman also mentioned the commitment by the American Left to quotas in employment and education, as well as the fact that certain elements on the left were voicing anti-Semitism and anti-Zionism. Friedman hoped Jewish professionals would recognize that many aspects of the welfare state were counterproductive and that their concern for the separation of church and state would not blind them to legitimate fears concerning crime, pornography, abortion on demand, and drugs.

The Jewish community, Friedman contended, was threatened far more by the "breakdown of the orderly norms of our society" than by minor breaches in the wall of separation between church and state. He was particularly disturbed by the opposition of Jewish spokesmen to tuition tax credits and vouchers for parents electing to send their children to nonpublic schools. In concluding his call for a new direction for American Jews, Friedman argued on behalf of "a moderate conservatism" aimed at bringing inflation under control, reviving the economy, and strengthening social norms and civilized discourse. As of yet Jewish professionals had failed to develop new strategies and policies to meet the growing doubts regarding liberalism. They had not confronted "some of the implications and consequences of their activities, their policies, and their ideas, let alone to ponder what will be required of them in the years ahead."[10]

Jews such as Friedman believed that much of the political inheritance from their parents was now irrelevant, anachronistic, and contrary to American interests in general and to Jewish interests in particular. The result was the articulation by a group of Jewish neoconservative intellectuals of what Friedman aptly called "a moderate conservatism," which challenged the leftward tilt of most Jewish intellectuals. One noteworthy aspect of this intra-ethnic debate within the Jewish intelligentsia involved Timerman's *Prisoner Without a Name.*

The most prominent case for Timerman's volume was Anthony Lewis's review in the May 10, 1981, *New York Times Book Review.* Intemperately titled "The Final Solution in Argentina," the review focused on the anti-Semitic aspect of Timerman's ordeal. Claiming the volume to be "the most important book I have read in a long time," Lewis asserted that it provided an unforgettable picture of state terrorism and of a "sophisticated society falling into irrationality and savagery." One week after his review appeared, Lewis returned to the Timerman case with a *Times* column asking, "What Kind of Country Are We?" Here Lewis attacked the Reagan administration for making overtures to Argentina, where, he wrote, anti-Semitism has become virtually an official policy of the government. He called upon American Jews to make their opposition to any rapprochement with Buenos Aires known. The issue was "one of our own soul. Are things at such a point that we Americans must enlist torturers and murderers as our allies and proclaim their values . . . as ours? . . . How must we appear to ourselves? What kind of country are we?"[11]

Timerman had provided the American Left with a timely issue to condemn the Reagan government. If Jacobo Timerman had not existed, the Left would have had to invent him or somebody like him. The distinction of the Reaganites between right-wing authoritarian governments and left-wing totalitarian regimes, which was basic to the outlook of the administration, was for Lewis "pseudo-academic rubbish." Lewis argued in this manner despite the fact that the distinction between totalitarianism and authoritarianism had been familiar to historians and political scientists for several decades.[12]

Irving Kristol answered Lewis's questions in a controversial essay published in the May 29, 1981, issue of the *Wall Street Journal.* Kristol claimed that Timerman's lofty position in American public opinion was due less to his sufferings and more to the fact that he had become a symbol of opposition to Reagan's efforts to mend fences with rightist regimes. Describing Timerman as a "Solzhenitsyn-of-the-Left," Kristol was troubled both by the Argentinian's failure to discuss in his book his relationship with David Graiver and by his analysis of the Argentinian Jewish community. Graiver, a bank swindler on a gigantic scale, had owned 45 percent of the stock of *La Opinion,* Timerman's newspaper. Kristol asserted that the Argentine government suspected Graiver of being the investment banker for Argentina's left-wing urban terrorists and that Timerman had been implicated in Graiver's activities. Kristol claimed that Timerman knew he had been arrested because of his association with Graiver. He failed to mention Graiver in his book because he did not want to detract from his role as a martyr to the right-wing government of Buenos Aires.

Kristol was also troubled by Timerman's attacks on the leadership of the Argentinian Jewish community for not being more vigorous in protesting violations of human rights and anti-Semitism. Kristol wondered whether these leaders did not have a better appreciation of the situation of Argentinian Jewry than Timerman. Timerman's description of Argentinian Jewry tottering on the edge of another Holocaust was "irresponsible and dishonest demagogy." The Argentinian regime, "for all its ugly aspects, is authoritarian, not totalitarian," and it was doing its best to eliminate anti-Semitism. Kristol predicted that the quiet diplomatic attempts of the Reagan administration would prove successful in moving Buenos Aires in the direction of liberalization, contrary to the predictions of Timerman and his leftist supporters.[13]

Suspicions about Timerman's relationship with Graiver were not original with Kristol. They had surfaced in December 1980 when Benno W. Varon, a former Israeli diplomat with four decades of experience in Latin America, published "Don't Rescue Latin American Jews!" in the right-of-center Zionist magazine *Midstream*. Through this and later writings Varon would become the leading debunker of Timerman. Varon denied that Argentinian Jewry was in any danger or that the Argentine government was a terrorist regime. Jews, in fact, were prospering in Argentina, and their leaders did not share Timerman's paranoia. For Varon, Timerman was neither a Dreyfus nor a Sharansky. Rather, he was the hapless associate of Mr. David Graiver.[14]

Varon's essay provoked much comment, both critical and favorable. Morton M. Rosenthal, director of B'nai B'rith's Anti-Defamation League's Department of Latin American Affairs, accused Varon of appeasing anti-Semites, of acquiescing in the "suffering of the just," and of writing a piece of "garbage." Rosenthal also described Kristol's essay as "character assassination." Varon responded to Rosenthal by claiming that he had no personal animus against Timerman, that he wished him well, and that he felt he had treated him fairly. It would be difficult to make such claims a few months later after Varon's review of *Prisoner Without a Name* appeared in *Midstream*.[15]

"The Canonization of Jacobo Timerman" accused Timerman of conveying a grotesque caricature of Argentina and Argentinian Jewry, of exaggerating the importance of his ordeal, of deliberately omitting any mention of David Graiver, and of playing fast and loose with the truth. Varon was particularly annoyed by Timerman's comparison of Argentina's Jewish leaders with the subservient Jewish councils established by the Nazis in Eastern Europe. Timerman, Varon wrote, "cannot forgive the Jews of Argentina for not considering his tragedy a Jewish tragedy, for not identifying themselves with one who was champion of revolutions and would-be king maker, for considering him not their hero but Graiver's victim." Timerman was being used by the American Left for their own purposes. His rise to prominence was sponsored by those who favor "a guerrilla victory in El Salvador, and intend to influence events in all of Latin America."[16]

Varon was undoubtedly correct that Timerman had assumed mythic proportions within the American Left, particularly among Jewish leftists. Anthony Lewis described the neoconservative attacks on Timerman as mere "pinpricks" and evidence of moral bankruptcy. Alfred Kazin argued in the *New Republic* that Timerman had become such an embarrassment to the Reagan administration that "right-wing Jewish salesmen" had resorted to using "every possible slur" against him. Theodore Solotaroff's review in the *Nation* described Timerman as a "prophet" and "an extraordinary man: reflective, humane, righteous and withal extremely brave, resourceful and hardheaded." He has made Jews "feel proud and protected." Michael Walzer's discussion in the *New York Review of Books* noted Timerman's "political and moral stature," while his suffering gave the lie to the Reaganite distinction between good authoritarians and bad totalitarians. The neoconservative critique of Timerman was "beneath contempt," the product of "great simplifiers." "These public statements," Walzer wrote, "suggest that even where there are no royal courts, there are still court Jews."[17]

Dissent's contribution to the discussion of Timerman was Leon Wieseltier's essay "The Many Trials of Jacobo Timerman." Wieseltier, a graduate student at Harvard, pictured Timerman as a principled foe of all human rights violators and "a democrat, pleading vainly for a return to legality." His memoir was "one of the century's great works of conscience." His critics, by contrast, lacked "political judgment and moral authority," undermined the anticommunist cause, and encouraged fascism and anti-Semitism. "Perhaps the most disgraceful aspect of the campaign against Timerman," Wieseltier went on, "is that it was begun by Jews." This, he claimed, stemmed from the confusion of neoconservative Jewish intellectuals regarding the Argentinian situation and the nature of anti-Semitism, as well as from their support of the Reagan administration, particularly its foreign policy.[18]

Jewish Frontier, the American organ of the socialist Zionist movement, came to its compatriot's defense in its August/September 1981 issue. A long editorial by Mitchell Cohen, the magazine's editor, accused Jewish conservatives of willingness to sacrifice Jewish interests on behalf of petty, self-interested politics. Irving Kristol's essay was an "outrageous" effort in character assassination. Fortunately, Timerman "does not bow before neo-conservative claptrap." This is his "triumph." *Prisoner Without a Name* is "a passionate account of the violation of human dignity by the fascists who control and abuse the people of Argentina today." Cohen's editorial accompanied an article by Elliot King, a New York journalist, that asked, "Who's Afraid of Jacobo Timerman?" He termed Varon's original *Midstream* essay "a shameful whitewash of anti-Semitic activity in Argentina" and contended that the critics of Timerman were encouraging Argentinian anti-Semitism.[19]

The Labor Zionists were not the only Jewish group that came to Timerman's defense. The Reform movement honored Timerman for struggling on behalf of human rights. The American Jewish Congress publication *Congress Monthly* strongly attacked Timerman's detractors and the Reagan administration's human rights stance. Timerman was living witness to "the moral bankruptcy of a policy which embraces torturers rather than the tortured." Kristol and other Jewish conservatives, *Congress Monthly* said, have sown "divisiveness and confusion in the Jewish community" and have done "a disservice to Jewish concerns and to human rights." The time had come for Jews to reaffirm their support for human rights, which "has long been part of our religious tradition, part of our self-esteem, woven into our history, pursued in causes often unpopular, often perilous."[20]

Moment, a Jewish monthly edited by the liberal political scientist Leonard Fein, reprinted Lewis's "What Kind of Country Are We?" Fein himself discussed "The Timerman Conspiracy," which he described as comprised of intellectuals engaged in a "smear" campaign against Timerman. Included among the smearers were Varon, Kristol, and Mark Falcoff, the author of an anti-Timerman essay in the July 1981 *Commentary*. The conspirators were united by the belief that anti-Sovietism should be the overriding goal of American diplomacy. "The stakes here are very large," Fein wrote. If the Reaganites have their way, "both American law and the American soul" would be subsumed under the anti-Soviet banner. Thus Timerman had to be discredited in order to court favor with the anti-Soviet regime in Argentina. "The most eloquent rebuttal to Kristol and his ilk," Fein claimed, "is a renewed commitment to the defense of human rights wherever they are systematically violated, whoever the victim of their abuses." For Fein, Timerman was a courageous "liberal" and thereby deserving of American Jewish support. In fact, "liberal" is a political category with little or no relationship to the Argentinian situation. Timerman was certainly no "liberal." He was either a political opportunist, as his critics charged, or a long-standing socialist and a man of the Left as he described himself in *Prisoner Without a Name*.[21]

The American Jewish Forum, a short-lived conservative organization created by Professor Seymour Siegel of the Jewish Theological Seminary, lent its support to Timerman's foes. Timerman's comparison of Argentina to Nazi Germany, it asserted, was "an error of the grossest sort." Not only was it wrong, but the Argentinian publisher knew it was wrong. The refusal of Argentinian Jews to take their property and leave their country was a more accurate indication of the status of anti-Semitism in Argentina than Timerman's overheated and self-serving fantasies. Rabbi Siegel suggested that the American government should support the Argentinian military junta and quietly attempt to move it along the path of democracy and liberty. This, and not the moralizing of the Carter administration or the feverish rhetoric of Timerman, would keep the strategically located and economically powerful Argentinians on the side of the West.[22]

The most important conservative analyses of the Timerman book appeared in *Contentions* and *Commentary*. *Contentions*, the organ of the Committee for the Free World, a hard-line anticommunist group headed by Norman Podhoretz's wife, Midge Decter, charged that the American Left was less interested in Timerman himself than in using him to indict America's anticommunist allies, particularly since this would divert attention from the atrocities committed by America's enemies. "Articles employing the man and his book as a stick with which to beat the government of the United States continue to pour from the presses," while "millions suffering far more than Timerman ever did continue to go unchampioned—because they have had the ill fortune to be victims of regimes it does not suit the purposes of the liberal press at this moment to get excited about."[23]

The most detailed and sophisticated conservative analysis of the Timerman controversy was Mark Falcoff's "The Timerman Case," published in the July 1981 issue of *Commentary*. Here Falcoff, then a professor of Latin American history at the University of Oregon, predicted that *Prisoner Without a*

Name could be "a propaganda windfall for the foreign-policy establishment of the American Left" if the American people remained ignorant about the political situation in Argentina and the circumstances surrounding Timerman's imprisonment. Falcoff described Argentina as a tolerable place in which to live. The Jews in Argentina were prospering and had a lively communal life. Buenos Aires might be an authoritarian regime. But it certainly wasn't a totalitarian one, nor did it resemble Nazi Germany. Timerman's comparison of Argentina with Hitler's Germany, Falcoff wrote, "cheapens the lives of those exterminated in Central and Eastern Europe, while doing less than nothing to alleviate the suffering of those political prisoners who happen to be Jewish."[24]

It is difficult for nonspecialists and outsiders to evaluate the arguments spawned by the Timerman controversy. Did he exaggerate Argentinian anti-Semitism and the complicity of Argentinian public officials? Was he arrested because of his association with David Graiver? Was the quiet diplomacy of the Reagan administration more effective than the public chastisements of the Carter regime in ameliorating conditions in Argentina? And yet there was no reluctance on the part of Timerman's supporters and detractors in making categorical and seemingly definitive judgments about these and other questions. Clearly Timerman's saliency within American public opinion was due less to the situation in Argentina and more to the relevance of his experiences to the political circumstances within the United States, including the emergence of the heavily Jewish neoconservative movement and the turn to the right by a minority of American Jews.

The reasons for these developments are many and complex. Part of the explanation is the gradual acculturation and assimilation of Jews into the American mainstream. Inevitably, the political attitudes of Jewish businessmen, workers, intellectuals, and professionals will gradually approximate those of their Gentile counterparts, although this could take several generations. The disparity between the Jewish social and economic profile and Jewish voting patterns cannot continue indefinitely, especially when the sources of Jewish liberalism are becoming historically more and more remote. In addition, many Jews have turned away from liberalism because they perceive that some of its manifestations have been hostile to both American and Jewish interests.

Most American Jews are professionals or involved in business. It certainly is not in their interest to favor liberal policies, which increase their taxes, stifle their opportunities, and regulate their activities. Despite the arguments of European Jewish radicals of the nineteenth and early twentieth centuries, Jews and economic leftism have never mixed very well. Jewish welfare and prosperity have been in direct relationship to the extent of economic freedom within the host society. Countries that have experienced socialist revolutions invariably have witnessed an exodus of Jews. Conversely, countries where capitalism and economic opportunity predominate, such as Canada and the United States, are precisely those nations with the most stable and prosperous Jewish communities.

Furthermore, Jews, like other Americans, are coming to realize that many of the liberal programs of the past, despite the compassionate rhetoric justifying them, have been counterproductive and have actually harmed the very individuals they were designed to aid. This tendency for even the best-intentioned reforms to go astray has been the central motif of *Public Interest,* the stimulating quarterly founded in the mid-1960s. The majority of *Public Interest*'s editors have been Jewish intellectuals skeptical of popular liberal panaceas for housing, taxation, crime and punishment, and welfare. Conservative Jews have been especially troubled by the tendency of the modern liberal welfare state to foster dependency. As Rabbi Seymour Siegel has pointed out, the highest form of charity within the Jewish tradition is providing opportunities for the poor "to help themselves escape from the bondage of poverty and dependence."[25]

Jews have also been troubled by the increasingly frequent attempts of the American Left to categorize Americans along racial and ethnic lines. Jews clearly remember the Jewish quotas in employment and universities in Europe and the United States. They are unable to view with equanimity what Nathan Glazer has termed "affirmative discrimination." Conservatives today are more clearly committed than liberals to the merit principle, a principle that has served Jews well in the past.

Prior to the late nineteenth century, Jews were not part of the political Left. Political activity was proscribed for Jews. As a result, they directed their energies inward. Later the unique historical circumstances surrounding Jewish emancipation from the ghetto attracted Jews to leftist movements of all sorts. Now, exactly one century after the vast migration of Jews from Eastern Europe to the United States commenced, the ties binding Jews and the political Left have become frayed. The Jews are one of America's most strategically located minority groups. Numbering approximately six million, they reside mainly in the states with the highest number of electoral votes. They turn out in high numbers at election time and are generous in their political contributions. The majority of adult Jews are college graduates and employed in business and the professions. Many are found in the publishing, communications, and academic fields. Up to now this vocal, affluent, and influential minority has been a vital cog in the liberal coalition. A change in Jewish political orientation to the right would help ensure the triumph of conservatism for the foreseeable future. Such an eventuality is not on the immediate horizon, although the long-term prospects are another matter.[26]

FOURTEEN

Pat Buchanan and the Jews

THE CENTRAL ROLE OF LIBERALISM in American Jewish identity has made Jews acutely sensitive to political movements and individuals who have challenged the underlying assumptions of modern liberalism. This has been particularly true regarding movements and individuals insensitive to Jewish concerns. Such insensitivity confirmed the assumption of most Jews that liberalism was the best guarantor of Jewish security and Jewish interests.

Few contemporary American political figures have been viewed so negatively by Jews as the conservative columnist Patrick J. Buchanan. This is not mainly because of the columnist's position on such matters as immigration, multiculturalism, the "cultural war," church-state relations, foreign trade, and overseas military involvements. What impresses Jews, rather, are his attitudes toward the Holocaust, Israel, and his Jewish critics. They believe his comments on these topics reflect more than foolishness, stubbornness, an excessively polemical and pugnacious style, and what William F. Buckley Jr. described as "clumsy forensic manners," an attraction "to mischievous generalizations," and "an iconoclastic temperament." They are, Jews believe, the rantings of an anti-Semite.[1]

It is doubtful that a man as politically experienced and astute as Buchanan has ever believed that he would be nominated by the Republican Party for president. Rather, as he has indicated on several occasions, his ultimate objective has been to control the American conservative movement. The tensions between Buchanan and American Jews are thus part of a larger story—the quarter-of-a-century-long struggle between "neoconservatives" and "paleoconservatives" such as Buchanan to dominate American conservatism.

Neoconservative intellectuals view Buchanan with contempt. For exam-

This chapter was previously published in *Judaism* 45 (spring 1996): 226–34. Reprinted by permission.

ple, Norman Podhoretz, the former editor of *Commentary* and now its editor-at-large, wrote that Buchanan was part of a conservative faction that would "release into the political air the viruses of xenophobia and nativism, and the derivative diseases of anti-Semitism and old fashioned racism." For Podhoretz, Buchanan has put the conservative movement at risk. "Having been carried triumphantly into the mainstream by Ronald Reagan," a Buchanan political victory would drag the movement "back into a marginal sectarian status with very little appeal to anyone outside its own fever swamps."[2]

Buchanan, for his part, is a longtime opponent of the neoconservatives, and his leading supporters have been drawn from the ranks of the paleoconservatives. Since the emergence of neoconservatism—a name and movement defined by Irving Kristol in the 1960s and 1970s—over three decades ago, paleoconservatives have claimed that the neoconservatives were not true conservatives. They were simply liberals who, without relinquishing their liberal mind-set, had moved to the right as a result of the excesses of the Great Society and the perilous status of the state of Israel. Russell Kirk, the leading traditionalist conservative intellectual, described the neoconservatives as "a little sect, distrusted and reproached by what we may call mainline conservatives." Buchanan agreed. The tactics of the neoconservatives, "including the smearing of opponents as racists, nativists, fascists, and anti-Semites—left many conservatives wondering if we hadn't made a terrible mistake when we brought these ideological vagrants in off the street and gave them a warm place by the fire," he wrote in 1991. "Like the fleas who conclude they are steering the dog, their relationship to the movement has always been parasitical."[3]

The differences between the paleoconservatives and the neoconservatives have involved four major areas. The first was religion. Many of the paleocons, including Buchanan, had come to conservatism through religion, and they identified conservatism with the values and institutions of Christendom. While many of the prominent Jewish neoconservatives recognized the importance of religion, few were religious themselves. If the major division in the world for the neocons was between freedom and tyranny, for the paleocons it was between naturalism and religion.

Buchanan and other paleos were correct that neoconservatism embodied the spirit of modernism. The neocons, in fact, did not yearn for a premodern golden age, nor were they hostile to science, capitalism, the experimental outlook, individualism, or secularism. Adam Meyerson, a neoconservative intellectual affiliated with the Heritage Foundation, noted that neoconservatives "have a sense of progress" and "welcome more than we fear advances in technology." Such statements confirmed for the paleoconservatives that the neoconservatives were essentially utilitarians with little sense of a transcendent religious and moral order or of the philosophical and theological underpinnings of traditional conservatism.[4]

The second area of conflict between the paleocons and the neocons concerned the welfare state. The neocons were not philosophically opposed to the welfare state, although they believed that it had gone too far during the 1960s. Neoconservatives such as Kristol supported a welfare state purged of paternalism and statism. For the neoconservatives, the modern liberal welfare state did not work; for the paleoconservatives, it was philosophically wrong. Paul Gottfried, a paleoconservative historian, accused the neoconservatives of being statists. "Their hearts, in most cases, are with the Left, even if their expense accounts come from the Right."[5]

The third area of conflict between the neocons and the paleocons stemmed from the latter's belief that, after laboring for decades in the vineyards of conservatism, they had been cruelly thrust aside by the neocons during the conservative ascendancy of the 1980s. As the historian Clyde Wilson complained in 1986, "Our estate has been taken over by an impostor, just as we were about to inherit." The paleos believed the neoconservatives had captured the major conservative foundations, had blacklisted their paleoconservative rivals, had received the best jobs within the Reagan administration, and, perhaps most important, had been accepted by the general public as the authentic voice of modern American conservatism. Traditional conservatives, Buchanan declared in May 1991, would have to take their movement back from the neoconservatives, "the ex-liberals, socialists, and Trotskyists who signed on in the name of anti-communism and now control our foundations and set the limits of permissible dissent."[6]

The final area of contention between the paleocons and the neocons concerned foreign policy. Buchanan and his fellow paleos were essentially isolationists. They rejected President Bush's "new world order," were skeptical of foreign aid, the World Bank, and the United Nations, favored high tariffs on products from the Third World, and dissented from the moralistic thrust of neoconservative foreign policy pronouncements. The paleos were particularly antagonistic to proposals by some neoconservatives that Washington should seek to spread democracy throughout the world. This worship of democracy, Buchanan said in May 1991, was "liberal idolatry masquerading as conservative orthodoxy," and he called the National Endowment for Democracy, a government agency strongly supported by neoconservatives, the "Comintern of the neo-conservatives." By contrast, Buchanan described himself as a "neo-isolationist." In his famous article "America First—and Second, and Third," published, interestingly enough, in Kristol's *The National Interest,* Buchanan called for a new nationalist and isolationist foreign policy purged of neoconservative "globabaloney."[7]

Buchanan's opposition to Desert Shield and Desert Storm—the military build-up in Saudi Arabia and the war against Iraq in 1991—was a logical outgrowth of his isolationism and the intramural struggle within the conservative movement. The war against Iraq, he contended, was an example of neoconservative foreign policy in action, and he referred to defenders of Bush's Persian Gulf policy as "neo-conservatives" eager to bring down an enemy of Israel. Buchanan claimed that the major foreign interest of the neoconservatives had always been Israel. "This *Commentary* crowd . . . didn't come around to our way of thinking," he told conservatives in 1983, "until the Soviet threat to Israel became apparent." He was mistaken. *Commentary* had been strongly anticommunist since its founding shortly after World War II.[8]

Adding to the tension between Buchanan and his neoconservative critics has been the columnist's pugnacious personality and his take-no-prisoners rhetorical style. His adult years are of a piece with his youth. His autobiography, *Right from the Beginning,* recounts his father's efforts to teach his seven sons to box and Pat's frequent fistfights and run-ins with the law while growing up in Washington, D.C. It was from his father that Buchanan inherited what he called "my combative proclivities." While Buchanan can be quite charming in private, his scrappy public posture has become an important element in his political image, and he glories in the epithet "pit bull of the Right." He admires such discredited figures as Joe McCarthy and Spiro Agnew in part because they were brawlers. In 1974, Buchanan was one of the most vigorous defenders of Richard Nixon during the Watergate crisis, not because he believed the president was innocent, but because when "they" come for one of "us" there can be only one possible response: lock and load.

Buchanan grew up in a devout Roman Catholic family, attended a parochial elementary school and Gonzaga High School, the Washington Jesuit high school, and graduated from Georgetown University, another Jesuit institution, in 1961. Georgetown's undergraduates were then required to take eight courses in metaphysics, logic, and natural theology, all, of course, taught from a Thomistic and Jesuit perspective. Here they learned that the greatest evils facing America were secular humanism and ethical relativism. In the 1950s, Roman Catholicism was moving into the American cultural and intellectual mainstream, and Roman Catholics such as Jacques Maritain, Thomas Merton, Christopher Dawson, Graham Greene, and Flannery O'Connor were entering the canon of modern Western thought and literature. With the fear of atheistic communism at its height, the fifties were an auspicious time for Catholics to demonstrate their Americanness and to escape from their self-imposed intellectual ghetto by taking the lead in the struggle against communism.

Buchanan recounts in his autobiography that he was taught by the nuns in parochial school that "America was God's country; there was no conflict then between nation and church." In fact, Catholics came to view themselves as the defenders of what was best in the American political tradition. John Courtney Murray and other Catholic intellectuals were then claiming that American democracy itself was ultimately derived from the Catholic conception of natural law, and they elevated the seventeenth-century Jesuit cardinal Robert Bellarmine and other Catholic political thinkers into the ranks of Locke, Trenchard, and Gordon as formative influences on the American Revolution and Constitution.[9]

The conservative intellectual movement that emerged in the 1950s had a major effect on Buchanan's thought. Russell Kirk's *The Conservative Mind* was published in 1954, when Buchanan was a junior in high school. The first issue of William F. Buckley Jr.'s *National Review* appeared the next year. Roman Catholics such as Buckley, Francis Graham Wilson, John Lukacs, and Ross Hoffman made up a disproportionate number of America's most influential conservative intellectuals. Communism, the major enemy of their church, was now also the major enemy of the United States, and Catholic conservatives believed they were better equipped intellectually than other Americans to oppose the naturalism, pragmatism, ethical relativism, and secular liberalism that were sapping America's will to resist communism.[10]

Buchanan recalled the impact that Buckley's *National Review* had on him. "My reaction was not unlike that of John Keats, 'On First Looking into Chapman's Homer,' " he wrote. "Here was stated, with style and grace, but especially with fire and wit, the political philosophy in which I, too, believed. . . . For us, what *National Review* did was take the word 'conservatism,' then a synonym for stuffy orthodoxy, Republican stand-pat-ism and economic self-interest, and convert it into the snapping pennant of a fighting faith."[11]

Buchanan's politics were an extension of his father's. Pop Buchanan had been an ardent America Firster prior to World War II, and the nativism and isolationism that permeated the America First movement would also pervade his son's politics. The elder Buchanan's greatest political heroes were Francisco Franco, Charles Lindbergh, Douglas MacArthur, Westbrook Pegler, and Joe McCarthy, and these were among Pat's heroes as well. Age did not mellow the conservative Catholicism that Buchanan inherited from his family. His Catholicism would remain pre–Vatican II, and he has only contempt for the ecumenical and liberalizing tendencies released in the church during the 1960s and for their ecclesiastical advocates.[12]

The charge that Buchanan was an anti-Semite was first widely publicized following the comments he made in August 1990 on television after the Iraqi invasion of Kuwait. He then claimed that the only proponents of war with Iraq were the Israeli defense ministry and its American "amen corner." "The Israelis want this war desperately because they want the United States to destroy the Iraqi war machine," Buchanan claimed. "They want us to finish them off. They don't care about our relations with the Arab world." A few weeks later he singled out as members of the amen corner four Jews: Henry Kissinger, the former secretary of state, Richard Perle, a Defense Department official and a well-known critic of arms control agreements with the Soviet Union, Charles Krauthammer, a prominent neoconservative commentator on foreign affairs, and Abe Rosenthal, a columnist for the *New York Times.*

This was patent nonsense. None of the leading advocates for Desert Shield or Desert Storm within the Bush administration were Jews, and Desert Shield and Desert Storm had widespread support throughout the country. Also, some of the Arab states, Great Britain, and most American conservatives favored ejecting Iraq from Kuwait and dispatching American military forces to Saudi Arabia. Nevertheless, Buchanan predicted that the casualties in any war with Iraq would have names such as McAllister, Murphy, Gonzales, and Leroy Brown. Intentionally absent from this list were Cohen, Goldberg, or Levy. Abe Rosenthal accused Buchanan of propagating a modern version of the infamous medieval "blood libel" that charged Jews sacrificing the blood of Christians during Passover.[13]

In March 1992, Buchanan replied to a group of Jewish hecklers while campaigning in Georgia's Republican presidential primary that he was speaking to "a rally of Americans, by Americans, and for the good old U.S.A." The clear implication was that his Jewish critics were un-American, had no concern for the national interest of the United States, and were only interested in the welfare of Israel. Jewish spokesmen accused Buchanan of seeking to resurrect the old anti-Semitic canard of dual loyalty.[14]

Buchanan's attitude toward Israel was driven by the same considerations of real politik, anticommunism, isolationism, and fear of increased executive authority that motivated his opposition to a war with Iraq. During the 1970s and early 1980s, he had praised Israel as a staunch ally of the United States in the struggle against communism and radicalism. The 1976 Israeli raid on Entebbe, he wrote, "was done in the noblest of causes—the rescue of unarmed civilians from cutthroats and thugs." Israel, Buchanan claimed on the occasion of the state's thirty-fifth anniversary in 1983, was "a tough, resourceful energetic nation, an offspring of the West, a strategic asset to the West, whose current struggle merits sympathy and support, not only because it mirrors our own, but because its resolution will likely presage the outcome of our own."[15]

Such praise, however, was less frequent after 1983. Increasingly Buchanan questioned whether American support of Israel was in the national interest. A March 13, 1991, Buchanan column asserted that Israel was "a strategic albatross draped around the neck of the United States." And in a column six months later he commended Bush's opposition to loan guarantees for Israel. Even if Bush's veto of these guarantees was overridden, Buchanan wrote, "he will have won high marks for his courage, and exposed Congress for what it has become, a Parliament of Whores incapable of standing up for U.S. national interests, if AIPAC is on the other line."[16]

Even more troubling to Jews than Buchanan's attitude toward Israel were his statements regarding the Holocaust. When considered alongside his comments regarding Israel and her Jewish supporters, these comments appeared to be sinister rather than merely eccentric and provocative. In 1985, Buchanan was director of the White House communications office when President Reagan announced that his upcoming trip to Germany would include a wreath-laying ceremony at a military cemetery in Bitburg, which contained the graves of SS veterans. Reagan then compounded the administration's embarrassment by stating that the German soldiers buried at Bitburg were as much victims of the Nazi regime as the inmates of the concentration camps. According to a report in the *Washington Post*, Buchanan was responsible for Reagan's maladroit statement.[17]

A barrage of criticism ensued after Reagan's itinerary was announced, and many Republicans begged Reagan to drop the visit to Bitburg. Buchanan, however, was a vigorous opponent of any revision in the president's travel plans. He seemed unaware of, or unconcerned with, the political implications. He also seemed oblivious to the reasons why some Americans would be outraged by a ceremony at Bitburg, and why they sought to keep alive the memories of Nazi atrocities more than four decades after the end of World War II. He wondered why there was not the same concern with atrocities committed by the communist states. "To what end," he asked, "all this wallowing in the atrocities of a dead regime when there is scarcely a peep of protest over the prison camps, the labor camps, the concentration camps operating now in China and Siberia, in Cuba and South Vietnam?" Given the state of American public opinion at the time, this was a bizarre response. Certainly he could not have been unaware of the constant criticism of China, Cuba, the Soviet Union, and South Vietnam during the 1980s for their treatment of political dissidents, and that much of this criticism emanated from neoconservatives.[18]

During the 1930s the isolationist Old Right had argued that the most fundamental challenge facing the United States came not from Nazi Germany but from the Soviet Union. While the Old Right was not sympathetic to National Socialism, many of its spokesmen believed Germany was providing a valuable service by checking Soviet expansionism. Buchanan's admiration for the Old Right helps explain his attitude toward the Holocaust. While he is not a Holocaust denier, he has played down its significance when compared with, say, the struggle against communism. He has frequently pointed out that there seemed to be a double standard at work. Accused Nazis were assumed guilty until proven innocent, while accused communists were assumed innocent until proven guilty. "There is political cowardice so thick you can cut it with a knife," he remarked once when discussing his defense of accused Nazi war criminals. "If these guys were accused of being communist spies on behalf of the Soviet Union in World War II . . . there would be ten thousand reporters working on their behalf demanding a hearing." Buchanan also believed that the evidence against accused Nazi war criminals was necessarily tainted because it came from Soviet archives. Almost by definition, any target of the Soviet Union must have some redeeming value.[19]

Buchanan repeatedly claimed that accused Nazi war criminals such as John Demjanjuk were victims of a frame-up. The Demjanjuk case, he wrote, was "an official lynching choreographed by the KGB." In March 1989, Buchanan criticized the ostracizing of Kurt Waldheim for his actions while in the German army during World War II. He even questioned whether the gas chambers at Treblinka could have killed as many persons as scholars claimed. His proof for this was an incident in a Washington, D.C., tunnel in which a train broke down and the passengers survived despite noxious fumes supposedly similar to those at Treblinka. Such a comparison was easily refuted by historians and chemists who pointed to the obvious differences between the two cases. Buchanan further claimed that a so-called Holocaust Survivor Syndrome involving "group fantasies of martyrdom and heroics" was partially responsible for this continual harping on the sins of the Nazis, as if their sins did not speak for themselves. Buchanan's newspaper column also vigorously defended the presence of the Carmelite convent at Auschwitz and bitterly attacked those Catholics opposed to it, including New York's Cardinal O'Connor, for seeking to appease Jews over this issue.[20]

All of this was too much for American Jews. The American Jewish Congress, for example, described Buchanan as being as "genuine and authentic an anti-Semite as they come." Buchanan, for his part, has vigorously denied that he is anti-Semitic, and he has claimed that the accusation of anti-Semitism was being used by rivals within the conservative movement to discredit him and like-minded paleoconservatives. Those who know Buchanan best, including fellow Washington journalists Jack Germond, Al Hunt, and Mark Shields, have denied that Buchanan is anti-Semitic, and certainly there was nothing in Buchanan's career prior to 1985 to indicate otherwise. His autobiography is free of anti-Semitic musings, and its scattered references to Jews and Israel are complimentary. Here he mentioned the admiration of his father, a prominent Washington, D.C., accountant, for the city's Jewish entrepreneurs, some of whom were his clients. Buchanan also stated in his memoir that he supported the American commitment to the survival of Israel.[21]

The question remains: is Buchanan an anti-Semite and, if so, what is the nature of his anti-Semitism? And if he is an anti-Semite, to what extent is this due to his paleoconservatism rather than other, more personal factors? Buchanan's personal relationship with Jews has always been cordial, and from childhood he has had close friendships with Jews. There is no evidence that he believes Jews as individuals to be different from others. In the face of accusations of anti-Semitism directed at Buchanan by *Commentary*, the Anti-Defamation League of B'nai B'rith, and even Bill Buckley, his Jewish conservative supporters, including Allan H. Ryskind, Paul Gottfried, and Murray Rothbard, have continually denied that Buchanan is an anti-Semite. If Buchanan is an anti-Semite, and there is some doubt on this score, it is not because he finds Jews as individuals to be undesirable. Rather, it is because Buchanan has taken positions that have conflicted with Jewish interests, and he has done so in a manner that has led fair-minded persons to conclude that he has a problem when it comes to matters of Jewish concern.

Even if Buchanan could not be charged personally with anti-Semitism,

Jews, as well as other Americans, are wise to oppose him. He has assumed leadership of a conservative faction permeated with xenophobia, isolationism, and a rancor directed at ethnic and cultural minorities. His is a politics of fear that appeals to estranged Americans nursing economic and cultural grievances but does not provide any sensible answers to alleviate their problems. Conservatives, in particular, have a further reason for distancing themselves from Buchanan since his brand of conservatism marginalizes the movement. As the conservative writer David Frum asked, "How deeply into kookery can a man who claims to speak for conservatism go before other conservatives are obliged to repudiate him?" Irving Kristol noted correctly that should Buchanan be successful in taking over the conservative movement, it will have suffered "its greatest defeat since the election of 1964." Buchanan's history of political failures indicates that this is not likely to occur.[22]

FIFTEEN

American Jewry and the State of Israel

THE STATE OF ISRAEL, particularly since 1967, has been, along with liberalism, the most important factor in shaping modern American Jewish identity. Jews often have found it difficult to articulate what the establishment of the state, coming nineteen hundred years after Masada and three years after the end of the Holocaust, meant to them. Certainly public opinion polls have failed to reveal the depth of attachment of American Jews to the Jewish state or the significance of Israel to American Jewish identity. It is not surprising therefore that the greatest challenge confronting contemporary Christian-Jewish relations in the United States over the past half century would involve Israel.

For American Jews anything less than wholehearted Christian backing of Israel is evidence of a lingering anti-Semitism. Many Christians, on the other hand, resent the Jewish demand for all-out support of Israel, seeing it as a form of blackmail in which a pro-Israel attitude is the Jewish price for continuing the Christian-Jewish dialogue. Christians find it difficult to comprehend this intense American Jewish commitment to Israel, while American Jews are often unable to explain the reasons for this commitment or the depth of their concern. What neither American Christians nor American Jews perhaps understand fully is the extent to which Israel has become the religion of a large percentage of American Jews. One of the most popular ways to be Jewish today and to identify with other Jews is by supporting Israel.

Israel has partially filled the vacuum created by the diminishing importance of traditional religious practices and beliefs and by the atrophying of Jewish ethnicity. Secularism has affected American Jewry more deeply than it has American Protestantism or American Catholicism. Public opinion surveys

This chapter was previously published in *Journal of Ecumenical Studies* 14 (winter 1977): 1–16. Reprinted by permission of *JES*; copyrighted 1977.

have revealed that American Jews attend religious services far less frequently than do American Christians, and that, compared to Christians, a smaller percentage of Jews accept such basic religious dogmas as the existence of a personal God, an afterlife, and the efficacy of prayer. A variety of sociological studies have shown that religious observance among second- and third-generation Jews is less frequent than among the immigrant generation. Another indication of the weakening hold of traditional religion on American Jews is an increasing intermarriage rate, a phenomenon that has led many American Jewish leaders to question whether Judaism, in the long run, will be able to survive in the United States.[1]

Even the High Holy Days of Rosh Hashanah and Yom Kippur reflect this growing secularism and acculturation of American Jewry. And the nature of that identification is best revealed on Yom Kippur, the Day of Atonement. During this most important day of the Jewish calendar, when more Jews will be at prayer than at any other time of the year, an appeal is made in countless synagogues for the purchase of Israel bonds. In the modern version of Yom Kippur personal atonement thus involves a financial commitment for the well-being of the state of Israel.[2]

This decreasing religious commitment has been accompanied by a still strong, although diminishing, ethnic consciousness. While the ties binding American Jews to Judaism have been attenuated, the ties binding them to one another have remained firm. It is significant that two Jewish religious rites retaining their popularity in the United States have been the lighting of Chanukah lights and the partaking of the Seder meal during Passover. Both of these rituals celebrate events having a nationalistic as well as a religious dimension. But even more important than the Chanukah lights and the Seder in what the sociologist Charles S. Liebman has called "the celebration and ritualization of communal ties" is the state of Israel.[3]

Israel has become for American Jews a screen upon which they project their dreams and aspirations, as well as a panacea for relieving their anxieties and frustrations. For American Jewry, Israel is all things to all people. For Jews whose major contact with the Jewish community is through the various self-defense organizations, Israel provides the most important opportunity for fighting anti-Semitism.

Israel provides patriotic American Jews an outlet for expressing their patriotism. By portraying Israel as the only democracy in the eastern Mediterranean, as a staunch ally of the United States, and, prior to 1991, as a barrier to the spread of communism and Soviet influence in the Middle East, Jews have viewed the national interests of Israel and America as essentially congruent. Israel has been pictured as a miniature United States in which Western values such as democracy, industrialization, capitalism, and technology predominate. The classical argument against Zionism, that it led to dual loyalties and prevented the full acceptance of Jews into American society, is thus turned on its head. Zionism now becomes a handmaiden of Americanism, and for a Jew to be a complete American patriot and a defender of American national interests he or she must, by necessity, also be a Zionist.

Support for Israel is found among both religious and nonreligious American Jews. The religious profess to see in Israel's establishment the hand of God, a fulfillment of biblical prophecy regarding the ingathering of the exiles and the coming of the messianic age. To the nonreligious, Zionism is a means to express a Jewish identity, although within a secular and even, at times, an antireligious context. Zionism thus can be a substitute religion and a surrogate for Judaism.[4]

Radical Jews, although embarrassed by the role of the Israeli religious establishment and fearful of the eventual effect of militarism on Israeli society, nevertheless have pointed to Israel as the most successful example of a modern democratic and socialist state experiencing rapid economic growth and social modernization. Such is the theme of sociologist Irving Louis Horowitz's book *Israeli Ecstasies/Jewish Agonies,* written during its author's radical days. Horowitz focused on what he described as "those problems of deepest concern to those of the younger generation possessing a radical persuasion." He was responding particularly to those on the left who viewed Israel as a capitalistic and militaristic bastion of Western imperialism. He reassured his readers that one could be both radical and pro-Israel at the same time. Not only was Israel "dedicated to principles of social egalitarianism as well as to a higher degree of public ownership of basic means of production," but it also shared with third-world nations a "deep and desperate sense of national autonomy and national liberation." Israel's natural home, Horowitz claimed, was among the third-world countries, and it was only because of the international situation that it has been forced to forge unnatural economic and military ties with the United States.[5]

Horowitz argued that the close relationship between Israel and the affluent, bourgeois Jewish communities of the West was artificial and disguised the Jewish state's true character as an increasingly secular and socialistic country, whose natural allies were the struggling nations of Africa and Asia. "It is more important," Horowitz contended, "that a Uganda ruler opens up a legation in Jerusalem than that ninety conferences between American Jews and Israeli Jews are held in Israel. The State needs legations more than conferences, needs Africans at least as much as Americans, needs support from poor nations no less than from wealthy Jews." Horowitz proposed that Israel should not only be a model for the proper treatment of oppressed minorities but that it should also eliminate all vestiges of official religious authority. If these things were not done and if Israel was unable to assume its natural place in the camp of the third-world and socialistic countries, "fundamental issues will never be addressed, much less resolved; and thus the unique place of Israel in the covenant of nations will become sheer myth, lost in the rubble of geographical determinism."[6]

Horowitz's volume illustrates the tendency of American Jews to project their own values upon Israel. In his discussion of the relationship between Israel and American Jewry, for instance, Horowitz did not stress what American Jews have done for Israel by providing financial aid and engaging in political lobbying. Disdaining the secure, affluent, and complacent American Jewry, Horowitz instead emphasized the example Israel provided American Jews of a socially concerned Jewish community. Thus he recommended closer ties between Israel and the black African states not only because this would aid Israel but also because it would strengthen "the ties between American Jews and American black people, not automatically, not *ipso facto*, but it would help to a considerable degree."[7]

One interesting aspect of this pro-Israel sentiment among American Jews is its relatively recent vintage. Indeed, prior to the 1930s Zionism was a decidedly minority position within American Jewry, and even in the mid-1960s Israel had a far less important place on the American Jewish agenda than it does today. Classical Zionism had little appeal in the United States because what Zionism hoped to achieve for European Jews had already been obtained by American Jews. Zionism emerged as an answer to the problem of European Jews who, in the late nineteenth and early twentieth centuries, found themselves in an increasingly hostile environment. Migration to Palestine offered the European Jew the prospect of a life free from the seemingly endemic anti-Semitism of Europe. American Jews, however, already lived in such an environment and thus saw little need for emigration to Palestine or, later, Israel. Little wonder then that when American Jews referred to "the golden land" they had the United States in mind, not Palestine.[8]

The energies of American Jews centered on achieving economic and social mobility and in assimilating into the mainstream of American life. Zionism, they feared, would hinder their complete acceptance by Gentile Americans. Fearful of being accused of having dual loyalties, American Jews went out of their way to assert their complete commitment to the United States and their rejection of European Zionist ideology. Thus in 1904 the prominent Jewish leader Louis Marshall proclaimed, "May we never prove recreant to this holy obligation, to this tremendous trust, and may our descendants never forget the debt of gratitude we owe to the God of our fathers, Who has led us out of Egypt into this land of freedom." Marshall was echoing what a number of Reform rabbis had declared two decades earlier in the famous Pittsburgh Platform: "We consider ourselves no longer a nation, but a religious community, and therefore expect neither a return to Palestine, nor a sacrificial worship under the sons of Aaron, nor the restoration of any of the laws concerning the Jewish state."[9]

If any one person was responsible for transforming American Zionism into a mass movement it was Adolf Hitler. It is difficult to exaggerate the impact the Holocaust has had on American Jewry. Despite its affluence and influence, the American Jewish community is insecure and fearful of another holocaust, if not in the United States then in the Middle East. Minor as well as major anti-Semitic incidents trigger nightmares among American Jews. The Jewish calendar in Israel and America is replete with events commemorating the martyrs to the Holocaust; Jewish youths are repeatedly taught the lessons of World War II; an inordinate number of Jewish organizations are continually looking for evidence of anti-Semitism here and abroad; and there is a continual flow of books and motion pictures focusing on the Holocaust. It is through the prism of the Holocaust that Israel is viewed today by American Jews.[10]

The decimation of the European Jews along with the supposed failure of the Western nations to do anything meaningful to rescue them convinced most American Jews that a Jewish state was a necessity. Israel has become for modern Jewry the answer to Auschwitz. The continued existence of Israel ensures that the martyrdom of the six million was not in vain. Israel is the guarantee that Jewish history still has meaning, the answer to those who argue that God died in the gas chambers. Because of World War II, American Jews are psychologically unable to view the situation of Israel and its Arab antagonists as a normal conflict between competing sovereign states. When they talk about the "survival and security" of Israel, it is with the memories of the Holocaust still fresh in their minds.

The term "survival and security" is not a mere rhetorical flourish; rather, it expresses the fear that what happened in the 1940s can occur again. American proposals for settling the Middle East crisis, whether they emanate from a President Carter, Reagan, Bush, or Clinton, or George W. Bush arouse concern in American Jewish circles that the United States is going to betray Israel for the sake of Arab oil and influence in the Arab lands, just as Neville Chamberlain sold Czechoslovakia down the river in 1938. American Jews compare the position of Israel to that of the helpless European Jews of the Holocaust, overlooking the fact that Israel has on several occasions shown that she is more than a military match for her adversaries. The thinking of American Jewry, however, is dominated not by evidence of Israeli military supremacy but by fears regarding the imminent destruction of another Jewish community.

The wars of 1967 and 1973 further accentuated the tendency of American Jewry to see the Middle East situation in apocalyptic terms. Never has American Jewry been as united as it was during June 1967 and October 1973, and this was because Jews believed the survival of Israel to be at stake. The genocidal rhetoric of the Arabs merely confirmed what American Jews had long correctly suspected to be the Arabs' ultimate objective. The response of American Jewry to the two crises, both in terms of fund-raising and of volunteering among the young to work in Israel, surprised both the leaders of the American Jewish establishment and the Israelis. Rabbi-historian Arthur Hertzberg, writing two months after the Six Day War, noted that the crisis had united American Jews "with deep Jewish commitments as they have never been united before, and it has evoked such commitments in many Jews who previously seemed untouched by them." He concluded that "there are no conventional Western theological terms with which to explain this and most contemporary Jews experience these emotions without knowing how to define them. . . . Israel may . . . now be acting as a very strong focus of worldwide Jewish emotional loyalty and thereby as a preservative of a sense of Jewish identity."[11]

In June 1967, more than seventy-five hundred inquiries were received by various Jewish officials from American Jews volunteering to take over the civilian jobs of those serving in the Israeli armed forces. One official of the Jewish Agency was approached on the day the war broke out by a man followed by his two sons who said, "I have no money to give but here are my sons. Please send them over immediately." The outpouring of money by American Jews to help Israel pay for the 1967 war was unprecedented in the history of American Jewish philanthropy. Whereas in 1966 $136,500,000 was pledged to the various Jewish community fund drives, the figure was $317,000,000 in 1967. In less than one month, $100,000,000 was raised by the United Jewish Appeal. Money came in faster than it could be tabulated, and individuals, overcome by the urgency of the situation, often insisted on giving cash rather than checks. Numerous persons donated the cash-surrender value of life insurance policies. Contributions were made to the UJA in lieu of anniversary, birthday, graduation, bar mitzvah, and Father's Day gifts. Jewish youth organizations turned over their treasuries to the UJA. In Essex County, New Jersey, the golf course at a Jewish country club was even closed on a Sunday morning so that a fund-raising meeting could take place, while in Washington, D.C., a Jewish belly dancer at a Middle Eastern nightclub donated several nights' pay to the cause.[12]

The response of American Jews in 1967 was dwarfed by their reaction to the Yom Kippur War of 1973. Once again American Jewry was engulfed by the memories of World War II, and this time more than thirty thousand persons volunteered to work in Israel. There occurred an outpouring of money the likes of which American philanthropy had never previously witnessed. During the first week of the war, $107,000,000 was pledged, and the total of United Jewish Appeal pledges reached $675,000,000. This included $1,000,000 raised by Jewish university students, as well as two gifts of $5,000,000 each.[13]

The solidification of American Jews behind Israel has not, however, been accompanied by any widespread acceptance of classical Zionist ideology. According to David Ben-Gurion and other Israeli Zionist spokespersons, Jews living outside the state of Israel were living in exile and should migrate to Israel. The essence of Zionism, Ben-Gurion claimed in 1950, is "a complete solidarity with the state and the people of Israel." Although the Israelis have contended that Israel is the homeland of the Jewish people and that every Jew is obligated to become a citizen of the state, only a small number of Jews have migrated to Israel for religious or ideological reasons. Migration has generally occurred because persecutions forced Jews to flee their native lands. Few Jews have felt the need to leave the comfort and security of Great Britain, Canada, and the United States and resettle in Israel, and most of those who did emigrate to Israel eventually returned. Zionist leaders view this refusal to leave the fleshpots of the West with a mingling of contempt and fright. It not only deprives Israel of the increased Jewish population that is the guarantor of its existence, but it also denies the fundamental tenet of Zionist ideology regarding the abnormality of Diaspora life once the Jewish state has been established. The result is, as the Zionist Nahum Goldmann stated in 1954, that Israel is the only state in the world where 90 percent of its people live outside its borders.[14]

Despite their reluctance to exchange Great Neck for Jerusalem and Beverly Hills for Tel Aviv, American Jews do not view themselves as Zionists manqué. Seeing no reason why they themselves should make aliyah, America's Jews have perceived Zionism as a movement to create a refuge for persecuted Jews, rather than a national homeland for all Jews. As far as American Zionism is concerned, there is much truth to the rather cynical description of Zionism as a movement in which one person gives money to a second person to send a third person to Israel.

No person was more important in the history of American Zionism than Louis D. Brandeis. Brandeis's greatest contribution was to Americanize Zionism, to reconcile the desire of American Jews to become an integral part of American life with their wish to create a refuge for Jews in Palestine. Brandeis provided a rationale for Zionism that blunted charges of dual loyalty and reassured American Jews fearful of the foreign taint surrounding Zionism. According to Brandeis, Americanism and Zionism shared common ideals of brotherhood, social justice, democracy, and liberty. For Brandeis the best Americans were those who deeply believed in the universality of these ideals. This meant that American Jews had a patriotic duty to help establish in the Middle East a society based on these American (and Zionist) principles. "To be good Americans," he claimed, "we must be better Jews, and to be better Jews we must become Zionists." Brandeis did not restrict his transnational view of Americanism to Zionism. "Every Irish-American who contributed toward advancing home rule," he maintained, "was a better man and a better American for the sacrifices he made."[15]

Brandeis's interpretation of Zionism as a movement to secure freedom and justice for Jews did not require American Jews to settle in Palestine, since American Jews were already living in a free and just society. Zionism's raison d'àtre was in providing a refuge for those less fortunate Jews who were being persecuted for racial and religious reasons. Brandeis defined Zionism as "a movement of freedom, a movement to give the Jew more freedom, not less, to give to him the same freedom which the other peoples enjoy, the freedom to go to the land of his fathers or to remain or go to some land as he may choose, the freedom which is enjoyed by every people and nation practically in all the world, be that nation small or large." As good Americans, American Jews could not stand aloof from this "movement of freedom."[16]

Under Brandeis's leadership American Zionism deemphasized Jewish nationalism and the goal of a Jewish state, and stressed instead philanthropic and humanitarian activities in Palestine. The stamp that Brandeis and his followers placed on American Zionism was the only one that could have appealed to a large number of American Jews, and it also legitimized Zionism in the eyes of non-Jewish Americans. This resulted in the enmity of European Zionists, who belittled American Zionism as mere philanthropy and accused the Brandeisians of ignoring the fundamental question of Jewish nationality. Chaim Weizmann, Brandeis's major opponent, accused American Zionists of "lacking in historic understanding of Jewish life and wanting in Jewish soul." They were ignorant of "all those imponderabilia which form a national movement of which Palestine is only a territorial aspect of a national political upheaval."[17]

The failure of Weizmann and his successors to convince American Jewry that Zionism involved something more than political and charitable efforts on behalf of Israel has not, however, diminished the fervor of American Jewry's commitment to the Jewish state. The impact of Israel on American Jewry is pervasive. Organizations such as the American Jewish Committee, which previously were non-Zionist, today stand in the forefront of Israel's supporters. The Reform rabbinate, which until the 1930s was a center of anti-Zionism, now requires candidates for ordination to spend at least one year studying in the movement's seminary in Jerusalem. Even Jewish organizations that are not directly concerned with Israel spend time and money on Israeli-oriented programs and organize tours to Israel because they realize these are necessary if they are to retain and increase their membership. The American Council for Judaism, which was founded in 1943 and has been the major American Jewish anti-Zionist organization, is virtually defunct. It is doubtful today whether any Jew who is not a staunch supporter of Israel could occupy a responsible position in a major American Jewish organization.[18]

This love affair between American Jews and Israel is evident no matter where one turns in American Jewish life. It is seen in the annual "Salute to Israel" parade up New York City's Fifth Avenue commemorating the establishment of the state. It is found in the gift shops of synagogues and in stores in Jewish neighborhoods where Israeli art objects are sold. These items are placed in American Jewish homes, where they assume a quasi-religious character because, after all, they are from Israel. It is reflected in the emphasis of synagogue Hebrew schools on Israeli dances and songs, and in their attempt to inculcate in their students a close identification with Israel. It is revealed by the popularity of Israeli movies and theatrical productions, and by the interest in books about Israel. This commitment to Israel is also seen in the round of lectures on Israel and Israeli cultural events that dot Jewish communal calendars. At Jewish communal banquets it is now common to sing the Israeli national anthem "Hatikvah" along with the "Star Spangled Banner." This desire to be a vicarious Israeli provides also the clientele for the Israeli nightclubs in New York City.

American Jewry's romance with Israel is responsible for the many college students who spend one or more years in Israeli universities and the large number of American tourists who go to Israel every year. It is now normal for students at Jewish day schools to spend a year studying at a yeshiva or seminary in Israel after graduating from high school. If an American Jew has not already been to Israel, he or she is probably thinking about going and is perhaps feeling guilty for not already having done so. Visiting Israel is not a matter of ordinary tourism. Jews feel duty-bound to go to Israel: first, because it helps the Israeli economy; secondly, because it is a form of personal identification with the people of Israel and lets them know they are not alone; and thirdly, to see what the Israelis have made out of "our" land. Visiting Israel resembles a religious pilgrimage more than a vacation.[19]

Even the most bizarre events involving American Jews frequently have a pro-Israel aspect. One such example took place in May 1974 in New York City. A man named David F. Kamaiko hijacked a helicopter and demanded that $2,000,000 in ten-dollar bills be placed in valises and delivered to him by a bikini-clad girl. The pilot of the helicopter later related that Kamaiko had been quite distraught by the recent massacre of Israeli children at Maalot by Arab terrorists, and that he planned to use the money to buy guns for the Jewish Defense League.[20]

By providing a new image of the Jew to replace the old image of the Jew as martyr and sufferer, Israel has been partially responsible for a new pride among many American Jews in their Jewishness. The Israelis have shown that Jews need not be passive victims who are slaughtered like sheep. One of the posters produced during the euphoria immediately after the Six Day War showed a Hasidic Jew stepping into a telephone booth where he takes off his long black coat to reveal a Jewish superman costume underneath. The new image of super-Jew is reflected in the spate of cheap novels picturing the Israelis as superspies and supercounterespionage agents. The back cover of one of these books, *Operation Kuwait* by Harry Arvay, describes the book's scenario. "On the edge of an oil-rich desert, Black September has established X19, a secret base where the art of sky sabotage is taught to paramilitary terror troops. While it operates, no plane can fly anywhere in the world free of fear. But Israel's Security Branch has other ideas. Their daredevil team of counterspy commandos has launched an operation that will smash X19 bullet by bullet, gun by gun, terrorist by terrorist." The publishers also promised that there would soon be published another novel by Mr. Arvay titled *The Piraeus Plot*, which is portrayed as "another dynamic adventure of the undercover war in the Middle East, matching the crack Israeli Secret Service vs. International Terrorists!"[21]

American Jews have vicariously shared in Israel's military and economic triumphs. The greater the victories, the more pride Americans have in Israel and themselves for, in their opinion, the Israelis are struggling on behalf of Jews throughout the world. This new pride in Jewishness is reflected in the fact that Jews have gone public. No longer do Jewish comedians, singers, and novelists hide their identity; instead they capitalize on it. To be Jewish is to be "in," so much so that a few years ago Truman Capote complained of a Jewish literary mafia. "The creation of the state of Israel," wrote Marshall Sklare, the prominent sociologist of American Jewry, "has had a profound effect on the American Jew, particularly on his psychological make-up. It has given him a heightened sense of morale—morale that enables him to abide newer challenges of the American scene to Jewish status and security." The great psychic investment of American Jews in Israel has led some to question whether in the face of the destruction of the state, American Jewry could continue to exist as a viable community.[22]

This pride in Israel and fear for its security is the spur to the intense political activity on its behalf on the part of American Jews. Statements and actions of prominent American political leaders are carefully scrutinized to ensure there is no weakening of the Israeli position in Congress or in the executive branch. Jewish organizations can, at a moment's notice, inundate the president and Congress with a deluge of telegrams and letters. American Jews finance the work of the American Israel Public Affairs Committee, a Washington lobbying organization, to shepherd through Congress legislation favorable to Israel. Jewish financial contributions to political candidates are contingent on their positions on Israel. George McGovern found it difficult to finance his presidential campaign in 1972 in part because some Jews were suspicious of his Middle East stance. Conversely, Richard Nixon received an unprecedented amount of money from Jewish sources because he was viewed as reliable regarding Israel. Jewish political activity in 1972 was so intense and prominent that the journalist Stephen D. Isaacs dubbed 1972 the "Year of the Jew."[23]

The most dramatic indication of this American Jewish commitment to Israel is through gifts to the state via the United Jewish Appeal and other organizations, or through the purchase of Israeli bonds. This financial aid was vital for Israel's economic growth during its early years. In the 1950s, for example, 47 percent of Israel's importation of capital represented the loans, investments, and donations of foreign Jews, mostly Americans. American Jewish giving to Israel has shown a tendency to rise during periods of crisis. In the wake of the emotions engendered by the Yom Kippur War, the sale of Israeli bonds in the United States combined with the charitable contributions of American Jews to Israel totaled nearly one billion dollars. By the 1970s much of Jewish communal work involved raising funds for Israel, and status within the American Jewish community depended in part on the size of one's annual gift to the United Jewish Appeal and to the various independent fund-raising organizations such as the American Friends of Hebrew University, the American Technion Society, and the American Committee for the Weizmann Institute.[24]

This intense psychological and financial stake in Israel combined with the fact that support for Israel has become for many the major reason for remaining Jewish makes it difficult, if not impossible, for American Jews to view Israel in a dispassionate manner. It is a truism of social science that people are most intolerant of matters that mean the most to them, and this is confirmed by the attitude toward Israel of the American Jewish community. Deviance among American Jews is now largely defined as something other than a wholehearted enthusiasm for Israel. American Jewry was horrified by the phenomenon of the New Left in the 1960s, mainly because some of its most prominent spokespersons were Jews indifferent or hostile to Israel. That any Jew could be anti-Israel was seen as a major failing of Jewish education in the United States. There is far more criticism of the Israeli government and Israel's social system inside Israel than among American Jews, and it is virtually impossible for American Jews to critically examine the nature of their identification with Israel. This identification goes to the heart of the functional religion for many American Jews, and no one is comfortable with a re-examination of his or her fundamental beliefs.[25]

An interesting by-product of American Jewry's relationship with Israel is a new definition of anti-Semitism. In 1974 two officials of the Anti-Defamation League of B'nai B'rith published a book titled *The New Anti-Semitism,* which argued that anti-Semitism included indifference and apathy toward Jewish concerns, especially "a widespread incapacity or unwillingness to comprehend the necessity of the existence of Israel to Jewish safety and survival throughout the world." Among those described as indifferent toward Israel, and hence anti-Semitic, were Senator J. William Fulbright, columnists

Jeffrey St. John, Rowland Evans, and Robert Novak, the leaders of the National Council of Churches and the American Catholic Council of Bishops, and the editors of the *Christian Science Monitor. The New Anti-Semitism* also singled out for attack a small book published by the American Friends Service Committee in 1970 titled *Search for Peace in the Middle East.*[26]

This Quaker document was, as one would expect, a rather Olympian-like and politically naïve view of the Middle East conflict. Its authors claimed that polarized attitudes regarding the Middle East made a dispassionate discussion of the issues quite difficult, and they predicted that their formula for settling the clash would be attacked by both sides as one-sided. The response of American Jews justified their fears. American Jews were particularly disturbed by the gratuitous advice offered to them to reassess the character of their support for Israel and the nature of their role in American politics.

> As free American citizens members of the American Jewish community have every right to utilize all the instruments of a free society to register their convictions and desires, and to try to influence legislative and executive actions. However, the nature of some of these pressures and their extensiveness have sometimes served to inhibit calm public discussion of the issues in the Arab-Israeli conflict, and, on occasion, to induce public officials to endorse policies concerning Israel in which they do not believe and which they in fact regard as likely to be counter-productive for Israel as well as for the cause of peace. This is not a new phenomenon in American politics, but it is nonetheless disturbing. No one who is truly concerned about the long-term fate of Israel and the long-term threats to inter-faith harmony and brotherhood can be indifferent to these dangers.[27]

Stung by these and other assertions, *The New Anti-Semitism* not surprisingly described the Friends' volume as an unfortunate attempt to rewrite history, "a pro-Arab document masquerading under repeated claims of objectivity." In 1971 a response to the Quaker analysis was published by several Jewish academicians under the title *Truth and Peace in the Middle East: A Critical Analysis of the Quaker Report.* They accused the Quakers of having "displayed a blatant bias, repressed facts, distorted history and presented a slanted and one-sided set of conclusions." They attributed this to Christian theological anti-Semitism disguised as anti-Zionism. "The basic attitude of some Christians, theologians as well as laymen," the Jewish professors charged, "is still deeply rooted in the postulate that because the Jews refused to accept Jesus as the Messiah, they are eternally damned and condemned to wander the earth as homeless witnesses to their sin." It is natural that Christians such as the Quakers failed to comprehend the sources of this fervent American Jewish support of Israel and were unable to share in American Jewry's concern for the future of the state.[28]

Jews were also bitterly disappointed and disillusioned by Christianity's seeming indifference to Israel's plight during the Middle East crisis of June 1967. Neither the National Conference of Catholic Bishops nor the National Council of Churches made a forthright statement on Israel's behalf at that time. This was far more important for Jews than the numerous interfaith dialogues and the frequent declarations of Christian good will toward Judaism and Jews that had occurred prior to the Six Day War. For Jews, June 1967 was proof that anti-Semitism still infected Christianity. Jews failed to realize that for most Christians Israel is simply another country. Jews did not ask themselves how they could expect Christians, who approached Israel from a different perspective, to view Israel in any other way.[29]

As for American Jews, they have frequently allowed their support for Israel to destroy their sense of historical and political perspective. The aid American Jewry has provided Israel is one of the great chapters in American Jewish history, but the price of this support has been a tendency to absolutize the state. Israel is, after all, a secular political body. The difficulty of distinguishing between the sacred and the secular, while at the same time recognizing the centrality of Israel for contemporary Jews, was illustrated by an address given at the December 1974 national conference of the United Jewish Appeal by Rabbi Walter S. Wurzburger, an Orthodox Jew and a professor of philosophy at Yeshiva University. The speech was titled "The Religious Significance of the State of Israel," and it analyzed the role of Israel in modern Jewish faith. While acknowledging that it was impossible to be certain whether the establishment of Israel marked the beginning of the messianic era, Rabbi Wurzburger refused to rule out the possibility that this might, in fact, be the case. "Granted that for a variety of reasons the State of Israel falls short of Messianic expectations," he argued, "there is no reason why even a purely Jewish State cannot serve as a preliminary phase in the unfolding of the Divine redemption." He then asked:

> Does not the partial return of our people to the Land of Israel strengthen our faith in the feasibility of the ultimate ingathering of all the exiles? Moreover, can we imagine what the spiritual plight of our people would have been after the Holocaust, had the State of Israel not come into being? . . . It was because of the invigorating hope, strength, and vitality which the State of Israel has instilled within Jews everywhere, that

we were able to witness such unprecedented resurgence of commitment to Jewish survival. Indeed, the breathtaking developments in the Land of Israel have confirmed our belief that the Jewish people will endure, return to Zion and eventually become the vehicle for the redemption of mankind.

Jews would do well to heed the advice of Reinhold Niebuhr, the Protestant theologian and Zionist supporter, who wrote in 1944 that "no society . . . is great enough or good enough to make itself the final end of human existence."[30] Christians, for their part, must make a greater effort to see Israel within the context of the tragic history of twentieth-century Jewry. Christians, in particular, should remember the warning of Dante that divine justice weighs the sins of the cold-blooded and the sins of the warm-hearted on different scales, as well as the words of Henri Amiel that "moral indifference is the malady of the cultivated classes."[31]

SIXTEEN

Blacks and Jews Entangled

OF THE MANY PIETIES of American Jewry, few have been so easily and widely accepted or have been so influential in the shaping of Jewish identity as the assumption that blacks and Jews share vital interests and a common identity arising out of what Arthur Hertzberg has termed the "comradeship of excluded peoples." Thus in her 1991 autobiography, *Deborah, Golda, and Me,* Letty Cottin Pogrebin argued that the black-Jewish relationship rested on a common history of oppression. "Both blacks and Jews have known Egypt," she wrote. "Jews have known it as certain death (the killing of the firstborn, then the ovens and gas chambers). Blacks have known it as death and terror by bondage." The political commentator Paul Berman agreed. "It was the past that made the blacks and the Jews almost the same," he wrote in the February 28, 1994, issue of the *New Yorker,* "and the past has the singular inconvenience of never going away."

The dismay of American Jews regarding the contemporary fraying of black-Jewish relations arises from the presumption that blacks and Jews should stand side by side through thick and thin. "The truth is that Jews do feel different vis-a-vis the black community," Abraham Foxman, national director of the Anti-Defamation League of B'nai B'rith, stated. "There is a history, there is a kinship, and it goes beyond the rhetoric. Look, there's never going to be a crisis in Irish-black relations or Italian-black relations, because they have no relations. But we do." Rabbi David Saperstein, head of the Religious Action Center of Reform Judaism and a member of the governing board of the National Association for the Advancement of Colored People, agreed. "Each day across the nation," he said, "blacks and Jews are working together for social justice, addressing problems of hunger and racism and dis-

This chapter was previously published in *First Things,* no. 45 (Aug.–Sept. 1994): 29–35. Reprinted by permission of the Institute of Religion and Public Life.

crimination and the challenges to education and health care in America. We are clearly joined at the hip." Judging from the comments of Foxman and Saperstein, Jews and blacks are also joined at the lip.

This identity of interest between two of America's most important victim groups was the underlying assumption of *CommonQuest,* a magazine that first appeared in 1996. Jointly sponsored by the American Jewish Committee and Howard University, *CommonQuest* had an editorial advisory board comprised of prominent blacks and Jews, including Clayborne Carson, Leonard Fein, Henry Louis Gates, Irving Greenberg, Paula Hyman, Julius Lester, Joseph Lieberman, Kweisi Mfume, Hugh B. Price, Jim Sleeper, Michael Walzer, Cornel West, and William Julius Wilson. The magazine's masthead noted that it sought to enlist the shared vision of blacks and Jews in order to serve "the African-American and Jewish communities in their pursuit of mutual understanding and a just society." The early issues of *CommonQuest* contained articles on the relationship of Al Jolson, Irving Berlin, and George Gershwin to black culture, the role of Jews in popularizing black rhythm-and-blues artists, and the black-Jewish political alliance.

For a century Jews have assumed that they, more than any other group of whites, could and did empathize with the plight of blacks, and that blacks recognized this. Jewish newspapers early in the twentieth century compared the black movement out of the South to the exodus from Egypt, noted that both blacks and Jews lived in ghettos, and described antiblack riots in the South as pogroms. Even European Jews voiced compassion for the American black. *Uncle Tom's Cabin* was translated into both Yiddish and Hebrew. In his 1902 book *Old New Land,* Theodore Herzl had one character say, "There is still one other question arising out of the disaster of the nations which remains unsolved to this day, and whose profound tragedy only a Jew can comprehend. This is the African question. . . . I am not ashamed to say, though I may expose myself to ridicule in saying so, that once I have witnessed the redemption of the Jews, my people, I wish also to assist in the redemption of the Africans." Zalman David Levontin, a prominent European Zionist of the late nineteenth century, argued that Jews should try to emulate the experience of the blacks who founded the Republic of Liberia. In his autobiography he noted that while a child he asked, "If the Negroes could found a free republic for themselves, why should we not go and found a state for ourselves too in the land of our ancestors?"

For Jewish leaders, if not the Jewish man-in-the-street, it became an article of faith that the fates of blacks and Jews were intertwined. Jews were propelled into the civil rights movement in part by the belief that Jews and blacks shared the same agenda. Joel and Arthur Spingarn helped found the National Association for the Advancement of Colored People, Jack Greenberg succeeded Thurgood Marshall as head of the NAACP Legal Defense Fund, and Jewish organizations such as the American Jewish Committee, the American Jewish Congress, and the ADL have been in the forefront in the campaign against racial prejudice. The financial contributions of Jews were crucial in the work of the NAACP, the Urban League, the Congress of Racial Equality, the Student Non-Violent Coordinating Committee, and other civil rights organizations. More than half of the whites who went to Mississippi in 1964 to challenge Jim Crow were Jews, and about half of the civil rights attorneys in the South during the 1960s were Jews. No white ethnic group has voted more readily for blacks than have Jews. This was true in Philadelphia and Los Angeles, and in Chicago and New York. Tom Bradley, Harold Washington, and David Dinkins would not have been elected mayor of Los Angeles, Chicago, or New York City had Jews voted the same as Italians, Poles, and the Irish.

Jews have been far more interested in blacks than blacks have been interested in Jews. George Gershwin wrote "Porgy and Bess," and Eddie Cantor and Al Jolson spent much of their stage careers in black face. In academia there is not one black scholar, apart from Julius Lester, a convert to Judaism, whose major field of interest is Jewish studies. By contrast, many of the most prominent authorities on black history and black sociology have been Jews. One thinks of Melville J. Herskovits (*The Myth of the Negro Past*), Frank Tannenbaum (*Slave and Citizen*), and Charles Silberman (*Crisis in Black and White*), among others. The field of black history is studded with such names as Herbert Aptheker, Ira Berlin, Philip Foner, Herbert Gutman, Lawrence W. Levine, Leon F. Litwack, Gilbert Osofsky, George Rawick, and Seth M. Schemer. Robert W. Fogel, cowinner of the 1993 Nobel Prize in Economics, coauthored the most controversial economic analysis of slavery, *Time on the Cross,* while Stanley Elkins wrote *Slavery: A Problem in American Institutional and Intellectual Life,* the most debated study of the impact of slavery on blacks.

The historian Peter Novick, in his 1988 volume *That Noble Dream: The "Objectivity Question" and the American Historical Profession,* noted a difference in the way that Gentile and Jewish historians have approached black history. Those white historians who wrote of white attitudes and behavior toward blacks—George Fredrickson, Winthrop Jordan, C. Vann Woodward—were usually Gentiles, while those white historians who wrote of blacks as subjects were generally Jews. Herbert Gutman wrote a mammoth history of the black family, and Lawrence Levine wrote an outstanding book on Afro-American folk culture. Nell Painter, a contemporary black historian, claimed that although most white historians wrote from a white perspective, historians such as Levine and Gutman "are able to think about history in what I'd call 'black' ways."

Jewish spokesmen emphasized that this interest of Jews in blacks stemmed not only from idealism but also from self-interest. Jews would benefit the more America moved toward a society of merit in which religious, ethnic, and racial barriers were unimportant. One year before the Supreme Court outlawed school segregation in the 1954 Brown decision, the Jewish Community Relations Advisory Council declared, "In a still imperfect society, Jews, together with many other groups, suffer from inequalities of opportunity and other forms of discrimination." Jewish leaders stressed the similarities rather than the differences between the Jewish and the black experience in America. Both groups, they asserted, were powerless and victims of persecution. Both included in their ranks martyrs to American intolerance, Leo Frank in the case of Jews and Emmett Till in the case of blacks. The murder of James Chaney, Andrew Goodman, and Michael Schwerner in Mississippi in 1964 strengthened the presumption that the fates of blacks and Jews were intertwined.

This presumption has continued to resonate among American Jews. One manifestation of this was the Public Broadcasting System documentary film *Liberators: Fighting on Two Fronts in World War II*. This film, and the book that appeared simultaneously with the movie's release, described the role of black soldiers in liberating Jews from the Buchenwald and Dachau concentration camps in April 1945. The film opened on November 9, 1992, the fifty-fourth anniversary of Kristallnacht, at Alice Tully Hall in Lincoln Center with Jesse Jackson and other luminaries in attendance. One month later it was screened at the Apollo Theater in Harlem under the sponsorship of a group calling itself the Liberators Commemoration Committee. This screening was followed by a reception attended by black leaders, black veterans of World War II, and Holocaust survivors.

Liberators could not have appeared at a more fortuitous time for New York City politicians and black and Jewish leaders. Mayor David Dinkins hoped that it would lessen the tensions between blacks and Jews that had been exacerbated by the 1991 riots in Crown Heights and the refusal in October 1992 of a Brooklyn jury to convict Lemrick Nelson of the murder of Yankel

Rosenbaum, who had been killed during the riots. Dinkins had been elected in 1989 as the city's first black mayor, and he had emphasized during the election campaign that he could best heal the city's ethnic and racial divisions. Dinkins's hope for reelection depended on support among Jewish voters, and *Liberators,* with its premise that Jews and blacks shared a common agenda, was grist for his political mill. The New York City Board of Education planned to distribute copies of the documentary to all of the city's public junior and senior high schools, and Jewish philanthropists competed for the privilege of funding the operation. They hoped that the film could help stem the tide of increasing black anti-Semitism and repair the badly frayed black-Jewish liberal coalition.

Liberators received an Academy Award nomination for best documentary even after doubts had been raised by black World War II veterans, Holocaust survivors, and Holocaust historians regarding the film's veracity. It soon was revealed that black soldiers had never liberated Dachau and Buchenwald, although they had been in the vicinity of the camps. Chris Ruddy of the *New York Guardian* blew the whistle on *Liberators* in his December 1992 article "PBS Documentary Lies about Liberation of Concentration Camps." Ruddy also published an article in *Newsday* on December 15, 1992, which described *Liberators* as "an out-and-out lie" propagating "romantic, invented history." Jeffrey Goldberg, the New York bureau chief for the *Forward,* followed with a widely read essay in the *New Republic.* Titled "The Exaggerators," it appeared in the magazine's February 8, 1993, issue. Goldberg quoted the denials of both black soldiers and survivors that blacks had liberated Dachau and Buchenwald. Shortly after Goldberg's article appeared, the American Jewish Committee issued a fifteen-page report, which concluded that *Liberators* contained "serious factual flaws well beyond what can be written off as 'artistic license.' "

Indicative of the great emotional investment of some people in the film and in the black-Jewish alliance was the fact that *The Liberators* was aired on public television station WNET in New York City even though the station had been alerted that the movie was peddling a falsehood. The black veterans of the 761st Tank Battalion were particularly angry regarding the liberties that had been taken with the truth. "I first went to Buchenwald in 1991 with PBS," one black soldier who appeared in the film told Goldberg. The black soldiers had had an enviable record of service in Europe in 1944 and 1945, and they did not want it sullied by fantasies that, once discredited, could bring into question their wartime performance. E. G. McConnell, one of the black soldiers, said, "We had been stripped of our history in our slavery, and I didn't want to come up with anything that could tarnish our record. But apparently some other people didn't mind a few lies." The black World War II veterans were not the only blacks who objected to the film. Blacks who had been involved in making the film complained that their artistic integrity had been compromised for the sake of a politically correct political and social agenda.

One of the more interesting aspects of the controversy surrounding *Liberators* was the continuing refusal of Nina Rosenblum, the film's Jewish cocreator, to recant even after the movie's misrepresentations had been exposed and the film had been withdrawn from circulation. She described as racists those whites who would deprive the black units of credit for liberating Dachau and Buchenwald. She argued this even though it had been the black veterans themselves who had first raised doubts about the film. In order to discredit McConnell, she said that he was "severely brain-damaged" as a result of being hit in the head with shrapnel during the war. She also charged that the criticism of her film "only serves to denigrate the courageous concentration camp survivors and their heroic liberators."

Rosenblum was not the only Jew unwilling to allow the minor point of historical accuracy to detract from the laudable effort to cement black-Jewish relations. If the film was not factually true, they seemed to be saying, so much the worse for truth. Peggy Tishman, one of the cohosts for the Apollo showing, asked rhetorically, "Why would anybody want to exploit the idea that this is a fraud? What we're trying to do is make New York a better place for you and me to live." The truth of the film was subsidiary to its role in reviving the black-Jewish alliance. For Jews on the left, the revelations concerning *Liberators* were a disaster not because it was a fraud but because they encouraged those elements within the Jewish community skeptical of the black-Jewish alliance.

Pogrebin, writing in the radical Jewish magazine *Tikkun,* feared that the controversy created by the film played into the hands of political forces seeking to capitalize on black-Jewish enmity. For her, the dispute mandated a search for truth "at a level deeper than facts." "The film presents us with a problem of ethical slippage and well-intentioned embellishment," she wrote, but it was not a hoax. "Truth must be defended, yes; but so must the liberal vision of Black advancement and the struggle for Black-Jewish harmony."

It is precisely because Jews believe in this "Black-Jewish harmony" that they have been so disappointed by the reluctance of Jesse Jackson and other black leaders to strongly condemn the anti-Semitic rantings of Louis Farrakhan and his ilk. This disappointment stems not merely from the belief that blacks have not shown the proper gratitude for all that Jews have done for them. More important is that evidence of black anti-Semitism throws doubt on an important element of the Jewish identity of American Jewish liberals and radicals—the presumption that blacks and Jews comprise a community of the oppressed and that Jews are never acting more true to their religious and ethnic heritage than when they are working side by side with blacks to create a society free of racial and religious prejudice.

If anything, this belief of Jews that they have a special relationship with blacks stimulates anti-Semitism. As Arch Puddington has argued (in "Black Anti-Semitism and How It Grows," *Commentary,* April 1994), anti-Semites such as Farrakhan are encouraged in their anti-Semitism "in the knowledge that Jews, unlike other whites, will react not simply with anger, but with wounded innocence and appeals for 'dialogue' and 'healing.' Abandoning the fiction of the special relationship might thus have the paradoxical effect of contributing to a reduction of racial tensions."

Black anti-Semitism, however, is simply incomprehensible to liberal Jews, who would like to believe that their own history of affliction, culminating in the Holocaust, has made them incapable of racism. This ignores the sociological and historical context within which black-Jewish relations have evolved. A curious effort in such denial was the editorial "Victims and Victimizers" in the March–April 1994 issue of *Tikkun.* It argued that the color of people's skins was determined not by pigmentation but by political correctness. "Who gets labeled 'white' and who gets labeled 'persons of color' derives not from the color of one's skin . . . but from the degree to which one has been a victim of Western colonialist oppression. By that measure, Jews have been the greatest victims of Western societies throughout the past two thousand years and must certainly be understood to be one of the 'peoples of color.' Our literature was systematically excluded from the academic canon and so deserves to be part of the multicultural corpus. And our history ought to be studied as a prime example of oppression." Michael Lerner, the founder of *Tikkun,* also denied that Jews were white. "Jews can only be deemed 'white' if there is massive amnesia on the part of non-Jews about the monumental history of anti-Semitism." Leonard Fein agreed. Jews, Fein said in 1968, "are not white symbolically and we are not white literally. . . . We are too much an oppressed people, still, and too much a rejected people, even in this country, to accept the designation 'white.' "

The belief that Jews have shared a victimhood status with blacks was responsible for the similarities Jews have drawn between their condition and that of the blacks. In 1917 the *Forward* compared the East St. Louis race riot to the Kishinev pogrom of 1903. "Kishinev and St. Louis—the same soil, the same people. It is a distance of four and a half thousand miles between these two cities and yet they are so close and so similar to each other." Even Gentiles noted the similarities between blacks and Jews. Henry Ford's anti-Semitic newspaper, the *Dearborn Independent,* described jazz as "Yiddish moron music."

For Jews on the Left an entente with blacks was necessary in order to fulfill their sense of self. This entente vindicated Jewish liberalism and radicalism and encouraged a Jewish identity free of religious obscurantism. "We are all forced to confront . . . the question of what is a Jew and what does this all mean," Ellen Willis, a Jewish radical, said in 1982. "And to me the status of Jews as outsiders and as persecuted outsiders is the core of what Judaism and Jewishness is all about." It is this Jewish need for close cooperation with blacks that accounted for the Jews' strong response to the bluster of Khalid Abdul Muhammad. Catholics had every right to feel equally aggrieved by Muhammad since he called the pope a "cracker." But most Catholics ignored such comments, perhaps because they don't expect much better, or perhaps because they did not believe their Catholicism to be dependent on an alliance with blacks.

Jews have continued to call for the maintenance of the black-Jewish alliance despite the vast socioeconomic differences between the two groups. Leonard Fein has been among the most eloquent spokesman for this position. In his 1988 book *Where Are We? The Inner Life of America's Jews,* he admitted that American Jews were no longer among the oppressed. Nevertheless, Jews should continue to identify with blacks because of "our continuing need to see ourselves among the miserable—or, at least, the still-threatened." The involvement of Jews in the civil rights movement, he concluded, "has helped preserve our sense of ourselves as still, and in spite of all the successes we've known, among the oppressed, hence also among the decent, the just, the virtuous." Fein was wrong. The history of anti-Semitism in Europe, the Middle East, and the United States has not shown that the oppressed are necessarily virtuous. The oppressed peasants of Russia were among the most rabid anti-Semites.

As the religious and ethnic elements of Jews' identity have become increasingly attenuated, Jews increasingly emphasized the importance of working in behalf of civil rights in defining Jewish identity. Thus Rabbi Abraham

Joshua Heschel, speaking in the 1960s, claimed that "the plight of the Negro must be our most important concern. Seen in the light of our religious tradition, the Negro problem is God's gift to America, the test of our integrity, a magnificent spiritual opportunity."

Even a cursory examination of the history of black-Jewish relations in the United States reveals that they were never as warm as Pogrebin, Fein, and Heschel believed they were or should be, nor are they today as frigid as alarmists claim. If support for blacks is an ineluctable result of Jewish values, then one would expect that the most Jewish of American Jews—the Orthodox of Brooklyn—would be the most sympathetic toward blacks. The exact opposite, however, is true. Secure in their Jewish identity, they do not require close relations with blacks to define it. Their Jewishness rests on more substantial grounds.

One does not have to be Orthodox to be wary of blacks. Norman Podhoretz's 1963 essay "My Negro Problem—and Ours" reveals how wide was the cultural gulf between immigrant Jews and their children who resided in the solidly Jewish neighborhood of Brownsville in Brooklyn and the blacks in adjacent neighborhoods. Podhoretz and his friends were simultaneously repulsed by and attracted to the superior athleticism and sexuality of the blacks, an attitude expressed also in Norman Mailer's famous essay "The White Negro."

If the most Jewish of Jews are the least receptive to blacks, the Jews most supportive of blacks have often been alienated from Jewish culture and religion. It is difficult to find any connection between the fact that the parents of Andrew Goodman and Michael Schwerner were Jews and the fact that their children risked and ultimately lost their lives working on behalf of blacks in Mississippi. Goodman and Schwerner evidenced little attachment in their daily lives to things Jewish. Goodman's parents were radicals, and his father was president of the board of directors of the radical New York City radio station WBAI. Schwerner professed to be an atheist. It was fitting that, just as they had lived their lives remote from Jewish concerns, so neither Goodman nor Schwerner had Jewish funerals.

What was true of Goodman and Schwerner was also true of many prominent Jews in the civil rights movement. The Spingarns were hardly ardent Jews. William Chafe's biography of Allard Lowenstein describes Lowenstein's embarrassment over his Jewish background, evidenced by his decision to attend the University of North Carolina rather than a northern university where there would be a sizable Jewish enrollment. Jack Greenberg did not participate in Jewish political or social affairs, and he seldom set foot in a synagogue. Indeed, for Greenberg and Lowenstein, as well as for Howard Zinn, William Kuntsler, and others, an involvement in black causes was a surrogate identity that helped fill the vacuum in their lives stemming from their estrangement from things Jewish.

The myth of black-Jewish identity also mistook the nature of black-Jewish relations and the attitude of blacks toward Jews. It is true that in a variety of ways ever since the time of slavery, blacks have drawn on the Jewish experience. In spirituals such as "Go Down, Moses," blacks drew parallels between their own situation in the South and that of the Jews in Egypt. Just as Jews escaped from slavery and inflicted punishment on their taskmasters, so blacks anticipated flight from slavery and the chastisement of southerners. The popularity of "Zion" in the names of black churches shows how the experience of the Exodus resonated among blacks. Black nationalists used the Zionist movement as a model for their own back-to-Africa movement. Finally, blacks pointed to the example of the upward social and economic mobility and bourgeois values of Jews as a model for their own people. For groups such as the Black Jews of Harlem, this admiration for Jews led to syncretic religious cults containing Jewish elements.

Blacks, however, never forgot that there was a vast racial gulf separating them from Jews. No matter how much Jews did for blacks, Jews were still Caucasians with all the privileges accruing to people with white skin. For blacks, the great fault line in America was between whites and blacks. The rapid decline of American anti-Semitism after 1945 combined with the nation's continuing pervasive racism was proof to blacks, if they needed any such proof, that the condition of American Jews bore little resemblance to that of blacks.

Blacks have been rightfully skeptical of the effort to conflate the black and Jewish experiences. The relationship between Jews and blacks does not have the cosmic moral significance for them that it has for Jews on the left. Blacks are naturally more impressed by the social and economic differences between themselves and Jews than by any ideological similarities between the two groups. No American black, the novelist James Baldwin wrote, wanted "to be told by an American Jew that his suffering is as great as the American Negro's suffering. It isn't, and one knows that it isn't from the very tone in which he assures you that it is."

Even during the first two decades after World War II—the supposed "golden age" of black-Jewish relations—Baldwin, Kenneth Clark, and other blacks warned liberal Jews that their image of a close black-Jewish relationship was a fiction and that candor and realism were now required when speaking of blacks and Jews. As Baldwin noted, "Georgia has the Negro and Harlem has the Jew." Whenever the black paid rent to a Jewish apartment house owner, or shopped at a Jewish-owned store, or was taught by a Jewish schoolteacher, or was supervised by a Jewish social worker, or was paid by a Jewish employer, the reality of black subservience to Jews was driven home.

The constant advice to blacks to look to the Jewish experience as a model exacerbated the difficulties between the two peoples. That advice assumed that if Jews could make it in American society, then presumably so could blacks; but this assumption ignored the crucial fact that Jews, *pace* Lerner and Fein, were white. Furthermore, the Jewish social and economic advance was painful to blacks in the face of their own less rapid progress. It was as if Jewish success was a constant insult, drawing continual attention to black inadequacies and failures. One could hardly think of a more effective way to increase black anti-Semitism than to encourage blacks to emulate Jews and to harp continually on the disparity between black and Jewish economic and social development. If Jews and blacks were really oppressed brothers, how could one account for the disparities in their social and economic conditions?

One can imagine the psychological impact on blacks of Eric Hoffer's comparison of blacks and Jews. The example of Jews, Hoffer wrote, "shows what persistent striving and a passion for education can do . . . even in the teeth of discrimination. This is a fact which the Negro vehemently rejects. It sticks in his gullet. . . . The Jew impairs the authenticity of the Negro's grievances and alibis. He threatens the Negro's most precious possession: the freedom to fail." For Hoffer, the success of the Jew was a continual refutation of the cult of victimization fostered by black spokesmen.

Blacks have had a far more realistic attitude toward the black-Jewish connection than Jews, and they were not as concerned as Jews by the unraveling of the black-Jewish alliance in the 1960s and 1970s. Jews needed blacks to authenticate their image of themselves as liberals, but blacks did not need Jews to authenticate their image of themselves as blacks. They merely had to look in the mirror. "Jews interested in rebuilding coalitions," Julius Lester said, "had to get to know blacks better, had to get to know them as people instead of as liberal icons."

Blacks also realized that they were hardly the social and economic equals of Jews, and that relations between the two groups reflected this disparity in economic and social status. As much as Jews might have done for blacks, the relationship was essentially one of paternalism. A paradigm of their association was the one between Jack Benny and Rochester on the popular radio and television show of the 1940s and 1950s. As close and warm as the dealings between the two men might be, there was never any mistaking the fact that Benny was the boss and Rochester the servant.

Blacks have resented Jews not because they did not do enough for them but because they did too much. This gave rise to the joke about the man who was shocked to find himself attacked by blacks. "I haven't done anything *for* them," he exclaimed. Harold Cruse's 1967 book *The Crisis of the Negro Intellectual* was an eye-opener for Jews, revealing the extent to which blacks resented Jewish involvement in black affairs. The pervasive anti-Semitism of the book stemmed from Cruse's bitterness that the black drive for self-determination had been deflected by Jewish radicals into communism and other causes that had little relevance to black nationalism.

For decades sensitive observers had warned Jews that black-Jewish relations were not what Jews presumed. In 1964, Rabbi Richard C. Hertz discussed the "Rising Tide of Negro-Jewish Tensions" in the black magazine *Ebony,* and two years later the sociologist Dennis Wrong prophesied that "Negro anti-Semitism is not a passing phenomenon." This prediction has come to pass. Recent polls have indicated that 63 percent of New York City's blacks believe Jews have too much influence in the city, and that nationally blacks are twice as likely to hold anti-Semitic views as other Americans. Gary E. Rubin of the American Jewish Committee has raised serious questions about the methodology of these polls, and he has argued that they overestimate the extent of overall American anti-Semitism. Still, there seems little doubt that anti-Semitism is more widespread among blacks than whites. American blacks are the only major American ethnic group that has leaders who are clearly anti-Semitic.

Black anti-Semitism seems to have repealed the traditional sociological laws regarding anti-Semitism. Whereas for whites anti-Semitism has been more prevalent among the older, less affluent, less educated, and more religious, among blacks the exact opposite is true. Within the black community there is a positive correlation between youth, schooling, income, and lack of religiosity on the one hand, and anti-Semitism on the other. Yet are these results so surprising? Is it really so strange that upwardly mobile blacks would see Jews as part of an undifferentiated mass of whites bent on limiting their advancement? Is it so odd that blacks, after contrasting their economic and social status with that of Jews (or Asians), would be frustrated and resentful?

Nevertheless, Jews continue to assume that black anti-Semitism is irrational and transitory. Since blacks and Jews have supposedly been close in times past, black anti-Semitism appears incongruous. Hence Gary Marx's 1967 book, *Protest and Prejudice,* which discounted the presence of black anti-Semitism.

Some Jews on the left would prefer to explain away black anti-Semitism because its existence casts doubt on the myth of black-Jewish comradeship. Thus one participant in a roundtable on "Beyond Crown Heights," published in the January–February 1993 issue of *Tikkun,* asserted, "It's no surprise that we might expect a problem with anti-Semitism after twelve years of Reagan and Bush in which social inequalities have grown." Jews were forced to resort to such bizarre arguments because they consistently misunderstood the history of black-Jewish relations and the relative status of the two communities.

Hillel Levine and Lawrence Harmon's *The Death of an American Jewish Community: A Tragedy of Good Intentions* (1992) exemplifies another attempt to hold on to the black-Jewish alliance. This study of the transformation of the Jewish neighborhood of Roxbury-Dorchester-Mattapan in Boston into a black slum blamed the hostility of blacks and Jews on outsiders, particularly unscrupulous bankers, realtors, and politicians, who presumably were only too happy to pit the two groups against each other.

The problems between Jews and blacks go much deeper than this. American Jews, whatever their problems with prejudice, have never experienced anything remotely resembling the enslavement, discrimination, and racism encountered by blacks, while blacks have never known the economic and social prosperity of Jews. Blacks and Jews derived different lessons from American history. "The Jewish travail occurred across the sea and America rescued him from the house of bondage," Baldwin wrote in 1967. "But America *is* the house of bondage for the Negro, and no country can rescue him." Their own experiences convinced Jews that America was an open society in which education and merit would eventually win out, hence their firm opposition to affirmative action. By contrast, blacks learned from history that American society was irredeemably stacked against them and that something more than the merit principle was necessary if the legacy of three and a half centuries of racism was to be overcome.

On every possible social and economic index, blacks have lagged far behind Jews. While Jews constitute an economic and social elite group within contemporary America, a significant minority of blacks comprise what sociologists call an "underclass." The disparities between Jews and blacks involving crime, family breakdown, drug addiction, alcoholism, and educational achievements are well known. There is nothing in the American Jewish experience similar to the culture of poverty found in the inner city. Jewish criminality, such as that on the Lower East Side of New York and in Brownsville, Brooklyn, back in the 1920s and 1930s, was largely a one-generation phenomenon, as was the Jewish working class. While the major problem facing America's Jews today is maintaining Jewish identity in the midst of affluence, acculturation, and declining anti-Semitism, the major problems facing most blacks are the more immediate ones of economic survival, family breakdown, and continuing racial prejudice. If the comradeship of Jews and blacks revolving around a common victimhood status was not a mirage in times past, it certainly is one today.

Black-Jewish relations can never be on a sound footing as long as Jewish leaders remain wedded to romantic notions regarding the natural links between the two groups. On a whole host of issues the interests of Jews and blacks diverge. There is nothing unusual or surprising about this. It is demeaning to both blacks and Jews to argue that each must reflexively support the other's agenda in order to avoid antagonisms. Michael Meyers, a black leader in New York City, has told Jews that they should recognize "the tough realities." "It's true that Jews and Blacks have been allies, but we've also been rivals," he noted. "To many Jews racial quotas are anathema, for many nonwhites affirmative action must be distinguished from exclusionary quotas. We have rivalry about housing. . . . We have disagreements about how and where there are double standards in the criminal justice system." It is hardly surprising that blacks would not have a visceral attachment to Israel, or that Jews would be more critical than blacks of national liberation movements in Africa and Asia. Nor is it unexpected that Jews would be more optimistic regarding American society, or that they would favor the impartial standards for judging merit that have served them so well.

Two centuries ago George Washington in his Farewell Address laid down the standards by which the United States should conduct itself with other nations. Here he warned American citizens not to take sides in the European conflicts resulting from the French Revolution. "In the execution of such a plan nothing is more essential than that permanent, inveterate antipathies against particular nations and passionate attachments for others should be excluded, and that in place of them just and amicable feelings toward all should be cultivated. The nation which indulges toward another an habitual hatred or an habitual fondness is in some degree a slave. It is a slave to its animosity or to its affection, either of which is sufficient to lead it astray from its duty and its interest. . . . Sympathy for the favorite nation, facilitating the illusion of an imaginary common interest in cases where no real common interest exists . . . gives to ambitious, corrupted, or deluded citizens (who devote themselves to the favorite nation) facility to betray or sacrifice the interests of their own country without odium, sometimes even with popularity. . . . I hold the maxim no less applicable to public than to private affairs that honesty is always the best policy."

Washington's advice—that honesty above all is the best policy—is equally applicable to relations between blacks and Jews. To recognize that Jews have romanticized their relationship with blacks is not to say that they were wrong in becoming so closely identified with the civil rights movement after World War II. Jews and blacks had common enemies, and both groups benefited from their relationship, which helped open up American society to hitherto excluded minorities. Involvement in the civil rights movement was a bright shining movement for American Jewry. The error for Jews was to become so enamored of this relationship that they lost track of their true interests and to give the relationship a centrality in Jewish identity that it did not warrant.

NOTES

BIBLIOGRAPHY

INDEX

Notes

INTRODUCTION

1. Henry L. Feingold, *Lest Memory Cease: Finding Meaning in the American Jewish Past* (Syracuse, N.Y.: Syracuse Univ. Press, 1996), 23–33. An earlier version of this essay appeared in *American Jewish History* 71 (June 1982): 421–31.

2. WORLD WAR II AND AMERICAN JEWISH IDENTITY

1. Charles C. Alexander, *Nationalism in American Thought, 1930–1945* (Chicago: Rand-McNally, 1969), 201.

2. Lucy S. Dawidowicz, *On Equal Terms: Jews in America, 1881–1981* (New York: Holt, Rinehart and Winston, 1981), 129–30.

3. *New York Times,* Sept. 12, 1941; Wayne S. Cole, *Charles A. Lindbergh and the Battle Against American Intervention in World War II* (New York: Harcourt Brace Jovanovich, 1974), chaps. 19–21.

4. *New York Times,* Feb. 14, 1938; *Congressional Record,* 77th Cong., 1st sess., Feb. 28, 1941, 1513–14; idem, July 31, 1941, 6498–99; Wayne S. Cole, *Roosevelt and the Isolationists, 1932–1945* (Lincoln: Univ. of Nebraska Press, 1983), 474–76; Judd L. Teller, *Strangers and Natives: The Evolution of the American Jew from 1921 to the Present* (New York: Delacourt, 1968), 186–90.

5. Senate Subcommittee of the Committee on Interstate Commerce, *Propaganda in Motion Pictures: Hearing before the Committee on Interstate Commerce,* 77th Cong., 1st sess., 1942, 6–48.

6. *Congressional Record,* 76th Cong., 2d sess., Nov. 1, 1939, 1939–40; idem, 76th Cong., 1st sess., Apr. 24, 1941, 3279–81.

7. *Congressional Record,* 77th Cong., 1st sess., June 4, 1941, 4726–27; *New York Times,* June 4, 1941.

8. *Congressional Record,* 77th Cong., 1st sess., June 4, 1941, 4727; idem, June 18, 1941, A2910–11, A3337–38; *Memorial Services Held in the House of Representatives of the United States, Together with Remarks Presented in Eulogy of Morris Michael Edelstein, Late a Representative of New York* (Washington, D.C.: Government Printing Office, 1943), passim.

9. *New York Times,* June 7, 1941; *Congressional Record,* 77th Cong., 1st sess., June 18, 1941, A3056.

10. Charles E. Silberman, *A Certain People: American Jews and Their Lives Today* (New York: Summit, 1985), 57; Dawidowicz, *On Equal Terms,* 97–99.

11. John Morton Blum, *V Was for Victory: Politics and American Culture During World War II* (New York: Harcourt Brace Jovanovich, 1976), 172–75.

12. Silberman, 28–31.

13. Ibid., 62–64.

14. Jerome N. Frank, "Red, White, and Blue Herring," *Saturday Evening Post* 214 (Dec. 6, 1941): 9–11.

15. Milton S. Mayer, "The Case Against the Jew," *Saturday Evening Post* 214 (Mar. 28, 1941): 18–19.

16. Stephen J. Whitfield, *American Space, Jewish Time* (Hamden, Conn.: Archon Books, 1988), 61–62.

17. Ibid.; Alexander Bloom, *Prodigal Sons: The New York Intellectuals and Their World* (New York: Oxford Univ. Press, 1986), 22–26.

18. Leonard Dinnerstein, "Antisemitism Exposed and Attacked, 1945–1950," in *Uneasy at Home: Antisemitism and the American Jewish Experience* (New York: Columbia Univ. Press, 1987), 178–96; Blum, 175.

19. Patricia Erens, *The Jew in American Cinema* (Bloomington: Indiana Univ. Press, 1984), 173–75.

20. Ibid., 176–80; Lester D. Friedman, *Hollywood's Image of the Jew* (New York: Ungar, 1982), 125–30; K.R.M. Short, "Hollywood Fights Anti-Semitism, 1945–1947," in *Feature Films as History,* ed. K.R.M. Short (Knoxville: University of Tennessee Press, 1981), 174–80.

21. Dinnerstein, 181–85.

22. Robert H. Abzug, *Inside the Vicious Heart: Americans and the Liberation of the Nazi Concentration Camps* (New York: Oxford Univ. Press, 1985), 66–67; Meyer Levin, *In Search: An Autobiography* (New York: Horizon, 1950), 232.

23. Susan Sontag, *On Photography* (New York: Farrar, Strauss, 1977), 19–20.

24. Dawidowicz, *On Equal Terms,* 110.

25. Henry Popkin, "The Vanishing Jew of Our Popular Culture," *Commentary* 14 (July 1952): 51–55; Stuart Samuels, "The Evolutionary Image of the Jew in American Film," in *Ethnic Images in American Film and Television,* ed. Randall M. Miller (Philadelphia: Balch Institute, 1978), 27–28; Alan Spiegel, "The Vanishing Act: A Typology of the Jew in Contemporary American Film," in *From Hester Street to Hollywood: The Jewish-American Stage and Screen,* ed. Sarah Blacher Cohen (Bloomington: Indiana Univ. Press, 1983), 260–61.

26. Herman Wouk, *The Caine Mutiny: A Novel of World War II* (Garden City, N.Y.: Doubleday, 1951), 441–42.

27. Peter C. Rollins, " 'Victory at Sea': Cold War Epic," *Journal of Popular Culture* 6 (spring 1951): 463–78.

28. Susan Dworkin, *Miss America, 1945: Bess Myerson's Own Story* (New York: Newmarket, 1987), 7–8, 106–11, 132.

29. Norman Podhoretz, *Making It* (New York: Random House, 1967), 100, 134–35.

30. Elliot E. Cohen, "An Act of Affirmation," *Commentary* 1 (Nov. 1945): 1–3.

31. Abram L. Sachar, *A Host at Last* (Boston: Little, Brown, 1976), 14–25.

32. Gilbert Klaperman, *The Story of Yeshiva University: The First Jewish University in Amer-*

ica (New York: Macmillan, 1969), 150–51; Jeffrey S. Gurock, *The Men and Women of Yeshiva: Higher Education, Orthodoxy, and American Judaism* (New York: Columbia Univ. Press, 1988), 92–93.

33. Klaperman, 151.

34. Dorothy Thompson, "America Demands a Single Loyalty," *Commentary* 9 (Mar. 1950): 210–19; the quotations from Oscar Handlin are in the revised version of his *Commentary* essay that was republished as "Israel and the Mission of America" and appears in Oscar Handlin, *Race and Nationality in American Life* (Garden City, N.Y.: Doubleday, 1957), 193–200. Handlin makes an even stronger case for multiple loyalties in this revision.

35. Will Herberg, *Protestant-Catholic-Jew: An Essay in American Religious Sociology* (Garden City, N.Y.: Doubleday, 1955), esp. chap. 5.

3. THE JEW AS PATRIOT: HERMAN WOUK AND AMERICAN JEWISH IDENTITY

1. Pearl K. Bell, "Good, Bad and Bad-Bad," *Commentary* 66 (Dec. 1978): 70–72.

2. Paul Fussell, review of Herman Wouk, *War and Remembrance,* in *New Republic* 179 (Oct. 14, 1978): 32–33. The most recent history of the Battle of Leyte Gulf also has high praise for Wouk as a historian. "My former colleagues in the Naval Academy's history department and professional historians everywhere will cringe at what I am about to say, but a truly wonderful (accurate and insightful) account of the battle is included in Herman Wouk's novel *War and Remembrance.*" Thomas J. Cutler, *The Battle of Leyte Gulf, 23–26 October, 1944* (New York: HarperCollins, 1994), 299.

3. Arthur M. Schlesinger Jr., "*Time* and the Intellectuals," *New Republic* 135 (July 16, 1956): 15–16; Harvey Swados, "Popular Taste and *The Caine Mutiny,*" *Partisan Review* 20 (Mar.–Apr. 1953): 248–56; Leslie A. Fiedler, *To the Gentiles* (New York: Madison Books, 1972), 107.

4. Fiedler, *To the Gentiles,* 108; Leslie A. Fiedler, *Love and Death in the American Novel,* rev. ed. (New York: Stein and Day, 1966), 151–53.

5. Norman Podhoretz, "The Jew as Bourgeois," *Commentary* 21 (Feb. 1956): 186–88.

6. "The Wouk Mutiny," *Time* 66 (Sept. 5, 1955): 48–52.

7. Fiedler, *To the Gentiles,* 107.

8. Arnold Beichman, *Herman Wouk: The Novelist as Social Historian* (New Brunswick, N.J.: Transaction, 1984), 10–11; "The Wouk Mutiny," 52.

9. Wouk, *Caine Mutiny,* 87–97.

10. Ibid., 426–30.

11. Ibid., 483–90.

12. Ibid., 490–97, 518–19.

13. William H. Whyte Jr., *The Organization Man* (New York: Simon and Schuster, 1956), 269–75.

14. Herman Wouk, *This Is My God* (Garden City, N.Y.: Doubleday, 1959), 52.

15. Wouk, *The Winds of War* (Boston: LB Books, 1972), 25–27, 31–32.

16. Ibid., 19, 25, 160.

17. Ibid., 61, 255–57.

18. Ibid., 240–43.

19. Ibid., 768.

20. Ibid., 102–3.

21. Ibid., 448.

22. Ibid., 1046.

23. Wouk, *War and Remembrance* (Boston: LB Books, 1978), 30, 797–801, 966, 1021, 1087, 1307.

24. Ibid., 49, 574, 1068, 1096.

25. Ibid., 585, 1375.

26. Jonathan Netanyahu, *Self-Portrait of a Hero: From the Letters of Jonathan Netanyahu, 1963–1976,* intro. Herman Wouk (New York: Random House, 1980), v–xi.

27. Herman Wouk, *Inside/Outside: A Novel* (Boston: Little, Brown, 1985), 630; Joseph Lowin, "Herman Wouk and the Liturgical Novel," *Jewish Book Annual* 44 (1986): 43–54.

28. Wouk, *Inside/Outside,* 4–5, 9–11, 599–600.

29. Herman Wouk, *The Hope* (Boston: LB Books, 1993), 33–34, 85, 425, 456.

30. Ibid., 56–57, 615.

31. Ibid., 108–10.

32. Wouk, *This Is My God,* 2; Wouk, *War and Remembrance,* 465.

33. Wouk, *The Hope,* 640; Herman Wouk, *The Glory* (Boston: LB Books, 1994), 48, 485.

34. Wouk, *The Glory,* 367–69, 406, 440, 453, 456.

35. Ibid., 605–7.

36. Ibid., 672.

37. "What Do American Jews Believe?" *Commentary* 102 (Aug. 1996): 18–96. Wertheimer's comments are on pages 91–93.

38. Hillel Halkin, *Letters to an American Jewish Friend: A Zionist's Polemic* (Philadelphia: Jewish Publication Society of America, 1977), 52; Jerrold S. Auerbach, *Rabbis and Lawyers: The Journey from Torah to Constitution* (Bloomington: Indiana Univ. Press, 1990), x–xi, 206.

4. JEWISHNESS AND THE NEW YORK INTELLECTUALS

1. C. Vann Woodward, *The Burden of Southern History* (Baton Rouge: Louisiana State Univ. Press, 1960), 31–32.

2. Alexander Bloom, *Prodigal Sons: The New York Intellectuals and Their World* (New York: Oxford Univ. Press, 1986), 142–55; Terry A. Cooney, *The Rise of the New York Intellectuals: "Partisan Review" and Its Circle* (Madison: Univ. of Wisconsin Press, 1986), 242; Alan Wald, *The New York Intellectuals: The Rise and Decline of the Anti-Stalinist Left from the 1930s to the 1980s* (Chapel Hill: Univ. of North Carolina Press, 1987); David J. Hollinger, "Ethnic Diversity, Cosmopolitanism and the Emergence of the American Liberal Intelligentsia," *American Quarterly* 27 (May 1975): 133–51.

3. Stephen J. Whitfield, "After Strange Gods: Radical Jews in Modern America," *Forum* 56 (summer 1985): 34–35; Cooney, 14; Isaac Deutscher, "The Non-Jewish Jew," in *"The Non-Jewish Jew" and Other Essays,* ed. Tamara Deutscher (New York: Oxford Univ. Press, 1968), 25–41.

4. Cooney, 14, 240; Leonard Fein, *Where Are We? The Inner Life of America's Jews* (New York: Harper and Row, 1988), 189.

5. Irving Howe, *A Margin of Hope* (New York: Harcourt Brace Jovanovich, 1982), 151–61.

6. Ruth R. Wisse, "The New York (Jewish) Intellectuals," *Commentary* 74 (Nov. 1987): 34–38.

7. Norman Podhoretz, *Making It* (New York: Random House, 1967), 118–22; Alfred Kazin, *New York Jew* (New York: Alfred A. Knopf, 1978), 26–34.

8. Howe, *Margin of Hope,* 247–51.

9. Irving Howe, "The Range of the New York Intellectual," in *Creators and Disturbers: Reminiscences by Jewish Intellectuals of New York,* ed. Bernard Rosenberg and Ernest Goldstein (New York: Columbia Univ. Press, 1982), 285–86.

10. Howe, *Margin of Hope,* 260–80.

11. Wald, 28; Sidney Hook to Joseph J. Jacobs, Jan. 9, 1984, Hook Papers, Hoover Institution, Stanford University.

12. Sidney Hook, "Our Country and Our Culture," *Partisan Review* 19 (Sept.–Oct. 1952): 570.

13. Sidney Hook, *Out of Step: An Unquiet Life in the 20th Century* (New York: Harper and Row, 1987), 33.

14. Hook, *Out of Step,* 33–34; Tom Bethell, "A Stroll with Sidney Hook," *American Spectator* 20 (May 1987): 12–13.

15. The outline of this speech is in the Hook Papers: Sidney Hook, "Promise Without Dogma: A Social Philosophy for Jews," *Menorah Journal* 25 (Oct.–Dec. 1937): 273–88.

16. Hook, "Promise Without Dogma"; Hook to Edward S. Shapiro, May 11, 1988, letter in possession of author. For two different responses to Hook's essay, see Shlomo Grodzensky, "Sidney Hook Faces the Jewish Problem," *Labor Zionist News Letter,* Jan. 15, 1938, 5–9; and Alvin Johnson, "A Social Philosophy for Jews," *Menorah Journal* 26 (Jan.–Mar. 1938): 1–5; Hook's response to Johnson at idem, 103–4.

17. Hook, *Out of Step,* 33.

18. *New York Times,* Dec. 4, 1948; Sidney Hook, "Israel and American Jewry," unpublished manuscript, Hook Papers.

19. A copy of Sidney Hook, "The National Council of Jewish Women on the Present-Day Jewish Scene: A Program Survey of the Organization," is in the Hook Papers.

20. Sidney Hook, "Reflections on the Jewish Question," *Partisan Review* 16 (May 1949): 466; Hook to Leonard R. Sussman, Mar. 7, 1957, Hook Papers.

21. Hook to Joseph P. Bachman, undated, Hook Papers; Hook to Jonathan Harlen, Nov. 24, 1982, Hook Papers.

22. Sidney Hook, "The Tragedy of German Jewry," *New Leader* 21 (Nov. 26, 1938): 8.

23. Ibid. For a general discussion of the response of American intellectuals to totalitarianism, see Stephen J. Whitfield, "American Jewish Intellectuals and Totalitarianism," in *Voices of Jacob, Hands of Esau: Jews in American Life and Thought* (Hamden, Conn.: Archon Books, 1984), 9–29.

24. Sidney Hook, "Hitlerism: A Non-metaphysical View," *Contemporary Jewish Record* 7 (Feb. 1944): 146–55.

25. Sidney Hook, "The New Medievalism," *New Republic* 103 (Oct. 28, 1940): 602–6; Sidney Hook, "The New Failure of Nerve," *Partisan Review* 10 (Jan.–Feb. 1943): 2–23.

26. Hook, "Reflections," 475, 479; Sidney Hook, "The Plural Sources of Jewish Life in America," unpublished manuscript, Hook Papers. Hook delivered this twenty-one-page paper at the 1947 conference of the American Jewish Committee.

27. Hook, "Reflections," 482.

28. Hook, "Plural Sources"; Hook, "National Council of Jewish Women."

29. Hook, "Reflections," 476.

30. Hook, "National Council of Jewish Women"; Hook, "Plural Sources."

31. Hook, "National Council of Jewish Women."

32. Ibid.

33. Fein, *Where Are We,* 168.

34. Ibid., 160–61.

5. THE ORDEAL OF SUCCESS: AMERICAN JEWRY SINCE WORLD WAR II

1. For the relationship between American Jews and Greenberg, see William M. Simons, "The Athlete as Jewish Standard Bearer: Media Images of Hank Greenberg," *Jewish Social Studies* 44 (spring 1982): 95–112; and Hank Greenberg, *Hank Greenberg: The Story of My Life,* ed. Ira Berkow (New York: Times Books, 1989).

2. For Myerson and the events of September 1945, see Susan Dworkin, *Miss America, 1945: Bess Myerson's Own Story* (New York: Newmarket, 1987).

3. Andrew Kopkind, "Bess Bets," *Village Voice,* Nov. 12, 1979, 19–20.

4. Jenna Weissman Joselit, *New York's Jewish Jews: The Orthodox Community in the Interwar Years* (Bloomington: Indiana Univ. Press, 1990), 21.

5. Silberman, 360–66.

6. Chaim I. Waxman, *America's Jews in Transition* (Philadelphia: Temple Univ. Press, 1983), 116–18, 156; Seymour Martin Lipset, "Jewish Fear, Black Insensitivity," *New York Times,* Mar. 9, 1990.

7. Charles Stember, "The Recent History of Public Attitudes," in Charles Stember and others, *Jews in the Mind of America* (New York: Basic Books, 1966), 156–69.

8. Dinnerstein, 17; Stember, 126–34; Earl Raab, "The Black Revolution and the Jewish Question," in *Black Anti-Semitism and Jewish Racism,* ed. Nat Hentoff (New York: Richard W. Baron, 1969), 15.

9. Nathan Perlmutter and Ruth Ann Perlmutter, *The Real Anti-Semitism in America* (New York: Arbor House, 1982), 72–78; Stember, 104–6.

10. Arnold Forster and Benjamin R. Epstein, *The New Anti-Semitism* (New York: McGraw-Hill, 1974), 3–5, 324.

11. Silberman, 180; Lawrence Bloomgarden, "Our Changing Elite Colleges," *Commentary* 29 (Feb. 1960): 152.

12. Stuart E. Rosenberg, *The New Jewish Identity in America* (New York: Hippocrene, 1985), 252–56; Seymour Martin Lipset, "A Unique People in an Exceptional Country," in *American Pluralism and the Jewish Community,* ed. Seymour Martin Lipset (New Brunswick, N.J.: Transaction, 1990), 4; Silberman, 99.

13. Henry James, *The American Scene* (New York: Harper and Brothers, 1907), 130–39.

14. Peter Novick, *That Noble Dream: The "Objectivity Question" and the American Historical Profession* (Cambridge: Cambridge Univ. Press, 1988), 172, 369.

15. Whitfield, *American Space, Jewish Time,* 46; Norman L. Friedman, "Orientation of Jewish Professors to the Jewish Community," *Jewish Social Studies* 35 (July–Oct. 1973): 269; Everett Carll Ladd Jr. and Seymour Martin Lipset, *The Divided Academy: Professors and Politics* (New York: McGraw-Hill, 1975), 162–67; Stephen Steinberg, *The Academic Melting Pot: Catholics and Jews in American Higher Education* (New York: McGraw-Hill, 1974), 15–46.

16. Morris N. Kertzer, *Today's American Jew* (New York: McGraw-Hill, 1967), 23; Silberman, 84.

17. Silberman, 88.

18. G. William Domhoff and Richard Zweigenhaft, "Jews in the Corporate Establishment," *New York Times,* Apr. 24, 1983.

19. Wouk, *This Is My God,* 252–56, 281–82; Philip Roth, *"Goodbye, Columbus" and Five Short Stories* (New York: Bantam, 1963), 184, 200–201.

20. Harold Mehling, "Is Miami Beach Jewish?" in *A Coat of Many Colors: Jewish Subcommunities in the United States,* ed. Abraham D. Lavender (Westport, Conn.: Greenwood, 1977), 118–22.

21. Thomas Sowell, *Ethnic America: A History* (New York: Basic Books, 1981), 88–98.

22. Irving Howe, *A Margin of Hope* (New York: Harcourt Brace Jovanovich, 1982), 341–42.

23. David Singer, "Living with Intermarriage," *Commentary* 68 (July 1979): 48.

24. Nathan Glazer, "On Jewish Forebodings," *Commentary* 80 (Aug. 1985): 36; Ze'ev Chafets, *Members of the Tribe: On the Road in Jewish America* (New York: Bantam, 1988), 250.

25. Daniel J. Elazar, *Community and Polity: The Organizational Dynamics of American Jewry* (Philadelphia: Jewish Publication Society of America, 1976), 76; Hillel Halkin, *Letters to an American Jewish Friend: A Zionist's Polemic* (Philadelphia: Jewish Publication Society of America, 1977), 25.

6. AMERICAN JEWS AND THE BUSINESS MENTALITY

1. Selma C. Berrol, "Education and Economic Mobility: The Jewish Experience in New York City, 1880–1920," *American Jewish Historical Quarterly* 65 (Mar. 1966): 257–71.

2. Moses Rischin, *The Promised City: New York Jews, 1870–1914* (Cambridge, Mass.: Harvard Univ. Press, 1962), 56; Thomas Kessner, *The Golden Door: Italian and Jewish Immigrant Mobility in New York City, 1880–1915* (New York: Oxford Univ. Press, 1977), 65.

3. Ronald Sanders, *The Downtown Jews: Portraits of an Immigrant Generation* (New York: Harper and Row, 1969), 219.

4. Marshall Sklare, "The Sociology of Contemporary Jewish Studies," in *The Jew in American Society,* ed. Marshall Sklare (New York: Behrman House, 1974), 19–25.

5. Stanley Kaufmann, "Stanley Kaufmann on Films," *New Republic* 173 (Oct. 18, 1975): 21; Robert F. Horowitz, "Between a Heartache and a Laugh: Two Recent Films on Immigration," *Film and History* 6 (Dec. 1976): 75.

6. Dan Isaac, "Some Questions about the Depiction of Jews in New Films," *New York*

Times, Sept. 8, 1974; David Weinberg, "The 'Socially Acceptable' Minority Group: The Image of the Jew in American Popular Films," *North Dakota Quarterly* 40 (autumn 1972): 63–65.

7. JEWS WITH MONEY

1. Paul Berman, "East Side Story: Mike Gold, the Communists and the Jews," *Radical America* 17 (July–Aug. 1983): 39–53; Allen Guttmann, *The Jewish Writer in America: Assimilation and the Crisis of Identity* (New York: Oxford Univ. Press, 1971), 140–42.

2. Paul Gottfried, "Sombart's *The Jews and Modern Capitalism* Revisited," *This World* 3 (fall 1982): 138–44.

3. John Higham, *Send These to Me: Jews and Other Immigrants in Urban America* (New York: Atheneum, 1975), 179.

4. Irving Kristol, *Reflections of a Neo-Conservative* (New York: Basic Books, 1983), 316.

5. Silberman, 329.

6. Stephen Birmingham, *"The Rest of Us": The Rise of America's Eastern European Jews* (Boston: Little, Brown, 1984), xvi, 57.

7. Nathan Glazer and Daniel P. Moynihan, *Beyond the Melting Pot: The Negroes, Puerto Ricans, Jews, Italians, and Irish of New York City* (Cambridge, Mass.: M.I.T. Press, 1963), 151–55; Silberman, 133–36.

8. THE FRIENDLY UNIVERSITY: JEWS IN ACADEMIA SINCE WORLD WAR II

1. Silberman, 99, 180.

2. Bloomgarden, 152; Arthur Hertzberg, *The Jews in America: Four Centuries of an Uneasy Encounter, a History* (New York: Simon and Schuster, 1989), 311.

3. Cleveland Amory, *The Proper Bostonians* (New York: E. P. Dutton, 1947), 27.

4. For the selection of Rudenstine, see *Harvard Magazine* 93 (May–June 1991): 31–36, 69–71.

5. Barbara M. Solomon, *Ancestors and Immigrants: A Changing New England Tradition* (Cambridge, Mass.: Harvard Univ. Press, 1956), 123; Marcia Graham Synott, *The Half-Opened Door: Discrimination and Admissions at Harvard, Yale, and Princeton, 1900–1970* (Westport, Conn.: Greenwood, 1979), 196; Amory, 35.

6. Louis Joughlin and Edmund M. Morgan, *The Legacy of Sacco and Vanzetti* (Chicago: Quadrangle, 1964), 39–40; Alan M. Dershowitz, *Chutzpah* (Boston: Little, Brown, 1991), 66–67.

7. Bloomgarden, 152; Silberman, 30–31; Seymour Martin Lipset and David Riesman, *Education and Politics at Harvard* (New York: McGraw-Hill, 1975), 144–49; Steinberg, *Academic Melting Pot,* 26–27.

8. Amory, 303.

9. Stephen Steinberg, *The Ethnic Myth: Race, Ethnicity and Class in America* (New York: Atheneum, 1981), 233.

10. Walter Goodman, "Bicker at Princeton: The Eating Clubs Again," *Commentary* 25 (May 1958): 406–10; Synott, 196.

11. Goodman, 406–7.

12. Ibid., 409–15; Marianne Sanua, "Stages in the Development of Jewish Life at Princeton University," *American Jewish History* 76 (June 1987): 397.

13. Synott, 150.

14. Dan A. Oren, *Joining the Club: A History of Jews and Yale* (New Haven, Conn.: Yale Univ. Press, 1985), 43; Synott, 17, 130, 155.

15. Synott, 159.

16. Ibid., xix, xx, 209; Oren, 243–45.

17. Sanua, 391–415.

18. James Yaffe, *The American Jews: A Portrait of a Split Personality* (New York: Random House, 1968), 52.

19. A. H. Halsey and M. A. Trow, *The British Academics* (London: Faber and Faber, 1971), 43–45.

20. Fritz K. Ringer, *The Decline of the German Mandarins: The German Academic Community, 1890–1933* (Cambridge, Mass.: Harvard Univ. Press, 1969), 3, 135–36, 143, 224, 229.

21. Ladd and Lipset, 1–2, 56, 88–89.

22. Lipset and Riesman, 149–50; Rosenberg, *New Jewish Identity,* 252–56; Hertzberg, *Jews in America,* 309; Steinberg, *Academic Melting Pot,* 123; Ladd Jr. and Lipset, 150–53.

23. Ari L. Goldman, *The Search for God at Harvard* (New York: Times Books, 1991), 11–12.

24. Bradley J. Longfield, " 'For God, for Country, and for Yale': Yale, Religion, and Higher Education Between the World Wars," in *The Secularization of the Academy,* ed. George M. Marsden and Bradley J. Longfield (New York: Oxford Univ. Press, 1992), 151–58.

25. David Bebbington, "The Secularization of British Universities since the Mid-Nineteenth Century," in Marsden and Longfield, 267–74; George M. Marsden, "The Soul of the American University: A Historical Overview," in Marsden and Longfield, 8–10; George M. Marsden, *The Soul of the American University: From Protestant Establishment to Established Nonbelief* (New York: Oxford Univ. Press, 1994), 265, 417. For the rise of the modern research university, see Laurence R. Veysey, *The Emergence of the American University* (Chicago: Univ. of Chicago Press, 1965), esp. chaps. 2–3.

26. Nathan Glazer, *Affirmative Discrimination* (New York: Basic Books, 1975).

27. Steinberg, *Ethnic Myth,* 249–52.

28. Randolph Bourne, *Youth and Life* (Boston: Houghton, Mifflin, 1913), 318.

9. ORTHODOXY IN PLEASANTDALE

1. Albert I. Gordon, *Jews in Suburbia* (Boston: Beacon, 1959), 148; Marshall Sklare and Joseph Greenblum, *Jewish Identity on the Suburban Frontier* (Chicago: Univ. of Chicago Press, 1967), 167–71.

2. Solomon Poll, "The Persistence of Tradition: Orthodoxy in America," in *The Ghetto and Beyond: Essays on Jewish Life in America,* ed. Peter I. Rose (New York: Random House, 1969), 119; William B. Helmreich, *The World of the Yeshiva: An Intimate Portrait of Orthodox Jewry* (New York: Free Press, 1982).

3. Stuart E. Rosenberg, "Suburban Judaism," *Midstream* 29 (Nov. 1983): 30–32. This is

excerpted from Rosenberg's *The Real Jewish World: A Rabbi's Second Thoughts* (New York: Philosophical Library, 1984).

4. Samuel C. Heilman, *Synagogue Life: A Study in Symbolic Interaction* (Chicago: Univ. of Chicago Press, 1976), 266.

5. Samuel C. Heilman, "Inner and Outer Identities: Sociological Ambivalence among Orthodox Jews," *Jewish Social Studies* 39 (summer 1979): 227–38.

6. For Orthodox divisiveness, see Heilman, *Synagogue Life*, chap. 1.

7. Charles S. Liebman, "Orthodoxy in American Jewish Life," *American Jewish Year Book, 1965*, ed. Morris Fine and Milton Himmelfarb, 66 (Philadelphia: Jewish Publication Society of America, 1965), 60.

8. Heilman, *Synagogue Life*, 103.

9. Charles Selengut, "By Torah Alone: Yeshiva Fundamentalism in Jewish Life," in *Accounting for Fundamentalisms: The Dynamic Character of Movements*, ed. Martin E. Marty and R. Scott Appleby (Chicago: Univ. of Chicago Press, 1994), 259.

10. Samuel C. Heilman and Steven M. Cohen, *Cosmopolitans and Parochials: Modern Orthodox Jews in America* (Chicago: Univ. of Chicago Press, 1989), 189.

10. THE MISSING ELEMENT: NATHAN GLAZER AND MODERN ORTHODOXY

1. Eric F. Goldman, *The Crucial Decade—and After* (New York: Vintage Books, 1960), 305–6; Martin E. Marty, *Righteous Empire: The Protestant Experience in America* (New York: Dial, 1970), 257–59.

2. William E. Leuchtenburg, gen. ed., *The Unfinished Century: America since 1900* (Boston: Little, Brown, 1973), 745–46.

3. Herberg.

4. Marty, 259; Herberg, chap. 5.

5. Nathan Glazer, "Religion Without Faith," *New Republic* 133 (Nov. 14, 1955): 18–20.

6. Eric F. Goldman, 306.

7. Nathan Glazer, *American Judaism* (Chicago: Univ. of Chicago Press, 1957), 130–34.

8. Marshall Sklare, *Conservative Judaism: An American Religious Movement* (New York: Schocken, 1955, 1972); Herberg, 209; Abraham J. Karp, "The Conservative Rabbi—'dissatisfied but Not Unhappy,' " *American Jewish Archives* 35 (Nov. 1983): 255; Abraham J. Karp, "A Century of Conservative Judaism in the United States," in *American Jewish Year Book, 1986*, ed. Milton Himmelfarb and David Singer, 86 (Philadelphia: Jewish Publication Society of America, 1986), 42.

9. Glazer, *American Judaism*, 97–98, 125–40.

10. Ibid., 116–21.

11. Sklare, *Conservative Judaism*, 43–46.

12. H. Richard Niebuhr, *The Social Sources of Denominationalism* (New York: Meridian Books, 1929, 1957), chaps. 2, 3, 8.

13. Howard W. Polsky, "A Study of Orthodoxy in Milwaukee: Social Characteristics, Beliefs, and Observances," in *The Jews: Social Patterns of an American Group*, ed. Marshall Sklare (New York: Free Press, 1958), 25–35.

14. Glazer, *American Judaism,* 109–10.

15. Ibid.

16. Ibid., 147.

17. Ibid., 142–47.

18. Leuchtenburg, 750–54.

19. Milton M. Gordon, *Assimilation in American Life: The Role of Race, Religion, and National Origins* (New York: Oxford Univ. Press, 1964), 173–95.

20. Poll, 119.

21. Sklare, *Conservative Judaism,* 262–67.

22. Karp, "Conservative Rabbi," 243; Mordecai M. Waxman, "Conservative Judaism Confronts Its Future," *Judaism* 36 (spring 1987): 179.

23. Rosenberg, *New Jewish Identity,* 35, 190–93.

24. Louis Bernstein, "Orthodoxy: Flourishing but Divided," *Judaism* 36 (spring 1987): 174–78. See also the chapter "Orthodoxy: Triumphalism on the Right," in Jack Wertheimer, *A People Divided: Judaism in Contemporary America* (New York: Basic Books, 1993).

25. Sklare, *Conservative Judaism,* 266.

26. Nathan Glazer, "A Middle Way," *Commentary* 20 (Sept. 1955): 277–80.

27. Glazer, "On Jewish Forebodings," 32–36; Glazer, "The Dream Fulfilled," *New York Times Book Review,* Sept. 1, 1985, 1, 17–18.

28. Reuven P. Bulka, "Orthodoxy Today: An Overview of the Achievements and the Problems," in *Dimensions of Orthodox Judaism,* ed. Reuben P. Bulka (New York: KTAV, 1983), 8–17.

11. POLITICS AND AMERICAN JEWISH IDENTITY

1. Samuel C. Heilman, *Portrait of American Jews: The Last Half of the 20th Century* (Seattle: Univ. of Washington Press, 1995), 164.

2. Alan M. Dershowitz, *The Vanishing American Jew: In Search of Jewish Identity for the Next Century* (Boston: Little, Brown, 1997), 2.

3. Jack Wertheimer, "Judaism Without Limits," *Commentary* 104 (July 1997): 24–27.

4. Craig Horowitz, "Are American Jews Disappearing?" *New York* 30 (July 14, 1997): 30–37, 101, 108.

5. Charles S. Liebman, *The Ambivalent American Jew: Politics, Religion, and Family in American Jewish Life* (Philadelphia: Jewish Publication Society of America, 1976), 157.

6. Charles S. Liebman and Steven M. Cohen, *The Two Worlds of Judaism: The Israeli and American Experiences* (New Haven, Conn.: Yale Univ. Press, 1990), 9; Elliott Abrams, *Faith or Fear: How Jews Can Survive in a Christian America* (New York: Free Press, 1997), 128.

7. Dominique Schnapper, *Jewish Identities in France: An Analysis of Contemporary French Jews,* trans. Arthur Goldhammer (Chicago: Univ. of Chicago Press, 1983), xxviii, 48; Paula Hyman, *From Dreyfus to Vichy: The Remaking of French Jewry, 1909–1939* (New York: Columbia Univ. Press, 1979), 3–7.

8. Brookhiser quoted in J. J. Goldberg, *Jewish Power: Inside the American Jewish Establishment* (Reading, Mass.: Addison-Wesley, 1996), 25; Heilman, *Portrait of American Jews,* 104ff; Steven M. Cohen, *American Modernity and Jewish Identity* (New York: Tavistock, 1983), 32.

9. Milton Himmelfarb, "The Case of Jewish Liberalism," in *Emerging Coalitions in Amer-*

ican Politics, ed. Seymour Martin Lipset (San Francisco: Institute for Contemporary Studies, 1978), 301; Seymour Martin Lipset and Earl Raab, "The American Jews, the 1984 Elections, and Beyond," in *Survey of Jewish Affairs, 1985,* ed. William Frankel (Cranbury, N.J.: Fairleigh Dickinson Univ. Press, 1985), 141–48; *New York Times,* Nov. 5, 1992, and Nov. 7, 1996.

10. The historian Ezra Mendelsohn has noted that the impact of the culture of East European Jews on "the Eastern European Jewish diasporas in Palestine and America can hardly be exaggerated. . . . For better or worse, the old association with the Left still has an impact—hard to measure but palpable—on the modern Jewish 'mentality.' " Mendelsohn, introduction to *Essential Papers on Jews and the Left,* ed. Ezra Mendelsohn (New York: New York Univ. Press, 1997), 9–12.

11. David Biale, *Power and Powerlessness in Jewish History* (New York: Schocken, 1986), 130–44.

12. Peter Y. Medding, "Toward a General Theory of Jewish Political Interests and Behavior in the Contemporary World," in *Kinship and Consent: The Jewish Political Tradition and Its Contemporary Uses,* ed. Daniel J. Elazar (Washington, D.C.: University Press of America, 1983), 317–18.

13. Willis quoted in Abrams, 156; Jean-Paul Sartre, *Anti-Semite and Jew,* trans. George J. Becker (New York: Schocken, 1948), 91, 143.

14. Gerald Sorin, *Tradition Transformed: The Jewish Experience in America* (Baltimore: Johns Hopkins Univ. Press, 1997), 220; J. J. Goldberg, 375.

15. Michael Selzer, *Zionism Reconsidered: The Rejection of Jewish Normalcy* (New York: Macmillan, 1970), xvii.

16. Jonathan Boyarin, *Thinking in Jewish* (Chicago: Univ. of Chicago Press, 1996), 16–31, 51–52; Daniel Boyarin, *A Radical Jew: Paul and the Politics of Identity* (Berkeley: Univ. of California Press, 1994), 235–60, 35–38.

17. Heilman, *Portrait of American Jews,* 138.

18. Cohen quoted in J. J. Goldberg, 26.

19. Biale, 181.

20. Ibid., 199; Dershowitz, *Vanishing American Jew,* 7; Liebman, *Ambivalent American Jew,* 159.

12. CHARLES S. LIEBMAN AND AMERICAN JEWISH LIBERALISM

1. Charles S. Liebman, "American Jews: Still a Distinctive Group," *Commentary* 64 (Aug. 1977): 57–60.

2. Liebman and Cohen, 97.

3. Arthur Hertzberg, "Behind Jews' Political Principles," *New York Times,* Nov. 2, 1984; Leonard Fein, *Where Are We? The Inner Life of America's Jews* (New York: Harper and Row, 1988), 199.

4. Liebman, *Ambivalent American Jew,* 20.

5. Ibid.

6. Liebman and Cohen, 122; Liebman, *Ambivalent American Jew,* viii.

7. Liebman, *Ambivalent American Jew,* vii–viii, 194–97.

8. Ibid., 96.

9. Ibid., 197.

10. Liebman, "Toward a Theory of Jewish Liberalism," in *The Religious Situation 1969,* ed. Donald R. Cutler (Boston: Beacon, 1969), 1037–42.

11. Liebman, "Toward a Theory," 1044.

12. Ibid., 1045.

13. Ibid., 1047–50, 1055.

14. Ibid., 1044, 1055.

15. Ibid., 1057.

16. Ibid.; Liebman, *Ambivalent American Jew,* 97.

17. Liebman and Cohen, 100.

18. Wise quoted in Stephen J. Whitfield, "The Jewish Vote," *Virginia Quarterly Review* 62 (winter 1986): 10–11.

19. Liebman and Cohen, 116.

20. Irving Kristol, "The Future of American Jewry," *Commentary* 92 (Aug. 1991): 24.

21. Alan Fisher, "Iraq, the U.S., and Two Jewish Questions Revisited," *Comment and Analysis* (newsletter of the Susan and David Wildstein Institute of Jewish Studies) 2 (June 1991): 3.

22. Charles S. Liebman, *Deceptive Images: Toward a Redefinition of American Judaism* (New Brunswick, N.J.: Transaction, 1988), 17.

23. Heilman and Cohen, 113, 166.

24. Liebman and Cohen, 117.

13. THE WAR AMONG THE JEWS

1. Jacobo Timerman, *Prisoner Without a Name, Cell Without a Number* (New York: Alfred A. Knopf, 1981), 139.

2. *New York Times,* June 25, 1981. At a meeting in New York City, Timerman called Begin a fascist. *Midstream* 28 (Feb. 1981): 35. For Timerman's opinion of the Begin government and the Jewish leaders of Argentina and the United States, see his "The Silence of the Jews," *Harper's* 263 (Nov. 1981): 20–23.

3. Jeane Kirkpatrick, "Dictatorships and Double Standards," *Commentary* 68 (Nov. 1979): 34–35; Eric P. Saltman, "Torture? On TV?" *New York Times,* May 26, 1981.

4. Irving Louis Horowitz, *Israeli Ecstasies/Jewish Agonies* (New York: Oxford Univ. Press, 1974), 109.

5. Deborah Dash Moore, *At Home in America: Second Generation New York Jews* (New York: Columbia Univ. Press, 1981), chap. 8; Stephen D. Isaacs, *Jews and American Politics* (Garden City, N.Y.: Doubleday, 1974); Werner Cohn, "The Politics of American Jews," in *The Jews: Social Patterns of an American Group,* ed. Marshall Sklare (New York: Free Press, 1958), 614–26; Lawrence H. Fuchs, "Sources of Jewish Internationalism and Liberalism," in Sklare, *The Jews,* 597ff; Irving Kristol in *Congress Bi-Weekly* 40 (Apr. 13, 1973): 18–19; Daniel J. Elazar, "American Political Theory and the Political Notions of American Jews: Convergences and Contradictions," in *The Ghetto and Beyond: Essays on Jewish Life in America,* ed. Peter I. Rose (New York: Random House, 1969), 203–27.

6. Bernard Rosenberg and Irving Howe, "Are American Jews Turning to the Right?" in *The*

New Conservatives: A Critique from the Left, ed. Lewis A. Coser and Irving Howe (New York: New American Library, 1977), 64–67.

7. Ibid., 69–89.

8. Norman Podhoretz, *Breaking Ranks* (New York: Harper and Row, 1979), 63–68.

9. Bernard Avishai, "Breaking Faith: *Commentary* and the American Jews," *Dissent* 28 (spring 1981): 236–56.

10. Murray Friedman, "A New Direction for American Jews," *Commentary* 72 (Dec. 1981): 37–44.

11. Anthony Lewis, "The Final Solution in Argentina," *New York Times Book Review,* May 10, 1981, 1, 30–32; Anthony Lewis, "What Kind of Country Are We?" *New York Times,* May 17, 1981.

12. Anthony Lewis, "Accomplice to Terror," *New York Times,* Mar. 22, 1981.

13. Irving Kristol, "The Timerman Affair," *Wall Street Journal,* May 29, 1981.

14. Benno Weiser Varon, "Don't Rescue Latin American Jews!" *Midstream* 26 (Dec. 1980): 11–16.

15. Rosenthal quoted in *New York Times,* June 3, 1981. See also Rosenthal and Varon in *Midstream* 27 (May 1981): 62–64. For evidence that Timerman knew his involvement with Graiver was responsible for his incarceration, see Seth Lipsky, "A Conversation with Publisher Jacobo Timerman," *Wall Street Journal,* June 4, 1981.

16. Benno Weiser Varon, "The Canonization of Jacobo Timerman," *Midstream* 27 (Aug.–Sept. 1981): 36–44. For reactions to this article and Varon's response, see "Last Word on Timerman," *Midstream* 28 (Feb. 1982): 34–42. For the attitude of Mario Gorenstein, president of the Delegation of Jewish Associations of Argentina, toward Timerman, see *New York Times,* May 22, 1981.

17. Anthony Lewis, "The Timerman Affair," *New York Times,* June 14, 1981; Alfred Kazin, "The Solitude of Jacobo Timerman," *New Republic* 184 (June 20, 1981): 32–34; Theodore Solotaroff, review of *Prisoner Without a Name, Cell Without a Number,* in *Nation* 232 (June 13, 1981): 733–36; Michael Walzer, "Timerman and His Enemies," *New York Review of Books* 29 (Sept. 24, 1981): 10–18.

18. Leon Wieseltier, "The Many Trials of Jacobo Timerman," *Dissent* 28 (fall 1981): 425–35.

19. Mitchell Cohen, "Bankrupt: A New Chapter," *Jewish Frontier* 48 (Aug.–Sept. 1981): 3–5; Elliot King, "Who's Afraid of Jacobo Timerman?" *Jewish Frontier* 48 (Aug.–Sept. 1981): 6–9.

20. *New York Times,* June 3, 1981; Jerome J. Shestack, "Jacobo Timerman: The Perils of Silence," 48 *Congress Monthly* (Sept.–Oct. 1981): 9, 11.

21. Leonard Fein, "The Timerman Conspiracy," *Moment* 6 (July–Aug. 1981): 61–63.

22. Richard Freund, "Anti-Semitism and Metaphors of the Holocaust," *Forum Newsletter* 1 (summer 1981): 2; Seymour Siegel, "Remarks about Argentina," *Forum Newsletter* 1 (summer 1981): 2, 7.

23. "The Uses of Jacobo Timerman," *Contentions* 1 (Aug. 1981): 1–3, 6–8.

24. Mark Falcoff, "The Timerman Case," *Commentary* 42 (July 1981): 15–23. For letters prompted by Falcoff's essay and Falcoff's response, see *Commentary* 62 (Dec. 1981): 14–23.

25. Seymour Siegel, "Right Turn," *Sh'ma* 11 (Apr. 17, 1981): 89–91.

26. Robert G. Kaiser, "The Jewish Voter: Giving Up on Carter," *Washington Post,* Aug. 17, 1980.

14. PAT BUCHANAN AND THE JEWS

1. William F. Buckley Jr., *In Search of Anti-Semitism* (New York: Continuum, 1992), 29, 44.

2. Norman Podhoretz, "Buchanan and the Conservative Crackup," *Commentary* 93 (May 1992): 34.

3. Jacob Weisberg, "Hunter Gatherers," *New Republic* 205 (Sept. 2, 1991): 14; John Ehrman, *The Rise of Neoconservatism: Intellectuals and Foreign Affairs* (New Haven, Conn.: Yale Univ. Press, 1995), 186; Fred Barnes, "Heir Apparent," *New Republic* 206 (Mar. 30, 1992): 20.

4. R. Emmett Tyrrell Jr., *The Conservative Crack-Up* (New York: Simon and Schuster, 1992), 97–98.

5. Paul Gottfried, "Notes on Neoconservatism," *World and I* 1 (Sept. 1986): 578.

6. Clyde Wilson, "The Conservative Identity," *Intercollegiate Review* 21 (spring 1986): 6–7; David Frum, *Dead Right* (New York: Basic Books, 1994), 125.

7. Gary Dorrien, *The Neoconservative Mind: Politics, Culture, and the War of Ideology* (Philadelphia: Temple Univ. Press, 1993), 342; Patrick J. Buchanan, "America First—and Second and Third," *National Interest* 19 (spring 1990): 77ff.

8. Daniel Bell, "Our Country—1984," *Partisan Review* 51 (fall 1984): 630.

9. Patrick J. Buchanan, *Right from the Beginning* (Boston: Little, Brown, 1988), 53.

10. The role of Catholics in the post–World War II American conservative movement is clearly told in Patrick Allitt, *Catholic Intellectuals and Conservative Politics in America* (Ithaca, N.Y.: Cornell Univ. Press, 1993).

11. Buchanan, *Right from the Beginning,* 218–21.

12. Charles Lane, "Daddy's Boy," *New Republic* 214 (Jan. 22, 1996): 15–25.

13. Joshua Muravchik, "Patrick J. Buchanan and the Jews," *Commentary* 91 (Jan. 1991): 29–30; Abe Rosenthal, "Forgive Them Not," *New York Times,* Sept. 14, 1990.

14. Benjamin Ginsberg, *The Fatal Embrace: Jews and the State* (Chicago: Univ. of Chicago Press, 1993), 232.

15. Allan H. Ryskind, letter to the editor, *Commentary* 91 (May 1992): 4–5; Anti-Defamation League, *From Columnist to Candidate: Pat Buchanan's Religious War,* Special Research Report (1992), 7–8.

16. Anti-Defamation League, *Anger on the Right: Pat Buchanan's Venomous Crusade,* Special Research Report (1991), 3–4.

17. Muravchik, 33.

18. Anti-Defamation League, *From Columnist to Candidate,* 17.

19. Eric Alterman, "Semite and Anti-Semites: The Pat and Abe Show," *Nation* 251 (Nov. 5, 1990): 520.

20. Jacob Weisberg, "The Heresies of Pat Buchanan," *New Republic* 203 (Oct. 22, 1990): 26; Muravchik, 33, 36.

21. Abraham H. Foxman, "Antisemitism in America: A View from the Defense Agencies,"

in *Antisemitism in America Today: Outspoken Experts Explode the Myths,* ed. Jerome A. Chanes (New York: Birch Lane Press, 1995), 331; Buchanan, *Right from the Beginning,* 277–78.

22. David Frum, "The Conservative Bully Boy," *American Spectator* 24 (July 1991): 14; Buckley, 125–27.

15. AMERICAN JEWRY AND THE STATE OF ISRAEL

1. Marshall Sklare, *America's Jews* (New York: Random House, 1971), 110–12; Sidney Goldstein, "American Jewry: A Demographic Analysis," in *The Future of the Jewish Community in America,* ed. David Sidorsky (New York: Basic Books, 1973), 81–89.

2. Arnold Lasker, "Motivations for Attending High Holy Day Services," *Journal for the Scientific Study of Religion* 10 (fall 1971): 241–48.

3. Liebman, *Ambivalent American Jew,* 67, 75, 102; Sklare and Greenblum, chap. 3; Nathan Glazer, "A Jewish Community," *Commentary* 46 (Aug. 1968): 67–68; Arnold Dashefsky and Howard M. Shapiro, *Ethnic Identification among American Jews: Socialization and Social Structure* (Lexington, Mass.: Lexington Books, 1974), 46–47; Sidney Goldstein and Calvin Goldscheider, *Jewish Americans: Three Generations in a Jewish Community* (Englewood Cliffs, N.J.: Prentice-Hall, 1968), 201–4.

4. Robert Silverberg, *If I Forget Thee O Jerusalem: American Jews and the State of Israel* (New York: William Morrow, 1970), 451–52; Liebman, *Ambivalent American Jew,* 88, 94–108; Sklare and Greenblum, chap. 6.

5. Irving Louis Horowitz, viii, 43, 75–85, 104.

6. Ibid., 79, 84–85.

7. Ibid., 84.

8. Joseph P. Sternstein, "Reform Judaism and Zionism, 1895–1904," in *Herzl Year Book,* ed. Raphael Patai, vol. 5 (New York: Herzl Press, 1963), 11–31.

9. Melvin I. Urofsky, *American Zionism from Herzl to the Holocaust* (New York: Anchor, 1975), 78, 95.

10. For the impact of the Holocaust on Israelis, see Amos Elon, *The Israelis: Founders and Sons* (New York: Bantam, 1971), 258–78.

11. Arthur Hertzberg, "Israel and American Jewry," *Commentary* 44 (Aug. 1967): 72.

12. Lucy S. Dawidowicz, "American Public Opinion," *American Jewish Year Book 1968,* ed. Morris Fine and Milton Himmelfarb, 69 (Philadelphia: Jewish Publication Society of America, 1968), 203–18; Silverberg, *If I Forget Thee,* 1–10, 574–77, 582; Marshall Sklare, "Lakeville and Israel: The Six-Day War and Its Aftermath," *Midstream* 14 (Oct. 1968): 4–21; S. P. Goldberg, "Jewish Communal Services: Programs and Finances," *American Jewish Year Book 1972,* ed. Morris Fine and Milton Himmelfarb, 73 (Philadelphia: Jewish Publication Society of America, 1972), 238–39.

13. Norman Podhoretz, "Now, Instant Zionism," *New York Times Magazine,* Feb. 3, 1974; Daniel J. Elazar, "United States of America: Overview," in *The Yom Kippur War: Israel and the Jewish People,* ed. Moshe Davis (New York: Arno, 1974), 1–35; Isaacs, 267; Meir Moshe, "The Yom Kippur War in Middle America," *Midstream* 20 (June–July 1974): 74–79.

14. Isaacs, 253; Silverberg, *If I Forget Thee,* 467–69.

15. Urofsky, 129–30.

16. Ibid., 131.

17. Ibid., 269, 297.

18. Liebman, *Ambivalent American Jew,* vii.

19. Ibid., 89–92; Sklare, *America's Jews,* 21–22.

20. *New York Times,* May 24, 1974.

21. Harry Arvay, *Operation Kuwait* (New York: Bantam, 1975).

22. Sklare, *America's Jews,* 222; Silverberg, *If I Forget Thee,* 460.

23. Isaacs, passim.

24. Silverberg, *If I Forget Thee,* 323, 456–58; Isaacs, 119. For the impact of American philanthropy on the decision-making process within the Zionist movement, see Ernest Stock, "The Reconstitution of the Jewish Agency: A Political Analysis," *American Jewish Year Book 1972,* 178–93.

25. Liebman, *Ambivalent American Jew,* 94.

26. Forster and Epstein, 18, 127–28, 312–24.

27. *Search for Peace in the Middle East* (Philadelphia: American Friends Service Committee, 1970), vi–vii.

28. Forster and Epstein, 85–88; Arnold M. Soloway with Edwin Weiss and Gerald Caplan, *Truth and Peace in the Middle East: A Critical Analysis of the Quaker Report* (New York: Friendly House, 1971), 70–71.

29. For Christian attitudes toward Israel, see Hertzel Fishman, *American Protestantism and the Jewish State* (Detroit: Wayne State Univ. Press, 1973), and Esther Feldblum, "On the Eve of a Jewish State: American-Catholic Responses," *American Jewish Historical Quarterly* 64 (Dec. 1974): 99–119.

30. Reinhold Niebuhr, *The Children of Light and the Children of Darkness* (New York: Charles Scribner's Sons, 1944), 133.

31. *Journal Intime,* Oct. 26, 1870, listed in *The Macmillan Book of Proverbs, Maxims, and Famous Phrases,* ed. Burton Stevenson (New York: Macmillan, 1948), 1236.

Bibliography

Abrams, Elliott. *Faith or Fear: How Jews Can Survive in a Christian America.* New York: Free Press, 1997.

Abzug, Robert H. *Inside the Vicious Heart: Americans and the Liberation of the Nazi Concentration Camps.* New York: Oxford Univ. Press, 1985.

Alexander, Charles C. *Nationalism in American Thought, 1930–1945.* Chicago: Rand-McNally, 1969.

Allitt, Patrick. *Catholic Intellectuals and ConservativePolitics in America.* Ithaca, N.Y.: Cornell Univ. Press, 1993.

Alterman, Eric. "Semite and Anti-Semites: The Pat and Abe Show." *Nation* 251 (Nov. 5, 1990): 517–20.

American Friends Service Committee. *Search for Peace in the Middle East.* Philadelphia: American Friends Service Committee, 1970.

Amory, Cleveland. *The Proper Bostonians.* New York: E. P. Dutton, 1947.

Anti-Defamation League. *Anger on the Right: Pat Buchanan's Venomous Crusade.* New York: Special Research Report, 1991.

———. *From Columnist to Candidate: Pat Buchanan's Religious War.* New York: Special Research Report, 1992.

Arvay, Harry. *Operation Kuwait.* New York: Bantam, 1975.

Auerbach, Jerrold S. *Rabbis and Lawyers: The Journey from Torah to Constitution.* Bloomington: Indiana Univ. Press, 1990.

Avishai, Bernard. "Breaking Faith: *Commentary* and the American Jews." *Dissent* 8 (spring 1981): 236–56.

Barnes, Fred. "Heir Apparent." *New Republic* 206 (Mar. 30, 1992): 20–22.

Bebbington, David. "The Secularization of British Universities since the Mid-Nineteenth Century." In *The Secularization of the Academy,* edited by George M. Marsden and Bradley J. Longfield, 259–77. New York: Oxford Univ. Press, 1992.

Beichman, Arnold. *Herman Wouk: The Novelist as Social Historian.* New Brunswick, N.J.: Transaction, 1984.

Bell, Daniel. "Our Country—1984." *Partisan Review* 51 (fall 1984): 620–37.

Bell, Pearl K. "Good, Bad and Bad-Bad." *Commentary* 66 (Dec. 1978): 70–72.

Berman, Paul. "East Side Story: Mike Gold, the Communists, and the Jews." *Radical America* 17 (July–Aug. 1983): 39–53.

Bernstein, Louis. "Orthodoxy: Flourishing but Divided." *Judaism* 36 (spring 1987): 174–78.

Berrol, Selma C. "Education and Economic Mobility: The Jewish Experience in New York City, 1880–1920." *American Jewish Historical Quarterly* 65 (Mar. 1966): 257–72.

Bethell, Tom. "A Stroll with Sidney Hook." *American Spectator* 20 (May 1987): 12–13.

Biale, David. *Power and Powerless in Jewish History.* New York: Schocken, 1986.

Birmingham, Stephen. *"The Rest of Us": The Rise of America's Eastern European Jews.* Boston: Little, Brown, 1984.

Bloom, Alexander. *Prodigal Sons: The New York Intellectuals and Their World.* New York: Oxford Univ. Press, 1986.

Bloomgarden, Lawrence. "Our Changing Elite Colleges." *Commentary* 29 (Feb. 1960): 150–54.

Blum, John Morton. *V Was for Victory: Politics and American Culture During World War II.* New York: Harcourt Brace Jovanovich, 1976.

Bourne, Randolph. *Youth and Life.* Boston: Houghton, Mifflin, 1913.

Boyarin, Daniel. *A Radical Jew: Paul and the Politics of Identity.* Berkeley: Univ. of California Press, 1994.

Boyarin, Jonathan. *Thinking in Jewish.* Chicago: Univ. of Chicago Press, 1996.

Buchanan, Patrick J. "America First—and Second and Third." *National Interest* 19 (spring 1990): 77–82.

———. *Right from the Beginning.* Boston: Little, Brown, 1988.

Buckley, William F., Jr. *In Search of Anti-Semitism.* New York: Continuum, 1992.

Bulka, Reuven P. "Orthodoxy Today: An Overview of the Achievements and the Problems." In *Dimensions of Orthodox Judaism,* edited by Reuven P. Bulka, 7–32. New York: KTAV, 1983.

Chafets, Ze-ev. *Members of the Tribe: On the Road in Jewish America.* New York: Bantam, 1988.

Cohen, Elliot E. "An Act of Affirmation." *Commentary* 1 (Nov. 1945): 1–3.

Cohen, Mitchell. "Bankrupt: A New Chapter." *Jewish Frontier* 48 (Aug.–Sept. 1981): 3–5.

Cohen, Steven M. *American Modernity and Jewish Identity.* New York: Tavistock, 1983.

Cohn, Werner. "The Politics of American Jews." In *The Jews: Social Patterns of an American Group,* edited by Marshall Sklare, 614–26. New York: Free Press, 1958.

Cole, Wayne S. *Charles A. Lindbergh and the Battle Against American Intervention in World War II.* New York: Harcourt Brace Jovanovich, 1974.

———. *Roosevelt and the Isolationists, 1932–1945.* Lincoln: Univ. of Nebraska Press, 1983.

Cooney, Terry A. *The Rise of the New York Intellectuals: "Partisan Review" and Its Circle.* Madison: Univ. of Wisconsin Press, 1986.

Cutler, Thomas J. *The Battle of Leyte Gulf, 23–26 October, 1944.* New York: HarperCollins, 1994.

Dashefsky, Arnold, and Howard M. Shapiro. *Ethnic Identification among American Jews: Socialization and Social Structure.* Lexington, Mass.: Lexington Books, 1974.

Dawidowicz, Lucy S. "American Public Opinion." In *American Jewish Year Book, 1968,* edited by Morris Fine and Milton Himmelfarb, vol. 69 (Philadelphia: Jewish Publication Society of America, 1968): 203–18.

———. *On Equal Terms: Jews in America, 1881–1981.* New York: Holt, Rinehart and Winston, 1982.

Dershowitz, Alan M. *Chutzpah.* Boston: Little, Brown, 1991.

———. *The Vanishing American Jew: In Search of Jewish Identity for the Next Century.* Boston: Little, Brown, 1997.

Deutscher, Isaac. "The Non-Jewish Jew." In *"The Non-Jewish Jew" and Other Essays,* edited by Tamara Deutscher, 25–41. New York: Oxford Univ. Press, 1968.

Dinnerstein, Leonard. *Uneasy at Home: Antisemitism and the American Jewish Experience.* New York: Columbia Univ. Press, 1987.

Domhoff, G. William, and Richard Zweigenhaft. "Jews in the Corporate Establishment," *New York Times,* Apr. 24, 1983.

Dorrien, Gary. *The Neoconservative Mind: Politics, Culture, and the War of Ideology.* Philadelphia: Temple Univ. Press, 1993.

Dworkin, Susan. *Miss America, 1945: Bess Myerson's Own Story.* New York: Newmarket, 1987.

Ehrman, John. *The Rise of Neoconservatism: Intellectuals and Foreign Affairs.* New Haven, Conn.: Yale Univ. Press, 1995.

Elazar, Daniel J. "American Political Theory and the Political Notions of American Jews: Convergences and Contradictions." In *The Ghetto and Beyond: Essays on Jewish Life in America,* edited by Peter I. Rose, 203–27. New York: Random House, 1969.

———. *Community and Polity: The Organizational Dynamics of American Jewry.* Philadelphia: Jewish Publication Society of America, 1976.

———. "United States of America: Overview." In *The Yom Kippur War: Israel and the Jewish People,* edited by Moshe Davis, 1–35. New York: Arno, 1974.

Elon, Amos. *The Israelis: Founders and Sons.* New York: Bantam, 1971.

Erens, Patricia. *The Jew in American Cinema.* Bloomington: Indiana Univ. Press, 1984.

Falcoff, Mark. "The Timerman Case." *Commentary* 42 (July 1981): 15–23.

Fein, Leonard. "The Timerman Conspiracy." *Moment* 6 (July–Aug. 1981): 61–63.

———. *Where Are We?: The Inner Life of America's Jews.* New York: Harper and Row, 1988.

Feingold, Henry L. "American Jewish History and American Jewish Survival." *American Jewish History* 71 (June 1982): 421–31.

———. *Lest Memory Cease: Finding Meaning in the American Jewish Past.* Syracuse, N.Y.: Syracuse Univ. Press, 1996.

Feldblum, Esther. "On the Eve of a Jewish State: American-Catholic Responses." *American Jewish Historical Quarterly* 64 (Dec. 1974): 99–119.

Fiedler, Leslie A. *Love and Death in the American Novel.* Revised edition. New York: Stein and Day, 1966.

———. *To the Gentiles.* New York: Madison Books, 1972.

Fisher, Alan. "Iraq, the U.S., and Two Jewish Questions Revisited." *Comment and Analysis* (newsletter of the Susan and David Wildstein Institute of Jewish Studies) 2 (June 1991).

Fishman, Hertzel. *American Protestantism and the Jewish State.* Detroit: Wayne State Univ. Press, 1973.

Forster, Arnold, and Benjamin R. Epstein. *The New Anti-Semitism.* New York: McGraw-Hill, 1974.

Foxman, Abraham H. "Antisemitism in America: A View from the Defense Agencies." In *Antisemitism in America Today: Outspoken Experts Explode the Myths,* edited by Jerome A. Chanes, 311–36. New York: Birch Lane Press, 1995.

Frank, Jerome N. "Red, White, and Blue Herring." *Saturday Evening Post* 214 (Dec. 6, 1941): 9–11.

Freund, Richard. "Anti-Semitism and Metaphors of the Holocaust." *Forum Newsletter* 1 (summer 1981): 2.

Friedman, Lester D. *Hollywood's Image of the Jew.* New York: Ungar, 1982.

Friedman, Murray. "A New Direction for American Jews." *Commentary* 72 (Dec. 1981): 37–44.

Friedman, Norman L. "Orientation of Jewish Professors to the Jewish Community." *Jewish Social Studies* 35 (July–Oct. 1973): 264–82.

Frum, David. "The Conservative Bully Boy." *American Spectator* 24 (July 1991): 12–14.

———. *Dead Right.* New York: Basic Books, 1994.

Fuchs, Lawrence H. "Sources of Jewish Internationalism and Liberalism." In *The Jews: Social Patterns of an American Group,* edited by Marshall Sklare, 595–613. New York: Free Press, 1958.

Fussell, Paul. Review of Herman Wouk, *War and Remembrance,* in *New Republic* 179 (Oct. 14, 1978): 32–33.

Ginsberg, Benjamin. *The Fatal Embrace: Jews and the State.* Chicago: Univ. of Chicago Press, 1993.

Glazer, Nathan. *Affirmative Discrimination.* New York: Basic Books, 1975.

———. *American Judaism.* Chicago: Univ. of Chicago Press, 1957.

——— "The Dream Fulfilled." *New York Times Book Review,* Sept. 1, 1985.

———. "A Jewish Community." *Commentary* 46 (Aug. 1968): 67–70.

———. "A Middle Way." *Commentary* 20 (Sept. 1955): 277–80.

———. "On Jewish Forebodings." *Commentary* 80 (Aug. 1985): 32–36.

———. "Religion Without Faith." *New Republic* 133 (Nov. 14, 1955): 18–20.

Glazer, Nathan, and Daniel P. Moynihan. *Beyond the Melting Pot: The Negroes, Puerto Ricans, Jews, Italians, and Irish of New York City.* Cambridge, Mass.: M.I.T. Press, 1963.

Goldberg, J. J. *Jewish Power: Inside the American Jewish Establishment.* Reading, Mass.: Addison-Wesley, 1996.

Goldberg, S. P. "Jewish Communal Services: Programs and Finances." In *American Jewish Year Book, 1972,* edited by Morris Fine and Milton Himmelfarb, vol. 73 (Philadelphia: Jewish Publication Society of America, 1972): 236–87.

Goldman, Ari L. *The Search for God at Harvard.* New York: Times Books, 1991.

Goldman, Eric F. *The Crucial Decade—and After.* New York: Vintage Books, 1960.

Goldstein, Sidney. "American Jewry: A Demographic Analysis." In *The Future of the Jewish Community in America.* Edited by David Sidorsky, 65–126. New York: Basic Books, 1973.

Goldstein, Sidney, and Calvin Goldscheider. *Jewish Americans: Three Generations in a Jewish Community.* Englewood Cliffs, N.J.: Prentice-Hall, 1968.

Goodman, Walter. "Bicker at Princeton: The Eating Clubs Again." *Commentary* 25 (May 1958): 406–15.

Gordon, Albert I. *Jews in Suburbia.* Boston: Beacon, 1959.

Gordon, Milton M. *Assimilation in American Life: The Role of Race, Religion and National Origins.* New York: Oxford Univ. Press, 1964.

Gottfried, Paul. "Notes on Neoconservatism." *World and I* 1 (Sept. 1986): 572–82.

———. "Sombart's *The Jews and Modern Capitalism* Revisited." *This World* 3 (fall 1982): 138–44.

Greenberg, Hank. *Hank Greenberg: The Story of My Life,* edited by Ira Berkow. New York: Times Books, 1989.

Grodzensky, Shlomo. "Sidney Hook Faces the Jewish Problem."*Labor Zionist News Letter* (Jan. 15, 1938): 5–9.

Gurock, Jeffrey S. *The Men and Women of Yeshiva: Higher Education, Orthodoxy, and American Judaism.* New York: Columbia Univ. Press, 1988.

Guttmann, Allen. *The Jewish Writer in America: Assimilation and the Crisis of Identity.* New York: Oxford Univ. Press, 1971.

Halkin, Hillel. *Letters to an American Jewish Friend: A Zionist's Polemic.* Philadelphia: Jewish Publication Society of America, 1977.

Halsey, A. H., and M. A. Trow. *The British Academics.* London: Faber and Faber, 1971.

Handlin, Oscar. *Race and Nationality in American Life*. Garden City, N.Y.: Doubleday, 1957.

Harvard Magazine 93 (May–June 1991): 31–36, 69–71.

Heilman, Samuel C. "Inner and Outer Identities: Sociological Ambivalence among Orthodox Jews." *Jewish Social Studies* 39 (summer 1979): 227–38.

———. *Portrait of American Jews: The Last Half of the 20th Century.* Seattle: Univ. of Washington Press, 1995.

———. *Synagogue Life: A Study in Symbolic Interaction.* Chicago: Univ. of Chicago Press, 1976.

Heilman, Samuel C., and Steven M. Cohen. *Cosmopolitans and Parochials: Modern Orthodox Jews in America.* Chicago:Univ. of Chicago Press, 1989.

Helmreich, William B. *The World of the Yeshiva: An Intimate Portrait of Orthodox Jewry.* New York: Free Press, 1982.

Herberg, Will. *Protestant-Catholic-Jew: An Essay in American Religious Sociology.* Garden City, N.Y.: Doubleday, 1955.

Hertzberg, Arthur. "Behind Jews' Political Principles." *New York Times,* Nov. 2, 1984.

———. "Israel and American Jewry." *Commentary* 44 (Aug. 1967): 69–73.

———. *The Jews in America: Four Centuries of an Uneasy Encounter, a History.* |New York: Simon and Schuster, 1989.

Higham, John. *Send These to Me: Jews and Other Immigrants in Urban America.* New York: Atheneum, 1975.

Himmelfarb, Milton. "The Case of Jewish Liberalism." In *Emerging Coalitions in American Politics,* edited by Seymour Martin Lipset, 297–305. San Francisco: Institute for Contemporary Studies, 1978.

Hollinger, David J. "Ethnic Diversity, Cosmopolitanism and the Emergence of the American Liberal Intelligentsia." *American Quarterly* 27 (May 1975): 133–51.

Hook, Sidney. "Our Country and Our Culture." *Partisan Review* 19 (Sept.–Oct. 1952): 569–74.

———. "Hitlerism: A Non-metaphysical View." *Contemporary Jewish Record* 7 (Feb. 1944): 146–55.

———. "The New Failure of Nerve." *Partisan Review* 10 (Jan.–Feb. 1943): 2–23.

———. "The New Medievalism." *New Republic* 103 (Oct. 28, 1940): 602–6.

———. *Out of Step: An Unquiet Life in the 20th Century.* New York: Harper and Row, 1987.

———. Papers. Hoover Institution, Stanford Univ., Palo Alto, California.

———. "Promise Without Dogma: A Social Philosophy for Jews." *Menorah Journal* 25 (Oct.–Dec. 1937): 273–88.

———. "Reflections on the Jewish Question." *Partisan Review* 16 (May 1949): 463–82.

———. "The Tragedy of German Jewry." *New Leader* 21 (Nov. 26, 1938): 8.

Horowitz, Craig. "Are American Jews Disappearing?" *New York* 30 (July 14, 1997).

Horowitz, Irving Louis. *Israeli Ecstasies/Jewish Agonies.* New York: Oxford Univ. Press, 1974.

Horowitz, Robert F. "Between a Heartache and a Laugh: Two Recent Films on Immigration." *Film and History* 6 (Dec. 1976): 73–78.

Howe, Irving. *A Margin of Hope.* New York: Harcourt Brace Jovanovich, 1982.

———. "The Range of the New York Intellectual." In *Creators and Disturbers: Reminiscences by Jewish Intellectuals of New York,* edited by Bernard Rosenberg and Ernest Goldstein, 264–87. New York: Columbia Univ. Press, 1982.

Hyman, Paula. *From Dreyfus to Vichy: The Remaking of French Jewry, 1909–1939.* New York: Columbia Univ. Press, 1979.

Isaac, Dan. "Some Questions about the Depiction of Jews in New Films." *New York Times,* Sept. 8, 1974.

Isaacs, Stephen D. *Jews and American Politics.* Garden City, N.Y.: Doubleday, 1974.

James, Henry. *The American Scene.* New York: Harper and Brothers, 1907.

Johnson, Alvin. "A Social Philosophy for Jews." *Menorah Journal* 26 (Jan.–Mar. 1938): 1–5.

Joselit, Jenna Weissman. *New York's Jewish Jews: The Orthodox Community in the Interwar Years.* Bloomington: Indiana Univ. Press, 1990.

Joughlin, Louis, and Edmund M. Morgan. *The Legacy of Sacco and Vanzetti.* Chicago: Quadrangle, 1964.

Kaiser, Robert G. "The Jewish Voter: Giving Up on Carter." *Washington Post,* Aug. 17, 1980.

Karp, Abraham J. "A Century of Conservative Judaism in the United States," in *American Jewish Year Book, 1986,* edited by Milton Himmelfarb and David Singer, vol. 86 (Philadelphia: Jewish Publication Society of America, 1986): 3–61.

———. "The Conservative Rabbi—'Dissatisfied but Not Unhappy.' " *American Jewish Archives* 35 (Nov. 1983): 188–262.

Kaufmann, Stanley. "Stanley Kaufmann on Films." *New Republic* 173 (Oct. 18, 1975): 21.

Kazin, Alfred. *New York Jew.* New York: Alfred A. Knopf, 1978.

———. "The Solitude of Jacobo Timerman." *New Republic* 184 (June 20, 1981): 32–34.

Kertzer, Morris N. *Today's American Jew.* New York: McGraw-Hill, 1967.

Kessner, Thomas. *The Golden Door: Italian and Jewish Immigrant Mobility in New York City, 1880–1915.* New York: Oxford Univ. Press, 1977.

King, Elliot. "Who's Afraid of Jacobo Timerman?" *Jewish Frontier* 48 (Aug.–Sept. 1981): 6–9.

Kirkpatrick, Jeane. "Dictatorships and Double Standards." *Commentary* 68 (Nov. 1979): 34–45.

Klaperman, Gilbert. *The Story of Yeshiva University: The First Jewish University in America.* New York: Macmillan, 1969.

Kopkind, Andrew. "Bess Bets." *Village Voice*, Nov. 12, 1979, 19–20.

Kristol, Irving. "The Future of American Jewry." *Commentary* 92 (Aug. 1991): 21–26.

———. *Reflections of a Neo-Conservative*. New York: Basic Books, 1983.

———. "The Timerman Affair." *Wall Street Journal*, May 29, 1981.

Ladd, Everett Carll, Jr., and Seymour Martin Lipset. *TheDivided Academy: Professors and Politics*. New York: McGraw-Hill, 1975.

Lane, Charles. "Daddy's Boy." *New Republic* 214 (Jan. 22, 1996): 15–25.

Lasker, Arnold. "Motivations for Attending High Holy Day Services." *Journal for the Scientific Study of Religion* 10 (fall 1971): 241–48.

"Last Word on Timerman." *Midstream* 28 (Feb. 1982): 34–42.

Leuchtenburg, William E., gen. ed. *The Unfinished Century: America since 1900*. Boston: Little, Brown, 1973.

Levin, Meyer. *In Search: An Autobiography*. New York: Horizon, 1950.

Lewis, Anthony. "Accomplice to Terror." *New York Times*, Mar. 22, 1981.

———. "The Final Solution in Argentina." *New York Times Book Review*, May 10, 1981.

———. "The Timerman Affair." *New York Times*, June 14, 1981.

———. "What Kind of Country Are We?" *New York Times*, May 17, 1981.

Liebman, Charles S. *The Ambivalent American Jew: Politics, Religion, and Family in American Jewish Life*. Philadelphia: Jewish Publication Society of America, 1976.

———. "American Jews: Still a Distinctive Group." *Commentary* 64 (Aug. 1977): 57–60.

———. *Deceptive Images: Toward a Redefinition of American Judaism*. New Brunswick, N.J.: Transaction, 1988.

———. "Orthodoxy in American Jewish Life." In *American Jewish Year Book, 1965*, edited by Morris Fine and Milton Himmelfarb, vol. 66 (Philadelphia: Jewish Publication Society of America, 1965): 21–97.

———. "Toward a Theory of Jewish Liberalism." In *The Religious Situation 1969*, edited by Donald R. Cutler, 1034–61. Boston: Beacon, 1969.

Liebman, Charles S., and Steven M. Cohen. *The Two Worlds of Judaism: The Israeli and American Experiences*. New Haven, Conn.: Yale Univ. Press, 1990.

Lipset, Seymour Martin. "Jewish Fear, Black Insensitivity." *New York Times*, Mar. 9, 1990.

Lipset, Seymour Martin, ed. *American Pluralism and the Jewish Community*. New Brunswick, N.J.: Transaction, 1990.

Lipset, Seymour Martin, and Earl Raab. "The American Jews, the 1984 Elections, and Beyond." In *Survey of Jewish Affairs, 1985*, edited by William Frankel, 141–57. Cranbury, N.J.: Fairleigh Dickinson Univ. Press, 1985.

Lipset, Seymour Martin, and David Riesman. *Education and Politics at Harvard*. New York: McGraw-Hill, 1975.

Lipsky, Seth. "A Conversation with Publisher Jacobo Timerman." *Wall Street Journal,* June 4, 1981.

Longfield, Bradley J. " 'For God, for Country, and for Yale': Yale, Religion, and Higher Education Between the World Wars." In *The Secularization of the Academy,* edited by George M. Marsden and Bradley J. Longfield, 146–69. New York: Oxford Univ. Press.

Lowin, Joseph. "Herman Wouk and the Liturgical Novel." *Jewish Book Annual* 44 (1986): 43–54.

Marsden, George M. *The Soul of the American University: From Protestant Establishment to Established Nonbelief.* New York: Oxford Univ. Press, 1994.

———. "The Soul of the American University: A Historical Overview." In *The Secularization of the Academy,* edited by George M. Marsden and Bradley J. Longfield, 9–45. New York: Oxford Univ. Press, 1992.

Marsden, George M., and Bradley J. Longfield, eds. *The Secularization of the Academy.* New York: Oxford Univ. Press, 1992.

Marty, Martin E. *Righteous Empire: The Protestant Experience in America.* New York: Dial, 1970.

Mayer, Milton S. "The Case Against the Jew." *Saturday Evening Post* 214 (Mar. 28, 1942): 18–19.

Medding, Peter Y. "Toward a General Theory of Jewish Political Interests and Behavior in the Contemporary World." In *Kinship and Consent: The Jewish Political Tradition and Its Contemporary Uses,* edited by Daniel J. Elazar, 313–42. Washington, D.C.: Univ. Press of America, 1983.

Mehling, Harold. "Is Miami Beach Jewish?" In *A Coat of Many Colors: Jewish Subcommunities in the United States,* edited by Abraham D. Lavender, 118–27. Westport, Conn.: Greenwood, 1977.

Mendelsohn, Ezra, ed. *Essential Papers on Jews and the Left.* New York: New York Univ. Press, 1997.

Moore, Deborah Dash. *At Home in America: Second Generation New York Jews.* New York: Columbia Univ. Press, 1981.

Moshe, Meir. "The Yom Kippur War in Middle America." *Midstream* 20 (June–July 1974): 74–79.

Muravchik, Joshua. "Patrick J. Buchanan and the Jews." *Commentary* 91 (Jan. 1991): 29–37.

Netanyahu, Jonathan. *Self-Portrait of a Hero: From the Letters of Jonathan Netanyahu, 1963–1976.* New York: Random House, 1980.

Niebuhr, H. Richard. *The Social Sources of Denominationalism.* 1929. Reprint, New York: Meridian Books, 1957.

Niebuhr, Reinhold. *The Children of Light and the Children of Darkness.* New York: Charles Scribner's Sons, 1944.

Novick, Peter. *That Noble Dream: The "Objectivity Question" and the American Historical Profession.* Cambridge: Cambridge Univ. Press, 1988.

Oren, Dan A. *Joining the Club: A History of Jews and Yale.* New Haven, Conn.: Yale Univ. Press, 1985.

Perlmutter, Nathan, and Ruth Ann Perlmutter. *The Real Anti-Semitism in America.* New York: Arbor House, 1982.

Podhoretz, Norman. *Breaking Ranks.* New York: Harper and Row, 1979.

———. "Buchanan and the Conservative Crack-Up." *Commentary* 93 (May 1992): 30–34.

———. "The Jew as Bourgeois." *Commentary* 21 (Feb. 1956): 186–88.

———. *Making It.* New York: Random House, 1967.

———. "Now, Instant Zionism." *New York Times Magazine,* Feb. 3, 1974.

Poll, Solomon. "The Persistence of Tradition: Orthodoxy in America." In *The Ghetto and Beyond: Essays on Jewish Life in America,* edited by Peter I. Rose, 118–49. New York: Random House, 1969.

Polsky, Howard W. "A Study of Orthodoxy in Milwaukee: Social Characteristics, Beliefs, and Observances." In *The Jews: Social Patterns of an American Group,* edited by Marshall Sklare, 325–35. New York: Free Press, 1958.

Popkin, Henry. "The Vanishing Jew of Our Popular Culture." *Commentary* 14 (July 1952): 46–55.

Raab, Earl. "The Black Revolution and the Jewish Question." In *Black Anti-Semitism and Jewish Racism,* edited by Nat Hentoff, 15–41. New York: Richard W. Baron, 1969.

Ringer, Fritz K. *The Decline of the German Mandarins: The German Academic Community, 1890–1933.* Cambridge, Mass.: Harvard Univ. Press, 1969.

Rischin, Moses. *The Promised City: New York's Jews, 1870–1914.* Cambridge, Mass.: Harvard Univ. Press, 1962.

Rollins, Peter C. " 'Victory at Sea': Cold War Epic." *Journal of Popular Culture* 6 (spring 1951): 463–78.

Rosenberg, Bernard, and Irving Howe. "Are American Jews Turning to the Right?" In *The New Conservatives: A Critique from the Left,* edited by Lewis A. Coser and Irving Howe, 64–89. New York: Quadrangle, 1974.

Rosenberg, Stuart E. *The New Jewish Identity in America.* New York: Hippocrene, 1985.

———. *The Real Jewish World: A Rabbi's Second Thoughts.* New York: Philosophical Library, 1984.

———. "Suburban Judaism," *Midstream* 29 (Nov. 1983): 30–32.

Rosenthal, Abe. "Forgive Them Not." *New York Times,* Sept. 14, 1990.

Roth, Philip, *"Goodbye, Columbus" and Five Short Stories.* New York: Bantam, 1963.

Sachar, Abram L. *A Host at Last.* Boston: Little, Brown, 1976.

Saltman, Eric P. "Torture? On TV?" *New York Times,* May 26, 1981.

Samuels, Stuart. "The Evolutionary Image of the Jew in American Film." In *Ethnic Images in American Film and Television,* edited by Randall M. Miller, 23–34. Philadelphia: Balch Institute, 1978.

Sanders, Ronald. *The Downtown Jews: Portraits of an Immigrant Generation.* New York: Harper and Row, 1969.

Sanua, Marianne. "Stages in the Development of Jewish Life at Princeton University." *American Jewish History* 76 (June 1987): 391–415.

Sartre, Jean-Paul. *Anti-Semite and Jew.* Translated by George J. Becker. New York: Schocken, 1948.

Schlesinger, Arthur M., Jr. "*Time* and the Intellectuals." *New Republic* 135 (July 16, 1956): 15–16.

Schnapper, Dominique. *Jewish Identities in France: An Analysis of Contemporary French Jews.* Translated by Arthur Goldhammer. Chicago: Univ. of Chicago Press, 1983.

Selengut, Charles. "By Torah Alone: Yeshiva Fundamentalism in Jewish Life." In *Accounting for Fundamentalisms: The Dynamic Character of Movements,* edited by Martin E. Marty and R. Scott Appleby, 236–63. Chicago: Univ. of Chicago Press, 1994.

Selzer, Michael. *Zionism Reconsidered: The Rejection of Jewish Normalcy.* New York: Macmillan, 1970.

Shestack, Jerome J. "Jacobo Timerman: The Perils of Silence." *Congress Monthly* 48 (Sept.–Oct. 1981).

Short, K.R.M. "Hollywood Fights Anti-Semitism, 1945–1947." In *Feature Films as History,* edited by K.R.M. Short, 157–89. Knoxville: Univ. of Tennessee Press, 1981.

Siegel, Seymour. "Remarks about Argentina." *Forum Newsletter* 1 (summer 1981).

———. "Right Turn." *Sh'ma* 11 (Apr. 17, 1981): 89–91.

Silberman, Charles E. *A Certain People: American Jews and Their Lives Today.* New York: Summit, 1985.

Silverberg, Robert. *If I Forget Thee O Jerusalem: American Jews and the State of Israel.* New York: William Morrow, 1970.

Simons, William M. "The Athlete as Jewish Standard Bearer: Media Images of Hank Greenberg." *Jewish Social Studies* 44 (spring 1982): 95–112.

Singer, David. "Living with Intermarriage." *Commentary* 68 (July 1979): 48–53.

Sklare, Marshall. *America's Jews.* New York: Random House, 1971.

———. *Conservative Judaism: An American Religious Movement.* 1955. New, augmented edition, New York: Schocken, 1972.

———. "Lakeville and Israel: The Six-Day War and Its Aftermath." *Midstream* 14 (Oct. 1968): 4–21.

———. "The Sociology of Contemporary Jewish Studies." In *The Jew in American Society,* edited by Marshall Sklare, 1–27. New York: Behrman House, 1974.

———, ed. *The Jews: Social Patterns of an American Group.* New York: Free Press, 1958.

Sklare, Marshall, and Joseph Greenblum. *Jewish Identity on the Suburban Frontier.* Chicago: Univ. of Chicago Press, 1967.

Solotaroff, Theodore. Review of *Prisoner Without a Name, Cell Without a Number,* by Jacobo Timerman. In *Nation* 232 (June 13, 1981): 733–36.

Solomon, Barbara M. *Ancestors and Immigrants: A ChangingNew England Tradition.* Cambridge, Mass.: Harvard Univ. Press, 1956.

Soloway, Arnold M., with Edwin Weiss and Gerald Caplan. *Truth and Peace in the Middle East: A Critical Analysis of the Quaker Report.* New York: Friendly House, 1971.

Sontag, Susan. *On Photography.* New York: Farrar, Strauss, 1977.

Sorin, Gerald. *Tradition Transformed: The Jewish Experience in America.* Baltimore: Johns Hopkins Univ. Press, 1997.

Sowell, Thomas. *Ethnic America: A History.* New York: Basic Books, 1981.

Spiegel, Alan. "The Vanishing Act: A Typology of the Jew in Contemporary American Film." In *From Hester Street to Hollywood: The Jewish-American Stage and Screen,* edited by Sarah Blacher Cohen, 257–75. Bloomington: Indiana Univ. Press, 1983.

Steinberg, Stephen. *The Academic Melting Pot: Catholics and Jews in American Higher Education.* New York: McGraw-Hill, 1974.

———. *The Ethnic Myth: Race, Ethnicity and Class in America.* New York: Atheneum, 1981.

Stember, Charles, ed. *Jews in the Mind of America.* New York: Basic Books, 1966.

Sternstein, Joseph P. "Reform Judaism and Zionism, 1895–1904." In *Herzl Year Book,* edited by Raphael Patai, vol. 5 (New York: Herzl Press, 1963): 11–31.

Stevenson, Burton, ed. *The Macmillan Book of Proverbs, Maxims, and Famous Phrases.* New York: Macmillan, 1948.

Stock, Ernest. "The Reconstitution of the Jewish Agency: A Political Analysis." In *American Jewish Year Book, 1972,* edited by Morris Fine and Milton Himmelfarb, vol. 73 (Philadelphia: Jewish Publication Society of America, 1972): 178–93.

Swados, Harvey. "Popular Taste and *The Caine Mutiny.*" *Partisan Review* 20 (Mar.–Apr. 1953): 248–56.

Synott, Marcia Graham. *The Half-Opened Door: Discrimination and Admissions at Harvard, Yale, and Princeton, 1900–1970.* Westport, Conn.: Greenwood, 1979.

Teller, Judd L. *Strangers and Natives: The Evolution of the American Jew from 1921 to the Present.* New York: Delacourt, 1968.

Thompson, Dorothy. "America Demands a Single Loyalty." *Commentary* 9 (Mar. 1950): 210–19.

Timerman, Jacobo. *Prisoner Without a Name, Cell Without a Number.* New York: Alfred A. Knopf, 1981.

———. "The Silence of the Jews." *Harper's* 263 (Nov. 1981): 20–23.

Tyrrell, R. Emmett, Jr. *The Conservative Crack-Up*. New York: Simon and Schuster, 1992.

Urofsky, Melvin I. *American Zionism from Herzl to the Holocaust*. New York: Anchor, 1975.

"The Uses of Jacobo Timerman." *Contentions* 1 (Aug. 1981): 1–3, 6–8.

Varon, Benno Weiser. "The Canonization of Jacobo Timerman." *Midstream* 27 (Aug.–Sept. 1981): 36–44.

———. "Don't Rescue Latin American Jews!" *Midstream* 26 (Dec. 1980): 11–16.

Veysey, Laurence R. *The Emergence of the American University*. Chicago: Univ. of Chicago Press, 1965.

Wald, Alan. *The New York Intellectuals: The Rise and Decline of the Anti-Stalinist Left from the 1930s to the 1980s*. Chapel Hill: Univ. of North Carolina Press, 1987.

Walzer, Michael. "Timerman and His Enemies." *New York Review of Books* 29 (Sept. 24, 1981): 10–18.

Waxman, Chaim I. *America's Jews in Transition*. Philadelphia: Temple Univ. Press, 1983.

Waxman, Mordecai M. "Conservative Judaism Confronts Its Future." *Judaism* 36 (spring 1987): 179–86.

Weinberg, David. "The 'Socially Acceptable' Minority Group:The Image of the Jew in American Popular Films." *North Dakota Quarterly* 40 (autumn 1972): 60–68.

Weisberg, Jacob. "The Heresies of Pat Buchanan." *New Republic* 203 (Oct. 2, 1990): 22–27.

———. "Hunter Gatherers." *New Republic* 205 (Sept. 22, 1991): 14–16.

Wertheimer, Jack. "Judaism Without Limits." *Commentary* 104 (July 1997): 24–27.

———. *A People Divided: Judaism in Contemporary America*. New York: Basic Books, 1993.

"What Do American Jews Believe?" *Commentary* 102 (Aug. 1996): 18–96.

Whitfield, Stephen J. "After Strange Gods: Radical Jews in Modern America." *Forum* 56 (summer 1985): 17–41.

———. *American Space, Jewish Time*. Hamden, Conn.: Archon Books, 1988.

———. "The Jewish Vote." *Virginia Quarterly Review* 62 (winter 1986): 1–20.

———. *Voices of Jacob, Hands of Esau: Jews in American Life and Thought*. Hamden, Conn.: Archon Books, 1984.

Whyte, William H., Jr. *The Organization Man*. 1956. New York: Anchor, 1959.

Wieseltier, Leon. "The Many Trials of Jacobo Timerman." *Dissent* 28 (fall 1981): 425–35.

Wilson, Clyde. "The Conservative Identity." *Intercollegiate Review* 21 (spring 1986): 5–8.

Wisse, Ruth R. "The New York (Jewish) Intellectuals." *Commentary* 74 (Nov. 1987): 34–38.

Woodward, C. Vann. *The Burden of Southern History.* Baton Rouge: Louisiana State Univ. Press, 1960.

Wouk, Herman. *The Caine Mutiny: A Novel of World War II.* Garden City, N.Y.: Doubleday, 1951.

———. *The Glory.* Boston: LB Books, 1994.

———. *The Hope.* Boston: LB Books, 1993.

———. *Inside/Outside: A Novel.* Boston: Little, Brown, 1985.

———."Introduction." In *Self-Portrait of a Hero: The Letters of Jonathan Netanyahu (1963–1976).* New York: Random House, 1980.

———. *This Is My God.* Garden City, N.Y.: Doubleday, 1959.

———. *War and Remembrance.* Boston: LB Books, 1978.

———. *The Winds of War.* Boston: LB Books, 1972.

"The Wouk Mutiny." *Time* 66 (Sept. 5, 1955): 48–52.

Yaffe, James. *The American Jews: A Portrait of a Split Personality.* New York: Random House, 1968.

Index